The Human Rights of Women

The Human Rights of Women: International Instruments and African Experiences

edited by Wolfgang Benedek, Esther M. Kisaakye
and Gerd Oberleitner

Zed Books
LONDON • NEW YORK

in association with

World University Service,
Austria

The Human Rights of Women: International Instruments and African Experiences was first published by Zed Books Ltd, 7 Cynthia Street, London N1 9JF, UK and Room 400, 175 Fifth Avenue, New York, NY 10010, USA, in association with World University Service Austria, Maiffredygasse 11, A-8010 Graz, Austria, in 2002.

Distributed in the USA exclusively by Palgrave, a division of St Martin's Press, LLC, 175 Fifth Avenue, New York, NY 10010, USA

Publication of this book had been made possible through funding by the Austrian Federal Ministry for Foreign Affairs, Department for Development Cooperation.

Cover designed by Andrew Corbett
Set in Monotype Ehrhardt and Franklin Gothic by Ewan Smith
Printed and bound in the United Kingdom by Biddles Ltd, www.biddles.co.uk

A catalogue record for this book is available from the British Library

Library of Congress Cataloging-in-Publication Data: available

ISBN 1 84277 044 6 cased
ISBN 1 84277 045 4 limp

Contents

Note by the Editors

This reader comprises lectures given at the annual Postgraduate Courses on Human Rights of Women from 1993 to 1999. The courses, of which two were held in Austria and four in Uganda, were organized by the Austrian Committee of World University Service together with World University Service Uganda, the Human Rights and Peace Centre of Makerere University in Kampala, the Ludwig-Boltzmann-Institute for Human Rights in Vienna, the United Nations Division for the Advancement of Women in New York, the Austrian Commission for UNESCO, the Austrian Study Centre for Peace and Conflict Resolution in Stadtschlaining, the Institute for International Law and International Relations at the University of Graz and the Austrian Federal Academy of Public Administration in Vienna. Since 1999, the European Training and Research Centre for Human Rights and Democracy (ETC) in Graz, Austria, has been involved in the follow-up process to this course and in publishing this book.

The Postgraduate Course was a regular teaching programme on the human rights of women. It aimed to make women – in particular in developing countries – aware of their legal situation, to inform them about their rights, to increase the legal literacy of women and to enhance the capacity of decision-makers in the economic, labour, political, social and cultural fields, as well as of legal experts, scholars and civil servants. It also aimed at raising the gender consciousness of the public and of law-makers in order to ensure compliance with international standards when laws are to be amended or new legislation is to be drafted.

The course provided information on human rights and gender issues, on international standards of equality, on the work of the United Nations, on the specialized agencies and regional organizations in this area, on women's rights under existing international standards of equality (legal instruments, ranging from the UN Charter to the Convention on the Elimination of All Forms of Discrimination against Women) and on the legal and administrative systems through which those standards are implemented nationally and examined internationally. In addition, specific topics such as female genital mutilation, human rights of women in armed conflict, refugee women as well as women and Islam were discussed with the aim of making participants better equipped for implementing international legal standards of equality in their home countries and to prepare them to address cases of inequality.

The first course was held for a period of six weeks in summer 1993 at the seat of the Austrian Study Centre for Peace and Conflict Resolution in Stadtschlaining and at the Federal Academy of Public Administration in Vienna. The following year a four-week course was held in Stadtschlaining. Subsequently, the course was moved to Uganda and was held for a period of four weeks in summer in Kampala from 1994 to 1999. Due to logistical reasons, no course took place in 1998. Following evaluations, which took place after each course, the content and faculty of the courses have been adjusted every year to better suit the needs of the participants.

The courses were funded by the Austrian Federal Ministry, Department of Development Cooperation. The first two courses received additional funding by the Commission of Science and Technology for Development at the Austrian Academy of Sciences. The courses were composed of lectures and working groups, which both required active participation. Experts and practitioners in the field of human rights of women were invited to give guest lectures. Excursions and visits to local governmental and non-governmental institutions and organizations active in the field of human rights of women, and – in Kampala – visits to women's prisons supplemented the training sessions.

The overall number of participants in all courses was 151. Their participation was made possible by about twenty-five fellowships granted by the Austrian Foreign Ministry for each course. While the first course saw participation from all continents, the following courses focused on anglophone African countries. All in all, men and women from 28 African countries had the opportunity to participate. Applicants, who had to hold a first degree in law, politics, sociology or related disciplines, came from academic or research institutions, legal professions, national or international non-governmental organizations, relevant development projects, civil service, labour administration or politics. Applicants who had practical experience and/or were engaged in relevant activities such as giving legal advice or teaching were given preference.

Each participant had to prepare a paper dealing with the situations of the human rights of women in his or her home country, focusing on *de jure* and *de facto* status of women, the regulations provided for under the respective national legal system and the implementation of universal and regional human rights instruments related to human rights of women. The papers had to be presented and were discussed at the end of the course with the consultation of the faculty. Upon their return to their countries the participants were expected to promote the issue of the human rights of women within their respective institutions and communities, and to use their knowledge in awareness-raising activities and teaching in formal and non-formal education at all levels. In some cases this led to the organization of training sessions in the students' countries of origin, or to the provision of more specific legal assistance and advisory services in the area of human rights of women.

The international faculty that taught and worked with the participants over the years consisted of Christine Ainetter Brautigam, United Nations Division for the Advancement of Women, New York; Fared Banda, School of Oriental and African Studies, London; Wolfgang Benedek, professor of international law, University of Graz; Chaloka Beyani, London School of Economics; Andrew Byrnes, professor of law, University of Hong Kong; E. V. O. Dankwa, professor of law, University of Legon, Ghana, and member of the African Commission on Human and Peoples' Rights; Seble Dewit, director of Alliances, African Women's Network, Washington; Khadija Elmadmad, professor of law, University of Casablanca; Dorothea Gaudart, honorary professor, University of Vienna, and member of the Austrian Commission for UNESCO; Dorota Gierycz, United Nations Division for the Advancement of Women, New York; Françoise Hampson, Dean, Department of Law, University of Essex; Barbara Harrel-Bond, visiting professor, Makerere Institute of Social Research, Makerere University Kampala; Deborah Kasente, lecturer, Department of Public and Comparative Law, Makerere University Kampala; Zdzislaw Kedzia, professor of law, Office of the UN High Commissioner for Human Rights; Edward Khiddu-Makubuya, professor of law, Makerere University Kampala; Renate Kicker, professor of international law, University of Graz; Itumuleng Kimane, lecturer, Department of Social Anthropology/Sociology, National University of Lesotho; Joy Kwesige, lecturer, Makerere University Kampala; Peter Leuprecht, director of human rights, Council of Europe, Strasbourg; Apollo Makubuya, lecturer in law, Makerere University Kampala; Christine Matovu, deputy director, Legal and Constitutional Affairs Division, Kampala; Esther Mayambala Kisaakye, lecturer in law, Makerere University Kampala, Valentine M. Moghadam, Coordinator, Research Programme on Women and Development, World Institute for Development Economics Research of the United Nations University, Helsinki; Rebecca Mukyala, Makerere University Institute of Social Research Kampala; Victoria Mwaka, professor of geography, Makerere University Kampala, deputy chairman, Constituent Assembly Uganda and founder head, Women's Studies Department of Makerere University; Kurt Neudek, assistant commissioner of prisons, Kampala; Manfred Nowak, professor of law at the University of Vienna and at the Austrian Federal Academy of Public Administration and director of the Ludwig-Boltzmann-Institute for Human Rights, Vienna; J. Oloka-Onyango, dean, Faculty of Law, Makerere University Kampala; Henry Onoria, lecturer, Department of Public and Comparative Law, Makerere University Kampala; Sonia Picado, professor of law, vice-president of the Inter-American Court of Human Rights and director of the Inter-American Institute of Human Rights; Ingeborg Schwarz, Ludwig-Boltzmann-Institute of Human Rights, Vienna, coordinator of NGO participation in the 1993 World Conference on Human Rights; Walter Suntinger, Ludwig-Boltzmann-Institute for Human Rights, Vienna; Sylvia Tamale, lecturer, Faculty of Law, Makerere University Kampala; Lilian Tibatemwa-Ekirikubinza, lecturer, Makerere University Kampala and Eleonora Zielinska, professor of law, director of the Institute of Penal Law, University of Warsaw.

The preparation, organization and conduct of the courses would not have been possible without the commitment, assistance, counselling, patience and efforts of many friends and colleagues. We thank Dorota Gierycz from the UN Division on the Advancement of Women; Dorothea Gaudart from the University of Vienna; Manfred Nowak, Renate Frech, Eva Wipler and Helmut Sax from the Ludwig-Boltzmann-Institute for Human Rights in Vienna, Samuel Tindifa, director of the Human Rights and Peace Centre in Kampala; Lilian Tibatemwa-Ekirikubinza from Makerere University Kampala, Reingard Hartmann-Waltersdorfer from the Institute of International Law and International Relations in Graz, and – in particular – Irene Kisuule from WUS Uganda for her dedication and tireless efforts over the years. Our thanks go also to the Austrian Regional Bureau for Development Co-operation in Kampala and in particular to Anton Mair and Barbara Nöst for their assistance and cooperation. We also have to thank Shereen Dawood from the University of Natal, South Africa, for her evaluation of the course undertaken in 1997.

The individuals' institutional affiliation referred to is the one that the lecturers and collaborators were holding at the moment of their involvement in the course. The contributions to this volume were prepared for the course, which ended in 1999. Although every effort has been made to update the text, the book reflects the issues as relevant at that time.

Wolfgang Benedek, Esther M.Kisaakye,
Gerd Oberleitner

Foreword

The idealism and thoughts encoded in the language of rights represent some of the highest aspirations of humankind. Yet many people around the world are still enchained by oppressive social, economic and political systems. The Austrian Development Cooperation is committed to the elimination of injustice and inequality and supports a number of programmes and projects that provide legal advice and legal education especially for women and law reform processes that recognize internationally agreed standards.

The category of gender, and, more especially, women's oppression and social disempowerment, emerged as an issue and as a priority for action on an international scale at the Nairobi Women's Conference in 1985. Empowering women to make the law relevant and real in their lives was identified as an imperative.

The realization of women's rights is not an easy task and is burdened with tensions, requiring the redefinition of concepts such as liberty, equality and freedom from a gender perspective. There are no easy answers or quick-fix solutions to realize this objective. While there is a strong commitment from human rights organizations and activists in various parts of Africa, the challenge remains that the international and national human rights laws are used and implemented by the representatives of juridical systems.

Since 1993 the Postgraduate Course on the Human Rights of Women in Africa has shown its potential by addressing the many tensions and challenges faced by human rights activists committed to the eradication of all forms of discrimination against women in the political, social and economic arena that are reflected in this publication.

Six of these courses have been held over the years. Two courses took place in Austria, the others in Kampala, Uganda. During this time, much experience has been gathered in relation to the content of the course and also in organizational matters. Altogether, some 151 participants have contributed to the success of the course, which has gained recognition among professionals and human rights activists. The Austrian Development

Cooperation wants to thank the project partners, the World University Service in Austria and Uganda, the Human Rights and Peace Centre and the Faculty of Law at Makerere University and all the lecturers, for taking on the challenges and for their contribution to the implementation of the rights of women in Africa.

Austrian Development Cooperation,
Vienna, March 2001

About the Authors

Christine Ainetter Brautigam works in the United Nations Division for the Advancement of Women, New York.

Wolfgang Benedek is professor of international law, University of Graz and chairperson of World University Service Austria.

Andrew Byrnes is professor of law, Australian National University.

Khadija Elmadmad is professor of law, University of Casablanca.

Dorothea Gaudart is professor of sociology, University of Vienna.

Dorota Gierycz is chief of the gender analysis section, United Nations Division for the Advancement of Women, New York.

Françoise Hampson is professor of law in the Department of Law and Human Rights Centre, University of Essex.

Esther M. Kisaakye is a lecturer in law, Makerere University Kampala.

Apollo Makubuya is a lecturer in law, Makerere University Kampala.

Kurt Neudek is assistant commissioner of prisons and special adviser to the commission of prisons, Kampala.

Manfred Nowak is professor of constitutional law, University of Vienna and director of the Ludwig-Boltzmann-Institute of Human Rights, Vienna.

Gerd Oberleitner is a lecturer in international law, University of Graz

J. Oloka-Onyango is dean of the faculty of Law, Makerere University Kampala.

Henry Onoria is a lecturer in the department of public and comparative law, Makerere University Kampala.

Part I

International Instruments

1

International Human Rights Law: The Relevance of Gender

Christine Ainetter Brautigam[1]

The Charter of the United Nations proclaims in its preamble faith in fundamental human rights and the equal rights of women and men. Among the purposes of the organization are the promotion of the respect for human rights and fundamental freedoms for all without distinction on a number of grounds, including sex. This commitment to women's equal rights formed the basis upon which a comprehensive body of international human rights law was subsequently developed to promote women's equality and non-discrimination, and to ensure their full enjoyment of human rights. It also formed the basis for the development of a global policy framework to complement the international legal regime in the pursuit of this goal.

This chapter will first outline the development of a women-specific regime in the United Nations. Attention will be paid to institutions and processes, and to norm development. The interplay in the development of the treaty-based and of the policy-based regime will be discussed. The shift from a women-specific to a gender approach will then be reviewed, and the importance of the gender approach to international human rights law will be considered. Finally, the chapter will assess recent developments in international human rights activities to mainstream a gender perspective as a strategy for ensuring the equal enjoyment by women of all human rights and fundamental freedoms.

Development of a Women-specific Regime in the United Nations[2]

Institutions and processes Under the Charter of the United Nations, responsibility for human rights is entrusted to the General Assembly and the Economic and Social Council (the Council) as the principal intergovernmental bodies. In its tasks, the Council is to be assisted by functional commissions in the economic and social field. Explicit reference is made to the establishment of such a commission in the area of human rights.

The Secretariat of the United Nations plays a key role in all United Nations programmes, including the work for the advancement of women. It provides the intergovernmental bodies with the necessary research and documentation in the form of reports and studies, and develops policy options and recommendations for their action. It is also responsible for implementing the decisions of such bodies, or for monitoring their implementation, as the case may be. The Secretariat also organizes and services the meetings of various bodies, prepares budgets, and facilitates interaction with non-governmental organizations and organizations of civil society. The Division for the Advancement of Women (DAW) serves as the Secretariat for the Commission on the Status of Women and for the Committee on the Elimination of Discrimination against Women (CEDAW). It also serves as the Secretariat for the Economic and Social Council and the General Assembly in their consideration of women-specific items on their respective agendas.

The Commission on the Status of Women (CSW) The Council recognized from its first session in 1946 that issues related to the status of women would require specific attention. It thus established a Sub-Commission on the Status of Women to submit proposals, recommendations and reports on the status of women to the Commission on Human Rights, including proposals for its own terms of reference. Following concern voiced by women representatives on the Sub-Commission and by members of non-governmental organizations that issues of concern to women would not receive the attention they required in light of the comprehensive work programme of the Commission on Human Rights, the Council elevated the Sub-Commission to a full-fledged functional commission reporting directly to it. As a consequence, the CSW was established in 1947, after only one session as a Sub-Commission.

One consequence of the establishment of a Commission on the Status of Women and of a Commission on Human Rights was the development of parallel tracks within the United Nations for human rights activities, on the one hand, and for activities dealing with the concerns of women, on the other. Over the years, these separate regimes resulted in the development of an ambiguous relationship between the promotion and protection of human rights in general, and the attention to the concerns of women, including their human rights concerns. Scholars and commentators have observed that the existence of these two regimes contributed to the historic neglect of women's human rights concerns in the general human rights activities.

At the same time, the existence of a separate regime for women ensured that focused and comprehensive attention was paid to the status of women. Over five decades, the United Nations women-specific machinery has worked to develop international legal norms of specific importance to women. In addition to elaborating legal measures, it has proposed political, economic and social measures to remedy the root causes as well as the consequences of systemic and systematic discrimination suffered by women in all parts of the world. In these tasks, cooperation with women's groups and non-governmental organizations provided the necessary support to bring many issues of concern to women on to the global and national agendas.

Mandate and composition of the CSW The Commission on the Status of Women takes a lead role among intergovernmental bodies of the United Nations in elaborating policies and strategies aimed at achieving gender equality in all parts of the world. The Commission develops recommendations and suggests courses of action for eliminating discrimination against women and achieving equality. It also plays a catalytic role throughout the United Nations system in focusing attention on the concerns of women.

The CSW derives its mandate from resolution 11 (II) of 21 June 1946.[3] This resolution encompasses the preparation of recommendations and reports to the Council on promoting women's rights in political, economic, civil, social and educational fields, and requests the Commission to make recommendations on urgent problems requiring immediate attention in the field of women's rights with the object of implementing the principle that women and men shall have equal rights, and to develop proposals to give effect to such recommendations. Since 1947, the Commission has also had the power to consider communications relating to the status of women (Council resolution 76 [V] of 5 August 1947). Amended in 1950, in 1983, and in 1993, this mandate enables the Commission to make recommendations on actions to be taken with regard to communications which appear to reveal consistent patterns of reliably attested injustice and discriminatory practices against women revealed by such communications (Council Resolution 1993/11 of 27 July 1993).

The original mandate of the Commission was expanded in 1987, in the aftermath of the Third World Conference on Women held in Nairobi in 1985.[4] Consequently, the Council broadened the Commission's terms of reference to include the functions of promoting the objectives of equality, development and peace, and of monitoring the implementation of measures contained in the Nairobi Forward-looking Strategies for the Advancement of Women. It was also entrusted with reviewing and appraising progress made in the advancement of women at the national, subregional, regional, sectoral and global levels.

In 1995 and 1996, once again following a World Conference on Women, the Commission's terms of reference were revisited to allow the Commission to pursue the new tasks resulting from the Conference, and to reflect gains made since the Nairobi Conference. Consequently, in its resolution 50/203 of 22 December 1995 on the implementation of the outcome of the Fourth World Conference on Women,[5] the General Assembly decided that the Assembly, the Council and the Commission, in accordance with their respective mandates, would constitute a three-tiered intergovernmental mechanism that would play the primary role in the overall policy-making and follow-up. These bodies also coordinate the implementation and monitoring of the Platform for Action adopted at the Conference. The pivotal role in this process was assigned to the Commission.

The Council, as the Commission's parent body, established the Commission's new terms of reference in resolution 1996/6 of 22 July 1996. It confirmed the CSW's past mandate and entrusted it to:

- assist the Council in monitoring, reviewing and appraising progress achieved and problems encountered in the implementation of the Beijing Declaration and Platform for Action at all levels, and to advise the Council thereon;
- continue to ensure support for mainstreaming a gender perspective in United Nations activities and develop further its catalytic role in this regard in other areas;
- identify issues where United Nations system-wide coordination needs to be improved in order to assist the Council in its coordination function;
- identify emerging issues, trends and new approaches to issues affecting the situation of women or equality between women and men that require urgent consideration, and make substantive recommendations thereon; and
- maintain and enhance public awareness and support for the implementation of the Platform for Action.

These terms of reference form the basis for the Commission's annual sessions. While the CSW met annually until 1970 (with the exception of 1964, when no session was held), a period of biennial meetings in the 1970s reduced the effectiveness of the Commission to act as catalyst for women's issues. Since 1987, the CSW has again met annually, usually in early March, for a period of two weeks. Since 1996, the Bureau of the Commission consisting of a chairperson, three vice-chairpersons and one rapporteur, one from each of the five geographical regions (Africa, Asia and Pacific, Latin America and the Caribbean, Eastern European Group of States, and Western European and Other Group of States), is taking on a more active role between the sessions to ensure more continuity.

The size of the CSW has increased over the years, in line with the expanding membership of the United Nations. Originally consisting of 15 members, it was increased successively to 18 in 1952, 21 in 1961, 32 in 1966, and 45 in 1989. Members are elected by the Commission's parent body, the Economic and Social Council, for a term of four years. They are representatives of governments. The seats are distributed on an equitable geographical basis, according to the following pattern: 13 members from African States; 11 members from Asian States; 9 members from Latin American and Caribbean States; 8 members from Western Europe and Other States; and 4 members from Eastern European States.

Participation by other actors in the work of the CSW The CSW is an intergovernmental body whose members represent governments and who are, in turn, elected by governments. Only members of the Commission have the right to vote on its decisions. This notwithstanding, all member and observer states of the United Nations have the right to participate in the Commission's work as observers with the right to speak during debate, and to participate in informal negotiations. In fact, the importance attributed by governments to the work of the CSW is reflected in the large number of observers who participate actively in its annual sessions.

In addition to governmental observers, representatives from intergovernmental organizations, such as the Organization of African Unity or the Council of Europe, are regularly present during the CSW's sessions.

The participation of non-governmental organizations has always been pivotal in the CSW's work. These organizations provide a different perspective but also the political pressure and visibility to ensure that the concerns of women from all parts of the world and all socio-economic strata are addressed. NGOs are a crucial lobby at the national level to ensure that attention is paid to women's issues and that international law and policy are translated into practical reality on the ground. NGOs have brought many new and emerging issues to the attention of the international community, sparking the search for global responses among all member states of the United Nations.

The global conferences convened by the United Nations in the 1990s, including the Earth Summit in Rio de Janeiro in 1990, the World Conference on Human Rights in Vienna in 1993, the International Conference on Population and Development in Cairo in 1994, the World Summit for Social Development in Copenhagen, and the Fourth World Conference on Women in Beijing in 1995, have contributed to a dramatic increase in the number and type of NGOs that participate actively in the work of the United

Nations. While in the past such participation was limited primarily to large international NGOs with consultative status, the conferences of the 1990s inspired many national NGOs from all regions with few or no ties to international groups to contribute actively to the work of the United Nations.

The advancement of women and the achievement of gender equality were never perceived to be the sole responsibility of the CSW. On the contrary: from the very beginning, the Commission sought cooperation from other entities, and in particular with the specialized agencies of the United Nations system, such as the ILO. With the growing understanding of women's role in development, and their crucial role in the well-being of their families, communities and societies, most of the entities of the UN family have put in place specific programmes on women, and participate in the work of the CSW. Among the funds and programmes, UNDP, UNICEF and UNFPA provide funding for women-specific projects and programming within their areas of responsibility. Others, such as the FAO, UNESCO and UNHCR increasingly pay attention not only to women's particular circumstances, but they are also starting to pay attention to gender aspects at all stages of policy-making and implementation processes. In these efforts, the catalytic role of the CSW as a policy-making body has become even more important.

The role of the CSW in developing international legal norms and global policies Throughout its 50-year history, the CSW has played the leading role in identifying concerns that required the attention of the global community. From an early emphasis on developing the international legal framework of women's rights, the CSW proceeded to championing a more holistic, developmental approach to addressing women's concerns. Women's role in development became the central focus of the Commission's work well into the 1980s and early 1990s. During the last several years, and within the framework of the major United Nations conferences of the 1990s, the Commission has emphasized and reinforced the shift in its conceptual approach from dealing with women's issues as well-defined but separate issues for which solutions were sought either separately from other societal questions or within existing parameters of political, economic and social discourse, to formulating women's issues in terms of gender. Rather than focusing on women only, the gender approach focuses on relations between men and women, and how men's and women's gender roles shape and influence women's access to rights, opportunities and resources with regard to all issues on the global and national agendas. This shift in conceptual approach, reflected mainly in the use of a gender mainstreaming strategy in pursuing the goal of gender equality, receives now the particular attention of the CSW.

The next section will provide an overview of the various stages of the Commission's work, with particular attention to its norm- and policy-development role.

The development of the international legal and policy framework for achieving women's equality From the outset, the Commission focused its attention on the unequal legal situation in which women in most countries found themselves when compared with men. Through a number of surveys, studies and questionnaires, the Secretariat gathered the data and information upon which the CSW then proceeded to develop international human rights norms to address discrimination against women and to achieve equality. In this regard, the CSW drafted several instruments covering specific issues such as women's political and nationality rights. It also elaborated the meaning of a comprehensive non-discrimination and equality norm for women, and developed international mechanisms to monitor its implementation.

International human rights law presents an essential tool for women in the pursuit of equal rights and opportunities at the national level. At the same time, the realization of women's equality does not solely depend on the existence of appropriate legal norms and standards. In fact, while the equal treatment of women in the law is an essential basis, the achievement of women's *de facto* equality depends greatly on women's role in society, and on attitudes, perceptions and stereotypes concerning that role. Such attitudes cannot be changed with the stroke of a pen alone. Thus work on the legal framework was soon complemented by a strategy that shifted the focus from the drafting of legal rights to the actual enjoyment of these rights through policy formulation and institutional development. This strategy puts particular emphasis on addressing the causes of women's inequality rather than dealing with the symptoms.

The series of international human rights treaties of particular relevance for women, an increased awareness of the causes of women's inequality and a comprehensive approach to development constituted the framework for the elaboration, in successively more detailed form, of an international agenda for women's equality. This policy framework was combined with a strategy of convening high-visibility events to focus attention on the issues that women were bringing to the global bargaining table, and that needed to be addressed directly by national and international policy-makers if the equal rights of women were to be achieved.

Through a series of global events and action plans on the advancement of women since the mid-1970s, the achievement of the goal of women's equality, development and peace moved steadily from the periphery of international and national attention towards its centre.

Development of women-specific international human rights norms Immediately following their establishment in 1946 and 1947, the Commission on Human Rights and the Commission on the Status of Women embarked on translating into more concrete terms the United Nations Charter's promise of the faith in equal rights of men and women, and in the protection and promotion of the human rights and fundamental freedoms for all without discrimination. The CSW pursued a two-fold strategy of developing norms of particular relevance to women, and of influencing the development of general human rights norms in a way that would clearly reflect their applicability to women and men alike.

A first step in the effort of the CSW to develop the international legal framework for women's equality was its contribution to the drafting of the Universal Declaration of Human Rights. The Commission's proposals ensured that women's equality was specifically included in the Declaration, including with regard to women's equal rights as to marriage, during marriage, and at its dissolution.[6]

ISSUE-SPECIFIC CONVENTIONS Using information gathered on the legal status of women, the CSW drafted several conventions in the late 1940s and early 1950s that address specific areas where women's unequal legal status when compared with men was most apparent. As a result of this work, the General Assembly was able to adopt three conventions establishing women's equal rights in particular areas.

The Convention on the Political Rights of Women is based expressly on the Charter of the United Nations, and the two other Conventions are couched in the language of the Universal Declaration of Human Rights. They therefore represent a further elaboration of the principles established in the constitutional framework of the United Nations.

The Convention on the Political Rights of Women was adopted in 1952, and entered into force in 1954, after the necessary number of ratifications had been received. Under this Convention, ratifying states commit themselves to grant women, on equal terms with men and without discrimination, the right to vote, to stand for election, and to hold public office.[7]

The Convention on the Nationality of Married Women was adopted in 1957, and entered into force in 1958. This Convention establishes that married women have the right to retain their own nationality, and that the loss or acquisition of nationality of a woman shall not be influenced as a result of marriage, dissolution of marriage, or change of nationality by the husband during marriage.[8]

The Convention on Consent to Marriage, Minimum Age of Marriage and Registration of Marriages was adopted in 1962 and entered into force in 1964. The main purpose of this Convention is to establish the requirement of the consent of both parties to entering marriage.[9]

The Commission on the Status of Women was thus successful in elaborating specific Conventions on the rights of women long before the Commission on Human Rights was able to draft the two Covenants on Economic, Social and Cultural Rights and on Civil and Political Rights, which were adopted by the General Assembly in 1966 and entered into force in 1976.[10] Both covenants are intended to apply on a non-discriminatory basis to women and men. The Covenant on Civil and Political Rights covers the rights that had previously been elaborated in greater detail in the women-specific Conventions.

DECLARATION ON THE ELIMINATION OF DISCRIMINATION AGAINST WOMEN Following the successful adoption and entry into force of these three Conventions, member states identified a need to address all issues that had been studied over the years and that revealed widespread lack of equality in a comprehensive way. The Declaration on the Elimination of All Forms of Discrimination against Women was adopted by the General Assembly in 1967.[11] It covered a broad range of rights in the civil, political, economic, social and cultural sphere. As a Declaration, it is not a legally binding instrument but does have political and moral force, reflecting the consensus of the CSW and the Assembly that despite the adoption of international legal instruments of a women-specific and of a general nature, such as the two Covenants, considerable discrimination against women continued to exist both in law and in practice.

CONVENTION ON THE ELIMINATION OF ALL FORMS OF DISCRIMINA-TION AGAINST WOMEN One of the major recommendations emanating from the World Conference on Women in Mexico City in 1975 was the call for the speedy completion of the work on a binding legal instrument on the elimination of discrimination against women. Such a Convention had been under consideration in the Commission since 1972.

The Convention on the Elimination of All Forms of Discrimination against Women was adopted by the General Assembly in 1979, and entered into force in 1981.[12] As an international human rights instrument, the Convention creates rights and obligations. The Convention is discussed in detail in a separate chapter of this reader, but its historical importance will be highlighted here.

The issue-specific Conventions, the 1967 Declaration, and the non-discriminatory scope of other international human rights treaties had left a strong sense that insufficient attention was being paid to the whole range of discriminatory laws and practices women continued to be subjected to in all parts of the world. The elaboration of a binding international treaty, comprehensive in scope and of a global nature, was seen as the necessary basis for establishing clear obligations and duties for states towards the elimination of discrimination and the achievement of equality between women and men.

The absence of any mandatory monitoring mechanism under the three issue-specific Conventions and under the (non-binding) Declaration made it desirable to proceed with a Convention that would include an effective international monitoring mechanism to ensure implementation of the Convention. Such a mechanism would need to go beyond the voluntary presentation of progress reports by governments.

As a result, member states adopted the Convention on the Elimination of All Forms of Discrimination against Women, which is often also called a 'Bill of Rights for Women'. This is the first Convention to explain the general prohibition of discrimination against women, establishing the general norm and a comprehensive obligation to eliminate discrimination against women in all its forms. It addresses both intentional and unintentional discrimination, extending its reach to actions beyond those of, or on behalf of, governments to the conduct of non-state actors. It covers a wide range of rights in the political, civil, economic, social and private spheres. The Convention aims at ensuring women's equality as a goal and as a binding legal obligation. In other words, the Convention aims to ensure that gender does not impede women's ability to exercise and enjoy rights protected by international human rights law.

DECLARATION ON THE ELIMINATION OF VIOLENCE AGAINST WOMEN A review of international standards and norms on the rights of women is completed by reference to the Declaration on the Elimination of Violence against Women,[13] adopted by the General Assembly in 1993. Like the other women-specific human rights instruments mentioned earlier, it had been drafted by the CSW for adoption by the Assembly.

The Declaration represents the culmination of the efforts spearheaded by NGOs to sensitize the international community to an issue that was known to be pervasive in all countries and all social strata, but had nevertheless remained relegated to the exclusive attention of governments at the national level. In turn, governments chose in many instances to ignore the problem as falling outside the regulatory realm of the state, or to regulate only its most serious forms in criminal law. Enforcement of existing laws was oftentimes perceived to be reluctant at best. As a consequence, the existence of violence against women, if acknowledged, remained a private matter outside the state's responsibility for protection. In their efforts, NGOs made explicit that violence against women was a deprivation of fundamental human rights.

With the adoption of the Declaration, which provides a definition of violence against women, major progress has been made in legitimizing systematic attention to this issue by the international community. The Declaration takes a comprehensive view of violence, encompassing any act of gender-based violence that results in, or is likely to result in, physical, sexual or psychological harm or suffering by women, including threats of such acts, coercion or arbitrary deprivation of liberty, whether occurring in public or in private life. The Declaration spells out many actions aimed at protecting women against such violence through prevention, at the establishment of remedial measures when it occurs, and at prosecuting and punishing its perpetrators. The Declaration's broad definition and comprehensive prescription for actions gives the international community, governments at the national level, and women's groups an effective tool in addressing violence against women with regard to both its causes and its consequences.

While the Convention on the Elimination of All Forms of Discrimination against Women does not explicitly refer to violence against women, its monitoring body, the Committee on the Elimination of Discrimination against Women (CEDAW), has left no doubt that the Convention covers violence against women. The CEDAW's General Recommendation No. 19 (eleventh session 1992) declares that the Convention's definition of discrimination includes gender-based violence, that is violence that is directed against a woman because she is a woman or that affects women disproportionately.[14] Detailed guidance is provided to states parties as to their obligations under the Convention and the types of action they are expected to undertake to implement the Convention with regard to violence against women.

Another mechanism provided by the international community to focus attention on violence against women is the appointment, by the Commission on Human Rights in 1994, of a special rapporteur on violence against women, including its causes and its consequences.[15] The special rapporteur, whose initial three-year mandate was extended in 1997 and 2000,[16] focused in her first three reports on the nature of the problem, on violence against women in the family and community, and on violence perpetrated by the state.[17]

IMPLEMENTATION AND MONITORING OF INTERNATIONAL NORMS AND STANDARDS   As in the case of all international human rights norms, the purpose of norms of particular interest to women is their realization and full enjoyment by beneficiaries at the national level. Primary responsibility for their implementation rests with governments. The obligations of governments in ensuring the full and equal enjoyment of all human rights and fundamental freedoms by all are usually categorized into obligations to respect, obligations to protect and obligations to fulfil[18] enjoyment of human rights.

International supervisory and monitoring procedures, as well as international complaints mechanisms, have been developed to ensure national compliance with international norms, and to establish accountability of governments for their human rights performance *vis-à-vis* the international community. Such mechanisms can be categorized into Charter-based and treaty-based mechanisms, depending on whether they are grounded legislatively in the Charter of the United Nations, or in a particular human rights treaty.

The most common among the treaty-based monitoring procedures is regular reporting by states parties to international expert bodies, a procedure contained in all the major international human rights instruments. For example, under the Convention on the Elimination of All Forms of Discrimination against Women all states parties are required to submit regular reports on legislative and other measures taken to implement the Convention. The first of these reports is due one year after the entry into force for the ratifying state, and thereafter every four years.[19] The reports are considered by independent expert bodies established under the terms of the treaty. The Convention on the Elimination of All Forms of Discrimination against Women established the Committee on the Elimination of Discrimination against Women, consisting of 23 experts who serve in their personal capacity.[20]

A second treaty-based monitoring mechanism is the complaints procedure. Examples of the latter are the individual communications procedure established under the first Optional Protocol to the Covenant on Civil and Political Rights, and similar provisions contained in the Convention on the Elimination of All Forms of Racial Discrimination,[21] and the Convention against Torture and Other Cruel, Inhuman or Degrading Treatment or Punishment.[22]

In establishing regular reporting by states parties as a treaty obligation, the Convention on the Elimination of All Forms of Discrimination against Women goes well beyond the voluntary approach that had characterized earlier women-specific Conventions. A proposal to include an individual complaints procedure into the Convention, along the lines of the Optional Protocol to the Covenant on Civil and Political Rights, did not come to fruition during the drafting of the Convention.

With a renewed emphasis placed on implementation of international treaty obligations by recent United Nations conferences, the CSW was entrusted with the development of an optional protocol to the Women's Convention. Work on such an optional protocol started in 1996, and was successfully completed in 1999. The draft of the optional protocol was being submitted for adoption to the General Assembly at its 54th session in the fall of 1999, at which point it will be opened for signature, ratification and accession. It will enter into force three months after the tenth instrument of ratification or accession has been deposited with the secretary-general of the United Nations.[23]

The optional protocol contains two procedures: a communications procedure allowing individual women, or groups of women, to submit claims of violations of rights protected under the Convention to the Committee on the Elimination of Discrimination against Women. The Protocol establishes that in order for individual communications to be admitted for consideration by the Committee, a number of criteria must be met, including that domestic remedies must have been exhausted. The Protocol also creates an inquiry procedure enabling the Committee to initiate inquiries into situations of grave or systematic violations of women's rights. In either case, states must be party to the Protocol. The Protocol included an 'opt-out clause', allowing states upon ratification or accession to declare that they do not accept the inquiry procedure. The Protocol explicitly provides that no reservations may be entered to its terms. Furthermore, the Protocol requires states to protect individuals from ill-treatment or intimidation when they act under the Protocol. States are also required to give publicity to this instrument. With its entry into force, the Optional Protocol will put the Convention on the Elimination of All Forms of Discrimination against Women on an equal footing with other international human rights instruments having individual complaints procedures (International Covenant on Civil and Political Rights, Convention on the Elimination of All Forms of Racial Discrimination, and Convention against Torture and Other Forms of Cruel, Inhuman or Degrading Treatment or Punishment) as well as inquiry procedures (Convention against Torture).

Development of an international policy regime for the advancement of women Just as the early work of the CSW was noted for its equal rights orientation, so the second phase has been noted for its development orientation, characterized primarily by the Women in Development movement. The rapidly changing membership of the United Nations in the late 1950s and 1960s shifted attention to the needs of developing countries, and emphasized the importance of achieving a more balanced economic and social development in all countries. The CSW followed these trends and responded with the elaboration of a long-term programme of concerted international action for the advancement of women in the late 1960s. During this second phase of its work, the CSW focused on the needs of the vast majority of the world's women – women in developing countries

– and on their role in the social and economic development of their countries. The goal was to improve the situation of women and increase their effective participation without discrimination and on a basis of equality in all sectors of national and international life.

The development of the core of global policies for women makes up a third phase in the work of the United Nations for the advancement of women. This phase carries the three-fold theme of equality, development and peace. The signposts in this phase are intensified action to promote equality between women and men; increase women's contribution to national and international development; and recognize the importance of women's increasing contribution to the development of friendly relations and cooperation among states and to the strengthening of world peace.

From the first three world conferences on women and the United Nations Decade for Women, three main lessons were drawn for the future. First, measures for women that are taken in isolation from general development strategies result in little progress for women. Second, legislative and developmental action for women cannot be fully effective unless they are accompanied by steps to change attitudes and prejudices. And third, special supportive measures are needed to enable women to benefit from equal rights and development opportunities. These lessons would be further reviewed and developed by the 1995 Fourth World Conference on Women: Action for Equality, Development and Peace.

UNITED NATIONS EVENTS BETWEEN 1975 AND 1985 International Women's Year 1975[24] was declared by the General Assembly in 1972. The objective of the IWY was to define a society in which women participated in a real and full sense in economic, social and political life and to devise strategies whereby such societies could be developed. In 1975, the United Nations also observed for the first time International Women's Day, on 8 March.

The first global conference on women was the World Conference of the International Women's Year, Mexico City, 19 June to 2 July 1975.[25] The most important outcome of this conference was the adoption of a World Plan of Action for the Advancement of Women, representing the first global assessment of the role and status of women. The plan contained key areas for national and international action to promote the three-fold theme of equality, development and peace. A marked increase was expected in areas such as women's literacy, vocational training and equal access to education; in women's employment opportunities and in the recognition of the economic value of women's work; in their participation in public life; in access to health services; and in parity under the law, among other aspects.

The conference highlighted the widespread deficiency in data and information collection and analysis of the situation of women at all levels and in all areas. The existence of such data was considered essential in formulating policies, evaluating progress and in effecting social change for women.

In line with the emphasis on institutional development as a tool for achieving women's equality, the Plan called for the establishment of national machinery, such as commissions or women's bureaux, as a means for accelerating the implementation of the plan at national level. Such machinery was intended to study the situation of women, to develop policies and make programme and legislative recommendations to translate the national goals into reality for women.

The conference led to the creation of two women-specific institutions within the United Nations system to strengthen implementation of the plan, namely the International Research and Training Institute for the Advancement of Women (INSTRAW), and a fund to support innovative and catalytic projects for women in developing countries (UNIFEM).

The conference encouraged the speedy finalization of the Convention on the Elimination of All Forms of Discrimination against Women, which was then being drafted by the CSW.

The United Nations Decade for Women: Equality, Development and Peace, 1976–85, was proclaimed by the General Assembly following the Mexico conference. Its purpose was to provide sustained and effective attention to the implementation of the Plan of Action adopted in Mexico City, nationally and internationally.

The mid-term World Conference of the United Nations Decade for Women, Copenhagen, 14–30 July 1980[26] was devoted to an assessment of the progress achieved in the implementation of the Plan of Action of Mexico City, whereby progress was considered to be insufficient to bring about the desired quantitative and qualitative improvements in the status of women. The link between the world economic crisis and the situation of women was made explicit. Governments were urged to set specific quantitative and qualitative targets for the second half of the Decade, and to focus their activities especially on improving women's employment, health and education.

Concluding the Decade, 157 countries met in Nairobi at the World Conference to Review and Appraise the Achievements of the United Nations Decade for Women: Equality, Development and Peace, Nairobi, 15–26 July 1985. The major purpose was to review the progress made during these ten years. The strength of the global women's movements and their growing impact on the national and international agenda were reflected also in the regional preparatory conferences, and in the unprecedented numbers of NGOs who participated in the Nairobi conference and in the parallel forum of NGOs.

The Nairobi Forward-looking Strategies for the Advancement of Women[27] were designed as a blueprint for measures to overcome obstacles women encountered in achieving equality by 2000. Particular attention was given to especially vulnerable and disadvantaged groups of women, such as rural and urban poor women, elderly, abused, and refugee and displaced women.

The Strategies concluded the shift from the approach of the 1960s and early 1970s, whereby social welfare and support measures for women were seen as the primary means for raising their status. The view of women as beneficiaries of development was replaced in the course of the Decade by an approach that firmly established a policy view that the goals of equality, development and peace could be achieved only through the equal participation of women in development. This approach emphasizes women's central role as intellectuals, policy- and decision-makers, and planners, contributors and beneficiaries of development.

UNITED NATIONS FOURTH WORLD CONFERENCE ON WOMEN, 1995 The Fourth World Conference on Women, held in Beijing from 4 to 15 September 1995, and the Beijing Declaration and Platform for Action[28] adopted at the event constitute the most recent steps in the elaboration of global policies for women. The participation of 189 governments, over 2,500 NGOs in the official conference, and some 30,000 participants in the forum for NGOs made it at the time the largest gathering ever to be organized by the United Nations. Preparations for the event had been under way nationally, regionally and internationally since 1992. The preparation of nearly 170 national action plans gives an indication of the almost universal involvement in this process. These national preparations, and the five regional preparatory conferences in 1994[29] and their regional plans and platforms for action, fed into the global preparatory process under the leadership of the CSW.

The conference can be assessed in terms of its contribution to the equality agenda as such, and its contribution to the new global consensus on economic and social development that is emerging from the series of global United Nations conferences and summits held in the 1990s.

THE CONFERENCE AND ITS IMPORTANCE IN THE GLOBAL AGENDA FOR GENDER EQUALITY Remarkable improvements in women's participation and an increase in women's options and opportunities occurred during the Decade and since its conclusion. However, decisive breakthroughs for women's equality were not readily apparent. Political and economic developments in the 1980s and early 1990s were accompanied by evidence indicating that in some regions, women were losing ground they had apparently gained, such as in economic and political participation in Eastern Europe, or in terms of persistent and increasing poverty in Africa. Since women's losses were frequently more pronounced than men's, the conclusion was drawn that women's gains had been of a less structural nature than had been assumed.

The uneven picture for women that was presented during the 1990 progress review of the NFLS in the CSW gave new weight to arguments, especially from development experts, that the issue at stake was not so much women's integration into development, but rather the type and nature of development that was being pursued. Consequently, women increasingly called for a transformation of development itself. The major argument was that the dominant development agenda and its goals had been designed without women's full and equal participation, and did not reflect their expectations and experiences. Since gender equality, both as an end, but also as a means towards the realization of sustainable, human-centred development, was not an integral part of the predominant development paradigm, only a transformation of that development paradigm to take into consideration the concerns of women and of men would establish the necessary framework for the achievement of gender equality.[30]

The preparatory process for the Fourth World Conference on Women consolidated this shift from a women-specific approach to a gender approach. While the gender approach as a conceptual framework may have originated in the Women in Development movement, its validity and applicability has since been demonstrated in many different areas, including in the area of human rights and economic policies.[31]

The Platform for Action abandoned the framework according to which a global agenda for gender equality can be subdivided into the three categories of equality, development and peace. Instead, it emphasized that many, if not all, areas of concern to women will have their causes, consequences or solutions in these categories. The Platform identified twelve critical areas of concern for action over the next five years: women and poverty; education and training of women; women and health; violence against women; women and armed conflict; women and the economy; women in power and decision-making; institutional mechanisms for the advancement of women; human rights of women; women and the media; women and the environment; and the girl child.

While a number of these areas, such as education and the economy, had been singled out for attention in previous policy instruments, the Platform incorporates the issues that had recently emerged as critical for women's equality. For example, the NFLS had devoted not more than two specific paragraphs (out of 367) to the issue of violence against women, in the chapter on peace. Having come to the fore as a major concern of women around the world, the Platform firmly established violence against women as a legitimate public concern of all countries. It also expanded substantially on the results of the Vienna Conference on Human Rights of 1993 with regard to women's human rights. The section on women and health, one of the most controversial topics in Beijing, was groundbreaking as it included women's reproductive and sexual health and rights.

Another distinguishing feature of the Platform is its emphasis on action. Previous instruments had provided much detailed analysis of the situation of women and what needed to be achieved, but had been much less clear on how actually to achieve the goals. By contrast, the Platform identifies under each of the critical areas of concern specific strategic objectives and agrees on a series of actions that need to be taken. It identifies the main actors responsible for such actions. While the Platform leaves no doubt that primary responsibility for its implementation rests with governments at the national level, the international community through development cooperation and other activities, various entities of the UN system, NGOs and organizations of civil society, including the private sector, are also targeted and assigned responsibility for action.

In addition to elaborating specific actions to be taken for women and identifying actors responsible for their implementation, another distinguishing feature of the Platform is the establishment of the gender approach as the new conceptual approach for the achievement of equality. The Platform establishes mainstreaming of a gender perspective as the major strategy and tool in this effort. To highlight this, governments committed themselves in the Beijing Declaration to the implementation of the Platform, and ensuring that a gender perspective is reflected in all policies and programmes.[32] This commitment to gender mainstreaming is reiterated in regard to each of the twelve critical areas of concern.[33]

The Platform constitutes the global agenda for gender equality, building upon past experiences, developing new areas for action, and outlining new conceptual approaches for achieving goals. It sets out a two-pronged approach to the achievement of gender equality: on the one hand, it endorses specific actions, policies and programmes for women as essential in addressing disadvantages and inequality women continue to experience in the twelve critical areas of concern identified in the Platform. These could be characterized as efforts to deal with the symptoms, designed primarily to remedy the consequences of disadvantage, discrimination and inequality. On the other hand, the Platform leaves no doubt that all policies and programmes in any field must be based on an assessment of their implications for women and men. As such, gender equality is no longer the responsibility of women and of women-specific institutions and processes alone. Rather, all policies and programmes are instrumental for the achievement of gender equality, through gender mainstreaming.[34]

As the gender mainstreaming approach is intended to take account of women's, as well as men's, experiences and concerns from the very outset of policy design and development, to its implementation, monitoring and evaluation, this approach makes gender equality an integral part of all public action. It is thus intended to ensure that public policies actively support the achievement of this goal as integral part, rather than paying attention to women's concerns as an afterthought, or as a special and isolated concern.

THE FOURTH WORLD CONFERENCE ON WOMEN IN RELATION TO UNITED NATIONS CONFERENCES OF THE 1990S It has been argued that the efforts of the CSW in the 1950s and 1960s to promote women's equality remained limited in their effectiveness largely because they were isolated efforts of the women-specific machinery that did not find resonance in mainstream political or development work. This was somewhat remedied by the Women in Development movement, which focused on women's participation in development, not simply as beneficiaries, but as actors and contributors. It was, however, not until the 1990s that attention to the situation of women began to spread more systematically into various sectoral areas.

Gender-specific recommendations are contained in the outcomes of all the recent conferences and summits. While this development is in and by itself striking and attests to the effectiveness of the global governmental and non-governmental women's movements, the conference results remain to some degree steeped in a women-specific approach dedicating special paragraphs or sections to women and their concerns, rather than reflecting in their entirety a gender mainstreaming approach. Nevertheless, when these documents are read in conjunction with the Beijing Platform for Action in the implementation process, the structures and processes that perpetuate systemic and systematic discrimination against women can be identified, and effective remedial and preventive mainstreaming policies can be designed.

From Women to Gender: A Shift in Conceptual Approach

Gender and gender relations The term 'gender' refers to the socially constructed roles of women and men that are ascribed to them on the basis of their sex. The word 'sex' refers to physical and biological characteristics of women and men. Gender roles reflect different social constructions of female and male identities which result from their different social positions, rather than innate female and male behaviour. Gender roles are contingent on the socio-economic, political and cultural contexts, and are thus usually specific to a given time and space. They can vary according to the specific context in which they occur, and are affected by other variables, such as class, age, race and ethnicity. Gender roles are learned, and vary widely within and between cultures. Like all social constructs, they can change. Gender roles and relations shape women's access to rights, resources and opportunities, in public and in private life.

Current political, economic and social institutions have largely been shaped without reference to gender dimensions. Traditional expectations of women's roles have an impact on the enjoyment of rights, on equal access to opportunities and resources, to participation in decision-making at all levels, to benefits and other goods and services offered in societal settings.

Gender analysis is the systematic effort to document and understand the roles of men and women within a given context, and how a particular activity, decision or plan will affect men and women. It moves analysis beyond focus on women as an isolated group, and to consideration of an issue and its effects and impact on men and women. Attitudes, prejudices, assumptions and expectations held by individuals and society about women's roles regarding an issue continue to be obstacles to the achievement of women's equality. Gender analysis makes visible the advantages and disadvantages experienced by either group in relation to an issue, and provides the basis for taking steps to address disadvantages, and for devising remedial and preventive intervention strategies. Systematic assessment of the implications for men and women of legislation, of a policy or of a programme ensures that there is a more complete and objective picture of the costs and benefits for men, as well as for women, of an initiative before it is taken. Gender analysis allows for more just and equal representation of all members in shaping human society. It is thus a means to an end, namely the achievement of gender equality.[35]

Gender equality cannot be achieved by treating women and men identically, or through protective measures for women alone. Identical treatment ignores women's and men's different social realities and gendered roles. Protective measures for women do not challenge the source and nature of women's subordination. A focus on gender recognizes that women's unequal status is based on, and is perpetuated by, structures of systemic inequality and discrimination against women.

The importance of the gender approach to international human rights law Human rights and fundamental freedoms, being inherent in the human person, belong to women and men alike. Mainstream human rights approaches have therefore long insisted that human rights norms are gender-neutral, or unaffected by gender. However, structural imbalances of power between women and men, the systemic nature of discrimination against women, and the general absence of women in law creation and implementation continue to reflect disproportionately the experiences of men and exclude the experiences of women. These factors have also influenced the generally accepted understanding of international human rights law where the structure and the substance of norms present or preserve obstacles to women's equality. Taken together, these processes contribute to a lack of enjoyment of human rights by women, which has at its roots gender-specific explanations.

A gender analysis of the processes and norms of international human rights law can make explicit gender-based biases that perpetuate disadvantages and inequality for women. Gender factors have an impact on the enjoyment of any human right by women. The impact of gender must therefore be assessed with regard to the conceptualization and full realization of rights, i.e. women's enjoyment of them. The current understanding of international human rights norms largely reflects men's experiences, and perpetuates inattention to gender-specific abuses predominantly suffered by women. Issues that are not part of the traditional human rights canon but are being raised by women as human rights concerns include the many forms of violence that women suffer in the domestic sphere or the workplace; their lack of, or prevention from obtaining, access to reproductive health services and information, or of very restrictive abortion laws that both may have an impact on their right to life; discriminatory laws justified by culture and tradition, such as those connected with marriage and family laws; or private interferences with women's exercise of freedom of movement, freedom of expression, and to seek, receive and impart information that have their basis in gender discrimination and women's gendered roles. The prevalent emphasis on civil and political rights to the disadvantage of economic and social rights perpetuates the systemic disadvantages women face in access to economic resources and opportunities. Inheritance rights, wages, pregnancy-related discrimination in access to, or at, work are areas where women continue to face gender-based disadvantages.[36]

Many of these rights are reflected in existing international human rights instruments, in particular the Covenant on Economic, Social and Cultural Rights and the Covenant on Civil and Political Rights, and in the Convention on the Elimination of All Forms of Discrimination against Women. The general, even abstract, formulation of these texts makes it necessary to determine their meaning and nature through the tools of interpretation and application.

In that regard, the standard of measurement for the realization of women's equality need not be the current male standard of equality, which would simply be a reaffirmation of the status quo. Rather, a new standard of equality should be envisaged based on a reconsideration of current assumptions and a reconceptualization of the meaning of equality from a gender perspective, reflecting the visions, interests and needs of women, as well as those of men, as an integral and inherent part of any human rights discourse. Such a new standard would recognize as legitimate and 'normal' the needs and aspirations of women and men, rather than classifying women's needs as 'special' or 'particular', thus pushing them outside the regular standards of consideration.

When the paramount purpose of human rights and fundamental freedoms is their enjoyment by *all*, without discrimination, then these rights must be conceptualized in such a way that women's and men's enjoyment finds its space in that interpretation and realization. The Platform for Action, as a recently adopted policy instrument, functions in a synergistic way with international human rights law in that it serves as an interpretive tool for the current realities and the political and economic dynamics in which women find themselves, and which should form the basis for the reading of international human rights law. Consequently, the gender approach established in the Platform should inform the interpretation and application of international human rights law in a progressive and forward-looking manner.

Recent Developments in International Human Rights Activities to Mainstream a Gender Perspective

In recent years, and in particular since the World Conference on Human Rights, there has been major progress in focusing on women's enjoyment of their human rights. Such efforts have emphasized a two-pronged strategy.

On the one hand, calls are made to strengthen the women-specific human rights regime represented by the Convention on the Elimination of All Forms of Discrimination against Women and its monitoring mechanism. The importance of the Convention and its expert body results from its global leadership role in addressing issues of particular concern to women at the national level. It also lies in CEDAW's ability to provide guidance and advice to mainstream institutions on the integration of gender issues structurally into their work.

There are a number of indicators that clearly point to the renewed importance and strength of the women-specific regime. In 1997, for the first time CEDAW was able to meet twice in a single calendar year to implement its responsibilities under the Convention, including to consider reports of states parties.[37] CEDAW's recent general recommendations are marked by a qualitative difference when compared to the resolution-like recommendations adopted in earlier years. The most recent general recommendations, particularly No. 19 on violence against women of 1992, No. 21 on equality in marriage and family relations (articles 9, 15 and 16), No. 23 on women in public life (articles 7 and 8), and No. 24 on women and health (article 12) are detailed and carefully crafted statements of the Committee reflecting its authoritative understanding of the meaning of these issues and articles of the Convention, and the obligations of governments to ensure compliance with the Convention.[38]

The development of a complaints procedure to allow individuals and other petitioners to approach CEDAW about alleged violations of the rights protected by the Convention is another indication of the power attributed to the Convention. The latter is, however, also a reflection of a pervasive sense that notwithstanding the gains made in terms of attention to women's human rights concerns in the general human rights activities, these concerns still need their own structures, mechanisms and advocates for effective consideration.

On the other hand, increasing attention is being focused on the extent to which general human rights activities are paying attention to the human rights of women. The primary target of gender mainstreaming in international human rights law is what has come to be described as 'the mainstream', i.e. the processes and institutions that currently shape the substance and interpretation of that law. Here, only very few examples can be provided as an indication of some of the work that is being done.

The World Conference on Human Rights, Vienna 1993, was a signal event in expanding the human rights agenda to include gender-specific violations.[39] While the Conference singled out violence against women and other forms of violence such as systematic rape, sexual abuse and forced pregnancy in armed conflict as violations of women's human rights, it must be underlined that gender-specific violations of human rights go well beyond these abuses and encompass any type of human rights violation that is either caused by gender or takes a particular form because the victim is a woman.

Following the Vienna conference, the Commission on Human Rights, as well as various mechanisms established under the Commission, have started to pay more attention to violations of women's human rights. While this is welcome, it must be acknowledged that these efforts remain largely *ad hoc*. They depend upon individuals' familiarity with the gender approach and their willingness to reflect this approach in their analysis and work. A systemic, structural shift has, however, not yet occurred.[40]

The human rights treaty bodies, prompted to no small extent by CEDAW, are increasingly paying attention to gender issues. During the annual meeting of the chairpersons of human rights treaty bodies, a discussion of the use of a gender perspective by the treaty bodies is included in the agenda.[41] Concluding comments/observations adopted by treaty bodies following consideration of states parties' reports indicate the experts' growing awareness of the impact of gender factors on the enjoyment of human rights.[42] The Human Rights Committee has elaborated a general comment on article 3, the obligation of states parties to ensure the equal right of men and women to the enjoyment of all the rights covered by the Covenant. This new general comment offers a welcome opportunity to conduct a thorough and systematic gender analysis of all the provisions of the Covenants. The Committee on the Elimination of Racial Discrimination has adopted a general recommendation No. XXV on gender-related dimensions of racial discrimination. Other indications include growing attention to the human rights situation of women during the consideration of states parties reports, and better information exchange between the various Committees and CEDAW.

Conclusion

Attention to the human rights of women has been a central focus of the work of the Commission on the Status of Women since its inception. Together with the Committee on the Elimination of Discrimination against Women, the Commission has developed a comprehensive understanding of the norm of non-discrimination. The general prohibition of discrimination has two aspects which are both reflected in the objectives of the Platform for Action and in the Convention on the Elimination of All Forms of Discrimination against Women: one, to ensure that gender does not impair women's ability to exercise their human rights; and two, to undertake specific efforts to change – transform – structures and processes that perpetuate women's inequality in all spheres of life.

Since the Fourth World Conference on Women, the shift in conceptual approach to achieving equality has been consolidated. The gender approach focuses on relations between women and men, and on the impact of gender roles in access to rights, opportunities and resources in societal settings, rather than on the situation of women alone. The gender approach is equally important in promoting women's enjoyment of their human rights as it allows for explicit attention to gender-based factors in the conceptualization of rights and in their full and equal enjoyment by women.

Notes

1. The views expressed in this chapter are those of the author and do not necessarily reflect those of the United Nations Secretariat.

2. Throughout this chapter, *The United Nations and the Advancement of Women,*

1945–1996, United Nations Sales Publication No. E.96.I.9, serves as an indispensable reference tool. This 850-page publication, Vol. VI of the United Nations Blue Books series, contains all essential legal and policy documents adopted by the United Nations since 1945, including, most recently, the Beijing Declaration and Platform for Action. Recent documents and reports of the secretary-general, resolutions, national action plans, reports of state parties to the Convention on the Elimination of All Forms of Discrimination against Women and of the Committee, documents and reports related to an optional protocol to the Convention, and so on, are posted on the website of the United Nations Division for the Advancement of Women at the following address: http://www.un.org/womenwatch/daw

3. Document 6 in the Blue Book.

4. Document 84 in the Blue Book reproduces the Nairobi Forward-looking Strategies for the Advancement of Women.

5. Document 135 in the Blue Book.

6. General Assembly resolution 217 A (III) of 10 December 1948. Document 12 in the Blue Book.

7. General Assembly resolution 640 (VII) of 20 December 1952. Document 26 in the Blue Book.

8. General Assembly resolution 1040 (XI) of 29 January 1957. Document 29 in the Blue Book.

9. General Assembly resolution 1763 A (XVII) of 7 November 1962. Document 31 in the Blue Book.

10. The two Covenants were adopted by General Assembly resolution 2200 A (XXI) of 16 December 1966.

11. General Assembly resolution 2263 (XXII) of 7 November 1967. Document 36 in the Blue Book.

12. General Assembly resolution 34/180 of 18 December 1979. Document 69 in the Blue Book.

13. General Assembly resolution 48/104 of 20 December 1993. Document 107 in the Blue Book.

14. See UN document A/47/38, Report of the Committee on the Elimination of Discrimination against Women at its eleventh session, 1992.

15 Commission on Human Rights resolution 1994/45 of 4 March 1994. Document 110 in the Blue Book.

16. Commission on Human Rights resolutions 1997/44 and 2000/45.

17. Document 115 in the Blue Book.

18. See, for example, Asbjorn Eide, 'Realization of social and economic rights and the minimum threshold approach', *Human Rights Law Journal*, Vol. 10, Nos 1–2, 1989.

19. Article 18 establishes that the reports are to cover the 'legislative, judicial, administrative and other measures' that have been adopted to give effect to the provisions of the Convention. The periodicity of reports is also established in this article.

20. Article 17 of the Convention.

21. Article 14.

22. Article 22.

23. The General Assembly adopted the Optional Protocol in resolution 54/4 of 6 October 1000. Having obtained the required ten ratifications, it entered into force on 22

December 2000. As of December 2001, 28 states have become party to the Optional Protocol. For the text, drafting history and materials see *The Optional Protocol: Text and Materials*, United Nations Publications, Sales No. E.00.IV.2.

24. Document 41 in the Blue Book (GA resolution of 1972 declaring 1975 International Women's Year).

25. Document 45 in the Blue Book.

26. Document 70 of the Blue Book.

27. See document 84 in the Blue Book.

28. See document 127 in the Blue Book.

29. The five regional conferences took place in Mar del Plata, Argentina, for the Latin American and Caribbean region; in Dakar, Senegal, for the African region; in Jakarta, Indonesia, for the Asia and Pacific region; in Amman, Jordan, for the Western Asian region; and in Vienna, Austria, for the European region.

30. The *World Survey on the Role of Women in Development 1994* discusses the gender approach in the framework of development. United Nations sales publication No. E.95. IV.1, pp. 1–4.

31. For the gender approach see below. The implications of gender analysis for economic policies have been discussed in a report of the secretary-general to the fifty-second session of the General Assembly, A/52/345.

32. Paragraph 38 of the Declaration.

33. Respectively, paragraphs 57, 79, 105, 123, 141, 164, 189, 202, 229, 238, 252 and 273 of the Platform for Action.

34. During its coordination segment in 1997, the Economic and Social Council considered the question of gender mainstreaming into all policies and programmes in the United Nations system. It adopted Agreed Conclusions 1997/2, proposing recommendations for action by intergovernmental bodies and at the institutional level. The Agreed Conclusions define gender mainstreaming as 'the process of assessing the implications for women and men of any planned action, including legislation, policies or programmes, in any area and at all levels. It is a strategy for making women's as well as men's concerns and experiences an integral dimension in the design, implementation, monitoring and evaluation of policies and programmes in all political, economic and societal spheres so that women and men benefit equally and inequality is not perpetuated. The ultimate goal is to achieve gender equality.' UN doc. A/52/3.

35. For the gender approach see *World Survey on the Role of Women in Development 1994*. The implications of the gender mainstreaming approach in terms of analysis are described in the Report of the Secretary-General on the follow-up to the Fourth World Conference on Women, A/51/322.

36. See Christine Ainetter Brautigam, 'Mainstreaming a gender perspective in the work of United Nations human rights treaty bodies', 91 ASIL PROC. 145 (1997).

37. Under the terms of the Convention, the Committee is entitled to meet for two weeks every year to consider states parties reports, and to make suggestions and recommendations. For many years, the General Assembly of the United Nations, which approves the Committee's budget, granted the Committee a three-week session, preceded by a one-week pre-sessional working group to prepare the questions to be raised with reporting states. Following the Committee's repeated requests to the Assembly, the Assembly granted the Committee, starting in 1997, two three-week sessions annually, each preceded by a one-week working group, ostensibly for the purpose of reducing the

backlog of reports awaiting consideration. By comparison, other human rights treaty bodies with comparable numbers of ratifications have for years had the right to meet up to twelve weeks annually to implement their treaty responsibilities.

38. Most of the treaty bodies elaborate general comments or recommendations. These are the authoritative views of the respective Committee on an article or issue covered by a treaty, and are based on a Committee's experience gained through the consideration of many states parties reports. These comments illustrate the meaning of the treaties, and provide essential guidance to states parties in the implementation of the treaty. On the purpose of general comments see the introductions to general comments by the Human Rights Committee and the Committee on Economic, Social and Cultural Rights. A compilation of all general comments/recommendations is contained in UN doc. HRI/GEN/1/Rev.2. CEDAW's general comments are also available on the DAW's website.

39. An excerpt of the Vienna Declaration and Programme of Action is contained in document 106 in the Blue Book.

40. For an overview of progress made so far see a recent report submitted to the Commission on Human Rights, E/CN.4/1997/40. While the report presents a very useful picture of the current attention paid to the human rights of women, it does not assess the implications of women's gendered roles for their enjoyment of human rights. The regular reports on follow-up to the Fourth World Conference on Women submitted to the CSW are useful in tracing progress in gender mainstreaming system-wide. See, most recently, the following reports: E/CN.6/1999/2, E/1999/54, and A/53/308, all available from the DAW's website.

41. See the most recent reports of the meeting of the chairpersons A/51/482, A/52/507, A/53/125 and A/53/432.

42. At the request of the eighth meeting of persons chairing human rights treaty bodies, the Division for the Advancement of Women prepared a study on the integration of a gender perspective in the work of United Nations human rights treaty bodies, UN doc. HRI/MC/1998/6, available from DAW's website.

2

Human Rights of Women at the Fiftieth Anniversary of the United Nations

Dorota Gierycz

In spite of the obvious fact that society is composed of women and men and that both belong to the category of 'human beings', the concept of 'human rights of women' is still subject to misunderstanding and mis-interpretation. In real life – at a time when the UN is celebrating its fiftieth anniversary – the human rights of women are far from being recognized and observed.

The following questions are often raised. Why do we talk about the human rights of women? Is it because their protection is not covered by the provisions on general human rights? And what about the rights of men? Moreover, why did the early international human rights instruments – for example, the Universal Declaration of Human Rights of 1948 – not refer directly to the human rights of women? Has something changed in the meantime?

All these questions have frequently been asked since the 1993 World Conference on Human Rights in Vienna, which explicitly placed the issue of the human rights of women on the international governmental agenda and incorporated that terminology in its Declaration and Programme of Action, stating that 'the human rights of women and of the girl-child are an inalienable, integral and indivisible part of universal human rights' (paragraph 18). Since 1993 the term has been increasingly used in the literature on the subject, as well as at governmental and non-governmental meetings, including its consistent application throughout the preparatory process to the Fourth World Conference on Women in Beijing in 1995 and in its final document 'Platform for Action'. However, for many the question remains – why 'human rights of women'?

International Standards of Equality and Protection of Human Rights of Women

The protection of the human rights of women is rooted in the international standards of equality and the protection of human rights, which are encompassed in both general international and regional instruments and the instruments that specifically address all or selected human rights in relation to women.

General standards The historical evolution of the concept of human rights led to the formulation of contemporary legal standards, set out, *inter alia*, in the United Nations Charter, the Universal Declaration of Human Rights and the International Covenants on Human Rights, and two Optional Protocols to the International Covenant on Civil and Political Rights, known as the International Bill of Human Rights. Those standards are derived from universally recognized principles, which state that human rights are attributed to human beings only; that they are attributed to all human beings equally, without any distinction as to race, ethnicity, sex, religion, social or civil status; and that they are rights of which no person can be deprived, and which no one can take away or violate without legal consequences.

The International Bill of Human Rights encompasses a broad catalogue of human rights and freedoms related to all spheres of life: political, economic, social, cultural, civil and personal. They include, *inter alia*, such rights as the right to life; the right to freedom of opinion and expression; the right to education; the right to health; and the right to work. Those general international human rights instruments, however, do not directly refer to the human rights of women. Rather, they set the standards of human rights protection for everyone, and explicitly state the principles of sex equality and non-discrimination . Thus they provide a strong foundation for the protection of the human rights of women.

The principles of respect for human rights and equality between women and men are enshrined in the United Nations Charter. The Charter re-affirms in its preamble 'faith in fundamental human rights, in the dignity and worth of the human person, in the equal rights of men and women and of nations large and small'.[1] Article 1, paragraph 3, of the Charter lists among the main purposes of the United Nations the achievement of 'international co-operation in promoting and encouraging respect for human rights and for fundamental freedoms for all without distinction as to race, sex, language or religion'.[2]

The Universal Declaration of Human Rights (1948) states that 'All human beings are born free and equal in dignity and rights' (Article 1) and that 'Everyone is entitled to all the rights and freedoms set forth in this Declaration, without distinction of any kind, such as race, colour, sex, language, religion, political or other opinion, national or social origin, property, birth or other status' (Article 2). Article 7 of the Declaration states that 'All are equal before the law and are entitled without any discrimination to equal protection of the law. All are entitled to equal protection against any discrimination in violation of this Declaration and against any incitement to such discrimination.'[3]

Similar provisions can be found in Article 26 of the International Covenant on Civil and Political Rights adopted on 16 December 1966 by General Assembly resolution 2200 (XXI). The article, which contains what is generally recognized as a non-discriminatory provision, states that 'All persons are equal before the law and are entitled without any discrimination to the equal protection of the law. In this respect, the law shall prohibit any discrimination and guarantee to all persons equal and effective protection against discrimination on any ground such as race, colour, sex, language, religion, political or other opinion, national or social origin, property, birth or other status.'[4]

Other international standards are related to some specific areas of human rights. The 1974 Universal Declaration on the Eradication of Hunger and Malnutrition, endorsed by GA res. 2248 (XXX), is a case in point. The Declaration states that 'Every man, woman and child has the inalienable right to be free from hunger and malnutrition in order to develop fully and maintain their physical and mental faculties' (paragraph 1).[5] The terms of the Declaration, however, have been particularly disregarded in relation to women. While many experience hunger, it has been documented that differential levels of feeding, nutrition and care of female children contribute to higher levels of female mortality, despite the fact that girls are biologically stronger. WHO and UNICEF reports indicate that in many countries the life expectancy for female infants is lower than that for boys; that girls are breast-fed for shorter periods of time; that they are fed less; and that the girls and women eat after the boys and males.[6]

The obvious lack of application of the international human rights standards to women, or their biased and discriminatory application, provides grounds for two kinds of actions: efforts to strengthen and sanction the implementation of those standards in regard to women, and the elaboration of specific regulations aimed at the elimination of discrimination against women and the full implementation of human rights of women in all spheres of life.

Specific regulations When the United Nations was established, it was clear to many that the historically inferior position of women in society called the implementation of the universal and gender neutral standards of human rights to women into question. The United Nations Charter and the organization itself were products of almost exclusively male negotiations, with Eleanor Roosevelt as the only, noble, exception. Owing largely to her efforts, in 1946 ECOSOC established the Commission on the Status of Women as a subsidiary body in order to implement in practice the principle that men and women have equal rights. At its first session, the Commission emphasized (in document E/90 of 1 July 1946) that its main purpose was to 'prepare recommendations and reports for ECOSOC on promoting women's rights in political, economic, social and educational fields' with the objective of ensuring *de facto* observance of the human rights of women.[7]

Passing years have proved that despite the catalogue of international human rights contained in the international instruments related to all human beings, women do not enjoy full and equal human rights and freedoms and suffer from both *de jure* and *de facto* gender discrimination in all spheres of life. The *de jure* situation at the national level in some countries and the *de facto* situation in all countries has been and remains one of discrimination compared to men. However, the degree of discrimination varies significantly from country to country and from region to region.

Consequently, new legal instruments have been developed in order to protect the human rights of women in the areas in which they are particularly neglected and in order to supplement the general provisions. The 1952 Convention on the Political Rights of Women, the 1957 Convention on the Nationality of Married Women, the 1974 Declaration on the Protection of Women and Children in Emergency and Armed Conflict, and the 1985 Nairobi Forward-looking Strategies are cases in point.

Although the Strategies were adopted by consensus at the Third World Conference on Women in 1985, they are not legally binding; rather, they reflect a moral consensus of the international community and provide an understanding of how equality and the human rights of women should be interpreted in practice. The Strategies strongly emphasize the necessity of fully observing the equal rights of women and eliminating *de jure* and *de facto* discrimination. In particular, they address the social, economic, political and cultural roots of *de facto* inequality. They assert that adequate legislation exists in the majority of countries and that it is ineffective implementation that is a major obstacle to the full participation of women in all spheres of life. The Strategies also provide a set of measures to improve the *de facto* human rights of women with regard to social and political participation, decision-making, role in the family, employment, education and training, equality under the law, health and social security.[8]

Among the international instruments specifically focused on the human rights of women, the most prominent and meaningful are the 1979 Convention on the Elimination of All Forms of Discrimination against Women and the 1993 Declaration on the Elimination of Violence against Women.

Convention on the Elimination of All Forms of Discrimination against Women

Its provisions and their meaning   The Convention on the Elimination of All Forms of Discrimination against Women, adopted by the General Assembly on 18 December 1979, constitutes the central and most comprehensive bill of human rights of women. The spirit and objectives of the Convention derive from principles of international law, general standards of equality and human rights and the goals of the United Nations. The Convention is also the product of more than thirty years of work by the United Nations Commission on the Status of Women.

The Convention explicitly states in its Preamble that 'extensive discrimination against women exists' and it defines discrimination as 'any distinction, exclusion or restriction made on the basis of sex which has the effect or purpose of impairing or nullifying the recognition, enjoyment or exercise by women, irrespective of their marital status, on the basis of equality of men and women, of human rights and fundamental freedoms in the political, economic, social, cultural, civil or any other field' (Article 1).[9]

It further condemns discrimination in all its forms and obliges states parties to pursue comprehensive policies and measures to eliminate discrimination against women at all levels, to apply sanctions and other measures to redress discriminatory situations, to repeal legal provisions and to modify discriminatory customs and regulations (Article 2). Its stated purpose is 'full development and advancement of women, for the purpose of guaranteeing them the exercise and enjoyment of human rights and fundamental freedoms on a basis of equality with men' (Article 3).[10] Subsequent provisions of the Convention (Articles 6–16) constitute a more detailed agenda for action towards equality of women which covers practically all aspects of human rights.

In Article 6 the states parties undertake an obligation to suppress all forms of traffic in women and exploitation of prostitution of women. Despite that provision, both forms of exploitation are prevalent worldwide, and in some regions they are on the increase. Poverty and economic crises in many parts of the world – for example, in many African countries and in some parts of Asia and Latin America – have been accompanied by growing prostitution. Women and, increasingly, children are being exploited by massive 'sex tourism' in many countries, with Thailand and the Philippines at the top of the list. A shocking record of daily incidents of forced prostitution – kidnapping girls; the selling of children, mainly girls, by poor families; and various forms of trafficking in women – is provided by daily media reports. For example, in Thailand about 800,000 girls under the age of 16, being sold at the age of 11, make their living from prostitution; in India 400,000 out of an estimated 2 million women in prostitution are minors. The hearings organized by NGOs during the World Conference on Human Rights in Vienna also provided important evidence in that respect that has shaken public opinion and forced governments at least to recognize the problem. The transition to democracy and a free market economy in Eastern Europe, with its high social and economic costs, brought similar consequences to that region, although those vary among the countries.[11]

Articles 7 and 8 of the Convention focus on the right of women to equal participation in political life, including decision-making at national and international levels. While Article 7 focuses on basic political rights, such as the right to vote, to participate in politics, including decision-making, and to hold public office, Article 8 reflects the new global reality, extending those rights to the international sphere, such as representation by women of their countries abroad, participation in meetings and negotiations at the international level and employment in international organizations.

Concerning the participation of women in politics and decision-making, the gap between *de jure* and *de facto* rights is one of the most significant. According to the latest data compiled by the Inter-Parliamentary Union (IPU) as of 30 June 1994, more than a hundred years after women's suffrage in New Zealand and Australia, the percentage of women in parliament, on average, was 10.51 per cent, with 10.8 per cent in a single or lower chamber and 8.6 per cent in other chambers.[12] Throughout history, there have been only 23 democratically elected female heads of state or government.[13] In 1994, on average, women constituted 6.2 per cent of cabinet ministers and 62 countries had no women ministers in the cabinet.[14] In the United Nations' fifty years of existence, of the 49 presidents of the General Assembly elected since 1945, only two were women. There has been no woman secretary-general of the organization, and in 1994, of 19 deputies to the secretary-general (under-secretaries-general) only two were women.[15] The participation of women at the highest ranks of bilateral and multilateral diplomacy has been almost invisible. Thus, although almost no country publicly disavows the right of women to political participation, their lack of participation is self-evident.

Articles 10–13 of the Convention reaffirm the human rights of women in the areas of education (Art. 10), employment (Art. 11), health (Art. 12), and economic and social activities (Art. 13) respectively and call for the elimination of ongoing discrimination. Article 14 pays special attention to the situation of women in rural areas with regard to those rights.

In spite of the progress achieved, the situation of women in all those areas remains one of discrimination. Although women have progressed towards equal education, huge gaps still exist between men's and women's educational achievements. Despite expanded literacy programmes for adults in many countries, the literacy rate for women is only two-thirds that of men.[16] According to UNESCO statistics, women constituted as much as 65 per cent of illiterates worldwide in 1993, with the highest illiteracy rates in Africa, Asia and Pacific. Even bigger discrepancies exist in terms of the level and quality of education, especially in some developing regions. Although the number of women in primary education has increased, the number of drop-outs remains unacceptably high. Young girls leave school because of socio-cultural constraints; in order to work in the household; to undertake paid employment to support their families; to care for siblings; because of early pregnancy and marriage; or because the families, facing constraints, decide to educate only boys. Young women are also often more influenced by the tradition and conditioning of their families, which make their choices more restricted.[17]

In terms of employment, the Convention obliges states parties to ensure, on the basis of equality of men and women, an inalienable right to work; the same employment opportunities; free choice of profession and employment; equal benefits, remuneration and conditions of service. There is no country in the world where all those conditions are met *de facto*. Existing data, although fragmented and often confusing because of the criteria applied and the indicators used, show that the participation of women in the labour market is increasing, however it lags far behind the participation rate of men. Neither is it matched by a qualitative improvement in the women's labour force where women are highly discriminated against.

According to recent UN and ILO data, 41 per cent of the world's women aged 15 and above are economically active. In the OECD countries, in 1990 women constituted 60 per cent of the labour force; in the developing countries, 31 per cent. However, if women's participation in the informal sector or in agriculture is included, the proportion increases significantly. For example, in India, the percentage of economically active women increases from 13 per cent to 88 per cent. In some countries in Africa, women produce 80 per cent of the food, but their contributions are often not remunerated or legally protected or honoured with proper contracts, work-related allowances, or even recognized as productive in terms of national economic development. Most women in the world work in underpaid, poorly regulated conditions, in occupations with low prestige and salaries. They are often denied equal remuneration and access to training, and face discrimination in their career development. Between 75 per cent and 80 per cent of female workers in the developed market economies are employed in the service sector; 15 per cent to 20 per cent in industry, mainly in the traditional women's occupational sectors such as textiles, food processing or clothing; and 5 per cent in agriculture.[18] Similar tendencies characterize women's paid work in the agricultural and informal sectors.

On average, women earn only 50 per cent to 80 per cent of men's wages.[19] They are poorly represented in decision-making positions in the public sector – at the governmental level and at the upper levels of the civil service. However, they are even worse off in the private sector, where there are almost no women in chief executive positions among managers of leading corporations (1 per cent).[20] An overwhelming majority of national military forces ban women from combat positions or relegate them exclusively to administrative and supportive positions. The situation in the police force is not much better.[21] Women are still legally excluded, or discriminated against by law in certain fields, or in certain jobs considered as particularly 'dangerous' or 'unhealthy' to female reproductive roles. It happens that those jobs are well paid.

The fact that adult female citizens are legally prohibited from certain occupations clearly indicates that women are not regarded as full citizens who, like men, can determine for themselves, on an individual basis, whether they want to accept such employment or assume certain positions. In the majority of countries, the state takes such decisions on behalf of women, who are largely absent or grossly under-represented at decision-making levels.

Women's right to health is also largely ignored. In general, much more attention is given to women as health and care providers than to their own health needs and status. In some parts of the world, women's health is addressed primarily in connection with reproductive roles and maternal–child health care services. There is no doubt that those services are very important to both women and children; however, the consideration of women's health exclusively in the context of family health care or in the capacity of nurturers shows the lack of focus on women's own right to health.

Limitations and cuts in health budgets and services, especially in rural areas, have a direct and negative impact on women's health. In the mid-1980s, 37 of the world's poorest countries cut their health budgets by half.[22] The health and nutritional status of many women, especially poor women and those in developing countries, are also seriously undermined by frequent pregnancies. Women who continuously become pregnant and give birth are at high risk of maternal mortality. The comparison of maternal mortality between developing and developed countries shows that, on average, in a developing country, one in 25 to 40 women dies in childbirth; in a developed country, one in 3,000. Female children also experience greater health risks than their male counterparts due to unequal health care. For example, some studies indicate that more boys than girls are brought to clinics when fees are charged, and four times as many boys as girls undergo paid immunization in clinics.[23]

The Convention points in Article 13 to the right to equal access of women to family benefits, credit, bank loans and mortgages, as well as to recreation and cultural life. The discrimination in that area is most visible in the case of rural women.

Article 14 of the Convention specifically focuses on the equal right of rural women, with men, to economic benefits, credit, loans and marketing facilities, as well as to education, health and social care, the right to participate in formulating developmental strategies and to have adequate living conditions. Thus the state parties should take appropriate measures to change the present situation in which the great majority of the poor in developed and developing countries are women, most of them in rural areas. More than 550 million women, 60 per cent of the rural population, live below the poverty line. Poverty among rural women is growing faster than among rural men. Over the last 20 years, the number of women in absolute poverty has risen by 50 per cent compared to the 30 per cent rise for rural men. In spite of their low status and poverty, rural women constitute 67 per cent of the agricultural labour force and produce on average 55 per cent of the food in developing countries.[24] Rural women are also increasingly responsible for income-generation and the daily survival of their families. Women in rural households are often more disadvantaged than other women due to a lack of access to health services, education, social services and child care. They are also in the disadvantageous position in their families, working on the farms, and carrying excessive work and household responsibilities. The poverty and the disadvantageous position of rural women is also strongly linked to the almost exclusive ownership of land by men in most developing countries, due to inheritance and other traditional practices, excluding women either *de jure* or *de facto* from the possession of property. As rural women do not own land, they consequently face major barriers in controlling it and getting credit, loans or access to affordable and appropriate technology for agricultural purposes.

That particularly discriminatory position of rural women with regard to their civil capacity and business matters also contradicts the obligations under Article 15 of the Convention, which stresses the full equality of women with men in a civil capacity and in business matters. Although discrimination in these areas affects rural women in most countries of the world, it also affects women, independently from their social position in some developing countries and regions, where the prevailing attitudes and regulations condition women's civil capacity by their family or marital status, or by treating women as 'extensions' of their husbands or other men in the family. Thus the equal right to civil capacity, like the right to equality in family and marriage (Article 16), points to the areas where most of *de jure* and *de facto* inequalities and acts of violence against women take place. The inequality of women in those spheres is strongly defended by fundamentalists. Attempts by some governments and human rights activists to change it to conform more closely with international standards are seen as attacks on tradition, customs that 'are protecting women', national sovereignty and religious freedom.

The articles in question, as well as Article 9 stating the equality of women with men in choosing nationality, irrespective of the woman's marital status, assert the equal rights and obligations of women and men with regard to basic personal decisions such as choice of spouse, conclusion and dissolution of marriage and of civil contracts, parenthood, profession, nationality, domicile, and command over property.

Discrimination and violations of those rights range from restriction on women's personal freedom of movement, and deprivation of property and parental rights, to direct violence, involving such 'cultural' and 'traditional' practices as suttee, dowry, female circumcision, and social, and sometimes even legal, permission to kill women who do not obey customs in terms of dress, behaviour or family relations.[25] In some countries and cultures, for example, women are confined to domesticity, and are not allowed to appear in public unattended; they are forbidden to socialize, and therefore to work and study with men, to drive a car, to travel or even to obtain basic identification documents, such as passports, without the consent of a husband or another senior male in the family. Women have no choice but to accept polygamous marriages and the status of one of several wives, because of legal, social and economic constraints. The economic motivations of those regulations and customs play an important role in preserving women's dependency and inequality and providing direct material gains to men and their families as a result. For example, the inheritance laws and practices, whereby property ownership and management pass to male family members only, exclude women from the ownership of property and from economic self-reliance. Under some legal systems, not only can women not inherit, but they themselves constitute part of an inheritance. For example, widows are not permitted to decide by themselves whether and whom to marry. It is determined without their consent by male members of the clan. The criminal practices of dowry-related 'kitchen accidents' and suttee also have strong economic roots. As the result of a woman's death, a dowry or other contribution to the marriage by the victim passes to the husband's family. Decisions on the custody of children, which rest with male family members, also serve as a means of strong pressure on a woman. If, for example, she does not obey and agree on another wife, or on divorce terms, or if she protests family violence and cruelty, she can be deprived of access to her children.

The areas covered by Articles 9, 15 and 16 of the Convention are also legally complicated in some developing parts of the world, particularly in countries with strong religious (mainly Islamic) influences and prevailing customs. In those countries, three different types of legal situation can be identified.

In some countries, the principal laws are based on religion or custom. They formally provide for unequal treatment of women and men. For example, despite differences among Islamic countries and their legal systems, Islamic Shari'a laws are based on the principle of male guardianship over women. Consequently, a man can take up to four wives, while a woman can be married to only one man at a time; a husband is entitled to the obedience of his wife and a wife who disobeys (taking, for example, employment against her husband's will or engaging in social or political activities outside the home) is not entitled to maintenance. Thus, in countries such as Iran or Sudan, the main conflict is between international legal standards and national laws exclusively applied in practice.[26]

In other countries, there are multiple and often conflicting legal systems: statutory, customary and religious. For example, in a number of countries in the Asia-Pacific region, personal and family law is not uniform, but varies between different social groups depending on their respective religion, culture and traditions. Thus the situation of women is determined mainly by the legal system, followed by the group to which they belong, and is, in general, disadvantageous.[27] In India, the Constitutional principles of equality and non-discrimination coexist with highly discriminatory personal and family laws, contradicting those principles. These laws are divided along religious lines reflected in Hindu, Muslim, Christian and Parsi legal regulations respectively and are highly discriminatory to women.[28] In a number of African countries, two or more legal systems are simultaneously in force. In some cases, clear priority is given to the statutory law, often reflecting international standards; in other cases, the relation between various legal systems is confusing and often conflicting, without a consistent indication as to their hierarchy.[29]

The third model relates to countries that had already introduced the statutory law, including international standards of equality, as the only obligatory legal system, but face difficulties with its implementation, due to the prevalence of custom and tradition, and the lack of proper mechanisms to enforce it. Zimbabwe and Ghana are cases in point. Thus, it is not incidental that most of the substantive reservations to the Convention were made on Articles 9, 15 and 16, as their full implementation would undermine the basis of male dominance, which constitutes part of the legal and political order in some developing countries. Consequently, although the situation is gradually changing *de jure*, at least in some countries, progress in the *de facto* situation of women in this respect is very slow.

The Convention also takes a stand on reproductive rights and family planning, obliging states parties to include them in education (Article 10, h) and to ensure legally the right of women to 'decide freely and responsibly on the number and spacing of their children and to have access to the information, education, and means to enable them to exercise these rights' (Article 16, e). In many parts of the world, the situation of women with regard to family planning is dramatic. That is especially the case of women with lower social status, income and level of education, as well as women in societies that inhibit family planning and sexual education because of religious, cultural or social constraints. Those women are unable to control their fertility and to make informed reproductive choices. The attempts by fundamentalist forces in recent years to limit the right of women to decide on their own reproduction, focusing instead on reproduction as a 'social, moral and national obligation', and promoting the role of women as only, or in the first place, mothers, further weakened the implementation of the reproductive rights of women at least in some regions. Instead of applying family planning measures, women resort to abortions, mainly unsafe or illegal. For example, despite the impact of the Catholic Church and restrictive laws, Latin America has the highest abortion rates among developing countries, one out of every four pregnancies. Some 125,000 to 170,000 women in Africa die annually as a result of unsafe or self-induced abortions.[30] One-quarter of 500,000 women who die every year from pregnancy or childbirth-related causes are teenagers.[31]

Social pressures related to women's reproductive role, and the traditionally submissive role of women to men with regard to sexual relations, in recent years has subjected women to the risk of HIV/AIDS infection. A decade ago, women appeared to be hardly affected by the epidemic. Recently, however, almost half of the newly infected are women, a great majority of whom are not drug addicts.[32]

In the context of Articles 9, 15 and 16, it should be noted that the Convention takes the stand on the impact of culture, tradition, stereotypes and images on restricting fundamental human rights of women and their freedoms.[33] That interrelationship, already noted in the Preamble, is further addressed in Article 5, in which the parties are called upon to work towards changing the traditional roles of men and women in society, and in the family, so as to eliminate prejudices and customary practices based on the idea of inferiority of either of the sexes or on stereotyped roles.

Its implementation The implementation of the Convention is monitored by the Committee on the Elimination of Discrimination against Women (CEDAW). Its mandate is defined in Articles 10–17.[34] Its main function is to review and discuss national reports on progress in the implementation of the Convention, submitted to the Committee every four years by the states parties. The reports are presented and defended by the representatives of the governments. The Committee makes recommendations to the states parties based on those reports and the situation of women in the country.

The Committee also makes general recommendations related to specific articles of the Convention, their interpretation and implementation. For example, at its thirteenth session, in 1994, the Committee adopted recommendation 21 on 'Equality in marriage and family matters', based on analyses of Articles 9, 15 and 16, which are especially relevant to the status of women in the family.

The Committee is composed of 23 experts in the field covered by the Convention, nominated by the governments and elected by the states parties for a period of four years, with the possibility of re-election. The Committee meets once a year for a period of three weeks. Although the Convention is the key instrument in the area of human rights of women it is necessary to stress that this powerful instrument has not been fully utilized and has been weakened by various factors.

One results from the nature of the Convention. Under the Convention, states parties assume obligations of results rather than obligations of means.[35] They oblige them to combat discrimination actively and to create guarantees for women to be able to enjoy all human rights. The Convention, however, leaves to the states parties the choice of the 'appropriate measures' that should be applied to achieve the goals stated in Article 3 and are spelled out in detail in the subsequent articles referring to the various human rights of women. The Convention also encourages the adoption of special temporary measures aimed at accelerating *de facto* equality between men and women (various forms of affirmative action, equal opportunity provisions), and adoption of special measures protecting maternity (Article 4), leaving to the states parties decisions as to whether and what kind of measures could be adopted.

That factor, combined with the inability of the Committee to establish measurable and consistent criteria to evaluate the implementation of the

Convention by the reporting governments; to take a stock of progress in the situation of women in the countries; to set deadlines and develop indicators for improvement; to make the reporting governments account-able for the information provided in their reports and for the promises and future-oriented policies outlined therein; and to monitor which promises were implemented in the subsequent reporting periods, seriously weakened implementation of the Convention.

A number of additional problems relate to the functioning of the Committee. They include insufficient time, staff and budget allocated to the Committee; weakness of the Secretariat servicing the Committee; lack of working cooperation with other human rights treaty bodies; uneven involvement of individual experts in the Committee's work and their often insufficient knowledge of the situation in the reporting countries; few lawyers among the members of the Committee, and even more minimal participation by human rights lawyers.

Politicization of the work of the Committee constitutes another problem. The states parties and the experts often tend to concentrate more on seeking compromises and cooperation with each other in order to be re-elected and to receive more favourable consideration of their own national reports. They hardly demand coherent and comprehensive information and answers to difficult questions which may antagonize the governments of reporting countries. The criterion of the submission of candidates to the Committee by governments excludes many outstanding women, ad-vocating human rights at the grassroots level, as they will never obtain the consent of their respective governments. Other problems weakening the implementation of the Convention include its lack of universality and limitation of scope with regard to some countries that adhered to the Convention with substantive reservations based on culture or tradition.

The figure of 139 states parties to the Convention as of May 1995 indicates that 50 states members of the United Nations were not yet parties and that the Convention is far from being universal. Among the permanent members of the UN Security Council and among the most industrialized countries, the USA is the only one that is not a party to the Convention. The largest group of countries that remains formally uncommitted to the Convention includes countries that have incorporated Muslim law in their civil or family codes and have large Muslim populations (for example, Algeria, Bahrain, Iran, Pakistan, Sudan). Other countries are not parties to the Convention because of religion and custom (mainly countries from sub-Saharan Africa, Asia and the Pacific Islands).

The practical applicability of the Convention is also severely limited in the countries that have ratified the Convention with reservations or declarations based on religious law or cultural tradition.[36] Those states do not consider themselves bound by Articles 2, 9, 15 and 16, which constitute a core of the Convention and are in conflict with their national laws or customs. Thus they rule out the applicability of international standards in their respective countries. Although the group of countries that had cultural reservations is composed of countries from all regions strongly influenced by religion or customs (for example, Bangladesh, Brazil, Egypt, Malta, Morocco, Maldives, Turkey), most of the countries with cultural reservations are Muslim.

It should be noted that the articles in question constitute the essence of the Convention and touch upon crucial areas of discrimination against women in many parts of the world. Thus many states parties to the Convention have declared that those reservations 'are incompatible with the object and purpose of the Convention' and that 'the reservations in question, if put into practice, would inevitably result in discrimination against women on the basis of sex, which is contrary to everything the Convention stands for' and that such incompatible reservations made to the Convention 'not only cast doubts on the commitments of the reserving States to the objects and purpose of the Convention, but moreover, contribute to undermine the basis of international contractual law'.

Declaration on the Elimination of Violence against Women

Another set of standards aimed at the protection of human rights of women is provided in the Declaration on the Elimination of Violence against Women, adopted by consensus by General Assembly resolution A/Res/48/104, on 20 December 1993. Although the universal standards of human rights, contained in the bill of rights, constituted the basis for equal protection against violence to all, for decades various forms of violence against women were considered 'private', 'domestic', or culturally and socially justified because the woman 'must have deserved it'. Various cruel, degrading and otherwise illegal acts, such as battering, rape and physical assault, were considered to be 'private disputes' and therefore different from criminal offences or torture, simply because the victim was female.

Thus it is important that the Declaration provided a comprehensive definition of violence against women as 'any act of gender-based violence that results in, or is likely to result in, physical, sexual or psychological harm or suffering to women, including threats of such acts, coercion or arbitrary deprivation of liberty, whether occurring in public, or in private life' (Article 1). The definition of violence against women encompassed, but did not limit itself to, physical, sexual and psychological violence occurring in the family and in society as well as that perpetrated or condoned by states (Article 3). As instances of violence the Declaration cites battering; sexual abuse; dowry-related violence; sexual harassment and intimidation at work, in educational institutions and elsewhere; rape, including marital rape; female genital mutilation and other traditional practices harmful to women; and trafficking in women and forced prostitution.

The Declaration stresses that women are entitled to equal enjoyment and protection of all human rights and fundamental freedoms in the political, economic, social, cultural, civil or any other field, including, *inter alia*, the right to life, to equality, to liberty and security of person; to equal protection under the law; to freedom from all forms of discrimination; to the highest standard attainable of physical and mental health; to just and favourable conditions of work; to freedom from subjection to torture or other cruel, inhumane or degrading treatment or punishment (Article 2).

As the Declaration correctly stated in its Preamble, 'violence against women is a manifestation of historically unequal power relations between men and women, which have led to domination over and discrimination against women by men and to the prevention of the full advancement of women ... violence against women is one of the crucial social mechanisms by which women are forced into a subordinate position compared with men'.

That statement marks the historical progress in the understanding of human rights of women and the requirements for their adequate protection and implementation. It also points to the roots of violence against women and clarifies, to some extent, why its recognition as a human rights issue, as a public matter and as a criminal offence has been refused for so many years.

Human Rights of Women at the Vienna Conference and Beyond

The World Conference on Human Rights held in 1993 in Vienna took certain important steps towards *de jure* and *de facto* incorporation of the human rights of women into the theory and practice of human rights. Consequently, the Conference:

- recognized the human rights of women and of the girl-child as an inalienable, integral and indivisible part of universal human rights;
- challenged the traditional qualification of human rights of women as private, therefore not deserving of public attention and proceedings, and the justification that culture, tradition and religion rule out the applicability of international legal standards, stating that 'Gender-biased violence and all forms of sexual harassment and exploitation, including those resulting from cultural prejudice and international trafficking, are

incompatible with the dignity and worth of the human person and must be eliminated';[37]

- considered all violations of the human rights of women in situations of armed conflict, such as murder, systematic rape, slavery and forced pregnancy, as violations of the fundamental principles of international human rights and humanitarian law.

The Conference also took steps towards strengthening the machinery and the regime of implementation of human rights of women. Thus it urged:

- universal ratification of the Convention on the Elimination of All Forms of Discrimination against Women by 2000 and withdrawal of reservations incompatible with the object and purpose of the Convention and with international treaty law;
- strengthening the structures and activities related to the protection of the human rights of women in the United Nations system (*inter alia*, the Commission on the Status of Women, Committee on the Elimination of Discrimination against Women, the Commission on Human Rights, Division for the Advancement of Women);
- the appointment of a special rapporteur on violence against women;
- the introduction of the right to individual petition through elaboration and adoption of an optional protocol to the Convention on the Elimination of All Forms of Discrimination against Women.

Those achievements would have not been possible if women from all over the world had not taken action in the defence of human rights and for their inclusion in the deliberations of the 1993 World Conference on Human Rights. In the petition to the secretary-general of the United Nations, signed by 65,000 people, they demanded that the Conference in Vienna should 'comprehensively address women's human rights at every level of its proceedings'.

This type of universal recognition, and broader interpretation of human rights of women, brought forth violent and consolidated opposition from those who refused to accept that women are equal and that as equals they should enjoy all human rights and freedoms. Opposition was visible in the conference halls, through numerous calls for women's return to the family and domesticity, and, in its extreme form, in the acts of violence against women rapidly increasing in almost all parts of the world. As part of that campaign, some governments began to argue at national and international fora that since they had not been a part of the historical legislative process leading to the formulation of international standards of equality and human rights of women, those norms could not be applied to them because they were culturally foreign and politically imposed.

Such attempts contradict the historical fact that all those instruments were intended to reflect and set out universally agreed norms. They were formed or adhered to by people from diverse cultures, religions and nationalities and therefore were intended to take into account such factors as religion and cultural traditions of countries. They were elaborated through the lengthy and open international process of negotiations and adopted by consensus. They contained provisions that were universally recognized. Neither in the process of negotiations nor in their adoption had any country argued against the principle of equality between men and women or considered it inconsistent or in conflict with national tradition, culture or religion. Those suddenly emerging cultural and moral considerations must therefore have other, political, grounds.

The attempts to undo the achievements of the last decades, including the 1993 Conference in Vienna, and to prevent full implementation of the international standards of equality and human rights of women, became particularly visible in the preparatory processes of the world conferences in Cairo (1994) and Beijing (1995). Attacks on women's reproductive rights and other human rights of women proved that the assertion of what was achieved and implementation of what was agreed upon are of primary importance. Without further, consolidated actions of non-governmental organizations, governments, individuals and other actors of civic society, led by women experts and activists in the area of human rights of women, further progress towards full *de jure* and *de facto* equality will be hindered. Efforts should also be made towards further broadening of the standards of human rights and full inclusion of women's rights and perspectives. As women did not participate in defining human rights and elaborating early human rights instruments it is time to fill this gap.

Notes

1. *Charter of the United Nations and Statute of the International Court of Justice*, Office of Public Information, United Nations, New York, p. 3.

2. Ibid.

3. *Human Rights. A Compilation of International Instruments*, Centre for Human Rights, ST/HR/1/Rev.4 (Vol. I, Parts 1 and 2), New York, 1993, p. 2.

4. Ibid., p. 30.

5. Ibid., p. 529.

6. World Health Organization, 'Women's health: towards a better world', Issues Paper prepared for the Global Commission on Women's Health, Geneva, 1994; 'Born unequal: the plight of the girl child', in *A Time for Action: Girls, Women and Human Rights*, Development Programmes for Women Unit, UNICEF, New York, 1991, Sales No: E.93.XX.USA.4.

7. Commission on the Status of Women, doc. E/90 of 1 July 1946 (terms of reference of the CSW).

8. *The Nairobi Forward-looking Strategies for the Advancement of Women*, United Nations, DPI/926-41761-September 1993-10M, p. 89.

9. *Human Rights. A Compilation*, p. 152.

10. Ibid., pp. 152–3. Citations of further articles of the Convention are based on the same source.

11. Global Campaign for Women's Human Rights, 'Women's tribunal judges issue recommendations to United Nations', *Women's Human Rights*/Vienna # 16, 1993; Georgina Ashworth, 'Women and human rights', *Terra Femina. Women and Human Rights*, 2, IDAC, Brazil, May/June 1993, p. 37.

12. Inter-Parliamentary Union, *Participation of Women in Parliaments*, Geneva, 1994.

13. *Participation of Women in Political Life and Decision-making*. Report of the Secretary-General, E/CN.6/1995/12, 21 February 1995, p. 4.

14. *Participation of Women*, pp. 4–5; source: Division for the Advancement of Women, from *World Government Directory, 1994* (Oxford, Oxford University Press, 1994).

15. *Participation of Women*, p. 7; source: Division for the Advancement of Women, compiled from Reports of the Secretary-General.

16. UNESCO, *World Education Report*, Paris, 1993.

17. Ibid.

18. 'Women in a changing global economy', *1994 World Survey on the Role of Women in Development*, Department of Policy Coordination and Sustainable Development, United Nations, New York, 1995, p. 49.

19. Ibid., p. 50.

20. Ibid., p. 80.

21. For further details, see *Participation of Women*, pp. 9–10.

22. World Health Organization, *Women, Health and Development*, Geneva, 1992.

23. 'Women in a changing global economy', pp. 40–1.

24. Ibid., pp. 34–5.

25. For further information see John Stratton Hawley, *Fundamentalism and Gender*, Oxford University Press, New York and Oxford, 1994, p. 220.

26. Abdullahi Ahmed An-Na'im, 'State responsibility under international human rights law to change religious and customary laws', in Rebecca J. Cook (ed.), *Human Rights of Women: National and International Perspectives*, University of Pennsylvania Press, Philadelphia, 1995, pp. 181–3; see also Asma Mohamed Abdel Halim, 'Challenges to the application of international women's human rights in the Sudan', in Cook (ed.), *Human Rights of Women*, pp. 397–422.

27. *Achievements of the United Nations Decade for Women in Asia and Pacific*, Economic and Social Commission for Asia and Pacific, 1987, pp. 9–10.

28. Kirti Singh, 'Obstacles to women's rights in India', *Human Rights*, pp. 375–97.

29. For further details see *Women's Legal Literacy: Obstacles and Measures*, Division for the Advancement of Women, EGM/IAWR/1992/WP.1, 12 May 1992.

30. 'Women and human rights', Ashworth, pp. 54–5.

31. 'Second review and appraisal of the implementation of the Nairobi Forward-looking Strategies for the Advancement of Women'. *Report of the Secretary General*, Addendum, E/CN.6/1995/3/Add.3, 27 February 1995, p. 8.

32. 'Second review and appraisal', p. 11.

33. Marsha A. Freeman, 'Women, development and justice: using the International Convention on Women's Rights', in Joanna Kerr (ed.), *Ours by Right: Women's Rights are Human Rights*, Zed Books, London, pp. 93–105.

34. For further information, see Andrew Byrnes, 'The "other" human rights treaty body: the work of the Committee on the Elimination of Discrimination against Women', *Yale Journal of International Law*, Vol. 14, No. 1, Winter 1989, pp. 1–67.

35. For further information, see Rebecca J. Cook, 'State accountability under the Women's Convention', in Cook, *Human Rights of Women*, pp. 228–57.

36. For detailed information, see Rebecca J. Cook, 'Reservations to the Convention on the Elimination of All Forms of Discrimination against Women', *Virginia Journal of International Law*, Vol. 30, No. 3, Spring 1990, pp. 643–716.

37. *World Conference on Human Rights*, United Nations DPI, DPI/1394 39399, August 1993-20M, p. 34, para. 18.

3

Charter-based Activities Regarding Women's Rights in the United Nations and Specialized Agencies

Dorothea Gaudart

In the context of the history of humanity or of that of human rights, the recognition of equality between women and men in all fields of social life is a very recent development. Recognition came first at the international level (Vogel-Polsky 1989). The principle of equal rights of men and women enshrined in the Charter of the United Nations gained ground much more slowly in national legal systems. The international cooperation aiming to promote the status and personal rights of women has interlinked in the last five decades the standard-setting activities in the various agencies of the United Nations system, which in the course of this time has been consolidated by each new standard-setting activity and, consequently, led to a tight network of international law regulations in favour of women's rights.

Society at large, however, continues to be badly informed on these international developments that moved women into the mainstream of social change in this century. With regard to women's rights under international conventions there is still a minority of experts in the international community that seeks to monitor and evaluate the implementation of these international standards while another minority seeks to apply them in national decision-making, in the negotiating assemblies of parliaments, interest groups, women's and other non-governmental organizations. However, the vast but rather silent majority of women still need to be empowered to claim these standards in their daily lives. Why is it that the legal framework of women's rights under international conventions falls short in this way and what can be done about it, particularly in view of the persistent violation of women's rights?

In 1985, the General Assembly of the United Nations adopted unanimously the Nairobi Forward-looking Strategies for the Advancement of Women up to the year 2000 (FLS). In 1990, after one-third of the time set for achieving the objectives of the FLS had elapsed, more progress would have been expected in order to remove the most serious obstacles to the implementation of the Strategies, in the first instance to achieve equality between men and women in all fields of political, social, educational, economic and cultural life.

The first review and appraisal of the implementation of the FLS had to recognize the interdependence of the different political and social sectors on the one hand, and the legal and social situation on the other. It stated in 1990:

> However, *de jure* equality constitutes only the first step towards *de facto* equality. Most countries have enacted legal measures to ensure that women have equal opportunities before the law, that is *de jure* equality. But *de facto* as well as *de jure* discrimination continues and visible political and economic commitment by Governments and non-governmental organizations will be required to eliminate it. One obstacle to eliminating *de facto* discrimination is that most women and men are not aware of women's legal rights or do not fully understand the legal and administrative systems through which they must be implemented.

Consequently, and related to the objective of equality between women and men, Recommendation I calls on governments, in association with women's organizations and other NGOs, to:

> take steps on a priority basis to inform women and men of women's rights under international conventions and national law and to prepare and/or continue campaigns for women's 'legal literacy' using formal and non-formal education at all levels, the mass media and other means; efforts to this end should have been undertaken by 1994. (ECOSOC Res. 1990/15)

Learning about rights and the proper utilization of the legal system in order to achieve those rights has been termed 'legal literacy'. Programmes or courses were set up to promote 'legal literacy' and dispel ignorance ('illiteracy') about basic legal rights (ESCAP 1989).

In this context, discussion usually emerged on whether the emphasis should not be primarily on grassroots women's education, while experience has shown that many graduates, particularly of law schools, lack knowledge and understanding of the effective implementation of international instruments, in particular of those on the rights of women, including reporting obligations under international instruments on human rights, particularly related to the Convention on the Elimination of All Forms of Discrimination against Women (CEDAW Convention).

In programmes for the promotion of legal literacy – for instance, as carried out among women in Bangladesh, Indonesia, the Philippines and Sri Lanka – it was widely accepted that to be effective, any legal literacy programme must involve both women and men and address itself to various groups in society. These groups include teachers, journalists, activists, social workers and members of the legal profession, among others (ESCAP 1989). In the European Community, for instance, in order to consolidate rights under European Community law and to improve the application of existing legal provisions, so far national-level conferences on the equality directives for judges and lawyers have been held in Athens, Oxford, Killarney, Rome, Lisbon, and Oporto, Hamburg and Barcelona (Commission of the European Communities 1988). Referring to the background ideas of these training models, the drafting group at the thirty-fourth session of the United Nations Commission on the Status of Women (CSW) finally added to the recommendations concerning formal and non-formal education 'at all levels' (Gaudart 1990, 1993).

Other conclusions drawn by the CSW from its first review of the implementation of the FLS indicate very clearly the need to become actively and more involved in the international cooperation over the realization of equality between women and men. Recommendation I of ECOSOC Res. 1990/15 continues:

> The work of the Committee on the Elimination of Discrimination against Women should be widely publicized through forms of communication that are accessible to women in order to make them aware of their rights. National reports to the Committee should be widely disseminated within the respective countries and discussed by governmental and non-governmental organizations. Organizations of the United Nations systems, particularly the International Labour Organization (ILO) and the United Nations Educational, Scientific and Cultural Organization (UNESCO), should be requested to examine national experience in promoting legal literacy with a view to assisting Governments, non-governmental organizations and women's movements in mounting successful campaigns.

At that time the CSW as well as CEDAW were serviced by the Division for the Advancement of Women and UN Secretariat located at the Centre for Social Development and Humanitarian Affairs (DAW/CSDHA), United Nations Office Vienna (UNOV).

In order to take advantage of the presence of this focal point for women's programmes and activities at UNOV two women experts from within and outside the UN system (Dorota Gierycz and Dorothea Gaudart) sat down by the bank of the Blue Danube and elaborated a project proposal for postgraduate training of women and men on women's rights under existing international standards of equality (legal instruments, ranging from the UN Charter to the Convention on the Elimination of All Forms of Discrimination against Women and the Declaration on the Elimination of Violence against Women). The purpose and objectives of this project in the field of humanities were welcomed by the Commission on Science and Technology for Development at the Austrian Academy of Science. The Commission supported until then mainly postgraduate training courses in natural sciences, for instance, in limnology (ecology of inland waters). The European University Centre for Peace Studies in Stadtschlaining (Austrian Province of Burgenland), developing its university-level programmes and courses in peace research and peace education towards a master of arts programme in Peace and Conflict Studies, was considered an appropriate location.

In order to take into consideration the important relationship between women's rights in the Convention on the Elimination of All Forms of Discrimination against Women and the mainstream of other human rights treaties, two male experts from the general human rights teaching at university level in Austria (Wolfgang Benedek and Manfred Nowak) were invited to join the efforts and took an active part in the furthering of the contents and methodology of the envisaged study programme and its faculty.

Considering the competence of the United Nations Educational Scientific and Cultural Organization (UNESCO) in the field of human rights education and bearing in mind UNESCO's three priority beneficiaries, namely the least developed countries, the member states of the Africa region, and women, the project proposal was further discussed with representatives of other regions in the framework of the Austrian Commission for UNESCO and finally organized with the support of the Austrian Government Development Cooperation Programmes by the World University Service – Austrian Committee.

The Austrian Development Cooperation Three-Year Programme 1994–96 aimed to concentrate on priority sectors. The Aid Review 1992/93 by the Development Assistance Committee (DAC) of the Organization for Economic Cooperation and Development OCDE/GD(93)76, 1993 – stated that education and energy received a share far above the DAC average. In this context education meant the costs for students from developing countries, which had been rising on an annual basis. Women in Development (WID)-specific activities were very limited, but several projects had a WID component as Austria believes that the protection of the environment, the role of women in the development process, democracy and human rights are important aspects. Consequently, the Three-Year Programme of Austria's Development Cooperation 1996–98 attaches importance to (i) democracy, human rights, good governance and development; (ii) Women and Development – Gender and Development; (iii) Environment and Development – Sustainable Development; and (iv) Social Justice and Development. The field of human rights forms an integral part of international cooperation, and Austria is, therefore, pursuing the necessary political dialogue within the context of development cooperation. As women have a key role in development cooperation, Austria's development cooperation seeks to scrutinize all programmes and project proposals in terms of their effects on and importance for women. Upgrading the role of women will largely depend on expanding education and training opportunities.

In summer 1993 and in 1994 the first two postgraduate courses on the human rights of women were convened in Austria, to be followed by courses in Uganda from 1995 onwards. It should be noted that the gender mix in the faculty and scholarship of those courses on human rights of women was enriching the discussions and understanding of women's rights in the workshops that followed the lectures. Men learned to gain professional and personal interest concerning the discrimination of women in various fields of life and to tackle these issues as violations of human rights. Women learned not only to accept but to appreciate the support of their male co-students and faculty.

The United Nations Commission on the Status of Women

This section emphasizes the importance of the international community in its achievements regarding gender equality. It starts with the origin and establishment of the United Nations Commission on the Status of Women (CSW) and highlights its role as a catalyst for action by others throughout and beyond the United Nations system. Relevant activities of the specialized agencies, namely the International Labour Organization (ILO) and the United Nations Educational, Scientific and Cultural Organization (UNESCO) are dealt with separately.

The institutional context of the international organizations, such as the United Nations, within which the international human rights law of women continues to evolve, was continuously and increasingly during the last decades influenced by women representatives around the globe. The public space of international meetings was crucial for development, and to the implementation and globalization of the human rights of women.

To start with, it should be mentioned, however, that the United Nations is not the first international and intergovernmental body to deal with questions affecting the status of women.

> During the years before the First World War, several international conferences attended by governments, while not discussing the status of women as such and not attempting to promote the principle of equality between the sexes, had nevertheless dealt with some specific problems affecting women.

For instance, in 1902 international conventions were adopted at The Hague dealing with conflicts of national laws concerning marriage, divorce and the guardianship of minors, and in 1904 and 1910 conventions were adopted dealing with the suppression of traffic in women and children. (UN 1961)

The Covenant of the League of Nations (adopted on 28 April 1919) included articles calling for humane working conditions for all, irrespective of sex or age, and for the suppression of traffic in women, and it opened the League Secretariat to women. At its sixteenth Assembly in 1935, the League, as a result of the initiative taken by the Latin American republics, particularly stemming from the Inter-American Commission of Women and the Liaison Committee of Women's International Organizations established in 1928, decided to consider the question of the status of women in its political and civil aspects. In 1937 the Assembly of the League of Nations resolved to publish a general study, 'giving detailed information on the status of women in the various countries of the world as established by national laws and their application'. This general survey was halted by the outbreak of the Second World War.

Origin and establishment At the founding Conference of the United Nations in San Francisco, non-governmental organizations (NGOs), women's organizations and women's representatives, particularly from the Inter-American Commission, lobbied for the inclusion of the principle of 'equal rights of men and women' in the Charter of the United Nations.

The first drafts agreed earlier at Dumbarton Oaks had not included any provisions on human rights or women's rights (Bruce 1968, 1971, 1993). The predominantly male drafters wanted the preamble to begin with 'We the Nations'. The words 'We, the peoples of the United Nations, determined to save succeeding generations from the scourge of war' were written by two American women professors of English literature, Virginia C. Gildersleeve, a member of the US delegation to the San Francisco UN Conference in 1945, and her assistant, Navy Lieutenant Commander Elizabeth Reynard.

In the Preamble of the Charter of the United Nations adopted in June 1945 the peoples of the United Nations reaffirm their faith in 'fundamental human rights, in the dignity and worth of the human person, *in the equal rights of men and women* and of nations large and small'. The principle of equality is specifically mentioned here, and in Article 8, which states: 'The United Nations shall place no restrictions on the eligibility of men and women to participate in any capacity and under conditions of equality in its principal and subsidiary organs.'

The Purpose and Principles of the Organizations set forth in Article 1 include the promotion and encouragement of respect 'for human rights and for fundamental freedoms for all without distinction as to race, *sex*, language, or religion'. Again under Article 55, the United Nations is to promote universal respect for, and observance of, human rights and fundamental freedoms for all without distinction as to race, *sex*, language or religion, and in Article 56 all member states pledge themselves to take joint and separate action in cooperation with the organization to achieve this purpose. Under the Charter the General Assembly and its Economic and Social Council (ECOSOC) are the organs of the UN that have primary responsibility for human rights, including the status of women. Women's rights, set forth in the Charter, received prominence when a member of the Brazilian delegation, Dr Bertha Lutz, proposed that ECOSOC should set up a commission of women to study their political status. (In 1945, when the UN was founded, women could vote or hold public offices in only 30 of the then 51 member states.)

In May 1946 the Nuclear Commission (members from Denmark, Dominican Republic, Lebanon, Poland, France, India and China, meeting at Hunter College, NY) met to discuss the fundamental principles, the scope and the programme of work of such a commission. The members stated that democracy was

> the only social order in which women could enjoy full rights as human beings; that freedom and equality were essential to human development and that the well-being and progress of society depended upon the development of the full personality of men and women aware of their responsibilities ... and ... that the work of the Sub-Commission should last until women had reached the point where they were on equal footing with men ... In practice priority had to be given to Political Rights since little progress could be made without them. (E/38/Rev.1)

On the women's request ECOSOC decided by its resolution 11(II) of 21 June 1946 to make the established Sub-Commission on the Status of Women a full commission reporting, like the Commission on Human Rights, directly to the Council.

At the first session of the Commission on the Status of Women (held at Lake Success, New York, from 10 to 24 February 1947, and attended by members from Australia, the Byelorussian Soviet Socialist Republic, China, Costa Rica, Denmark, France, Guatemala, India, Mexico, Syria, Turkey, the Union of Soviet Socialist Republics, United Kingdom, the United States of America, Venezuela and by representatives of ILO and UNESCO, the representative of the assistant secretary-general for social affairs, Mr Stanczyk, recalled in his opening statement that in building up the structure of the United Nations, one should not forget women's contribution to international co-operation and understanding. It was they who attempted to ease and correct, especially in times of war, the injustices and inequalities brought about in most cases by men. During the war women justified, by their readiness to defend freedom and justice, their predecessors who had struggled against discriminatory laws and age-old prejudices. (R/CN.6/SR.1)

Membership of CSW The Commission began with 15 members (as mentioned before at its first session held at Lake Success, NY). Membership increased to 18 in 1952, then to 21 in 1961, 32 in 1966 and 45 in 1989. To date the 45 members of CSW are elected by ECOSOC for four-year terms on the following basis: 13 from African states, 11 from Asian states; 4 from Eastern European states; 9 from Latin American and Caribbean states; and 8 from Western European and other states. The Commission meets normally on an annual basis for a period of eight working days.

Terms of reference of CSW The specific mandate of CSW set up in June 1946 was to prepare recommendations and reports to ECOSOC 'on promoting women's rights in political, economic, civil, social and educational fields' and to make recommendations 'on urgent problems requiring immediate attention in the field of women's rights'. The latter phrase was amended the following year to emphasize the principle of equal rights of men and women. In its amended form it reads: 'urgent problems requiring immediate attention in the field of women's rights with the object to implementing the principle that men and women shall have equal rights, and to develop proposals to give effect to such recommendations' (ECOSOC Res. 48[IV] of 29 March 1947).

The mandate of CSW was expanded in 1987 by the Council in its resolution 1987/22 to include the monitoring of the 1985 Nairobi Forward-looking Strategies for the Advancement of Women. Following the Fourth World Conference on Women, the General Assembly mandated CSW in 1996 to integrate into its work programme a follow-up process to the conference, regularly monitoring, reviewing and appraising progress achieved and problems encountered in the implementation of the 1995 Beijing Declaration and Platform for Action at all levels.

Relationships with Other Organizations

CSW as a functional commission of ECOSOC submits its recommendations, reports and so on directly to the Council and, through ECOSOC, to the General Assembly. It also addresses recommendations to governments through ECOSOC or its own. Based on the agreements concluded between the United Nations and the specialized agencies, ILO and UNESCO have been regularly represented at the sessions of CSW and reported on their activities concerning women as well as undertaking specific studies at the request of CSW on subjects within their competence. CSW was particularly interested in the consideration of the draft international bill of human rights and asked that a copy of the draft be circulated to members of CSW at the same time as it was made available to members of the Commission on Human Rights. CSW was represented at the Commission on Human Rights and at meetings of the Sub-Commission on the Prevention of Discrimination and Protection of Minorities until 1970 (when the Division of Human Rights was transferred to Geneva).

Relations with non-governmental organizations It is noteworthy to recall in view of the critical standpoints of the emerging autonomous women's organizations in the 1970s *vis-à-vis* the UN and CSW how the relations with NGOs were built up and supported already in CSW's first session in 1947. Article 71 of the Charter of the UN provided that ECOSOC may make suitable arrangements for consultation with NGOs that are concerned with matters within its competence; with international organizations and, where appropriate, with national organizations after consultation with the member of the UN concerned. ECOSOC set up a Committee on Arrangements for Consultation with NGOs. CSW took note of this article and decided, in view of the fact that ECOSOC had already set up a Committee on Arrangements for Consultation with NGOs, that all requests for consultative status from women's organizations be referred to that Committee, and 'that whatever decisions the Committee might take should be discussed by the CSW at its next session. This shall not affect the principle of recognizing national coordinating agencies.' This last decision must be explained because it proves the forward-looking strategies of these first women pioneering international cooperation. CSW expressed 'its desire that the ECOSOC should recommend that unless such agencies were already in existence, the Member States encourage the establishment within their respective countries of coordinating agencies of NGOs to which any organization dealing with the political, economic, social, educational and other problems relating to the status of women would be entitled to belong'. CSW further recommended that if such agencies – which we would call today 'national machinery' – were formed, 'their applications for consultative status should be duly considered' (E/281/Rev.1, original text Russian, as the rapporteur Mrs E. Uralova came from Byelorussian SSR).

Close working relationship were maintained with international NGOs, particularly women's organizations. The first contact between CSW and NGOs was established at the first session when representatives were heard from the following international women's organizations: the Women's International Democratic Federation, the Associated Countrywomen of the World, the International Alliance of Women, the International Co-operative Women's Guild, the International Federation of University Women, the Women's International League for Peace and Freedom, the International Union of Catholic Women's Leagues, the World Young Women's Christian Association, the International Federation of Business and Professional Women, the International Council of Women, the Pan-Pacific Women's Association and the World Women's Party (E/281/Rev.1). NGO participation has gained momentum in recent years, in relation to both CSW and CEDAW.

CEDAW decided in its Decision 16/II to invite the UN Secretariat to facilitate an informal meeting with NGOs, during each session, but outside the regular meeting time of the Committee. During that meeting, NGOs would be invited to offer country-specific information on the states parties to be reviewed by CEDAW. CEDAW recommended that states parties consult national NGOs in the preparation of their reports required by article 18 of the Convention. It recommended that international NGOs and UN agencies, funds and programmes be encouraged to facilitate the attendance at Committee sessions by representatives of national NGOs. It also recommended that specialized agencies and other UN entities with field representation work with NGOs to disseminate information on the Convention and the work of the Committee and call upon past and present experts of the Committee to participate in those efforts.

The UNIFEM–CEDAW booklet *Bringing Equality Home* (available from Internet site: http://www.unifem.undp.org/cedaw/cedawen9.htm) provides examples of good practices and explains as follows:

> Women's NGOs are not formally included in the CEDAW Committee sessions at which Government reports are presented, but their communication with the Committee is a crucial part of the reporting process. The Committee has welcomed independent information to help it assess Government claims and to determine where improvements are needed, and the Committee has called on NGOs to help provide that information. For this purpose, many NGOs have joined together in coalitions to prepare 'shadow reports' for the Committee, which describe the state of women's human rights in their countries and comment on their Governments' reports.
>
> Women's NGOs have used the reporting process to good effect: to hold their Governments accountable for the claims and commitment made at the CEDAW Committee sessions, to continue dialogue with their Governments

on implementing the CEDAW Committee's concluding comments, and as a vehicle to raise public awareness within their own countries.

Involvement of NGOs was in the work of CSW through the United Nations Division for the Advancement of Women (DAW). DAW sent out questionnaires to the government missions in New York in order to obtain information on the implementation of the Nairobi Forward-looking Strategies for the Advancement of Women and the Beijing Platform for Action, five years after its adoption. At the same time DAW invited non-governmental organizations, women's groups and other organizations of civil society to contribute to this preparatory process for the Special Session of the General Assembly to follow up the Beijing Conference held in New York from 5 to 9 June 2000. NGOs were encouraged to address in their forthcoming meetings or events the appraisal of progress achieved since the Beijing Conference within the context of the interest and expertise of each organization. These organizations were urged to identify further actions or initiatives that might be required to fully implement the Beijing Platform for Action beyond 2000.

CSW's secretariat A Section on the Status of Women established as part of the Department of Social Affairs was upgraded to a Branch for the Promotion of Equality of Men and Women within the Centre for Social Development and Humanitarian Affairs transferred to the United Nations Office, Vienna, in 1978. It was further upgraded to a Division for the Advancement of Women (DAW) and, with effect from 1 August 1993, moved back to the UN Headquarters in New York, where it now forms part of the Department of Economic and Social Affairs. Among the main responsibilities of the Division is the servicing of:

- the Commission on the Status of Women (CSW), the central inter-governmental body with the mandate to elaborate policies to achieve equality between women and men; and
- the Committee on the Elimination of Discrimination against Women (CEDAW/C), the expert treaty body that monitors the implementation of the legal standards in the Convention on the Elimination of All Forms of Discrimination against Women.

DAW is a catalyst for advancing the global agenda on women's issues and for mainstreaming gender in all sectors. Under the Division, there are four main branches:

1. the Gender Analysis Section conducts research and develops policy options, fosters interaction between governments and civil society and

provides substantive servicing for UN intergovernmental and expert bodies;

2. the Women's Rights Unit assists in breaking down the barriers between human rights and development and fosters the attainment of women's human rights as an integral part of development;

3. the Coordination and Outreach Unit raises awareness, promotes international standards and norms and sharing of best practices, and strengthening communication between the international and national policy-making processes and the women of the world; and

4. the Gender Advisory Services Unit provides governments with advisory services and technical support in the activities related to gender in development.

These services, together with those offered through the WomenWatch databank on the Internet, are supporting UN system-wide cooperation at country level in information-sharing, advisory support, policy development and institutional capacity development at various levels.

International Cooperation in Fact-finding and Standard-setting

CSW in its first session decided by eight votes to two to adopt the following guiding principles and aims in its future work. Fifty years of United Nations action might be the right moment to recall the wording of these Principles set up in 1947:

> Freedom and equality are essential to human development; since woman is as much a human being as man, she is entitled to share these attributes with him.
>
> The well-being and progress of society depend on the extent to which both men and women are able to develop their personalities and are cognizant of their responsibilities to themselves and to each other.
>
> Woman has thus a definite role to play in the building of a free, healthy, prosperous and moral society, and she can fulfill that obligation only as a free and responsible member of that society.
>
> Woman must take an active part in the struggle for the total elimination of the fascist ideology and for international co-operation directed towards the establishment of a democratic peace among the peoples of the world and the prevention of further aggression.
>
> In order to achieve this goal, the Commission intends to raise the status of women, irrespective of nationality, race, language or religion, to equality with men in all fields of human enterprise, and to eliminate all discrimination against women in the provisions of statutory law, in legal maxims or rules, or in interpretations of customary law. (Chapter V of the Report on the first session, E/281/Rev.1)

Consequently, CSW suggested amendments to the draft Covenants on Human Rights. Under Article 3 of each Covenant, for example, states parties undertake to ensure the equal right of men and women to the enjoyment of all the rights set forth in the present Covenant, and Article 2 provides that the rights set forth will be exercised without discrimination on grounds of sex, among other grounds.

CSW adopted numerous resolutions intended to draw attention to problems and existing inequalities of men and women. According to its mandate, CSW started to collect information (by means of questionnaires addressed to member states and NGOs) and to analyse the discrepancies between constitutional and legislative provisions and the real situation and conditions of women in member states, in consultation with the ILO as regards the economic and social fields and with UNESCO with regard to basic education for women.

The central part of CSW's work is the setting of universal standards regarding gender equality. Due to its efforts, women's rights have become the substance of international treaties and declarations, many of which set important precedents in the area of human rights, such as the following:

- Convention on the Political Rights of Women, 1952;
- Convention on the Nationality of Married Women, 1957;
- Convention and Recommendation on Consent to Marriage, Minimum Age for Marriage and Registration of Marriages, 1962, 1965;
- Declaration on the Elimination of Discrimination against Women, 1967;
- Convention on the Elimination of All Forms of Discrimination against Women, 1979; and
- Declaration on the Elimination of Violence against Women, 1993.

The Convention on the Elimination of All Forms of Discrimination against Women (CEDAW Convention) incorporates the norms against gender-based discrimination as well as all of the standards relating to women or having particular significance for women that had been set in earlier instruments. It is the most comprehensive codification of internationally accepted principles and measures to achieve equal rights for women in all fields – political, economic, social and educational, cultural and civil. It calls for national legislation to ban discrimination against women, recommends temporary special measures to speed equality between men and women, and indicates the actions necessary to modify social and cultural patterns that perpetuate sex-biased discrimination.

The CEDAW Convention was adopted by the General Assembly in its resolution 34/180 of 18 December 1979. Ratification was rapid and the treaty came into force on 3 September 1981. As of May 2001, 168 states (out of 189 member states of the UN) are party to the Convention. As of

May 2001, 168 states (out of 189 member states of the UN) are party to the Convention (latest ratification: Mauretania, 10 May 2001). The Convention is now the international human rights treaty with the second-largest number of ratifications, subsequent to the Convention on the Rights of the Child of 1989. However, it is also among those treaties with a rather high number of reservations by state parties. Out of 161 state parties that had ratified the Convention, 54 have entered reservations on substantive articles. Thus all relevant texts will repeat that states are urged to withdraw reservations that are contrary to the object and purpose of the Convention or are otherwise incompatible with international treaty law.

States parties are obliged to submit to the secretary-general of the UN, for consideration by the Committee on the Elimination of Discrimination against Women (CEDAW/C, consisting of 23 independent experts) 'a report on the legislative, judicial, administrative or other measures which they have adopted to give effect to the provisions of the Convention' – within one year after entry into force for the state concerned, and thereafter, at least every four years and further whenever the Committee so request (Article 18 of the CEDAW Convention). The treaty monitoring and examining CEDAW has adopted guidelines to help states prepare their initial as well as their following periodic reports. CEDAW issued General Recommendations on the articles of the Convention, also concerning reservations so that states parties could take note and act accordingly.

As an important step forwards, the international normative framework was reinforced by the Vienna Declaration and Programme of Action adopted at the World Conference on Human Rights in 1993. The Declaration, recalling the Preamble to the Charter of the UN, reaffirms faith in the equal rights of men and women, emphasizes that the human rights of women and of the girl-child are an inalienable, integral and indivisible part of universal human rights, and stresses that the full and equal participation of women in political, civil, economic, social and cultural life, at the national, regional and international levels, and the eradication of all forms of discrimination on grounds of sex are priority objectives of the international community. The Programme of Action states:

> The equal status of women and the human rights of women should be integrated into the mainstream of UN system-wide activity (paragraph 37).
>
> In particular, the World Conference on Human Rights stresses the importance of working towards the elimination of violence against women in public and private life, the elimination of all forms of sexual harassment, exploitation and trafficking in women, the elimination of gender bias in the administration of justice and the eradication of any conflicts which may arise between the rights of women and the harmful effects of certain tradi-

tional or customary practices, cultural prejudices and religious extremism ... Violations of the human rights of women in situations of armed conflict are violations of the fundamental principles of international human rights and humanitarian law. All violations of this kind, including in particular murder, systematic rape, sexual slavery, and forced pregnancy, require a particularly effective response (paragraph 38).

Treaty monitoring bodies should disseminate necessary information to enable women to make more effective use of existing implementation procedures in their pursuits of full and equal enjoyment of human rights and non-discrimination ... The Commission on the Status of Women and the Committee on the Elimination of Discrimination against Women should quickly examine the possibility of introducing the right of petition through the preparation of an optional protocol to the Convention on the Elimination of All Forms of Discrimination against Women (paragraph 40). (World Conference on Human Rights 1993)

In March 1994, the UN Commission on Human Rights agreed to appoint a special rapporteur on violence against women, Ms Radhika Coomaraswamy (Sri Lanka). Her mandate includes reporting to the Commission on Human Rights, fact-finding missions to specific countries, the assessment of individual allegations of violence being committed against women, the forwarding of complaints to governments with the purpose of receiving clarification and, in dialogue with states, the recommending of measures at all levels to eliminate violence against women. The process of collecting information with respect to the future programme of work had begun and governments were urged to provide information.

Communication Procedures

Private individuals, groups and NGOs have written to the UN since the early days of 1946 and 1947. From its inception onwards CSW received many communications, and at its first session in 1947 made the following recommendation to ECOSOC as to the manner of dealing with them:

(a) That the Secretary-General be requested to compile a confidential list of communications received concerning the status of women, before each session of the Commission;

(b) That this confidential list, which would also specify the contents of the communications, and give the names of the organizations from which they were received, be forwarded to the members of the Commission at least fourteen days before the opening of each session;

(c) That the members of the Commission, at their request, have the right to consult the originals of these communications;

(d) That the Secretary-General be requested to inform the authors of all such communications that they will be brought to the attention of the Commission on the Status of Women. (E/281/Rev.1 Report to the ECOSOC on the first session of the Commission, held at Lake Success, New York, 10 to 24 February 1947)

Many of these communications alleged violations of human rights by national authorities. How to handle them has always been a difficult and sensitive issue, reflecting the concern of governments to protect themselves against alleged violations that they feared might be exploited for political purposes. This was especially true at the time of the Cold War and the struggle of non-self-governing territories to attain their independence. A further concern was the protection from persecution of individuals for having complained to the UN that their rights had been infringed. Confidentiality was considered essential for both these reasons.

ECOSOC established identical procedures for both Commissions on Human Rights and on the Status of Women in resolutions 75 (V) and 76 (V) of 5 August 1947. Both resolutions state that the commissions have no power to take any action in regard to complaints. Confidential lists of communications were to be prepared and furnished to each Commission in a private meeting. In 1950 a distinction was made between communications dealing with principles which would be included in a non-confidential list, and 'other communications' (i.e. complaints), which would continue to be handled confidentially. At each session from 1951 to 1970 CSW set up a Committee on Communications to review both lists and any government replies received and to report back to the plenary of CSW and ECOSOC (Bruce 1993).

Meanwhile, beginning in 1966, the General Assembly, ECOSOC and the Commission on Human Rights modified the procedure and laid down details in Council resolution 1503 (XLVIII) of 27 May 1970 for dealing with communications that reveal 'a consistent pattern of gross and reliably attested violations of human rights'. What has become known as the '1503' procedure applies not to individual cases but only to situations that affect a large number of people over a protracted period of time. (However, complaints of alleged violations of rights by individuals may be handled under the Optional Protocol to the Covenant on Civil and Political Rights [1966] if the state complained against is a party to the Optional Protocol, and the alleged violation is covered by the terms of the Covenant, or under the other human rights conventions that allow for the receipt of complaints from individuals.)

CSW was not involved in the development of this new procedure or in its implementation. Furthermore, the views of its members were sharply divided on action to be taken. Some argued that communications were an important source of information and they also believed that the Commission had an obligation to review alleged violations of women's rights. Others were of the view that all human rights violations should be considered together, and in any case the Commission already had a very heavy workload during the UN Decade for Women. Finally, CSW decided to retain the consideration of communications as part of its work programme. ECOSOC reaffirmed in its resolution 1983/27 that the mandate of the CSW was to consider confidential and non-confidential communications on the status of women (paragraph 1).

The secretary-general was requested to submit reports to the CSW on such communications and to solicit the cooperation of the specialized agencies, regional commissions and other UN bodies in compiling that report (paragraphs 2 and 3). CSW henceforth appointed a Working Group consisting of not more than five of its members selected with due regard for geographical distribution, to meet in closed meetings during each session of the Commission.

In 1997, the Working Group on Communications on the Status of Women took note of ten confidential communications received directly by the Division for the Advancement of Women of the UN Secretariat, as well as the 41 communications that formed the confidential list received from the Centre for Human Rights of the UN Office at Geneva. Specific forms of violence against women continued to exist. Appreciation was expressed to governments for having sent in replies conducive to the clarification of the cases concerned. The Working Group noted, however, that some governments had not replied and the Working Group suggested that the CSW should encourage all Governments concerned to cooperate in order to make the communications mechanism more effective

Draft optional protocol to the CEDAW Convention The Vienna Declaration and Programme of Action adopted in 1993 by the World Conference on Human Rights and the Platform of Action adopted in 1995 by the Fourth World Conference on Women in Beijing have reaffirmed and strengthened the human rights of women as stipulated in the CEDAW Convention. It was also agreed to examine the possibility of introducing the right of petition through preparation of an optional protocol to the Convention. CEDAW gave the primary impulse to start the intergovern-mental process and the CSW runs the Open-ended Working Group on the Elaboration of a Draft Optional Protocol to the Convention on the Elimination of All Forms of Discrimination against Women.

On 12 March 1999 the forty-third session of the UN Commission on the Status of Women adopted the Optional Protocol to the CEDAW

Convention. The Protocol is the result of four years of negotiations in the Working Group, which was chaired by Ms Aloisia Woergetter of Austria. On 6 October 1999, in a landmark decision for women, the UN General Assembly, acting without a vote, adopted the 21-article Optional Protocol to the Convention and called on all states parties to the convention to become party to the new instrument as soon as possible. The Protocol, which was opened for signature, ratification and accession on 10 December 1999, includes an 'opt-out clause', allowing states upon ratification or accession to declare that they do not accept the inquiry procedures. Article 17 of the Protocol explicitly provides that no reservations may be entered to its terms. As of 22 September 2001 DAW counted 68 signatures to the Optional Protocol and 27 ratifications.

The Protocol makes it possible for women, as individuals or in groups, to submit complaints about alleged violations of the CEDAW Convention. The Protocol also entitles the Committee to initiate inquiries into situations of grave or systematic violations of women's rights. Although the Protocol includes an 'opt-out-clause', allowing states upon ratification or accession to declare that they do not accept the inquiry procedure, it explicitly provides that no reservations may be entered to its terms. Secretary-General Kofi Annan stated at the signing ceremony for the Optional Protocol on Human Rights Day, 10 December 1999:

> It is fitting that the Protocol has been adopted in 1999, the twentieth anniversary of the adoption of the Convention on the Elimination of All Forms of Discrimination against Women by the General Assembly. Together with the achievement of the goals of universal ratification of the Convention by the year 2000, the Optional Protocol is a major step forward in realizing Governments' commitments to women's human rights. I urge Member States to show the same commitment to speedy ratification of the Protocol, as they have shown to the Convention. I also urge those States which have not yet ratified the Convention to do so in this anniversary year.

In the African Platform for Action adopted by the Fifth Regional Conference on Women, held at Dakar from 16 to 23 November 1994, a proposed action calls for an optional protocol also to the regional instrument. The OAU (Organization of African Unity) should introduce the right of petition through the adoption of an optional protocol to the African Charter on Human and Peoples' Rights.

Evolution of Long-term Programmes for the Advancement of Women

The 1960s and 1970s saw a rapid increase in the membership of the United Nations and growing concern for the problems of the developing countries. It was also a period when the UN bodies concerned with the development issues began to place greater emphasis on balanced economic and social development and on the human factor. These changes had a marked impact on programmes, advisory services and technical assistance programmes affecting women, including topics such as community development, rural development, agricultural workers, family planning, the impact of scientific and technological advances on women, and, more especially, the expansion of assistance to help women in developing countries. The term 'status of women' was gradually replaced by 'advancement of women'.

The objective of the 'full integration of women in the total development effort' came into the programming when in 1972, on the proposal of CSW, the General Assembly of the UN, in its resolution 27/3010 of 18 December 1972, proclaimed 1975 as International Women's Year 'to intensify action with a view to promoting equality between men and women, ensuring the integration of women in the total development effort, and increasing the contribution of women to the strengthening of world peace'. Four World Conferences on Women and parallel NGO fora have strengthened the international women's movement and the global quest for women's rights.

Mexico City, Mexico 1975 The World Conference of the International Women's Year attracted 133 governments and adopted a World Plan of Action for the Advancement of Women for the coming decade. Helvi Sipilä (Finland) was the secretary-general of the Conference. For the first time, some 6,000 representatives of non-governmental organizations attended a parallel forum – the International Women's Year Tribune.

Copenhagen, Denmark 1980 One hundred and forty-five member states attended the World Conference of the UN Decade for Women. They called for improvements in women's employment, health and education. Lucille Mair (Jamaica) was secretary-general of the Conference. About seven thousand NGOs attended the NGO Forum.

Nairobi, Kenya 1985 One hundred and fifty-seven government delegations participated in the World Conference to Review and Appraise the Achievements of the UN Decade for Women: Equality, Development and Peace. Delegates adopted the Nairobi Forward-looking Strategies for the Advancement of Women as a blueprint to improve the status of women by the end of the century. Leticia Shahani (Philippines) was secretary-general of the Conference. Some 15,000 NGOs attended the NGO Forum.

Beijing, China 1995 The Fourth World Conference on Women attracted 189 government delegations. The Platform for Action proposed strategies and actions to remove obstacles to women's advancement in twelve critical areas. Gertrude Mongella (Tanzania) was secretary-general of the Conference. The NGO Forum attracted over thirty thousand activists from around the world.

The General Assembly, in resolution 52/23, decided to convene, from 5 to 9 June 2000, a Special Session to appraise and assess the progress achieved in the implementation of the Nairobi Forward-looking Strategies for the Advancement of Women (FLS) and the Beijing Platform for Action (PfA), five years after its adoption.

CSW was the Preparatory Committee for the Special Session entitled 'Women 2000: Gender Equality, Development and Peace for the Twenty-first Century' – obviously continuing the three interrelated objectives of the International Women's Year 1975. The subprogramme of the Special Session covered six areas, as follows:

1. gender mainstreaming in the work of intergovernmental forums, and in the UN Secretariat and system, as well as other intergovernmental organizations and member states;
2. policy analysis and monitoring activities related to the implementation of the FLS and Beijing Declaration and Platform for Action;
3. women's enjoyment of their human rights;
4. gender policy advisory services;
5. improving the status of women in the UN Secretariat; and
6. outreach activities and information exchange.

A review and appraisal of the implementation of the PfA was based on, *inter alia*, national action plans, reports of the states parties to CEDAW under Article 18 of the Convention, replies of member states to the questionnaire, statements made by delegations at relevant fora of the UN, reports from regional commissions and other entities of the UN system and follow-up to global UN conferences.

Research, data Before the UN Decade for Women (1976–85), separate statistics for men and women were scant. The UN Statistical Division, the UN International Research and Training Institute for the Advancement of Women (INSTRAW) and the ILO have been instrumental in developing methodology for gathering statistics that measure the value of women's work, both paid and unpaid, more accurately.

The Platform for Action (Beijing, 1995) marked a major shift in the emphasis from women as reproductive agents, important in the social sphere, to a more balanced emphasis that placed women as major economic actors in the national and global arenas. That shift in policy had brought an increased demand for research and data on women and work. Strengthening the statistical base and database was essential for informing an enabling policy. The UNDP 1995 *Human Development Report* had provided a major conceptual breakthrough in the development paradigm and accounting systems that underlie the equalization of both paid and unpaid work done by women.

The UN *World's Women 1995: Trends and Statistics* report shows that women have made significant progress in some areas since the First World Conference on Women was held in Mexico in 1975. However, the statistical report also makes it clear that greater efforts will be required to achieve social, political and economic equality between the sexes. The United Nations Women's Indicators and Statistics Database (Wistat, Version 3) is also available on CD-ROM and accompanied by a User's Guide and Reference Manual, 1997.

The International Labour Organization

Origin and establishment, Constitution and functions The Constitution of the ILO, established in 1919, introduced two fundamental innovations into international relations. First, the world community recognized the value of dealing collectively, not only with relations between states (not bilaterally but on a multilateral basis), but also with the very basis of the problems on which the progress, well-being and even the survival of humankind depended. In addition, a kind of legislative function was introduced at the international level. The Preamble to the ILO Constitution sets out the following three reasons for the establishment of an organization for the main purpose of adopting international labour standards:

1. The fact that 'universal and lasting peace can be established only if it is based upon social justice'. This was a prime motive for those who framed the ILO Constitution as an integral part of the 1919 peace treaty.
2. The existence of conditions of labour involving 'injustice, hardship and privation' and the need for their improvement. The reference to the 'sentiments of justice and humanity' was reaffirmed in 1944 by the passage of the Declaration of Philadelphia that 'all human beings, irrespective of race, creed or sex, have the right to pursue both their material well-being and their spiritual development in conditions of freedom and dignity, of economic security and equal opportunity'.
3. Fear of the social effects of international competition. The Preamble acknowledges that 'the failure of any nation to adopt humane conditions of labour is an obstacle in the way of other nations which desire to improve the conditions in their own countries'.

The most urgent problems of the time, on which the first ILO decisions were made, included the promotion of the eight-hour working day, the struggle against unemployment, social security, maternity protection and the working conditions of women and youth. International labour standards have been formulated since 1919 and have had to adapt to a rapidly changing world. By 1906 two international treaties had been adopted, one prohibiting the use of white phosphorus and the other regulating night work by women.

Between the two world wars the ILO was an autonomous part of the League of Nations. During the Second World War the ILO moved its headquarters from Geneva to Montreal, Canada. In Philadelphia, in 1944, the International Labour Conference helped prepare the ILO for the problems awaiting it after the war, and further defined the organization's aims and objectives in adopting the so-called 'Declaration of Philadelphia', which is now an annex to the Constitution.

In 1946 the ILO became the first specialized agency of the United Nations, recognized as having special responsibility for social and labour questions. Consequently, the ILO was represented at the sessions of the Commission on the Status of Women (CSW), later contributing also to the sessions of the Committee on the Elimination of Discrimination against Women (CEDAW). The ILO presented comparative surveys and data analyses relating to the improvement of working conditions of women workers, for example, on pay or labour relations. The ILO now has 174 member states, as compared with 45 at its foundation in 1919 and 58 immediately after the Second World War.

Structure and working methods The ILO accomplishes its work through three main bodies, all of which encompass the unique feature of the organization: its tripartite structure (government, employers, workers).

1. International Labour Conference: the member States of the ILO meet at the International Labour Conference in June of each year, in Geneva. Each member state is represented by two government delegates, an employer delegate and a worker delegate. They are accompanied by technical advisers. Employer and worker delegates can express themselves and vote according to instructions received from their organizations. They sometimes vote against each other or even against their government representatives. The Conference acts as a forum where social and labour questions of importance to the entire world are discussed. The Conference establishes and adopts international labour standards. It also adopts the budget of the organization and elects the Governing Body.

2. The Governing Body is the executive council of the ILO and meets three times a year in Geneva. It is also tripartite and takes decisions on ILO's policy. It establishes the programme and the budget which it then submits to the Conference for adoption. It also elects the director-general.

3. The International Labour Office is the permanent secretariat of the International Labour Organization and is based in Geneva. It prepares the overall activities under the scrutiny of the Governing Body and under the leadership of a director-general, who is elected for a five-year renewable term. The Office runs field offices around the world. Experts undertake missions under the programme of technical cooperation.

The organization also works through other bodies such as regional conferences, industrial committees and panels of experts. The ILO remains a standard-setting body, but today there is also a marked emphasis on operational programmes and on educational work. This has resulted, in particular, in the establishment of the International Institute for Labour Studies (IILS) in Geneva in 1960 and of the International Centre for Advanced Technical and Vocational Training in Turin in 1965. The Institute specializes in higher education and research in the fields of social and labour policy.[1] The Turin Centre provides key personnel with training at a higher level than they can obtain in their home countries in areas such as vocational training, management development and training for trade unionists (ILO 1994).

International labour standards and women workers International Labour Standards are Conventions and Recommendations adopted by the International Labour Conference. Each Convention is a legal instrument regulating aspects of labour administration, social welfare or human rights. Its ratification involves a dual obligation for a member state: it is both a formal commitment to apply the provisions of the Convention, and an indication of willingness to accept a measure of international supervision. International Labour Recommendations are not open to ratification but lay down general or technical guidelines to be applied at the national level. They often contain detailed guidelines to supplement the principles set out in particular Conventions, or they provide guidance on subjects that are not covered by Conventions. Both Conventions and Recommendations define standards and provide a model and stimulus for national legislation and practice in member countries.

ILO standards cover a wide range of social and labour problems, including basic human rights issues (such as freedom of association, abolition of forced labour and the elimination of discrimination in employment), child labour, minimum wages, labour administration, industrial relations, employment policy, human resources development, working conditions, social security, occupational safety and health and employment at sea. It is evident from the pattern of international labour standards adopted that the scope of application of the principle of equality between women and men has continued to broaden with the realization that equality in one area can be achieved only through attainment of equality, dignity and respect in all aspects of life.

Relatively few conventions and recommendations apply exclusively to women. These instruments can be divided into two main groups: standards for improving the status of women and standards for the protection of women. Since the International Women's Year in 1975 and in the following United Nations Decade for Women (1976–85), standards for the temporary preferential treatment of women have been adopted.

The adoption in 1951 of a Convention (No. 100) concerning equal remuneration for men and women workers for work of equal value was inspired also by the United Nations Commission on the Status of Women (CSW). It provides that ratifying states must promote and, in so far as is consistent with the methods in operation for determining wages, ensure the application of this principle of equality, and that this should be done by means of legislation, collective agreements or wage-fixing machinery. Stress is laid, in this connection, on the importance of promoting the objective appraisal of jobs on the basis of the work to be performed.

In 1958 the International Labour Conference adopted both a Convention (No. 111) and a Recommendation (No. 111) on discrimination in employment and occupation. Both instruments refer to grounds of discrimination as diverse as race, sex or political opinion, for example. They cover discriminatory laws or acts in very general terms such as 'any discrimination, exclusion or preference ... which has the effect of nullifying or impairing equality of treatment', which can be the result not only of legislation but also of existing factual situations or practices. They reach into all sectors of employment and occupation, both public and private, and extend to vocational training and access to employment and to particular occupations, as well as to conditions of employment in general. The methods proposed in these texts to combat discrimination range from direct intervention through legislation to educational activities, and from action by the state to action by employers' and workers' organizations; individual countries are left a fairly wide margin of discretion.

The continuing increase in the number of women working outside their homes and having difficulty in reconciling their dual family and work responsibilities had led to the adoption in 1965 of a Recommendation (No. 123) on women with family responsibilities. This Recommendation was superseded in 1981 by Convention No. 156 and Recommendation No. 165, Concerning Workers with Family Responsibilities. The aim is to create equality of opportunity and treatment for women and men workers with family responsibilities. These instruments provide for the adoption of policies and measures in such fields as vocational guidance and training, hours of work, leave, child care facilities and social security to enable the workers concerned to exercise their right to engage in employment without being subject to discrimination and without conflict between their family and work responsibilities.

In the Report of the International Labour Organization, requested by the treaty-monitoring CEDAW, on the implementation of the CEDAW Convention in areas falling within the scope of their activities (CEDAW/C/1999/I/3/Add.4, dated 5 January 1999), the ILO's information on the provisions of Article 11 of the CEDAW Convention relates principally to the mentioned three ILO standards:

- the Equal Remuneration Convention, 1951 (No. 100), which has been ratified by 137 member states;
- the Discrimination (Employment and Occupation) Convention, 1958 (No. 111), which has been ratified by 131 member states; and
- the Workers with Family Responsibilities Convention, 1981 (No. 156), which has been ratified by 26 member states.

The ILO Report continues that, where applicable, reference is made to a number of other Conventions that are relevant to the employment of women:

Employment policy
- the Employment Policy Convention, 1964 (No. 122)
- the Human Resources Development Convention, 1975 (No. 142)

Maternity protection
- the Maternity Protection Convention, 1919 (No. 3)
- the Maternity Protection Convention (Revised), 1952 (No. 103)

Night work
- the Night Work (Women) Convention (Revised), 1948, (No. 89) [and Protocol]
- the Night Work Convention, 1990 (No. 170)

Underground work
- the Underground Work Convention, 1935 (No. 45)

Part-time work
- the Part-Time Convention, 1994 (No. 175)

Home work

• the Home Work Convention, 1996 (No. 177)

In June 1999, the International Labour Conference undertook the first discussion of the revision of the Maternity Protection Convention No. 103, and its accompanying Recommendation No. 95, which were adopted in 1952. The Convention is being revised to take into account changes in women's employment since its adoption and to bring it up to date. Important elements to be considered include: the extension of coverage to all employed women; stronger protection from dismissal during pregnancy; maternity leave and after return to work; and measures to remove maternity as a source of discrimination in employment.

As ILO surveys have shown, girls outnumber boys in the most vulnerable group of working children between five and eleven years of age – close to three girls for every two boys. The number would be much higher if children involved in full or near full-time housekeeping activities in their own parents' households are included. In addition, in many instances the girls work longer hours than the boys, particularly girls engaged in paid or unpaid domestic work.

In June 1999, the 174 states members of the ILO concluded the 87th annual International Labour Conference with the unanimous adoption of the Worst Forms of Child Labour Convention 1999. The new Convention applies to all persons under the age of 18. It defines the worst forms of child labour as: all forms of slavery or practices similar to slavery, such as the sale and trafficking of children, debt bondage, serfdom and forced or compulsory labour; forced or compulsory recruitment of children for use in armed conflict; use of a child for prostitution, production of pornography or pornographic performances; use, procuring or offering of a child for illicit activities, in particular for the production and trafficking of drugs; and work that is likely to harm the health, safety or morals of children.

The interlinkage of international standards The ILO has played a major role in the past eight decades in setting standards promoting equality for women workers. This international cooperation in favour of women has led to a tight network of legal regulations, which in the course of this time has been strengthened and consolidated by each new standard-setting activity. The consequent extension and deepening of this network of international law regulations can be seen from the example of remuneration, which occupies a central role in every system of labour law and labour relations.

With the adoption in 1951 of the Equal Remuneration Convention

No. 100, the International Labour Conference underlined its commitment to the principle of equal remuneration for work of equal value, which was already contained in the ILO Constitution of 1919. The following international instruments have paid tribute to the 'principle of equal remuneration for work of equal value'. For example, the International Covenant on Economic, Social and Cultural Rights (of 19 December 1966) calls for 'fair wages and equal remuneration for work of equal value without distinction of any kind, in particular women being guaranteed conditions of work not inferior to those enjoyed by men, with equal pay for equal work' – Article 7(a)(i).

In a regional context, for instance, Article 119 of the Treaty Establishing the European Economic Community (EEC) in 1957 merely provided for the application of the principle that men and women should receive equal pay for equal work. However, when referring to the objectives of the International Women's Year in 1975, the European Community had to bring its community law into line with the international standards laid down by the ILO. Consequently, the principle of 'equal pay for work of equal value' has been accepted in a number of directives: first of all in the Council Directive of 10 February 1975 on the approximation of the laws of the member states relating to the application of the principle of equal pay for men and women (75/117/EEC) and then in the Council Directive of 9 February 1976 on the implementation of the principle of equal treatment for men and women as regards access to employment, vocational training and promotion and working conditions (76/207/EEC).

Article 11, Paragraph 1 (d) of the CEDAW Convention (which was adopted by the United Nations in 1979) lays down 'the right to equal remuneration, including benefits, and to equal treatment in respect of work of equal value, as well as equality of treatment in the evaluation of the quality of work'.

The international obligations Conventions are communicated to the governments of member states of the ILO, which have to submit them to the competent national authorities. Each state remains free to decide whether it wishes to ratify a Convention or not, but when it does ratify any Convention, the state concerned is legally bound to take such measures as would be necessary to give full effect to all the provisions of the said Convention and to report to the ILO on these measures. The international obligations resulting from ratification not only mean the transformation of internationally agreed labour standards into domestic legislation, but also include their implementation in practice.

Governments, employers' and workers' organizations and other NGOs are encouraged to ensure women's increasing involvement in national development planning and programmes, in order to implement further the principles contained in ILO standards. As such, these obligations are directed not only at the state, but also at all social forces and national bodies. Accordingly, women and men are indirectly called upon to contribute to the achievement of gender equality in everyday life.

Originally, ILO Conventions contained relatively precise standards that could be taken over directly into national legislation. As concerns the so-called 'promotional' Conventions the individual ratifying states undertake to pursue stated objectives, but by methods that are left largely to their own discretion, as is the timing of the changes made. There can, of course, be no doubt of the value of such a legal commitment where the objective is defined with precision, and where progress towards its attainment can be measured with a fair amount of certainty. From this point of view, promotional Conventions such as the Equal Remuneration Convention, 1951 (No. 100), and the Discrimination (Employment and Occupation) Convention, 1958 (No. 111), have undoubtedly had a considerable effect in many countries. In other cases, in which the aim may be less easy to define with clarity, objective evaluation of the extent of compliance with the international commitment becomes difficult, and the use of the Convention form becomes more open to doubt; in such cases it might be preferable to cast proposed standards in the form of Recommendations, enjoying the authority of internationally accepted principles of social policy, but not involving a formal legal commitment in the event of ratification (ILO 1990).

The importance of a convention is reflected in the number of ratifications. The ILO publishes annually for the International Labour Conference Lists of Ratifications by Convention and by country (as at 31 December of the preceding year). This represents a global expression of a political will by governments, interest groups and other governmental and non-governmental organizations involved in these international opinion-forming processes, to achieve real equality for women.

The international reporting procedures The effectiveness of the conventions depends on the national and international bodies given the task of examining their observance. As has already been mentioned, a state party in its ratification simultaneously enters into the obligation of submitting periodic reports on the implementation of the ratified convention on the national level. The bases of these reporting procedures are laid down in the concluding articles of the respective convention. Guidelines are also designed to help the states parties in the preparation of their reports.

In the case of ILO conventions and recommendations, the periodic reporting is designed to ensure that the governments and the interest groups representing the employers and workers are regularly confronted with their responsibilities and shortcomings in the fulfilment of labour standards. The application of ratified Conventions is supervised in the ILO by the Committee of Experts on the Application of Conventions and Recommendations (CEACR), a body of independent experts from around the world, which meets annually. This international examination procedure is laid down in the Constitution of the ILO. Employers' and workers' organizations are included in the government's reporting activities. The Committee of Experts prepares a report on whether a government is fully complying with the requirements of a ratified Convention.

In the case of non-compliance, the governments are called upon to remedy deficiencies. The Committee of Experts can also make observations, which are published in its report, or can first of all address direct requests to the governments concerned who pass these on to the interest groups representing the employers and workers for comment. Observations are comments published in the CEACR's annual report, produced in English, French and Spanish. Direct requests (produced in English and in French, and, in the case of Spanish-speaking countries, also in Spanish) are not published, but are made public. The report is submitted to each annual session of the International Labour Conference, where it is examined and discussed by a specially appointed tripartite Conference Committee on the Application of Conventions and Recommendations.

In addition, the Committee of Experts carries out a general survey of the implementation of selected conventions and agreements (chosen by the governing body of the ILO) in the individual member states on the basis of the reports received from their governments. General Surveys of the Committee were on Equal Remuneration (1986); Equality in Employment and Occupation (1988), and Workers with Family Responsibilities (1993) (ILO 1986, 1988, 1993b).

As indicated at the beginning of this chapter, the ILO is the specialized agency in the UN system that contributed regularly and efficiently to the work of CSW and CEDAW, interlinking not only the standards but also the examination procedures of states parties. The ILO information submitted to the annual (since 1997 biannual) sessions of CEDAW consists of the mentioned observations and direct requests made by the ILO Committee of Experts to those states parties to CEDAW Convention to be considered at a particular session of CEDAW.

For example, on behalf of the Committee on the Elimination of Discrimination against Women, the Secretariat invited the International Labour Organization on 29 October 1998 to submit to CEDAW by 5 December 1998 a report on information provided by states to the ILO on the implementation of Article 11 and related articles of the CEDAW

Convention, which would supplement the information contained in the reports of those states parties to the CEDAW Convention and would be considered at the twentieth session of CEDAW.

At the twentieth session of CEDAW (19 January–5 February 1999) the ILO's indications concerning Algeria, China, Columbia, Greece, Kyrgyzstan, Thailand included (i) the position of the individual country in regard to ILO Conventions relating to women and (ii) comments by the ILO supervisory bodies, i.e. the pending comments of the ILO Committee of Experts on matters relevant to the provisions of the CEDAW Convention.

Accordingly, the reports provided by specialized agencies of the UN on the implementation of the CEDAW Convention in areas falling within the scope of their activities, in its Addendum of the International Labour Organization (CEDAW/C/1999/I/3/Add.5, dated 5 January 1999), submit in compliance with the above-mentioned request:

- Part I: information referring to activities, programmes and policy decisions undertaken by the ILO to promote the implementation of Article 11 and related articles of the CEDAW Convention; and
- Part II: indications concerning the situation of individual countries, containing the position of the states parties Algeria, China, Colombia, Greece, Kyrgyzstan and Thailand in regard to ILO Conventions relating to women. For each country, under review, the relevant ILO Conventions it has ratified are indicated.

In addition, the ILO supplements the report, wherever appropriate and possible, by referring to information supplied by the government in its reports to the ILO under Article 22 of the ILO Constitution on the application of the relevant ratified Conventions and in its reports under Article 19 of the ILO Constitution on the application of non-ratified Conventions and Recommendations. Where appropriate, reference is also made to observations or direct requests made by the ILO supervisory bodies – the Committee of Experts on the Application of Conventions and Recommendations, and the Committee on the Application of Standards of the International Labour Conference. This provides substantial information, usually prepared by different authorities in an individual country either for the ILO or for CEDAW/C, and supplements the examination of states parties reports in compliance with the CEDAW Convention.

The international reporting procedure has experienced an enormous upsurge in favour of women since the International Women's Year (1975). There have been several reasons for this. Public debate before 1975 was directed not towards gender equality, but rather towards the expansion of socio-political measures for mothers and families. Women themselves were barely or not yet active in key positions in the administration of government bodies or interest groups, which would have made it possible for them to have achieved a change in the preparation of reports and monitoring procedures. (Vogel-Polsky 1977)

In their reports, the states parties of conventions did not go beyond making general statements on the principles and quoting the legislation which dealt with the status of women. For both sides, both for the international assessors as well as for the national reporting bodies, it was relatively easy only to give information on legislative and other measures, while difficulties always arose if the social changes in the development of society were supposed to be revealed and evaluated (Gaudart 1984). As a result of the repeated inquiries of the international organizations and monitoring bodies during the United Nations Decade for Women (1976–85) concerning the existing of *de jure* and *de facto* obstacles and barriers facing equality of the sexes – particularly in the areas of employment and occupation – both reporting and monitoring on both the national and international levels became increasingly critical (ILO 1980a, 1980b; Eyraud et al. 1993; Martens and Mitter 1994).

Apart from the representation and complaints procedures set out in the ILO Constitution, governments of member states report on ratified conventions. Workers and employers' organizations have the right to provide additional or controversial information on the goverment report. Beyond appreciating and using all available procedures, the single most effective way to make their voices heard in this area would be for women to have a greater direct participation in all relevant structures of the ILO and in the international reporting procedures.

The institutional arrangements for the ILO strategy: mainstreaming gender concerns The institutional arrangements are made by the long-standing Office on Women Workers' Questions. It is the special adviser on women workers' questions who is responsible for the promotion and coordination of ILO policies, strategies, programmes and activities concerning equality for women in employment throughout the Office on women workers' questions; and for liaison on these matters with other international organizations, particularly in the UN system. Within the system-wide programming for the advancement of women, the ILO has adopted special resolutions relating to the objectives of the UN Decade for Women, in particular, preparing for the United Nations World Conferences on Women.

It is often forgotten that one of the most famous statistics on women quoted around the world originated from the ILO in 1975: 'while women and girls constitute one half of the world's population and one-third of the official labour force and perform nearly two-thirds of work hours, they receive only one-tenth of the world's income and they own less than one-hundredth of the world's property'. In this context the debate on 'protection or equality' is raised. 'Although protective measures for women have been viewed as necessary social protection, they have also been criticized as violations of equality of opportunity and treatment between men and women and as prejudicial to women's employment and career development. (ILO 1987).' However, the need to protect pregnant and nursing women from hazardous work and from jobs that involve potential exposure to toxic substances or can be harmful to the health of the mother or child remains undisputed (see ILO 1994).

A lack of awareness of women workers' rights has increasingly been recognized as a constraint on the effective use of the rights enshrined in both national laws and international standards. Dissemination of information about these rights is, therefore, a vital instrument for improving upon the status of women in society. It is in this context that the International Labour Office, through its Interdepartmental Project on Equality for Women in Employment, has produced a multimedia information kit and modular training package on women workers' rights to stimulate action in this area. The then special adviser on women workers' questions at the ILO, Maria Angélica Ducci, indicates in the Preface that the ILO is in a good position to contribute to the course of women workers' rights because of the following:

• The International Labour Standards act as an international labour code and set the principles and aims to be pursued.
• Its tripartite structure allows governments, employers and workers to agree on the basic rules of the game in the world of work.
• The ILO, as part of the UN system, is at the centre of a concerted effort to promote the advancement of women.
• The influence of the ILO in the world of work allows for an effective means of disseminating information on women workers' rights, to advocate them, to assist countries in reflecting them in national legislation and to promote its effective application and enforcement.

The Women Workers' Rights – Modular Training Package consists of:

• Introductory Module: Gender and Equality;
• Module 1: The role of the ILO and the UN in the Promotion of Women Workers' Rights;
• Module 2: International Labour Standards on Women Workers; and
• Module 3: Action at National Level to Promote Women Workers' Rights.

In addition, a general trainer's guide and audiovisual support materials have been prepared.

The International Labour Standards and Women Workers – Information Kit consists of:

- an ABC of Women Workers' Rights;
- a brochure;
- a pocket guide;
- six posters; and
- a video.

The materials can be used by the different ILO structures, governmental bodies, workers' and employers' organizations as well as non-governmental and other relevant groups working on women, gender and equality concerns. They can be adapted to local situations. The materials are available in English, French and Spanish, and the Information Kit also in German (ILO 1993a, 1994).

With regard to the critical areas identified by the Beijing Platform for Action (1995), the special adviser on women workers' questions, Jane Youyun Zhang, reported on programmes designed and implemented in ILO, such as:

- More and Better Jobs for Women;
- Women in Management, Breaking through the Glass Ceiling;
- Women in Export Processing Zones;
- Promoting Women's Employment and Participation in Social Funds;
- Capacity-building on Gender, Poverty and Employment; and
- the International Small Enterprise Programme and a number of others.

Some programmes are continuing today. The programme on More and Better Jobs for Women is just one example.

More Jobs	Better Job
means	means
• employment creation	• equal pay
• human resource development	• occupational desegregation
• entrepreneurship development	• occupational safety and health
• improvement in access to the labour market	• improvement in conditions of non-standard employment
• access to productive resources	• social security
• equality of opportunity	• family friendly workplaces
• poverty alleviation	• protection for vulnerable workers.
(ILO 1999)	

For further information please contact the International Programme on More and Better Jobs for Women, tel. +41.22.799.8276 or +41.22.799.7039; fax +41.22.799.7857, e-mail womemp@ilo.org (ILO 1999).

Integrating gender into the technical work of the ILO is promoting gender sensitivity in research, advisory and operational work and integrating gender aspects into programmes focused on the informal sector, small and medium enterprises, data collection, social security and promoting organizations of workers, training, employment creation schemes and proposing and evaluating standards, as well as in ILO branches and regional and area offices.

The Office of the Special Adviser on Women Workers' Questions (FEMMES) submitted the final draft of the ILO's contribution to the 1999 UN World Survey on the Role of Women in Development, a publication produced every five years by the United Nations Division for the Advancement of Women (DAW). One of the major UN publications, this survey presents an overall assessment of women's situation in the various aspects of social and economic life, covering the challenges, opportunities and obstacles faced by women. The 1999 issue focuses on globalization and women in the world of work. For more information contact the Office of the Special Adviser on Women Workers' Questions (FEMMES), tel. +41.22.799.6730, fax: +41.22.799.6388 or email: femmes@ilo.org

The United Nations Educational, Scientific and Cultural Organization (UNESCO)

Origin and establishment, constitution and functions When the first Conference of Allied Ministers of Education (London, 1942) proposed the establishment of an international organization within their field of competence, it was the British biologist Sir Julian Huxley who persuaded the founding fathers not to limit themselves to education and culture, but to introduce science as another main field that the new international organization aimed to foster. He became UNESCO's first director-general. The Constitution was adopted in London on 16 November 1945 and came into force when 20 states had accepted it by 4 November 1946. The Preamble starts with the often quoted phrase: 'The Governments of the States Parties to this Constitution on behalf of their peoples declare: That since wars begin in the minds of men, it is in the minds of men that the defences of peace must be constructed.'

Consequently, the purpose of the organization is to contribute to peace and security 'by promoting collaboration among the nations through education, science and culture in order to further universal respect for justice, for the rule of law and for the human rights and fundamental freedoms which are affirmed for the peoples of the world, without distinction of race, sex, language or religion, by the Charter of the United Nations'. Reciprocal representation was agreed between the United Nations and UNESCO and the function of UNESCO was to advise the UN on the educational, scientific and cultural aspects of matters of their concern.

Consequently, UNESCO was represented in the sessions of the UN Commission on the Status of Women (CSW) from its inception in 1946 and from 1982 onwards contributing also to those of the Committee on the Elimination of Discrimination against Women. UNESCO provided assistance and submitted comparative studies within its fields of competence, mainly concerning communication and recently also on science and culture as highlighted in the following overview of the main fields of activities of UNESCO.

Fields of activity

Education The organization's first reason for existence was education – the 'E' of the acronym. To begin with, the aim was to reconstruct the schools destroyed by the Second World War and to re-establish teacher exchanges disrupted by the conflict. Training teachers in the Third World soon became a top priority, with the launching of educational systems adapted to the particular needs of each country. In concrete terms, this meant enabling member states to devise and apply their own educational policies and to assess the results of such policies. The objective applied to three essential areas: the universalization of elementary education, the abolition of illiteracy and the democratization of education (UNESCO 1980a, 1981).

The Convention against Discrimination in Education adopted by the eleventh session of the General Conference of UNESCO in 1960 and entering into force in 1962 addresses – like the other human rights instruments of general application – the need to prevent discrimination among groups in society in the matter of education, but does not address the need to prevent gender-specific discrimination. Its Article 2 describes situations that are not deemed to constitute discrimination, such as the establishment or maintenance of separate educational systems or institutions for pupils of the two sexes, or for religious or linguistic reasons, or for being either a public or private institution, so long as the systems and institutions offer equivalent access to education and equivalent standards, equipment and premises. Article 3 obliges states parties to eliminate and prevent discrimination in stated ways. Article 4 obliges states parties to formulate, develop and apply national policies that will tend to promote equality of opportunity and of treatment in the matter of education. In line with the thinking of the day, such policies were defined as making primary education free and compulsory, making secondary education generally available, and so on; ensuring that standards of education are equivalent in all public education institutions of the same level; encouraging the education of persons who have not received any primary education and adult continuing education; and providing training for the teaching profession without discrimination.

In the following decades the emphasis of comparative studies carried out by UNESCO was primarily on the 'access' of women to education (1952), of girls to secondary education (UNESCO 1966), of girls and women to technical and vocational education (UNESCO 1968), or on women in the age of science and technology (UNESCO 1970), on school education of girls (Deblé 1980), on the opening up to women of vocational training and jobs traditionally occupied by men (UNESCO 1980c), on women in engineering and technological education and training (UNESCO 1986b), on women in engineering education (Michel 1988) or *Women's Education Looks Forward, Programmes, Experiences, Strategies* (Kotite 1989), Islam, perestroika and the education of women (UNESCO 1990c), to mention just a few examples of data analyses.

UNESCO has not developed special norms combating discrimination against girls and women as stipulated in the CEDAW Convention. In its Article 10 the Convention obliges states parties

> to take all appropriate measures to eliminate discrimination against women in order to ensure to them equal rights with men in the field of education and in particular to ensure, on a basis of equality of men and women: (a) The same conditions for career and vocational guidance, for access to studies and for the achievement of diplomas in educational establishments of all categories in rural as well as in urban areas, this equality shall be ensured in preschool, general, technical, professional and higher technical education, as well as in all types of vocational training.

The following sub-provisions in Article 10 concern access to the same curricula, same examinations, teaching staff, premises and equipment, scholarships and other study grants, programmes of continuing education, including adult and functional literacy programmes, particularly those aimed at reducing, at the earliest possible time, any gap in education existing between men and women. Article 10 (c) stipulates: 'The elimination of any stereotyped concept of the roles of men and women at all levels and in all forms of education by encouraging co-education and other types of education which will help to achieve this aim and, in particular, by the revision of textbooks and school programmes and the adaptation of teaching methods.'

As various recommendations relate to the importance of revising educational material and of teaching teachers how not to pass on the stereotype role models that they have learned, national studies on the images of women and of men projected by school textbooks and children's literature were carried out at the request of UNESCO in various regions of the world (Abu Nasr et al. 1983, 1986a). However, the UNESCO Convention on Technical and Vocational Education, adopted in 1989, does not tackle the need for non-sexist training and education materials.

The joint CEDAW/UNESCO Manifesto entitled *Towards a Gender-inclusive Culture through Education*, presented at the Beijing Conference 1995, appeals to the international community to reaffirm education as a fundamental human right of girls and women. This need is urgent because women comprise two-thirds of the 885 million adults in the world who are illiterate. Girls make up the majority of the more than 130 million children who have no access to primary schooling. The aims are mainly increased access to, and improvement of, the quality and relevance of basic education.

UNESCO runs programmes covering important aspects of education, such as teacher training, and under its promotion of 'access to education' for girls and women expands the subjects to vocational and technical as well as scientific and technological education, education for peace and international understanding (human rights education), environmental education, education for AIDS prevention, nutritional education under its 'Education for the Twenty-first Century' Programme. The report to UNESCO of the International Commission on Education for the Twenty-first Century under the presidency of Jacques Delors (former president of the EU), *Learning: The Treasure Within* (UNESCO 1996b), highlights four pillars upon which education throughout life is based: learning to know, learning to do, learning to live together and learning to be. Its recommendation concerning a policy of strong encouragement for the education of girls and women has to resort again to international action, following on the recommendations of the Fourth World Conference on Women (Beijing, September 1995).

In the field of higher education UNESCO runs programmes for information, documentation, and academic exchange between universities and institutes of higher education. Conventions have been adopted with the aim of recognizing studies, diplomas and degrees in higher education in order to provide students and teachers everywhere with equal opportunities, particularly at the regional level. Higher education management and academic staff development, support for university and scientific libraries, and higher-level distance education are some of the key features, including special programmes to promote the status of women in teaching, research and the administration of higher education.

UNESCO called experts from different regions to analyse the objectives, evaluate the principal characteristics and make prospective recommendations concerning women's studies. The *Report on Programmes of Research and of Teaching Related to Women* was presented in 1980 at the Second UN World Conference on Women in Copenhagen (UNESCO 1980b; Rendel 1980). Margherita Rendel discussed the purposes and implications of research and studies relating to women, examined intellectual, psychological and political aspects and traced their development in the United States, Europe and Third World countries.

Programmes launched in the 1990s with UNESCO acting as catalyst are the UNITWIN projects for inter-university cooperation at sub-regional, regional and interregional levels and the establishment of international university chairs for the promotion of international intellectual cooperation with the universities and with the support of various organizations, institutions and funding agencies in all regions of the world, initially in the developing countries. The UNITWIN/UNESCO Chairs Programme comprises (February 1999) over three hundred UNESCO Chairs in some 90 countries and 46 UNITWIN networks. (Detailed information of the UNESCO Chair Scheme and UNITWIN programmes may be obtained from the Division of Higher Education and Research, UNESCO, 7 place de Fontenoy, 75352 Paris 07 SP, France, tel. 33 1/4568 1031, fax 33 1/4568 5626, email m.grosjean@unesco.org).

In 1996 a UNESCO chair in women, society and development was established at the Institute of Sociology, University of Warsaw (Poland). The University of Swaziland is a shareholder of the chair.

Science UNESCO promotes international cooperation in the development of science and technology and its application within the framework of international/intergovernmental programmes, such as the International Geological Correlation Programme (IGCP), the International Hydrological Programme (IHP), and the Intergovernmental Oceanographic Commission (IOC), which supports projects such as the World Climate Research Programme, and implements, in conjunction with the World Meteorological Organization (WMO), the Global Ocean Observing System (GOOS).

Upon the initiative of the biologist Magda Staudinger performing microscopic observations on macromolecular substances, first in natural, then in polarized and UV light, later mainly using the electron microscope, the man and the biosphere programme (MAB) was launched in order to promote international cooperation in research, training and dissemination of information. An international network promotes 'Biosphere Reserves' (as of September 2001 there were 411 sites in 94 countries), which provide representative examples of approximately two-thirds of the world's land ecosystems, and serve as centres for conservation, development, research, demonstration, education, training, and ongoing biosphere monitoring.

The interdisciplinary programmes relating to social and human sciences were integrated and are now concerned jointly with activities and publications in the fields of human rights, particularly rights related to UNESCO's fields of competence: education, science, culture and communication. A central part of this programme is the struggle against all forms of discrimination, which also includes work to improve the status of women and to promote equality between men and women. This meant convening a special meeting of experts on the social and cultural factors that impede the promotion of equality and the application of the CEDAW Convention in Bakou, USSR, in 1987, on the one hand, and ignoring the principle of 'equal rights of men and women' and CEDAW in UNESCO's *Declaration on Education for Peace, Human Rights and Democracy*, adopted at the forty-fourth session of the International Conference on Education, Geneva, October 1994 on the other. On Austria's request in 1995, a reference to CEDAW and the Fourth World Conference on Women was finally included in this Declaration.

Nevertheless, efforts are made in line with the principle of equality between men and women concerning the revision of all basic texts of UNESCO with a view to the use of gender-neutral terminology and wording, although the famous Preamble of the Charter of UNESCO quoted at the beginning of this chapter remains unchanged (UNESCO 1993a; see also UNESCO 1988).

Obviously, there has been an undeniable increase in the recruitment of women scientists/engineers in recent years. The area to investigate is, however, the scientific community itself, and its knowledge – over a period of time – about women as applicants, project workers, project leaders, research objects, functionaries in the process of inspection (peer review system), members of executive boards designing research policy in general or for the body on which they serve, selection of boards, and so on (Sutherland 1990; Gaudart 1990; UNESCO/CEPES 1992, 1994; Stolte-Heiskanen 1991; UNESCO 1993b).

'The gender dimension describes the way in which culturally organized differences between men and women interact with historically and socially diverse scientific and technological practices and their meanings. Scientific and technological cultures and practices shape gendered social relations and, in turn, are shaped by them.' Sandra Harding and Elizabeth McGregor (1995) start their analysis with this conceptual framework and pose two key questions: science by whom? and science for whom? In most countries women are under-educated, have fewer credentials, are under-employed and clearly under-promoted. Women's presence is negligible in virtually any science and technology policy group. The publication analyses the range of obstacles to women's equal opportunities in science and technology, examines the differential impact of technological change on the lives of men and women, explores the role of women in traditional knowledge systems and reviews the history of women in science. Examples of strategies addressing issues of women in science policy are given throughout. 'The gender dimension of science and technology' is an extract from the UNESCO *World Science Report 1996* (Moore et al. 1996) and has been produced as a contribution towards the 1995 UN Fourth World Conference on Women in Beijing.

The Declaration on Science and the Use of Scientific Knowledge, adopted by the World Conference on 'Science for the Twenty-first Century: A New Commitment', assembled in Budapest, Hungary, from 26 June to 1 July 1999 under the aegis of UNESCO and the International Council for Science (ICSU) had to recognize in its Preamble that 'most of the benefits of science are unevenly distributed, as a result of structural asymmetries among countries, regions and social groups, *and between the sexes*'. The 'historical imbalance in the participation of men and women in all science-related activities' is explicitly addressed only 'in the fundamental role played by women in the application of scientific development to food production and health care'. However, the 'difficulties encountered by women, constituting over half of the population in the world, in entering, pursuing and advancing in a career in the sciences and in participating in decision-making in science and technology' are considered as an urgent need to be addressed towards meeting the needs of humankind.

Culture UNESCO's cultural activities are among its best known, such as securing and preserving the rock temples of Abu Simbel, the Sanctuary of Borobudur in Indonesia. The Convention for the Protection of the World Cultural and Natural Heritage (1972, covering the World Heritage List) highlights the interdisciplinary nature of its approach.

UNESCO also works actively to support the preservation of oral tradition, the promotion of books and reading, and the Universal Copyright Convention (1952) falls within its competence. The sign © is now used to protect books all over the world.

UNESCO publishes and distributes numerous periodicals, specialist journals, reviews, documents and books dealing with the various aspects of education. Many publications designed to be both thought-provoking and informative are available in several languages, including the monthly magazine the *UNESCO Courier* (published in 36 different languages and in Braille), *UNESCO Sources* (in French, English, Portuguese and Spanish; free of charge), *Prospects* (quarterly journal on education), the *International*

Social Science Journal, Impact of Science on Society, Nature and Resources, the *Copyright Bulletin* and the *Bulletin of the International Bureau of Education.*

However, repeated recommendations of, and references to, the international community preparing for the Fourth World Conference on Women (1995) were necessary to persuade UNESCO that, for instance, the 1995 edition of the *World Education Report* should focus on the education of women and girls statistics, male/female comparisons, and gender analysis and measures. Gender components are included – as mentioned before – in the *World Science Report* (Moore et al. 1996) and the *World Communication Report* 1996.

Equal rights of men and women are often ignored, forgotten or even put under taboo in this respect. UNESCO devoted its quarterly publication *Museum* No. 171 (Vol. XLIII, No. 3, 1991) to a 'Focus on women' and the editor was shocked on how bad things really were for women. The absence of women's history in many museums studied turned to the question of how can women fail to be alienated if their history is excluded, if they are deprived of contact with the cultural heritage of their gender? 'The historical fact is that the feminist movement in US during the early 1970s by-passed the museum world. More accurately, American museums have ignored this feminist movement since its inception.' In other regions, women's museums viewed themselves not as ghettos but rather as spearheads in altering attitudes and exhibitions – and in keeping the women/museums agenda visible until there is a better gender balance in traditional museums. Other fields of activities in this sector concern the concept of cultural identity, cultural exchange and intercultural studies (UNESCO 1982), also in the framework of the World Decade for Cultural Development (1988–97).

Some projects for 'the preservation of cultural identities' warrant further study from the point of view of social processes relating to the fact that the living and working conditions of women are changing in an evolutionary process in many regions of the world, accelerated since the International Women's Year 1975 and the activities during the UN Decade for Women (1976–85) and the adoption of the Nairobi Forward-looking Strategies in 1985. However, the dynamics of this evolution have not affected every woman, and much less every man. The dominant planners and decision-makers in education, science, culture and communication seem to ignore the realities of emerging women's roles and women's claims for 'parity democracy' in all fields of life. Some evidence relating, in particular, to migrant women proves that the search for cultural identity in the past can be perceived and used against the concerns and interest of women of today, i.e. against their gradually achieved legal equality with men, their individual and social self-fulfilment. Emerging cultural identities of many women clash with policies aiming to revitalize traditional values in this respect (UNESCO 1990a).

Progress towards equality can be noted in programmes and publications if they include an international dimension and do refer to international standards. The World Commission on Culture and Development under the presidency of Javier Perez de Cuellar (former secretary-general of the UN) included women experts, and its report *Our Creative Diversity* (1995) contains a chapter on 'Gender and culture' and an 'International Plan for Gender Equality'. The establishment of a research programme on the interface between women's rights, cultural specificities and socio-cultural change is to be followed.

As an educational organization, UNESCO plays a specific role in human rights education as well as in campaigning for a culture of peace that combines non-violence and respect for all human rights, cultural diversity, the promotion of democracy, tolerance and solidarity, sustainable development and gender equality. The Statement on Women's Contribution to a Culture of Peace, launched in Beijing 1995, gained support in various regions and in the preparations for the year 2000, which was proclaimed International Year for the Culture of Peace by the United Nations General Assembly on 20 November 1997. The signatories of the Statement made a commitment themselves, *inter alia*, 'to promote knowledge and respect for international normative instruments concerning the human rights of girls and women', 'to oppose the misuse of religion, cultural and traditional practices for discriminatory purposes', and 'to promote relevant quality education that imparts knowledge of the human rights of men and women, skills of non-violent conflict resolution, respect for the natural environment, intercultural understanding and awareness of global interdependence'. In its transdisciplinary project towards a culture of peace, however, it is stated that UNESCO will promote 'legal literacy' for women by assisting local NGOs and community groups in providing basic instruction on women's rights recognized in national legislation. This could lead to non-compliance with international recommendations and standards concerning the human rights of women. (For further information on women's roles as promoters of a culture of peace please contact Woman and a Culture of Peace, Culture of Peace Programme Unit, 7, place de Fontenoy, 75352 Paris 07 SP, France, tel. (+33.1) 4568 1212, fax (+33.1) 4568 5557, email i.breines@unesco.org, Director, CPP/WCP.)

Communication Although it does not figure in UNESCO's title, communication has been a field of work ever since its Constitution gave the task 'to promote the free flow of ideas by word and image'. The organization works in support of press freedom, pluralism, independence and diversity of both public and private media. Along similar lines, it is actively helping developing countries to enhance their means of communication and to apply new communication technologies so that they have a chance to make their voice heard internationally. The development of communication was enlarged by international programmes for general Information and Informatics set up in the last two decades (Ceulemans and Fauconnier 1979).

With regard to communication, in *Communication in the Service of Women: A Report on Action and Research Programmes 1980–1985*, Margaret Gallagher (1985) concluded:

> Priorities and strategies debated or implemented in the communication sector itself have – at both national and international levels – failed miserably to acknowledge the existence of women as a constituent group, with its own complex profile, exigencies and rights. Neither the McBride Report nor the International Programme for the Development of Communication (IPDC) – the two major substantive outcomes of the international debate of the 1970s on information and communication – place any particular emphasis on women's needs, although they are both part of an international response to the very issues which women themselves highlight as problematic in their relationship to the communication media: access, control, training needs, under-representation, marginalisation, distortion.

Strategies proposed in the communication sector as well as in other cultural fields distinguish always between (i) media or cultural industry-related issues (such as changing the portrayal [image] of women and men in the media or using the resources of our museums to build collections, to plan, design and show exhibitions addressing women in the arts and sciences as well as women's history) and (ii) women's participation in these fields growing out of a concern about job opportunities for women at all levels, particularly at decision-making level, based on the assumption that there is a link between the output of media or museums or cultural industries and the producers of that output.

Another impact evaluation of communication activities carried out for the benefit of women over the last decade (1981–91) (UNESCO 1992b) as well as comparative studies were carried out in all regions in view of the preparation for the Fourth World Conference on Women. In the concluding International Symposium: Women and the Media, Access to Expression and Decision-making, held in Toronto (Canada) from 28 February to 3 March 1995 the participants adopted the Toronto Platform for Action, which sums up global as well as specific and immediate actions in this communication field related to women (UNESCO 1995b).

How does UNESCO work? Before turning to the question of how UNESCO promotes the status of women in its fields of competence, in general, some consideration must be given to the working methods of the organization (UNESCO 1981, 1990b, 1992a, 1995a).

The General Conference, which brings together the representatives of the 186 member states every two years, lays down the organization's programme. The Executive Board, composed of 58 members, supervises the programme's implementation by the organization's Secretariat. The Secretariat is divided into sectors corresponding to its operational activities in education, science, culture and communication. The staff of the Secretariat, based at headquarters in Paris and in regional offices around the world, comprises professionals of the various disciplines. The post of general director has been filled by Koichiro Matsura (Japan) since 1999. UNESCO's activities are based on biennial (since 1976 also on mid-term) planning, which does not permit direct integration of research findings into the planning process. As a consequence each sector must incorporate its own research and evaluation dimensions.

UNESCO is the only agency in the United Nations systems with National Commissions (in 1997, in 180 out of its 186 member states), each with a task of involving the country's educational, scientific, cultural and communication circles, as well as its main institutions, in UNESCO's work. Unique in this respect within the United Nations system, the National Commissions participate in the elaboration, execution and evaluation of UNESCO programmes. As organs of liaison, information, discussion and implementation, the National Commissions, usually following the structure of competence of the organization, have set up special committees for education, natural sciences, social sciences and humanities, human rights and peace, culture and communication. In addition, regular meetings of the secretaries of National Commissions on the regional and interregional levels serve to keep UNESCO informed on local as well as global needs.

The 26th General Conference (1992) invited member states and their National Commissions to inform the director-general of the name of the person in their National Commission or other institution who was dealing with UNESCO's transverse theme 'Women', with a view to facilitating contacts between member states and UNESCO's Coordinating Unit for Activities Relating to Women (FEM), and at the same time provide him with information on the relevant institutions and organizations, governmental and non-governmental, which promote the advancement of women (Res. 26 C/11.1). Since that time more than one hundred National Commissions have nominated such 'focal points' on the theme 'women'.

Supporting UNESCO are also the UNESCO Associated Schools, set up to foster a spirit of international understanding in young people, and the UNESCO Club movement, whose aim is to involve the public in the activities of the organization and the United Nations. Today there are some 5,000 UNESCO Clubs, Centres and Associations in more than 120 countries, linking people of goodwill across the globe. More than 3,300 Associated Schools exist in 126 countries.

Over 585 non-governmental organizations maintain working and mutual information relations with UNESCO, some of which, like the International Council of Scientific Unions, play an important role in executing projects. The UNESCO Cooperative Action Programme provides a means for educators, scientists, artists, authors, librarians, museologists, computer specialists, journalists, publishers and voluntary associations to participate in projects.

In conclusion, UNESCO is its member states and the professionals in the educational, scientific, cultural and communication fields, which historically have not been at the forefront in promoting the human rights of women. The states, their representatives, delegates, and the huge number of independent or autonomous intellectuals from the educational, scientific, cultural and communication circles give the instructions, and the corresponding professionals in the Secretariat carry them out. UNESCO works in this specific international community of intellectuals, and it works through them and for them. Apparently, women have not yet reached a critical mass in these intellectual circles.

National Commissions for UNESCO and their focal points for the programmes on women: case study of Austria A survey carried out by the Austrian Commission for UNESCO in 1987 revealed that subcommittees or special committees on the status of women existed in Canada, Germany, Norway, France and Denmark, with coordinators in Spain, GDR, Ireland, Yugoslavia, Finland, Bulgaria, the USSR and Israel, while in 1987 no special units with responsibility for the status of women programmes were to be found in the CSSR, Luxembourg, Netherlands, Sweden, Ireland or Italy.

Accordingly, the Austrian Commission for UNESCO (hereafter ACU) set up a Special Committee on the Status of Women in 1987. In the functional period 1993–98 the mandate of the Special Committee was expanded, first, with the UN Charter-based principle of equality between men and women and second with the UN policy dimension of sustainable development. The Special Committee of ACU was consequently renamed 'Status of Women, Equality and Development'.

Within the Participation Programme an Interregional Consultation on the Transverse Theme 'Women' was convened by the ACU at the European

University Centre for Peace Studies in Stadtschlaining, in Austria, in 1993. It recommended in the field of social change, peace and human rights, *inter alia*:

- Research into the global values, interests, problems and concerns related to women's rights issues should be carried out on a multidisciplinary basis at all levels. Research and studies on the legal perspectives of women's rights should be carried out in all regions, e.g. in university cooperation programmes, by networking in relation with the UNITWIN and UNESCO Chairs programme.
- International instruments adopted before the International Women's Year 1975, particularly before the adoption by the General Assembly of the Convention on the Elimination of All Forms of Discrimination against Women in 1979, should be reviewed and adjusted to the CEDAW Convention, e.g. by an additional protocol.
- Furthermore, the promotion of knowledge and understanding of women's human rights instruments, their wide dissemination and translation into national languages, was considered essential for both women and men. (The inclusion of women's rights under international conventions in the curricula, textbooks and other teaching materials should provide the basis, in particular, for all actions related to international education.)
- UNESCO should ensure that from 1993 onwards all updated editions of UNESCO publications related to human rights teaching, peace and international education contain information and knowledge about existing instruments about women's human rights, in particular, the CEDAW Convention (Austrian Commission for UNESCO 1993).

Consequently, the Austrian Commission for UNESCO Special Committee decided to strengthen its work towards the promotion of knowledge and understanding of women's rights under international conventions, in co-operation with educational experts of the Austrian Federal Ministry of Education, in order to include the instruments relating to women's rights in curricula, textbooks and other teaching materials. This objective was strengthened in line with those of the Vienna Declaration and Programme of Action (adopted by the World Conference on Human Rights, June 1993), the United Nations Year for Tolerance 1995 and the United Nations Decade for Human Rights Education (1995–2004).

UNESCO's programme for the advancement of women UNESCO's activities concerning women are geared to several objectives, as demonstrated in this overview. They were grouped in the analysis by Nicole

Echard under two main headings: first, the development of knowledge, regarded as a necessary basis for action, about issues that are still shrouded in ignorance, having only recently come to the fore; second, the creation of a groundswell of reflection, promotion and action in the various formal bodies concerned by changes in gender relations. 'Clearly, the failure to disseminate the results prevents their effective utilization by the various social agents, while at the same time precluding the establishment of any discussion about them in the communities concerned' (UNESCO 1987). Annotated bibliographies on the status of women were disseminated mainly at the biennial sessions of the UNESCO General Conference (UNESCO 1983, 1986a, 1991).

Following the worldwide programming of the UN system, UNESCO started in the 1970s to articulate programmes for the advancement of women which were changing somewhat with each biennium. 'New targets are defined, different expectations of results are articulated, different activities are planned. What is clear, however, is that the programme for the advancement of women is consistently underfunded, understaffed, with many of its staff overstretched, and replacement not being made in time or at all' (UNESCO 1992b)

As a specialized agency in the UN system, the organization contributed to the system-wide programming, which started with the three objectives of the International Women's Year 1975: Equality, Development and Peace (A/Res/1972) and the United Nations Decade for Women (1976–85). From an initial collection of scattered activities aimed at 'improving the status of women' (a priority articulated by the First Medium-Term Plan 1977–82), in document 19 C/4 paragraph 1334, women's activities came, in the Second Medium-Term Plan (1984–89) under a separate programme, the Major Programme XIV, entitled 'The Status of Women' (24 C/4) (a cross-sectional chapter that brings together the activities planned under this heading in the 13 major programmes; a budgetary provision was included for the office of the coordinator for programmes concerning the status of women, being also served by an Intersectoral Committee. The objective was a twofold strategy: (i) developing activities specifically addressing the needs, concerns and interests of women, and (ii) integrating the female dimension into the planning, implementation and evaluation of all the organization's programmes. The Third Medium-Term Plan (1990–95) (document 25 C/4) was streamlined and activities foreseen were conceived as a transverse theme 'women'.

The following strategy relates to 'women' as one of the 'priority groups such as LDCs (least-developed countries), Africa and Youth' in the (Fourth) Medium-Term Strategy 1996–2001 (UNESCO 1996a; document 28 C/4, paragraphs 227–33). It is based on a three-pronged approach proposed by the Secretariat of the Consultative Committee on Women set up in the Directorate in order to prepare for the Fourth World Conference on Women:

1. to mainstream a gender perspective in all policy-planning, programming, implementation and evaluation activities;
2. to make full use of women's vision, competence, experience and potential; and
3. to develop specific programmes, projects and activities for the benefit of girls and women, geared towards promoting equality, endogenous capacity-building, and women's full citizenship.

The first approach 'will also entail the revision of normative instruments to bring them into line with the Convention on the Elimination of All Forms of Discrimination against Women (CEDAW Convention), the promotion of non-sexist terminology and the development of gender-sensitive indicators to monitor all UNESCO's projects' (paragraph 228 in 28 C/4).

The reference to the CEDAW Convention for inclusion in UNESCO's strategic planning was repeatedly – as mentioned before – proposed by the Special Committee on the Status of Women of the Austrian Commission for UNESCO. Evidently, UNESCO had not made use of its normative function so far. More recommendations and declarations than conventions were adopted. The normative activities of the organization are rather pragmatic and fragmented, as stated in the analysis of the normative function of the Organization by Pierre Michel Eisemann (1994).

Accordingly, the Report of the UNESCO Committee on Conventions and Recommendations (CR) concerning the implementation of the Convention and Recommendation against Discrimination in Education (156 EX/52, 7 June 1999) called for broadening the information base and changing the very nature of UNESCO's reports on the elimination of discrimination in education.

> Reports should critically reflect the situation regarding problems and practices persisting in the domain of discrimination in education, rather than provide short analytical summaries of the reports received from Member States. To that end, it would be pertinent, in particular, to *take into account the relevant reports submitted to the United Nations on the elimination of discrimination against women*, implementation of the Convention on the Rights of the Child and other United Nations instruments relating to the problem of discrimination, as well as reports of other intergovernmental organizations. (Paragraph 15 in 156 EX/52).

The outlook seems promising if UNESCO considers reporting and monitoring procedures of the kind established by the United Nations regarding the human rights of women.

In accordance with Article 22 of the CEDAW Convention (General Assembly resolution 34/180, annex) specialized agencies are invited to submit reports to CEDAW on the implementation of the Convention in areas falling within the scope of their activities. Accordingly, on behalf of CEDAW, the Secretariat invited UNESCO to submit to the Committee a report on information provided by states to UNESCO on the implementation of Article 10 and related articles of the Convention, which would supplement the information contained in the reports of those states parties to the Convention to be considered at the next session of the Committee. In compliance with the Committee's requests UNESCO is providing these reports – as are ILO, FAO and WHO – on the implementation of the CEDAW Convention in areas falling within the scope of their activities more and more accurately.

On 1 April 1996, the director-general established the Unit for the Promotion of the Status of Women and Gender Equality with the task of coordination all UNESCO programmes relating to women. This unit represents UNESCO at the Inter-Agency Committee on Women and Gender Equality in the United Nations Administrative Committee on Coordination. At its fourth session (February 1999) UNESCO, together with the UNDP Gender in Development Programme and the World Bank, joined the United Nations Internet gateway for information on women's and gender issues on the site WomenWatch.

The three entities in the United Nations system specifically devoted to women's issues – the Division for the Advancement of Women in the Department of Economic and Social Affairs (DAW/DESA), the United Nations Development Fund for Women (UNIFEM) and the International Research and Training Institute for the Advancement of Women (INSTRAW) – pooled efforts and resources to create WomenWatch, launched on International Women's Day, 8 March 1997. WomenWatch is a gateway to United Nations information and data on women worldwide. It is designed to serve as an important contribution to the outreach programme of its collaborating partners, providing a cost-effective means to expand outreach and networking, and streamlining access to information.

The information is organized in an Internet-accessible database to allow users in developing countries who do not have direct access to all Internet tools to retrieve the information. Efforts are made to repackage and redisseminate information to locations with no Internet access. Closer cooperation will be fostered with organizations that provide training in the use of electronic communication technologies. The Internet site is accessible through the World Wide Web at http://www.un.org/womenwatch, as well as through other Internet tools, such as the electronic mail (womenwatch @un.org) and the gopher (gopher://gopher,un.org).

Note

1. On the occasion of the International Women's Year 1975 the International Institute for Labour Studies convened a research symposium on Women and Decision-making: A Social Policy Priority (Geneva, November 1975). See International Institute for Labour Studies (ed.), Research Series No. 23, Geneva 1976, in Dorothea Gaudart, *Women and Social Policy Decision-Making: The Case of Austria*, pp. 59–74. On the occasion of the moving of the UN Branch for the Advancement of Women to the United Nations Office Vienna, the Austrian government convened jointly with the IILS an international symposium on Women and Industrial Relations (Vienna, September 1978). The design and themes are still relevant for women workers. See IILS, *International Symposium on Women and Industrial Relations* (Vienna, September 1978), Research Series 54–57, Geneva; IILS, *Women and Work, Selected Bibliography 1970–1978*, Geneva; IILS, *Women and Industrial Relations*, Research Series 54; Dorothea Gaudart, 'Framework paper'; Dorothea Gaudart and Rose Marie Greve, 'Analysis of the discussions'; No. 55 (French version); No. 56, *Working Papers of an International Symposium (Vienna, September 1978), Theme 1: The Representation of Women and their Interests in Industrial Relations Institutions*: Alice Cook, 'Women in trade unions'; Jacqueline Aubert, 'La position des femmes dans la gestion des entreprises et dans les associations patronales en France'; Elsa Hackl, 'Frauen im Management: Eine österreichische Fallstudie'; Peter Bowen, 'White collar jobs and the unionisation of women'; Friedrich Fürstenberg, 'Die Vertretung der Frauen und ihrer Interessen im Betriebsrat am Beispiel der Bundesrepublik Deutschland und Österreichs'; Stanislas S. Grozdanic, 'Representation of women and their interests under the workers' self-management system in Yugoslavia'; M. C. Endert-Baylé, 'Improving career possibilities for women in Shell in the Netherlands'. *Theme 2: Legislation and Collective Bargaining as Instruments for the Integration of Women in Industrial Relations*: Marion Janjic, 'L'évolution récente de la législation relative à l'emploi des femmes dans les pays industrialisés et son importance pour les relations professionelles'; Hiromasa Suzuki, 'La négociation collective et l'égalité de rénumération et de chances dans les pays industrialisés', Helga Stubianek, 'Die Entwicklung der Kollektivverhandlungen der Angestellten in Österreich und ihre Bedeutung für die Frauen'; No. 57, *Working Papers of an International Symposium (Vienna, September 1978), Part II, Theme 3: Employment and Quality of Working Life Issues for Women*: Ursula Engelen-Kefer, 'Beschäftigung und Qualität des Arbeitslebens: Auswirkungen für Frauen (dargestellt am Beispiel der Bundesrepublik Deutschland)'; Julie Loranger, 'Canadian policies for the promotion of women's employment conditions in the public service'; Magda Hoffmann, 'Employment and quality of working life: the situation of women in Hungary'; Christina Jonung, 'Policies of "positive discrimination" in Scandinavia in respect of women's employment'; Erwin Weissel, 'Die Ausbildung – Ein Instrument der Verbesserung der Beschäftigung und der Teilnahme der Frauen in den Arbeitsbeziehungen: Eine österreichische Fallstudie'; Hilda Scott, 'Women and employment: approaches in East and West'; *Theme 4: Repercussions of Industrial Relations Developments for Improving the Conditions of Women in Society at Large*: Françoise Latour da Veiga-Pinto, 'L'évolution de la notion de travail: perspectives du changement social et du travail des femmes en Europe occidentale'; Mino Vianello, 'Women's role in work and society: a note on a current research project on

women and power'; Joan M. McCrea, 'Retraining older women: needs and programmes', Geneva 1980, 2nd impression 1982.

References

Austrian Commission for UNESCO (1993) *Interregional Consultation on UNESCO's Theme 'Women'*, Burg Schlaining, Austria, 30 January–3 February, Vienna: ACU.

Bruce, Margaret (1968) 'An account of the United Nations actions to advance the status of women', *Annals of the American Academy of Political and Social Science*, Vol. 375, January, pp. 163–75.

— (1971) 'Work of the United Nations relating to the status of women', *Human Rights Journal*, Vol. IV, No. 2, pp. 365–412.

— (1993) 'The United Nations and the equal rights of men and women, 1946–1977', unpublished manuscript prepared for DAW.

Ceulemans, Mieke and Guido Fauconnier (1979) *Mass Media: The Image, Role, and Social Conditions of Women, a Collection and Analysis of Research Materials*, UNESCO/ Department of Communication Science, Catholic University of Leuven.

Commission of the European Communities (1988) *Implementation of the Medium Term Community Programme on Equal Opportunities for Women (1986–1990)*, Commission of the European Communities, 27 April.

Coomaraswamy, Radhika (1996) *Report of the Special Rapporteur on Violence Against Women, its Causes and Consequences*, E/CN.4/1996/53.

Deblé, Isabelle (1980) *The School Education of Girls: An International Comparative Study on School Wastage among Girls and Boys at the First and Second Levels of Education* (trans. into French, Spanish, Russian, Arabic) Paris: UNESCO.

Discrimination Against Women: The Convention and the Committee, Human Rights Fact Sheet No. 22 (1994), Geneva: Centre for Human Rights.

ECOSOC (1990) *Resolution 1990/15, Recommendations and Conclusions Arising from the First Review and Appraisal of the Implementation of the Nairobi Forward-looking Strategies for the Advancement of Women to the Year 2000*, New York: ECOSOC.

Eisemann, Pierre Michel (1994) 'Etude relative a l'action normative de l'UNESCO par Pierre Michel Eisemann, Professeur des Facultés de droit, Vice-President de l'Université de Paris XIII, on the basis of survey carried out in 1992', draft paper.

ESCAP (1989) *Guidelines on Upgrading the Legal Status of Women, Economic and Social Commission for Asia and the Pacific*, Bangkok, ST/ESCP/832, UN, to be obtained from Social Development Division, ESCAP, United Nations Building, Rajadamnern Avenue, Bangkok 10200, Thailand.

Eyraud, F. et al. (eds) (1993) *Equal Pay Protection in Industrialised Market Economies: In Search of Greater Effectiveness*, Geneva: ILO.

Federal Ministry for Foreign Affairs (1995) *Three-Year Programme of Austria's Development Cooperation 1996–1998*, Vienna: Federal Ministry for Foreign Affairs.

Gallagher, Margaret (1985) *Communication in the Service of Women: A Report on Action and Research Programmes 1980–1985*, COM.85/WS1, London: City University and Paris: UNESCO.

Gaudart, Dorothea (1984) 'Nationale und internationale Tätigkeiten zur Gleichbehandlung' (National and international activities concerning equality), in Oswin Martinek, Heribert Maier, Gerfried Schultheis and Josef Weidenholzer (eds), *Festschrift für Alfred Dallinger zum 60. Geburtstag, Sozialpolitik und Sozialplanung*, Vienna.

— (1990) 'Illiteracy in Europe?', *Higher Education in Europe*, Vol. XV, No. 3, Bucharest: CEPES/UNESCO, pp. 48–53.

— (1993) 'Introducing women's rights under international conventions in the development of human rights education in the Europe region', in *Human Rights and Human Rights Education in the Process of Transition to Democracy*, reports from the international expert meeting organized by the European Centre for Human Rights Education, Prague: European Information Centre of Charles University.

Harding, Sandra and Elizabeth McGregor (1995) *The Gender Dimension of Science and Technology*, London and Paris: UNESCO.

ILO (1980a) *ILO Standards and Policy Statements of Special Interest to Women Workers*, Geneva: ILO.

— (1980b) *Equality of Treatment between Men and Women in Employment. Changes in the Legislation in Selected Western Euopean Countries*, document prepared by Office for Women Workers' Questions, ILO.W.5/80, Geneva: ILO.

— (1986) *Equal Remuneration. General Survey of the Reports on the Equal Remuneration Convention (No. 100) and Recommendation (No. 90) 1951, by the Committee of Experts on the Application of Conventions and Recommendations, International Labour Conference, 72nd Session, Report III (Part 4B)*, Geneva: ILO.

— (1987) 'Women workers: protection or equality?', *Conditions of Work Digest*, Vol. 6, No. 2, Geneva: ILO.

— (1988) *Equality in Employment and Occupation. General Survey of the Reports on the Discrimination (Employment and Occupation) Convention (No. 111) and Recommendation (No. 111) 1958, by the Committee of Experts on the Application of Conventions and Recommendations, International Labour Conference, 75th Session 1988, Report III (Part 4B)*, Geneva: ILO.

— (1990) *International Labour Standards: A Workers' Educational Manual*, 3rd rev. edn, Geneva: ILO.

— (1993a) *Information Kit on International Labour Standards and Women Workers*, Geneva: ILO.

— (1993b) *Workers with Family Responsibilities: General Survey of the Reports on the Workers with Family Responsibilities Convention (No. 156) and Recommendation (No. 165), 1981, International Labour Conference, 80th Session, Report III (Part 4B)*, Geneva: ILO.

— (1994) *Modular Training Package on Women Workers' Rights*, Geneva: ILO.

— (1999) *More and Better Jobs for Women: An Action Guide*, ILO follow-up to the Fourth World Conference on Women and the World Summit for Social Development, Geneva: ILO.

Kotite, Phyllis (1989) *Women's Education Looks Forward: Programmes, Experiences, Strategies*, Paris: UNESCO.

Martens, Margaret Hosmer and Swasti Mitter (eds) (1994) *Women in Trade Unions: Organizing the Unorganized*, Geneva: ILO.

Methods of Measuring Women's Economic Activity (1993), Technical Report, Studies in Methods, Series F, No. 59, Department of Economic and Social Information and Policy Analyses, Statistical Division, ST7ESA/STAT/SER.F/59, New York: UN.

Michel, Andrée (1986) *Down with Stereotypes! Eliminating Sexism from Children's Literature and School Textbooks*, also trans. into French and Russian, Paris: UNESCO.

Michel, Jean (1988) 'Women in engineering education', with case studies prepared by Mariana Belis, Geoffrey E. Chivers and Colette Mathieu-Batsch, *Studies in Engineering Education*, 12, Paris: UNESCO.

Moore, Howard, Safoura Clément and Pascale Murugaiyan (eds) (1996) *World Science Report 1996*, Paris: UNESCO.

Nairobi Forward-looking Strategies for the Advancement of Women, The, Report of the World Conference to Review and Appraise the Achievements of the United Nations Decade for Women: Equality, Development and Peace, Nairobi, Kenya, 15–26 July 1995, E.85.IV.10, New York: UN.

Nasr, Julinda Abu, Irene Lorfing and Jamileh Mikati (1983) *Identification and Elimination of Sex Stereotypes in and from School Textbooks: Some Suggestions for Action in the Arab World*, ED-84/WS/31, Institute for Women's Studies in the Arab World, Beirut University College and Paris: UNESCO.

OECD (1993) *Aid Review 1992/93*, Report by the Secretariat and Questions for the Review of Austria, OCDE/GED(93)76, Paris: OECD.

Rendel, Margherita (1980) 'Report on programmes of research and of teaching related to women', presented to World Conference for the United Nations Decade for Women, Paris, 26 June, SS-80/WS/20; also in *Cultures*, Vol. VIII, No. 3, Paris, pp. 102–20.

Stolte-Heiskanen, Feride Acar, Nora Ananieva and Dorothea Gaudart (eds), in collaboration with Ruza Fürst-Dilic for the European Co-ordination Centre for Research and Documentation in Social Sciences (1991) *Women in Science, Token Women or Gender Equality*, ISSC/UNESCO/Berg.

Sutherland, Margaret (ed.) (1990) *The Fortunes of Highly Educated Women, Symposium on the Role of Women in Higher Education, in Research and in the Planning and Administration of Education*, Bucharest, October 1988, Strasbourg: UNESCO/CEPES, European Network on Women's Studies, Council of Europe.

UN (1961) *The United Nations and the Status of Women*, New York: UN.

— *The United Nations and the Advancement of Women, 1945–1996*, New York: UN.

— (1991) *The World's Women 1970–1990, Trends and Statistics, Social Statistics and Indicators*, Series K, No. 8, ST/ESA/STAT/SER-K/12, New York: UN.

— (1993) *World Conference on Human Rights, the Vienna Declaration and Programme of Action, June 1993*, with the opening statement of UN Secretary-General Boutros Boutros-Ghali, New York: UN.

— (1995) *The World's Women 1970–1990, Trends and Statistics, Social Statistics and Indicators*, Series K, No. 12, SGT/ESA/STAT/SER.K/12, New York: UN.

— (1997) *Women 1947–1997, Fifty Years: The United Nations Commission on the Status of Women*, brochure and video, New York: UN.

— *United Nations Women's Indicators and Statistics Database (Wistat)*, CD-ROM.

UNESCO (1966) *Access of Girls to Secondary Education*, UNESCO/EDF/2, Paris: UNESCO.

— (1968) *Comparative Study on Access of Girls and Women to Technical and Vocational Education*, ED/MD/3, Paris: UNESCO.

— (1970) 'Women in the age of science and technology', *Impact of Science on Society*, Vol. XX, No. 1, January–March.

— (1980a) *UNESCO, Backgrounder*, Paris: UNESCO.

— (1980b) *Meeting of Experts on Research and Teaching Related to Women: Evaluation and Prospects, Final Report and Recommendations*, SS-80/CONF.626/9, Paris: UNESCO.

— (1980c) 'International seminar on opening up to women of vocational training and jobs traditionally occupied by men', Frankfurt, 10–13 November.

— (1981) *UNESCO: What it is, what it does, how it works*, Paris: UNESCO.

— (1982) 'Women on the move – towards what?' *Cultures*, Vol. VIII, No. 4, Paris.

— (1983) *Bibliographic Guide to Studies on the Status of Women, Development and Population Trends*, Paris: Bowker/UNIPUB/UNESCO.

— (1986a) *UNESCO Publications Concerning the Status of Women, Annotated Bibliography for the Period 1965–1985*, BEP/87/WS/3, Paris: UNESCO.

— (1986b) *UNESCO Consultative Meeting on Women in Engineering and Technological Education and Training, Paris, 2–4 December, Final Report*, Paris: UNESCO.

— (1987) *Impact Evaluation (Category III Evaluation) of Activities Concerning the Status of Women and Promotion of the Status of Women (Programme XIII.4: Elimination of Descrimination Based on Sex)*, 11 September, 126 EX/INF.7, Paris: UNESCO.

— (1988) *Guidelines on Non-sexist Language/Pour un langage non sexiste*, Paris: UNESCO.

— (1990a) *Women in Cultural Development*, Bonn: Friedrich-Ebert-Stiftung/German National Commission for UNESCO.

— (1990b) *Basic Texts, Manual of the General Conference and the Executive Board*, biennial edns, Paris: UNESCO.

— (1990c) *Islam, Perestroika and the Education of Women: Principles and Possibilities*, International Seminar on Literacy and Lifelong Education for Women, Frunze, Kirghizstan, 26 November–1 December, ED/91/WS22, UNESCO/Kirghiz Teacher-Training Institute for Women.

— (1991) *UNESCO Publications Concerning the Status of Women, Annotated Bibliography for the Period 1965–1990*, FEM/91, Paris: UNESCO.

— (1992a) *What is UNESCO?*, Paris: UNESCO.

— (1992b) *Impact Evaluation of Communication Activities Carried Out for the Benefit of Women over the Last Decade (1981–1991)*, 139EX/5, 31 March, Paris: UNESCO.

— (1993a) *Report by the Director-General on the Revision of All the Basic Texts with a View to the Use of Gender-neutral Terminology and Wording*, 27th Session of General Conference, 27 C/34, 26 April, Paris: UNESCO.

— (1993b) *Women in Higher Education Management*, with the participation of the International Development Research Centre, the International Federation of University Women and the Standing Conference of Rectors, Presidents and Vice-Chancellors of the European Universities, Paris: UNESCO.

— (1995a) *Key UNESCO Data*, brochure and CD-ROM; 'Selected UNESCO documents in education', Documentation and Information Service, Education Sector, UNESCO, fax. (33.1) 45 68 45 83.

— (1995b) *Toronto Platform for Action*, adopted by participants in international symposium 'Women and the Media, Access to Expression and Decision-making', Toronto, 28 February–3 March.

— (1995c) *World Education Report 1995*, Oxford: UNESCO.

— (1996a) *Medium-term Strategy 1996–2001*, 28 C/4, Paris: UNESCO.

— (1996b) *Learning: The Treasure Within*, Paris: UNESCO.

UNESCO/CEPES (1992) 'Career patterns of men and women in research and development: conditions and perspectives', *Higher Education in Europe*, Vol. XVII, No. 2, Paris: CEPES/UNESCO.

— (1994) *Gains and Losses: Women and Transition in Eastern and Central Europe*, Paris: CEPES/European Network for Women's Studies.

Vogel-Polsky, Eliane (1977) 'The right of employed women to equal pay and to protection

(Theme No. III)', working paper for the Symposium on the European Social Charter and Social Policy Today, Strasbourg 7–9 December, AS/Coll/Charte 4-E.

— (1989) *Summary of the Study on Positive Action and the Constitutional and Legislative Hindrances to its Implementation in the Member States of the Council of Europe, EG(88)3, Les actions positives et les contraintes constitutionelles et législatives qui pèsent sur leur mise on oeuvre dans les Etats membres du Conseil de l'Europe, EG(89)1,* Strasbourg.

4

The Prohibition of Gender-specific Discrimination under the International Covenant on Civil and Political Rights[1]

Manfred Nowak

Since the Committee on the Elimination of All Forms of Discrimination against Women was only recently authorized to consider an individual complaints system,[2] victims of gender-based discrimination had to address their cases either to the Commission on the Status of Women or to the Human Rights Committee. The Commission on the Status of Women is, however, an inter-governmental body, and the procedure established by ECOSOC Resolution 1983/27 is directed at investigating situations that reveal a consistent pattern of reliably attested injustice and discriminatory practices against women rather than at providing relief to the individual victim.[3] To submit an individual complaint to the Human Rights Committee remained, therefore, the most efficient remedy for a woman (or man) who personally s/he is a victim of gender-based discrimination, provided that the state concerned is among the 101 (as of December 2001) states that have already ratified the first Optional Protocol (OP) to the United Nations Covenant on Civil and Political Rights (CCPR). The Covenant itself is presently binding on 197 (as of December 2001) states parties in all world regions and is generally regarded as the most important human rights treaty within the framework of the United Nations, comparable in significance only to the European and the American Convention on Human Rights. Together with the Covenant on Economic, Social and Cultural Rights of 1966 (which does not yet provide for an individual complaints system) and the Universal Declaration of Human Rights of 1948 (which is not a binding treaty), the CCPR forms the core of the United Nations human rights standards.

Both the Covenant and the first OP were adopted by the General Assembly on 16 December 1966[4] and entered into force on 23 March 1976. The 18-member international expert body entrusted with the task of monitoring state compliance with the Covenant by means of examining state reports, inter-state and individual complaints, the Human Rights Committee (hereinafter referred to as the Committee), was established in 1977.[5] Until the end of 1994, the Committee examined a total of 444 individual complaints[6] and rendered 197 decisions on the merits called 'final views'.[7] In roughly 50 per cent of these decisions the Committee found one or more violations of the Covenant, and in quite a few cases the respective government actually changed its laws and/or practice in order to comply with its obligations under the Covenant.

The merit of international complaints procedures lies both in the actual relief to the victim concerned and in the preventive effect on the legal system of the country concerned as well as other states. Because of its judicial or quasi-judicial nature, complaints procedures, unlike reporting procedures, force the international monitoring body concerned to rule in a given case whether the facts established actually disclose a violation of an international treaty provision or not. Even if such a decision is not legally binding under international law,[8] it puts a heavy pressure on the government concerned to ensure that similar violations do not occur in the future. In addition, international complaints procedures provide treaty monitoring bodies with the opportunity to elaborate a uniform interpretation of international legal standards which are to be complied with by domestic courts in their primary task of implementing these norms. By means of an evolutive or dynamic interpretation treaty monitoring bodies adopt international law in the light of current challenges and developments. Through its case law under the first OP the Human Rights Committee actually put life into many provisions of the Covenant.[9] In order to illustrate this point let us move on to analyse the Covenant's provisions and the Committee's case law on gender-based discrimination.

Equality and Non-discrimination under the Covenant

Along with liberty, equality is the most important principle imbuing and inspiring the concept of human rights. The principle of equality, including the prohibition of discrimination, therefore, runs like a red thread throughout the Covenant.[10] In Art. 2 (1) all states parties obligate themselves to ensure all rights of the Covenant without any discrimination to all individuals within their territory and subject to their jurisdiction. A number of provisions reiterate this obligation by means of an explicit reference to Art. 2 (1): the emergency clause in Art. 4 (1), the protection of children pursuant to Art. 24 (1) and the political rights in Art. 25. In Art. 20 (2), the states parties commit themselves to prohibit all advocacy of national, racial or religious hatred that constitutes incitement to discrimination, hostility or violence.[11] Other provisions contain specific rights of equality or specific prohibitions of arbitrary, i.e. discriminatory, interferences with Covenant rights.[12]

Last but not least, Art. 26 guarantees a general and comprehensive right to equality and non-discrimination. In practice this right turned out to be one of the most important and innovative provisions of the Covenant. It was the first provision in an international human rights treaty to contain all four historical states in the development of the principle of equality: the eighteenth-century principle of equality before the law, the nineteenth-century concept of equal protection of the law, and the twentieth-century achievements of equality expressed in terms of prohibition of discrimination by state action and protection against discrimination through positive state measures.[13] Unlike the accessory prohibition of discrimination in Art. 2 (1) of the Covenant or Art. 14 of the European Convention on Human Rights, Art. 26 constitutes an independent right to equality and non-discrimination. In other words, Art. 2 (1) can be violated only if somebody has been discriminated against in the exercise or enjoyment of one of the other civil and political rights recognized in the Covenant. On the other hand, Art. 26 protects against any type of discrimination, even if it is not related to any human right at all. For example, nobody has a human right to sit on a public park bench, but when a state enacts a law forbidding Jews, blacks or women from sitting on public park benches, then this law violates Art. 26.

Equality of Women and Men under the Covenant

Not every distinction between human beings amounts to discrimination. As has been elaborated in the case law of the Human Rights Committee and other monitoring bodies, a distinction constitutes discrimination only when it is not based on 'reasonable and objective criteria'. The decisive question of whether a specific legal distinction between various persons or groups of persons is based on 'reasonable and objective criteria' is ultimately subject to resolution only on a case-by-case basis by weighing all relevant circumstances. The wording of Art. 2 (1) and Art. 26 provides, however, some guidance by listing certain especially reprehended personal criteria.[14] Particularly problematic are statutory distinctions on the basis of inherent personal features not capable of being changed by the person concerned, such as race, colour, sex, birth or origin. In the practice of the Human Rights Committee, most violations of the right to equality have been found in relation to gender-specific statutory distinctions.

Gender-specific discrimination is not only prohibited by the general non-discrimination clauses in Art. 2 (1) and 26. In addition, states parties in Art. 3 undertake the specific obligation 'to ensure the equal right of men and women to the enjoyment of all civil and political rights set forth in the present Covenant'. Although this provision, like Art. 2 (1), is only of an accessory nature, it explicitly highlights equality between women and men, and equality means more than not making gender-specific distinctions. The Human Rights Committee, therefore, rightly emphasized that this provision calls for 'affirmative action designed to ensure the positive enjoyment of rights. This cannot be done simply by enacting laws.'[15]

Finally, states parties to the Covenant are required by virtue of Art. 23 (4) to 'take appropriate steps to ensure equality of rights and responsibilities of spouses as to marriage, during marriage and at its dissolution'. Although this provision constitutes the only merely progressive implementation duty of the Covenant on Civil and Political Rights,[16] its inclusion in the Covenant was a victory for the proponents of human rights of women. They had rightly stressed that the roots of manifest discrimination against women lay especially in the private sphere of marital and familial life.[17]

Selected Case Law of the Human Rights Committee

Sandra Lovelace* v. *Canada[18] Sandra Lovelace, a Maliseet Indian of Canadian nationality who was raised on the Tobique Reserve, lost her status as an Indian under the Canadian Indian Act and thus her right to live on the Reserve on account of her marriage to a non-Indian. Male Indians marrying a non-Indian did not face this legal consequence. Following divorce from her husband, Sandra Lovelace returned with her children to the Tobique Reserve, where she actually was protected by other Maliseet Indians against pending expulsion by the Canadian authorities. In her communication to the Committee of 29 December 1977 she claimed that the Indian Act was discriminatory on the grounds of sex and contrary to Arts 2 (1), 3, 23 (1) and (4), 26 and 27.

Since her marriage and loss of Indian status had taken place already in 1970, i.e. before the entry into force of the Covenant, the Committee decided to consider the case only in relation to her right, as a member of an ethnic minority, to enjoy her own culture in community with the other members of her group, i.e. her right to return to the Reserve, in accordance with Art. 27. In this respect, the Committee took the view that statutory restrictions affecting the minority concerned must have both a reasonable and objective justification and be consistent with the other provisions of the Covenant, in particular Arts 2, 3, 12, 17, 23 and 26. On the basis of such a systematic interpretation, the Committee found a violation of Art. 27 and, therefore, it deemed it 'unnecessary ... to examine the general provisions against discrimination'.

In a dissenting opinion the Tunisian member Néjib Bouziri expressed his view that 'also articles 2 (para. 1), 3, 23 (paras 1 and 4) and 26 of the Covenant have been breached, for some of the provisions of the Indian Act are discriminatory, particularly as between men and women. The Act is still in force and, even though the Lovelace case arose before the date on which the Covenant became applicable in Canada, Mrs Lovelace is still suffering from the adverse discriminatory effects of the Act in matters other than that covered by article 27.'[19] In July 1985 the Canadian government informed the Committee that all discriminatory provisions had been removed from the Indian Act and that Indian women who had lost their Indian status upon marriage to a non-Indian may once again be registered as Indians.[20]

Mauritian women case[21] The 1977 Immigration and Deportation Acts of Mauritius granted the alien wives of Mauritian men an unlimited residency right, but alien husbands of Mauritian women were required to obtain an official residence permit, which could be refused or removed at any time by the minister of the interior. On 2 May 1978 20 Mauritian women submitted a communication to the Committee by claiming that the enactment of both statutes constituted discrimination based on sex against Mauritian women, violation of the right to found a family and a home, and removal of the protection of the courts of law, in breach of Arts 2, 3, 4, 17, 23, 25 and 26 of the Covenant.

The Committee dismissed the claims of 17 unmarried women. With respect to the three women who were actually married to foreign husbands, the Committee expressed the view that not only the future possibility of deportation, but the existing precarious residence situation of foreign husbands in Mauritius represented an interference with the family life of the Mauritian wives and their husbands. The applicants were suffering from the adverse consequences of the statutes only because they were women. Since no sufficient justification for this gender-specific distinction had been given, the Committee found violations of Arts 2 (1), 3 and 26 in conjunction with the rights to respect for family life in Art. 17 and the protection of the family in Art. 23. The Committee made, however, no distinction between the accessory non-discrimination clauses in Arts 2 (1) and 3 and the independent right to equality in Art. 26.[22]

On 15 June 1983 the Government of Mauritius informed the Committee that the two impugned Acts had been amended by the Immigration and Deportation Amendment Acts of 1983, which were passed by parliament on Women's Day, so as to remove the discriminatory effects of those laws on grounds of sex.[23]

Dutch social security cases I: Broeks, Zwaan-de Vries and Vos The views of the Committee in the cases of *S. W. M. Broeks and F. H. Zwaan-*

de Vries v. *the Netherlands* of 9 April 1987 are probably the most widely known decisions regarding the Covenant.[24] In these decisions, the Committee commented on several long-disputed questions and established its jurisprudence concerning equality as an independent right. In both cases, the issue was gender-specific distinctions in the Dutch Unemployment Benefits Act. Under the law, married women received unemployment benefits only when they could prove that they were 'breadwinners', whereas this proof was not required of married men. Both applicants were married women whose unemployment benefits were terminated on the ground that they were not 'breadwinners'. The Dutch government considered it incompatible with the aims of both the CCPR and the first OP that an individual complaint with respect to the right of social security, as referred to in Art. 9 of the Social Covenant, could be dealt with by the Human Rights Committee by way of an individual complaint based on Art. 26 CCPR.

The Committee rejected this argument by noting that Art. 26 does not merely duplicate the guarantees already provided for in Art. 2. The principle of equal protection of the law rather prohibits discrimination in law or in practice in any field regulated and protected by public authorities. 'Although article 26 requires that legislation should prohibit discrimination, it does not of itself contain any obligation with respect to the matters that may be provided for by legislation. Thus it does not, for example, require any State to enact legislation to provide for social security. However, when such legislation is adopted in the exercise of a State's sovereign power, then such legislation must comply with article 26 of the Covenant.'[25] The Committee observed in this connection that what was at issue was not whether or not social security should be progressively established in the Netherlands, but whether the legislation providing for social security violated the prohibition against discrimination contained in Art. 26.

In applying the 'reasonable and objective criteria-test' the Committee considered that the distinction in the Dutch Unemployment Benefits Act placed married women at a disadvantage compared with married men which was not reasonable. Since both applicants were denied a social security benefit on an equal footing with men, the Dutch law was found to constitute a violation of Art. 26. Since the Covenant is directly applicable in the Netherlands, the Committee's rule in the Broeks and Zwaan-de Vries cases was later applied by Dutch courts in a number of cases, leading to major changes in the Dutch social security legislation and to strong political reactions, including serious consideration even given to a possible denunciation of the Covenant and re-ratification with a reservation to Art. 26.[26]

The impact of these decisions seems, however, to have been misjudged by some Dutch counsels, as a considerable number of communications based on Art. 26 have later been declared inadmissible or rejected on the merits by the Committee.[27] For instance, in the case of *Hendrika S. Vos v. the Netherlands*, the Committee found that certain gender-specific distinctions in other social security laws of the Netherlands were based on reasonable and objective criteria.[28] The General Disablement Benefits Act makes a distinction according to sex, in that a disabled woman whose (former) husband dies does not retain the right to a disability allowance but is entitled to a widow's pension under the General Widows and Orphans Act. In contrast, a disabled man whose (former) wife dies retains the right to a disability allowance. Normally, this traditional distinction constitutes preferential treatment for women. In the case of Mrs Vos, who had been divorced from her husband for 22 years and who had been providing for her own support when she became disabled nine years after her divorce, the replacement of the disability allowance by a widow's pension constituted a financial disadvantage. Nevertheless, the majority of the Committee agreed with the Dutch government that this distinction was a reasonable one, and only two Committee members found that it constituted discrimination contrary to Art. 26.[29]

Graciela Ato del Avellanal v. Peru[30] In September 1978, Graciela Ato del Avellanal, a Peruvian professor of music and owner of two apartment buildings in Lima, sued a number of tenants for having ceased to pay rent for their apartments. While the court of first instance had found in her favour and ordered the tenants to pay her the rent, the Superior Court in November 1980 reversed the judgment on the procedural ground that she was not entitled to sue, because, according to Article 168 of the Peruvian Civil Code, 'when a women is married only the husband is entitled to represent matrimonial property before the courts'. After the Supreme Court, in two different judgments, had upheld the decision of the Superior Court, Mrs Ato del Avellanal in January 1986 submitted a complaint to the Human Rights Committee. The Committee found that the application of Article 168 of the Peruvian Civil Code had resulted in denying her equality before the courts and constituted discrimination on the ground of sex. It decided, therefore, unanimously that Peru had violated Arts 3, 14 (1) and 26 of the Covenant.

Dietmar Pauger v. Austria[31] This is the first gender discrimination case submitted by a man. Dietmar Pauger is a law professor at the University of Graz who claimed to be a victim of discrimination as a widower (as compared to widows) under the Austrian Pension Act. Until 1985 widowers could receive pensions only if they did not have any other form of income, a requirement not applicable to widows. After the Austrian Constitutional Court in 1984 had declared this provision unconstitutional as gender-based discrimination, the Austrian parliament in 1985 introduced a general widower pension. However, in view of the financial burden on the state's budget, a three-phase pension scheme was set up, providing reduced benefits in the first two stages: one-third of the pension as of 1 March 1985, two-thirds as of 1 January 1989, and the full pension only as of 1 January 1995.

As Mr Pauger's wife, a teacher in Austrian public school, had died in 1984, he first did not receive any pension at all, and since 1985 only one-third compared to a widow in the same situation. His appeal to the Constitutional Court claiming a full pension and the annulment of the three phases of implementation, was dismissed in October 1989. On 5 June 1990 he therefore submitted a communication to the Committee.

The Committee referred to its constant jurisprudence established in the Dutch social security cases and found a discrimination based on sex in contravention of Art. 26 for this transitional period. In determining whether the amended Austrian Pension Act entailed a differentiation based on unreasonable or unobjective criteria, it noted that Austrian family law, as from 1976, had imposed equal rights and duties on both spouses, with regard to their income and mutual maintenance, whereas according to the amended Pension Act, widowers were entitled to full pension benefits on equal footing with widows only as of 1 January 1995. Such a differentiation between men and women whose social circumstances were similar was found not to be reasonable even for a transitional period.

Dutch Social Security Cases II: Cavalcanti Araujo-Jongen and Pepels

As in *Pauger* v. *Austria*, these two recent cases deal with state obligations in transitional periods. The case of *C. H. J. Cavalcanti Araujo-Jongen* v. *the Netherlands*[32] concerns a married Dutch secretary who was employed part-time from September 1979 to January 1983. As of 1 February 1983 she became unemployed and was granted unemployment benefits under the Dutch Unemployment Act for the maximum period of six months. Further (reduced) benefits under the Dutch Unemployment Provision Act (75 per cent of the last salary for a maximum period of two years) were at that time available only to men, unmarried women and married women who qualified as breadwinners.[33] As of 24 April 1984 she found new employment.

The discriminatory breadwinner provision in the Dutch Unemployment Provision Act was abrogated by a law of 24 April 1985 with effect from 23 December 1984, the ultimate date established by the Third Directive of the European Community for the elimination of discrimination between men and women. The provision remained, therefore, applicable in respect of married women who had become unemployed before 23 December 1984. Her application of 11 December 1986 for retroactive benefits for the period of her unemployment between 1 August 1983 and 24 April 1984 was therefore rejected.

As these transitory provisions were much criticized, they were abolished by an Act of 6 June 1991. As a result, women who had been eligible in the past to claim such benefits because of the breadwinner criterion can claim these benefits retroactively, provided they satisfy the other requirements of the Act. One of the other requirements is that the applicant be unemployed on the date of application. Since the applicant had been employed when she had applied for the benefits in December 1986, she was again not eligible for these retroactive benefits. She considered this as indirect discrimination against women and submitted a communication to the Committee.

The Committee observed that, 'even if the law in force in 1983 was not consistent with the requirements of article 26 of the Covenant, that deficiency was corrected upon the retroactive amendment of the law on 6 June 1991'. Since it also found that the requirement of being unemployed at the time of application for benefits was, as such, reasonable and objective, it concluded that the facts in this case did not reveal a violation of Art. 26.

The case of Mr *H. J. Pepels* v. *the Netherlands*,[34] comparably to *Pauger* v. *Austria*, concerns the question of a widower's pension in a transitional period. Together with the Cavalcanti Araujo-Jongen case it reflects the strong impact of the cases of Broeks and Zwaan-de Vries on the Dutch social security policy and jurisprudence. Pepels became a widower in 1978 and had to assume sole responsibility for the upbringing of his four young children. Since the General Widows' and Orphans' Act did at that time not provide for benefits to widowers, he did not apply.

Ten years later, on 7 December 1988, the Central Board of Appeal, the highest court in social security cases, decided on the basis of the Human Rights Committee's decisions in the Broeks and Zwaan-de Vries cases, that, despite the text of the law, widowers were also entitled to benefits under the General Widows' and Orphans' Act, since the legal provisions were considered to be in violation of the principle of non-discrimination.

One week later, on 14 December 1988, Mr Pepels applied for widower's benefits. In March 1989, he was informed that a benefit would be granted to him as of 1 December 1987, pursuant to Article 25 (3) of the law, which provides for the retroactive grant of benefits for a period of up to one year preceding the date of application. His appeal against this decision was finally dismissed by the Central Board of Appeal and the Maastricht District Court. On 25 November 1991 he submitted a communication to the Committee and claimed retroactive widower's benefits as of 11 March

1979, the date of entry into force of the Covenant in the Netherlands. He argued that the Covenant is directly applicable in the Netherlands and that the refusal of widower's benefits violated Art. 26 as of that date.

The Dutch government conceded before the Committee that social realities had changed and that the different treatment between widows and widowers could no longer be justified in present-day society. However, one could not apply present standards to past facts and circumstances, when other social realities were relevant. Since legislation necessarily lagged behind social development in society, the government argued that it was reasonable to allow for a certain amount of time to adjust legislation and practice. Mr Pepels replied that in 1979 this situation had already changed.

The Committee did not pronounce itself on Mr Pepel's retroactive claim for the period between 11 March 1979 and 1 December 1987 on the grounds that he had not attempted to challenge the law at the material time and that the law, therefore, was never applied in his particular case. Thereby the Committee evaded the difficult question as to from which date social reality in the Netherlands had changed to the extent that different treatment between widows and widowers could not any more be considered reasonable and therefore constituted discrimination in contravention of Art. 26.

Conclusions

The Human Rights Committee consists of 18 independent experts from all world regions elected by states parties to the Covenant.[35] According to Art. 31 (2) the CCPR, in its election, consideration is given 'to equitable geographical distribution of membership and to the representation of the different forms of civilization and of the principal legal systems'. Since women constitute only a small minority in the Committee's membership, one certainly cannot accuse it of being biased in favour of feminist ideas. Nevertheless, its case law, more than that of any other international human rights body, has had a considerable impact on the development of the principle of equality between women and men in international law. In view of the global composition of the Committee, of the fact that most of its decisions are reached by consensus,[36] as well as of the fact that the Covenant is legally binding on roughly two-thirds of the states of the present world, it is not an exaggeration to conclude that the jurisprudence of the Committee constitutes a kind of minimum universal consensus on gender-specific discrimination. Of course, not every dictum in the highly sophisticated Dutch social security cases can be directly applied to an Asian or African society with a different cultural or social background. But the cases of the Mauritian women and of *Ato del Avellanal* v. *Peru* clearly show that the Committee does not hesitate to apply the principle of equality between women and men with the same vigour to statutory distinctions in Africa and Latin America. In a case against Mauritius the statutory exclusion of women from jury service did not lead to a finding of a breach by Mauritius only because the applicant, a man who was convicted by an exclusively male jury of murder and sentenced to death, was not considered to be a 'victim' within the meaning of Art. 1 OP.[37] If the applicant had been a woman who could have shown that the absence of women on the jury actually had prejudiced the sentence, the decision would probably have been different. Undoubtedly, the most important safeguard against gender-specific discrimination is Art. 26 CCPR. The main principles derived from the Committee's case law in this respect may be summarized as follows:

a) Art. 26 CCPR is not an accessory but rather an independent right pertaining to any statutory or non-statutory distinction between women and men.
b) Not every gender-specific distinction is discriminatory.
c) A gender-specific distinction constitutes discrimination only when it is not based on 'reasonable and objective criteria'.
d) Whether a gender-specific distinction is based on 'reasonable and objective criteria' depends primarily on the social reality in the country concerned and can, therefore, be decided only on a case-by-case basis taking all relevant circumstances into consideration.
e) Most gender-specific violations found relate to statutory distinctions between women and men.
f) In European societies, such as the Netherlands and Austria, where family law provides for full equality between the spouses, this equality must also lead, within a reasonable period, to full equality regarding social security benefits. Disadvantages of women concerning, e.g., umemploy-ment benefits based on the 'breadwinner concept' or disadvantages of men in respect of, e.g., widowers' pensions constitute, therefore, a violation of Art. 26 CCPR.
g) Blatant gender-specific distinctions in family law, such as the inability of married women to represent matrimonial property before the courts, have been found to constitute gender-specific discrimination also in non-European societies. The holding in the case of *Ato del Avellanal* v. *Peru* might, therefore, have far-reaching consequences on gender-specific distinctions in the family law of Islamic states or in African customary law. Until now, these controversial issues have, however, not been brought to the attention of the Committee in the framework of individual complaints. This is primarily due to the fact that not too many Islamic, African and Asian states have ratified both the Covenant and the first

OP. Test cases might, however, originate from countries such as Algeria, Angola, Benin, Cameroon, the Central African Republic, Congo, Equatorial Guinea, Gambia, Korea, Libya, Madagascar, Mauritius, Mongolia, Nepal, Niger, the Philippines, Senegal, the Seychelles, Somalia, Togo, Zaire or Zambia.

h) The only gender-specific discrimination established by the Committee with respect to an African country concerned the Immigation Act of Mauritius. Although these types of statutory distinctions exist in the legislation of many states, the Committee did not hesitate to find a violation of the Covenant.

One may, therefore, conclude that the Committee has established fairly strict universal minimum standards for the admissibility of statutory distinctions between women and men. Governments, in both the North and the South, must show strong reasons to justify gender-specific distinctions to be based on 'reasonable and objective criteria'. It is now up to women and their lawyers, in particular in African and Islamic states, to challenge discriminatory laws and practices based on customs and religious traditions by means of submitting individual complaints to the Human Rights Committee.

Notes

1. This chapter was prepared in 1996 and has received only minor updating.

2. See, however, para. 40 of the Vienna Programme of Action of 25 June 1993 in which the World Conference on Human Rights called upon the Commission on the Status of Women and on CEDAW to 'quickly examine the possibility of introducing the right to petition through the preparation of an optional protocol' to the CEDAW Convention. As a first step, the Human Rights Law Group and the University of Limburg convened an expert seminar, which met in Maastricht from 29 September to 2 October 1994 and prepared a first draft of such an OP.

3. See, e.g., Helga Kaschitz, 'The Commission on the Status of Women (with particular reference to its work on communications)', *SIM Newsletter* 4/1988, 26 et seq.; Laura Renda, 'The Commission on the Status of Women', in Philip Alston (ed.), *The United Nations and Human Rights*, Oxford 1992, 295 et seq. For the text of ECOSOC Res. 1983/27 of 26 May 1983 see *SIM Newsletter* 4/1988, 87.

4. GA-Res. 2200 A; *UNTS* Vol. 999, 171. For the text see, e.g., United Nations, *Human Rights – A Compilation of International Instruments*, New York 1993, Vol. I (First Part), 20 and 41; Felix Ermacora, Manfred Nowak and Hannes Tretter (eds), *International Human Rights*, Vienna 1993, 24 and 34.

5. For the practice of the Committee see, e.g., Dominic McGoldrick, *The Human Rights Committee, its Role in the Development of the International Covenant on Civil and Political Rights*, Oxford 1991.

6. The OP actually uses the term 'communications'.

7. All inadmissibility decisions and final views are published in the Committee's

Annual Reports to the General Assembly, UN-Docs A/32/44 and A/33 to 49/40. See also the 'Selected decisions under the optional protocol' up to the 32nd session of the Committee (April 1988), UN-Docs. CCPR/C/OP/1 and 2. A summary of most decisions can also be found in Manfred Nowak, 'The effectiveness of the International Covenant on Civil and Political Rights – Stocktaking after the first eleven sessions of the UN-Human Rights Committee', *Human Rights Law Journal* (*HRLJ*) 136 (1980) and his periodic surveys of decisions, 2 *HRLJ* 168 (1981), 3 *HRLJ* 207 (1982), 5 *HRLJ* 199 (1984), 7 *HRLJ* 287 (1986), 11 *HRLJ* 139 (1990) and 14 *HRLJ* 9 (1993).

8. This is the case with decisions of all United Nations treaty monitoring bodies as opposed to judgments of the European and Inter-American Court of Human Rights.

9. For a systematic interpretation of all provisions of the Covenant based on, *inter alia*, the case law of the Committee, see Manfred Nowak, *U.N. Covenant on Civil and Political Rights – CCPR Commentary*, Kehl/Strasbourg/Arlington 1993.

10. Cf. B. G. Ramcharan, 'Equality and nondiscrimination' in Louis Henkin (ed.), *The International Bill of Rights – The Covenant on Civil and Political Rights*, New York 1981, 246; Christian Tomuschat, 'Equality and Non-Discrimination under the International Covenant on Civil and Political Rights', in *Festschrift für Hans-Jürgen Schlochauer*, Berlin/New York 1981, 691; Karl Josef Partsch, 'Fundamental Principles of Human Rights: Self-Determination, Equality and Non-Discrimination', in Karel Vasak and Philip Alston (eds), *The International Dimension of Human Rights*, Paris 1982, Vol. I, 61; Torkel Opsahl, 'Equality in human rights law, with particular reference to article 26 of the International Covenant on Civil and Political Rights', in *Festschrift für Felix Ermacora*, Kehl/Strasbourg/Arlington 1988, 51; Nowak, supra note 8, 43 et seq. and 458 et seq.

11. Interestingly enough, gender hatred is not included in this important provision.

12. Cf., e.g., equality before the courts in Art. 14 (1); prohibition of arbitrary deprivation of life in Art. 6 (1) and of the right to enter one's own country in Art. 12 (4); prohibition of arbitrary arrest or detention in Art. 9 (1); prohibition of any arbitrary interference with one's privacy, family, home or correspondence in Art. 17 (1).

13. Cf. the text of Art. 26: 'All persons are equal before the law and are entitled without any discrimination to the equal protection of the law. In this respect, the law shall prohibit any discrimination and guarantee to all persons equal and effective protection against discrimination on any ground such as race, colour, sex, language, religion, political or other opinion, national or social origin, property, birth or other status.'

14. Ibid.

15. General Comment 4/13 of 28 July 1981, para. 2. Cf. Nowak, supra note 8, 69 et seq., 850.

16. Obligations of conduct such as to 'take appropriate steps to ensure' usually only relate to economic, social and cultural rights. Cf., e.g., Art. 2 (1) of the International Covenant on Economic, Social and Cultural Rights.

17. Cf. Nowak, supra note 8, 416.

18. Comm. No. 24/1977, Views of 30 July 1981; UN-Docs A/36/40, 166 and CCPR/C/OP/1, 83; *HRLJ* 1981, 158; cf. also Anne F. Bayefsky, 'The Human Rights Committee and the case of Sandra Lovelace', *Canadian Yearbook of International Law* 1982, 244; Frank Newman and David Weissbrodt, *International Human Rights*, Cincinnati 1990, 69 et seq.

19. Individual opinion appended by Mr Néjib Bouziri, cf. also in this sense Bayefsky, supra note 17, 262; Nowak, supra note 8, 469.

20. Cf. Nowak, supra note 6, *HRLJ* 1984, 217; *HRLJ* 1986, 305.

21. *Shirin Aumeeruddy-Cziffra et al.* v. *Mauritius*, Comm. No. 35/1978, Views of 9 April 1981; UN-Docs A/36/40, 134 and CCPR/C/OP/1, 67; *HRLJ* 1981, 139; cf. also Vojin Dimitrijevic, 'The Roles of the Human Rights Committee', Saarbrücken 1985, 13; Alfred de Zayas, Jakob Th. Moller and Torkel Opsahl, Application of the International Covenant on Civil and Political Rights under the Optional Protocol by the Human Rights Committee, *German Yearbook of International Law* 1985, 9 at 60.

22. Cf. Nowak, supra note 8, 470.

23. Cf. Nowak, supra note 6, *HRLJ* 1984, 217.

24. Comm. Nos 172 and 182/1984, Views of 9 April 1987; UN-Docs A/42/40, 139 and 160, CCPR/C/OP/2, 196 and 209; *HRLJ* 1988, 256; cf. also the commentaries of Tom Zwart and A. W. Heringa in *NJCM* (Nederlands Juristen Comite voor de Mensenrechten) *Bulletin* 1987, 377, 405, 480; 1988, 98; see further A. W. Heringa, 'Article 26 CCPR and Social Security', 1/1988 *SIM Newsletter* 19; Christian Tomuschat, *Der Gleichheitssatz nach dem Internatinalen Pakt über bürgerliche und politische Rechte*, EuGRZ 1989, 37; Peter Kooijmans, *De internationale verplichting tot gelijke behandeling van man en vrouw*, The Hague 1988; Dimitrijevic, supra note 20, 13 et seq.; Opsahl, supra note 9, 61 et seq.; Nowak, supra note 8, 461, 466, 470.

25. Comm. Nos 172 and 182/1984, supra note 23, para. 12.4. Cf. also para. 12 of the Committee's General comment 18/37 of 9 November 1989 on non-discrimination, text in Nowak, supra note 8, 868.

26. Cf. the petition to the Dutch foreign minister signed by various Dutch human rights experts, in *SIM Newsletter* 1/1988, 128.

27. Cf., e.g., Comm. Nos 212 and 217/1986, 273/1988, 406, 418 and 426/1990, 477 and 478/1991, 501 and 509/1992, 548/1993; cf. Nowak, supra note 6, *HRLJ* 1990, 152 et seq.

28. Comm. No. 218/1986, Views of 29 March 1989; UN-Doc. A/44/40, 232; cf. Nowak supra note 6, *HRLJ* 1990, 150.

29. Individual opinion of Mr Aguilar Urbina (Costa Rica) and Mr Bertil Wennergren (Sweden) to Comm. No. 218/1986, supra note 27.

30. Comm. No. 202/1986, Views of 28 October 1988; UN-Doc. A/44/40, 196; *HRLJ* 1988, 262.

31. Comm. No. 415/1990, Views of 26 March 1992; UN-Doc. A/47/40, 333; cf. Manfred Nowak, *Österreichische Witwerpensions-Übergangsregelung verletzt Recht auf Gleichheit gem. Art. 26 IPBPR*, EuGRZ 1992, 344; ibid., supra note 6, *HRLJ* 1993, 18.

32. Comm. No. 418/1990, Views of 22 October 1993; UN-Doc. A/49/40.

33. As in the cases of Broeks and Zwaan-de Vries, the breadwinner requirement did not apply to married men.

34. Comm. No. 484/1991, Views of 15 July 1994; UN-Doc. A/49/40.

35. For the membership of the Committee between 1977 and 1993 see Nowak, supra note 8, 914.

36. For the principle of consensus, which is reflected in a footnote to Rule 51 of the Committee's Rules of Procedure, see Nowak, supra note 8, 541 and 835.

37. *Ponsamy Poongavanam* v. *Mauritius*, Comm. No. 567/1993; Inadmissibility Decision of 26 July 1994; UN-Doc. A/49/40.

The Convention on the Elimination of All Forms of Discrimination against Women

Andrew Byrnes

In the early 1970s the United Nations Commission on the Status of Women embarked on the elaboration of what was to become the Convention on the Elimination of All Forms of Discrimination against Women (the Convention or the CEDAW Convention).[1] Although there had been many statements in international instruments promising equality and non-discrimination on the basis of sex – some in binding instruments, others in non-binding declarations – there was no comprehensive and detailed charter of equality for women under international law.[2] The proponents of the Convention considered that the time had come for a comprehensive statement of women's entitlements to equality in a form that would be legally binding for states that became parties to a treaty containing those guarantees. The resulting Convention, adopted in 1979, thus moved beyond the 1967 Declaration on the Elimination of Discrimination against Women,[3] which had been a broad statement, in non-binding form, of women's rights to equality and non-discrimination in many areas of life.

This chapter is intended to provide an introduction to the Convention as an international legal instrument, an overview of the substantive content of the Convention, a brief outline of the international mechanism established by the Convention to monitor states parties' implementation of it (the *reporting procedure*), and a summary of recent developments to strengthen the Convention by adopting a procedure under which individuals may claim that their rights under the Convention have been violated. Finally, the chapter discusses a number of examples of how the Convention has been used at the national level, with a particular emphasis on its use in the courts but also referring to other uses.

The Convention: An Overview

The Convention on the Elimination of All Forms of Discrimination against Women was adopted by the United Nations General Assembly on

18 December 1979. The Convention was opened for signature during the mid-Decade Conference of the United Nations Decade for Women held in Copenhagen in 1980, and entered into force on 3 September 1981. As of 15 January 2002 there were 168 states parties to the Convention.[4]

The Convention contains guarantees of equality and freedom from discrimination by the state and by private actors in all areas of public and private life. To a large extent, it codifies the existing gender-specific and general human rights instruments containing guarantees of freedom from discrimination on the ground of sex, although it adds some significant new provisions.[5] It thus requires states parties to ensure that women enjoy equality in the fields of civil and political rights, as well as in the enjoyment of economic, social and cultural rights.

The Convention can be viewed from a number of perspectives. It is a political manifesto, clearly declaring the right of women to equality and non-discrimination; it is also an international legal instrument (a treaty), as well as providing a framework or point of reference for policy-making, lobbying and social activism.[6] The following discussion, however, focuses primarily on its status and potential use as an international legal instrument internationally and nationally.

A number of features of the Convention should perhaps be mentioned at the outset, since together these are what make it distinctive. The first is that the Convention addresses not discrimination on the basis of sex, but discrimination *against women*. Second, the Convention is comprehensive in its coverage of rights in that it explicitly guarantees equality in the enjoyment of civil and political, as well as economic, social and cultural rights. Third, the Convention imposes explicit obligations on states parties in respect of discrimination by *private* parties, not just by the state or public officials. The Convention is divided into six parts:

- Part I (Articles 1–6) contains definitions and sets out obligations of a general nature to eliminate discrimination;
- Part II (Articles 7–9) contains guarantees of equality in political and public life;
- Part III (Articles 10–14) contains guarantees of equality in social and economic fields;
- Part IV (Articles 15 and 16) contains guarantees of equality before and under the law, and of equality in marriage and family life;
- Part V (Articles 17–22) establishes the international monitoring mechanism; and
- Part VI (Articles 23, 24–30) deals with formal and procedural matters.

Under the Convention states parties assume different types of obligations with respect to the elimination of discrimination in a number of fields.[7] A number of provisions of the Convention require immediate steps to be taken to guarantee equality, while other provisions are of a more programmatic nature, under which states parties oblige themselves to take 'all appropriate measures' or 'all necessary measures' to eliminate particular types of discrimination.[8]

This chapter cannot attempt to give a detailed exegesis of the individual articles of the Convention. That task has been undertaken by other commentators,[9] as well as by the Committee itself in its examination of reports and elaboration of *General Recommendations*. It is perhaps sufficient to note in this context that, while most of the articles of the Convention deal with the elimination of discrimination against women in specific areas, the overarching impact of Article 2 means that all forms of public and private discrimination are reached by the Convention.[10]

In addition to the substantive obligations accepted by states that become parties to the Convention, under Article 18 of the Convention states also accept an obligation to submit regular reports on the steps they have taken to give effect to their obligations under the Convention. These reports are to be submitted within one year after the entry into force of the Convention for the state concerned and every four years thereafter. The reports are examined by the Committee on the Elimination of Discrimination against Women (CEDAW), a body established pursuant to Article 17 of the Convention and consisting of 23 independent experts elected to serve in their personal capacity by the states parties to the Convention. The reporting procedure is the only monitoring or enforcement procedure established under the Convention which is obligatory for states parties.[11] The Convention itself was supplemented by the adoption in 1999 of an optional protocol to the Convention that establishes both an individual complaints and an inquiry procedure.[12]

Interpreting the Convention

Since the Convention is a treaty under international law, the normal rules of treaty interpretation apply to it. For most purposes, those rules are to be found in the provisions of the Vienna Convention on the Law of Treaties.[13] Although the Vienna Convention does not as such apply to the interpretation of the CEDAW Convention,[14] the provisions of the Vienna Convention relating to interpretation of treaties, in particular Articles 31 and 32,[15] are generally considered as representing customary international law on the subject, and thus binding on all states.

Article 31 gives primacy in the interpretation of the treaty to the ordinary meaning of the words of the treaty in their context and in the light of the object and purpose of the treaty, in the process of interpretation. However, it is also permissible to take into account other matters, including any subsequent practice in the application of the treaty that establishes the agreement of the parties regarding its interpretation. Furthermore, Article 32 provides that it is permissible to refer to the preparatory works (*travaux préparatoires*) of the treaty in certain circumstances, most importantly in those cases where application of the rules set out in Article 31 leaves the meaning of a provision ambiguous or obscure.

In the case of a treaty (such as the CEDAW Convention) that does not provide for binding third-party interpretation of its terms, the primary power to interpret the treaty authoritatively is generally considered to lie with the states parties to it. The question of the authoritative interpretation of human rights instruments such as the Convention is complicated by the existence under the treaty of an independent expert body, the Committee on the Elimination of Discrimination against Women (CEDAW), which the Convention requires to perform functions which in practice involve the interpretation of the provisions of the treaty. This may take place as part of the Committee's examination of reports submitted by states parties or as part of its efforts to give detailed guidance to states parties and others as to meaning of the Convention through the adoption of general recommendations, or in the consideration of complaints made under a complaints procedure. The practice of the supervisory committees established under the human rights treaties – manifested in their discussion of, and concluding comments on, state reports and their general comments or recommendations – is of considerable practical importance for the interpretation of the treaties, though the exact legal status of those sources is less clear.

In the case of the CEDAW Convention, the reports submitted by states parties under the Convention, together with the discussion between the Committee and states concerned when those reports are reviewed, are a source of state practice in which agreement as to the meaning of provisions of the treaty – within the meaning of Article 31(3)(b) of the Vienna Convention – might be found. Due to the proliferation of states parties and reports under the Convention, this material is in practice of limited utility. However, the Committee's collective concluding comments on each state report (together with any response by the state to those observations) make the results of this process more focused and useful for interpreting the Convention, and these can be used to identify the Committee's view of the meaning of many provisions of the Convention.

The *General Recommendations* of the Committee[16] occupy a similarly ambiguous status as a guide to the meaning of the Convention. While entitled to due consideration as the considered pronouncement of the expert body established by states parties to monitor the Convention, they are not in themselves interpretations of the Convention that are legally binding on states parties as a matter of international law.[17] However, the Committee's *General Recommendations* are circulated to all states parties, which have the opportunity to comment on them. Accordingly, silence on the part of states parties following receipt of the Committee's interpretation may arguably be considered as acquiescence in the substance of those recommendations, and thus as constituting state practice that could be viewed as establishing the agreement of the states parties regarding the interpretation of particular provisions.

However, one may need to be cautious about drawing such a conclusion too readily. While some states may pay due regard to decisions and recommendations of CEDAW and other treaty bodies and promptly express their disagreement with interpretations put forward by the body concerned,[18] many do not do so. Frequently, a state party may first indicate its disagreement with the Committee's interpretation only when it appears before the Committee to review its report, rather than at the time when the Committee's recommendation is initially circulated to it.

In addition to the international sources which are related directly to the Convention, there are other sources that may provide assistance in the interpretation of the Convention. The practice under other international and regional treaties which contain the same or very similar provisions is relevant.[19] For example, the *General Comments* of the Human Rights Committee[20] established under the International Covenant on Civil and Political Rights (ICCPR)[21] and of the Committee on Economic, Social and Cultural Rights[22] established under the International Covenant on Economic, Social and Cultural Rights (ICESCR)[23] provide detailed elaborations of the rights guaranteed by those instruments, including rights to non-discrimination. Similarly, the interpretation of international labour conventions dealing with equality issues (such as ILO Nos 100[24] and 111,[25] which have close counterparts in Article 11 of the Convention) can throw light on the meaning of articles in the Convention. Likewise, the practice under regional treaties, such as the regional human rights conventions or gender-specific conventions (such as the Inter-American Convention on the Prevention, Punishment and Eradication of Violence against Women),[26] can also provide guidance in interpreting the Convention. Finally, national decisions on discrimination issues, whether applying the Convention or other international instruments or constitutional guarantees, can also be drawn on.

The Concept of Discrimination

Definition of discrimination (Article 1)   The concept of discrimination, defined for the purposes of the Convention in Article 1, is the thread that runs through the Convention's substantive provisions. The problem the Convention addresses is that of discrimination against women, rather than discrimination on the basis of sex.[27] Article 1 (which draws on the similar definition in the International Convention on the Elimination of All Forms of Racial Discrimination)[28] provides:

> For the purpose of the present Convention, the term 'discrimination against women' shall mean any distinction, exclusion or restriction made on the basis of sex which has the effect or purpose of impairing or nullifying the recognition, enjoyment or exercise by women, irrespective of their marital status, on a basis of equality of men and women, of human rights and fundamental freedoms in the political, economic, social, cultural, civil or any other field.[29]

Both *direct* and *indirect* discrimination are covered by the Convention. Thus, not only discrimination that is explicitly based on sex, but also apparently neutral practices or policies that have the effect of disproportionately excluding women from the enjoyment of opportunities (if not objectively justifiable), will amount to discrimination.[30] The definition thus focuses not just on the formal, *de jure* enjoyment by women of equality, but on the *de facto* situation, the extent to which women in practice enjoy those rights. As a corollary of this definition, Article 4 of the Convention provides that temporary special measures taken to ensure that women enjoy rights equally with men are not to be considered discrimination for the purposes of the Convention. It should also be noted that the Convention covers discrimination on the basis of marital status. This would cover both discrimination against married women in comparison with married men – although this is really straight sex discrimination – as well as discrimination against women who are single in relation to married women (or vice versa).

The Convention does not apply explicitly to discrimination on the basis of sexuality or sexual orientation and it does not appear that the matter was expressly considered during the drafting of the treaty. CEDAW has not stated a formal collective view on this question, although the Committee has been prepared to take up issues involving discrimination against lesbians, which in some cases would fall within the scope of the guarantee of protection from discrimination against women in so far as it involved a refusal to conform to stereotyped or gender-assigned roles.[31] While in other international contexts there have been suggestions that discrimination on the ground of sex should be interpreted as including discrimination on the ground of sexuality,[32] the issue is a contentious one, as a matter of both substance and interpretation. It seems unlikely, in the near future at least, that CEDAW will address this issue in a direct formal manner (such as by adopting a general recommendation on the rights of lesbians).

One important difference between the definition contained in the Racial Discrimination Convention and the CEDAW Convention is that the former is confined to 'public life'. This phrase was deliberately omitted from the CEDAW Convention, in recognition that many forms of inequality for women have their origin and are primarily experienced in the private sphere, in particular within the family. This premise is critical to the scheme of the Convention and its aspirations to ensure equality for women.[33]

Finally, one important aspect of the definition is its coverage of inequality in the enjoyment of 'human rights and fundamental freedoms in the political, economic, social, cultural, civil or any other field'. While the Convention explicitly refers to many of the rights guaranteed by other international instruments (in particular the two Covenants), it does not refer to all of them. For example, there is no express mention in the Convention of the obligation of a state party to eliminate discrimination in women's enjoyment of the right to freedom of expression, the right to privacy, or the right to be free from arbitrary detention. Nevertheless, these rights – and indeed all the rights guaranteed in the two Covenants and probably others besides – are incorporated by reference as a result of the terms of Article 1. This means that, although there may be no specific provision obliging a state party not to discriminate in relation to these rights, the general obligations in the Convention (especially Article 2) in effect impose that obligation.

A related point is that some violations of women's human rights are not covered by a specific article of the Convention, but are nevertheless covered by the Convention as a whole. One example of this is violence against women, which the Committee has interpreted as constituting discrimination within the meaning of the Convention and therefore being covered by a number of articles.[34] Similarly, the Committee has devoted considerable attention both in its consideration of reports and in its *General Recommendations* to subgroups of women who may face multiple forms of discrimination, such as disabled women, women with HIV/AIDS, women belonging to minority groups, and refugee women.

The Convention's concept of discrimination has been criticized by a number of commentators as embodying a male-based model of equality, in that the Convention guarantees women protection against discrimination which prevents them from enjoying rights 'on the basis of equality with men'. As a result, it is argued, the Convention guarantees to women those things to which men are entitled under existing androcentric human rights guarantees and may fail to reflect the particularities of women's experiences; in cases in which women's perspectives may be fundamentally different and are related to fundamental social patterns of disadvantage, a right to equality with men may fail to address the real problems and injustices.[35]

While there is a good deal of truth in this analysis, the provisions of the Convention and the practice under it suggest that the constraints may be less severe than might appear from the definition of discrimination itself. First, a number of provisions of the Convention appear to be less concerned with a male-based model of equality and more focused on addressing the gender-specific disadvantages that women suffer. For example, Article 5 of the Convention, a central provision, requires the modification of traditional practices and attitudes which are based on inferiority of women or the notion of stereotyped roles for the two sexes. Similarly, Article 6 addresses explicitly the problem of trafficking in women and the exploitation of prostitution of women, without any reference to the concept of discrimination or to equality with men.

Secondly, the Committee on the Elimination of Discrimination against Women, in interpreting discrimination as defined in Article 1, has laid considerable emphasis on the *de facto* enjoyment of rights by women and has construed 'discrimination' broadly so as to encompass patterns of disadvantage which women suffer, without adopting the type of unduly formalistic approach to the term that has been adopted by some domestic courts when considering whether discrimination exists. The Committee's approach to violence against women – which it had no difficulty in characterizing as a form of discrimination against women within the meaning of the Convention – is one of the clearest examples of this approach.

Nevertheless, the underlying concept of discrimination is still derived from an androcentric model (although it should not be forgotten that in some cases equal treatment, formally and substantively, can be of considerable importance, e.g. in the area of legal capacity). Despite this, CEDAW has been able to adopt a substantive approach to women's enjoyment of human rights and has not been constrained by an excessively formalistic approach in addressing issues of discrimination.

Reservations[36]   Many of the states that have become parties to the Convention have been unwilling to accept the full scope of obligations set out in the instrument. Accordingly, they have entered reservations to one or more of its articles, which purport to limit or qualify their obligations under those provisions. These reservations have ranged from specific reservations to individual provisions (in many cases subsequently lifted once the inconsistent law or practice has been removed)[37] to broad, sometimes vague reservations that appear to limit the state's obligations under the Convention in sweeping ways.

While states are generally free under international law to enter reservations when they become a party to a treaty, their freedom to do so is not unlimited. Article 28 of the Convention, reiterating the general international law standard,[38] provides that reservations may not be 'incompatible with the object and purpose of the treaty'. A number of the more sweeping reservations entered by states ratifying or acceding to the Convention appear to be clearly inconsistent with the object and purpose of the treaty. This is particularly true of those reservations which purport to make the state's acceptance of obligations under the Convention as a whole, or central provisions such as Article 2 and Article 16, subject to existing domestic law or customs or to a system of religious law. For example, the Maldives entered a reservation in the following terms: 'The Government of the Republic of the Maldives will comply with the provisions of the Convention except those which the Government may consider contradictory to the principles of the Islamic Sharia upon which the laws and traditions of the Maldives are founded.'[39]

Other countries have stated that their acceptance of obligations under the Convention is subject to existing constitutional or statutory provisions (especially in the area of family relations). While it is not clear in every case whether there are major inconsistencies, it is clear that, should there be such inconsistencies, then the reservation is likely to be incompatible. For example, Malawi made the following reservation (which it subsequently withdrew): 'Owing to the deep-rooted nature of some traditional customs and practices of Malawians, the Government of the Republic of Malawi shall not, for the time being, consider itself bound by such of the provisions of the Convention as require immediate eradication of such traditional customs and practices.' Upon acceding to the Convention, Pakistan made a declaration in the following terms: 'The accession by [the] Government of the Islamic Republic of Pakistan to the [Convention] is subject to the provisions of the Constitution of the Islamic Republic of Pakistan.'

While some of these reservations are almost certainly incompatible with the object and purpose of the Convention, the Convention provides no specific procedure for making a determination of incompatibility (unlike the Racial Discrimination Convention, under which a reservation is considered to be incompatible if two-thirds of the states parties object to it). Instead, the matter is left to be dealt with by individual states parties, the meeting of states parties and the Committee itself.

Although the question of reservations found its way on to the agenda of the meeting of states parties for some years, nothing much has been accomplished in that forum, or indeed in the other United Nations fora in which the very states that have entered offending reservations endorse calls for the review and removal of such reservations. The task of seeking to control the inroads that reservations make on the integrity of the Convention regime has in practice fallen to a small number of states parties, to the Committee and to NGOs.[40]

A number of states parties have regularly objected to sweeping reservations entered by new states parties, declaring that they are incompatible with the Convention, do not provide sufficient detail for a determination of their compatibility to be made, or involve an unacceptable attempt to limit the scope of international obligation by reference to the limits of national law. Particularly prominent in scrutinizing reservations have been Austria, Denmark, Finland, Germany, Mexico, the Netherlands and Sweden.[41] These objections (combined in some cases with criticism by CEDAW or non-governmental organizations) have led to the withdrawal or narrowing of some of these reservations. But many reservations that appear incompatible with the object and purpose of the Convention remain.

The approach taken by CEDAW to reservations entered by states parties has been primarily a pragmatic one, although it has in recent years expressed its views on incompatibility more forcefully in an effort to protect the integrity of the treaty regime. The Committee regularly questions states parties about the meaning and scope of reservations, the justification for them, and any timetable the state party has for reviewing or removing them. As part of its preparation for the examination of country reports, the Committee has asked to be briefed on reservations that states parties may have entered to similar guarantees in other human rights treaties. In many cases, states have not entered reservations to the equality guarantees of the ICCPR, ICESCR or Convention on the Rights of the Child (CRC),[42] yet have entered reservations to provisions of CEDAW that embody essentially identical obligations. In addition, the Committee now regularly includes in its concluding comments on individual country reports its views on the reservations entered by that State.[43]

In 1994 the Committee made the following statement:

Each State Party that has entered substantive reservations to the Convention should include information on them in each of its periodic reports.

In reporting on reservations, the State Party should indicate why it considered the reservation to be necessary and whether reservations the State Party may or may not have entered on obligations with regard to the same right in other conventions are consistent with the reservations to the Convention on the Elimination of All Forms of Discrimination against Women, as well as the precise effect of the reservation in terms of national law and policy. It should indicate the plans that it has to limit the effect of reservations and ultimately withdraw them and, whenever possible, specify a timetable for withdrawing them.

States Parties which have entered general reservations that do not refer to a specific article of the Convention or reservations to articles 2 and 3 should make a particular effort to report on the effect and interpretation of them. The Committee considers these to be incompatible with the object and purpose of the present Convention.[44]

The Committee returned to the subject in 1998, when it set out in some detail its views on the question of reservations to the Convention, once again expressing its concern about the number and scope of reservations and the impact these have on the goals of the Convention, and calling on states parties to review reservations in an effort to narrow or remove them.[45] An important role is also played at the national level, by non-governmental organizations, many of whom have put pressure on governments to review and remove reservations.[46]

The Committee on the Elimination of Discrimination against Women[47]

The composition of the Committee The supervisory mechanism established by the Convention was modelled on those adopted under the Racial Discrimination Convention[48] and the ICCPR.[49] The Convention provides for the establishment of a committee of 23 experts, to be elected by the states parties to serve in their personal capacity.[50] The members of the Committee are to be chosen with due regard to equitable geographical distribution and the representation of different forms of civilization and the principal legal systems.[51]

The Committee is established '[f]or the purpose of considering the progress made in the implementation of the Convention'. The Convention assumes that the major part of that task will be the examination of the reports submitted by states parties. The Committee is under an obligation to report annually on its activities to the General Assembly through the Economic and Social Council and it may make suggestions and general recommendations based on its examination of reports and information received from states parties.[52] The Convention also gives the Committee the power to invite the specialized agencies of the United Nations to supply it with relevant information.[53]

The membership of the Committee has generally corresponded to the description in the Convention, though regional balance has not always been exactly achieved and in a number of cases persons holding high executive government positions or diplomatic posts (and therefore arguably not having the quality of appearance of independence from government required of members) have been nominated and elected.[54] One noteworthy feature of the Committee's membership has been the wide range of occupational and disciplinary backgrounds of its members, as compared with the domination of some of the other treaty bodies by international lawyers. This has had advantages in making available to the Committee a breadth of knowledge that is important for assessing the extent to which the Convention has been implemented. On the other hand, it has also meant that the Committee was slow to conceive of itself as a member of the family of treaty bodies whose work was potentially of considerable legal significance (in addition to its other importance), and to ensure that its output was in a form that maximized the impact of the Committee's work.

The functions of the Committee The primary function of CEDAW is the consideration of reports submitted by states parties, and it is this task that takes up most of the Committee's time. However, in addition to the review of reports, the Committee has over the years expanded the range of its activities: it has devoted increasing amounts of time to the elaboration of general recommendations, to the formulation of input to the series of world conferences organized by the United Nations during the 1990s, and to liaison with specialized agencies and other human rights mechanisms of the United Nations system.[55] Following the entry into force of the optional protocol to the Convention, the ambit of the Committee's work will expand to include consideration of individual complaints and to conduct inquiries into gross or systematic violations of the Convention.

As of the end of January 2002, the Committee on the Elimination of Discrimination against Women had held 26 sessions since it began its work in 1982.[56] Under Article 20 of the Convention the Committee was expected to meet for only two weeks per year, a period that has turned out to be a gross underestimate of the meeting time needed by the Committee, and less than has been provided for the other treaty bodies. Following the entry into force of the Convention, more and more states became parties to the Convention, and the number of reports the Committee had to consider increased, leading to a backlog of reports awaiting consideration. As a result, from 1988 the Committee was permitted to meet for three weeks per year on an exceptional basis, and from 1997 the Committee was permitted two three-week sessions per year until the backlog of reports is cleared. While these solutions were adopted on an *ad hoc* basis, in May 1995 the states parties to the Convention adopted an amendment to Article 20; this amendment provides that CEDAW shall normally meet annually, but that the duration of its meetings would be determined by a meeting of states parties, subject to the approval of the General Assembly.[57]

As of 15 January 2002 the amendment was not yet in force, having been ratified by only 28 states parties. Two-thirds of the states parties must ratify the amendment before it enters into force, so it seems unlikely that the amendment will enter into force soon, if ever. Since it commenced its work, the Committee has reviewed dozens of reports submitted by states parties to the Convention on the measures that they have taken to give effect to their obligations under the Convention. In addition, the Committee has carried out a considerable amount of other work, contributing to international conferences focusing on women as well as on other themes, and the elaboration of suggestions and general recommendations under the Convention.

Reporting under the Convention[58]

The obligation to report Article 18 of the Convention obliges each state that becomes a party to the Convention to submit regular reports 'on the legislative, judicial, administrative or other measures which they have adopted to give effect to the provisions of the ... Convention and on the progress made' in that regard. Initial reports are due within one year after the entry into force of the Convention for the state concerned and thereafter every four years or whenever the Committee so requests.[59]

Functions of reporting procedures The reporting procedure is the central feature of the Convention's system of international supervision,[60] and is in fact the activity that absorbs most of the Committee's time. It also provides an important occasion for non-governmental organizations to focus debate at the national level on the extent to which the government has given effect to its obligations under the Convention.

The Committee on Economic, Social and Cultural Rights has identified a number of functions that a reporting procedure may serve under the ICESCR, functions that are equally applicable to the CEDAW Convention (*mutatis mutandis*):[61]

1. to ensure that a comprehensive review of national legislation, administrative rules and procedures, and practices is undertaken in an effort to ensure the fullest possible conformity with the Convention;
2. to ensure that the state party monitors the actual situation with respect to each of the rights on a regular basis and is thus aware of the extent to which the various rights are, or are not, being enjoyed by all individuals within its territory or under its jurisdiction;
3. to enable the government to demonstrate that principled policy-making involving the elaboration of clearly stated and carefully targeted policies for the implementation of the Convention's provisions has in fact been undertaken;

4. to facilitate public scrutiny of government policies with respect to the rights guaranteed in the Convention and to encourage the involvement of women in the implementation and review of the relevant policies;

5. to provide a basis on which the state party itself, as well as the Committee, can effectively evaluate the extent to which progress has been made towards the realization of the obligations contained in the Covenant; for this purpose, it may be useful for states to identify specific benchmarks or goals against which their performance in a given area can be assessed;

6. to enable the state party itself to develop a better understanding of the problems and shortcomings encountered in efforts to realize progressively the full range of rights guaranteed by the Convention; for this reason, it is essential that states parties report in detail on the 'factors and difficulties' inhibiting such realization; and

7. to enable the Committee, and the states parties as a whole, to facilitate the exchange of information among states and to develop a better understanding of the common problems faced by states and a fuller appreciation of the type of measures which might be taken to promote effective realization of each of the rights contained in the Convention.

While all of these functions may not have originally been envisaged by those who adopted the reporting procedures under human rights treaties, the reporting procedure under the Convention and the other treaties has evolved over the years into a mechanism that can be used effectively in some cases to promote the implementation of the Convention at the national level. In most cases this has been the result of government officials' actually having to prepare a report and thus having to focus on the provisions of the Convention, the spotlight of publicity that may result from an international hearing and, most importantly, the use made by NGOs of the occasion of the review of a report to focus attention on the issues and to put pressure on the government to make changes. The manner in which the process unfolds and the role that NGOs may play, formally and informally, are described below.

The contents of the report In order to help states parties to prepare their reports the Committee has approved a number of sets of guidelines indicating what it expects to be included in reports: these include the *Consolidated Guidelines* for the initial part of reports by states parties under the various treaties agreed to by all the UN treaty bodies (the core document),[62] and the *Guidelines for the Preparation of Reports* (covering initial and periodic reports).[63]

In addition to these guidelines, which are formulated in very general terms, CEDAW has given more detailed guidance to the material that should be included in reports in its *General Recommendations*, and these need to be taken fully into account in the preparation of a report.[64] In general terms, the initial report is meant to be a comprehensive description of the situation of women in the country and to provide a baseline against which progress can be measured in future reports. Subsequent reports are meant to identify the progress and other changes made since the earlier report. Of particular importance are the Committee's insistence that reports describe not just the *de jure* situation of women, but also the *de facto* situation, that reports include statistics disaggregated by sex wherever available, and that reports describe the difficulties or lack of progress as well as the advances.

Status of submission of reports The situation under the Convention is similar to that under the other United Nations human rights treaties: many states have fallen behind with their reporting obligations and are overdue in their submission of reports (in many cases owing more than one report). As of 1 August 2001, over 100 states parties were overdue with one or more reports, and over 60 owed more than one report.[65] Of particular concern was the fact that 53 states parties had failed to submit their initial reports by that date. Of these more than half were five years or more overdue with their initial report and 13 states parties were more than ten years overdue with their initial report.[66] The reporting procedure may therefore not be too unfairly described as a 'non-reporting system' for many states parties.[67]

The useful functions that can be served by the reporting procedure can be exploited only if states do in fact report. Since a third of states parties have yet to submit their first report, and over two-thirds of states parties are delinquent, it must be a priority for the Committee and the United Nations system, and also for non-governmental organizations in delinquent states parties, to find ways to encourage or pressure governments to file their reports.

The Committee has explored a number of ways to facilitate submission by states of their reports. One measure the Committee has taken to encourage states to catch up on overdue reports (as well as to help with the backlog) is to permit states 'on an exceptional basis and as a temporary measure' to combine up to two reports (and in some cases more than two);[68] many states have done so.[69] The Committee is also exploring the option of asking states to submit focused second and later reports dealing with a limited number of issues, in an effort to relieve the reporting burden on states.[70]

If the Committee permits states to continue to combine reports in this way, there is a real risk that many states will end up submitting reports to the Committee only once every eight years, and more likely no more than once a decade. While it may be preferable to have states submit reports according to this extended cycle (rather than not reporting at all), such lengthy delays will significantly dilute the impact that international scrutiny of a state's performance may have. Other options open to the Committee include rescheduling the due dates for reports but not allowing a state to combine reports, so that a state's next report will be due no later than four years after the consideration of its last report by the Committee.[71]

Even these measures seem unlikely to have a major impact on the record of delinquency, and the Committee may also need to take more energetic steps, such as scheduling a state for review in the absence of a report, basing its examination on information available from official sources and NGOs. Although the Committee on Economic, Social and Cultural Rights has adopted this approach for states that have submitted an initial report,[72] the CEDAW has not so far been prepared to adopt this course, either for overdue initial reports or for overdue periodic reports.

Even though there is a high level of delinquency, the Committee has for some time had a backlog of reports that it *has* received but has not yet been able to consider. There have been many reports submitted by states (including a number of combined or multiple reports) that have not yet been considered by the Committee. This has led in many cases to delays in the consideration of reports,[73] although a number of those delays are due to the states parties that withdrew reports and substituted new ones or put off being scheduled for consideration by the Committee.

The Committee considered a total of 16 reports in 1998, 14 reports in 1999, 15 reports in 2000 and 16 in 2001. Since this is roughly keeping pace with the number of new reports received, it looks as if the Committee is likely to be facing a backlog for some time. The irony is that this backlog can be kept under control only if states fail to carry out their obligations under the Convention. Yet the Committee is insistent on encouraging states to report, and it is critical to the effectiveness of the monitoring procedure that they do so.

It can be seen that the reporting procedure in practice has fallen far short of its original goals, both as regards the proportion of states parties that actually submit reports, and the cycle of four-yearly reporting that the Committee has laid down. Whatever improvements can be made seem unlikely to change the situation radically. While the reporting procedure can be (and has been) used effectively by national NGOs to advance implementation of the Convention, the experience so far underlines the point that the major impact of the Convention must come at the national level. While the reporting process can provide additional stimulus to those efforts (and even catalyse them), much can be achieved by using the Convention domestically quite apart from the reporting procedure – in the courts and legislatures, and as a framework for activism; indeed, innovative and effective applications of the Convention have occurred in countries that have not reported under the Convention.

Review of reports by the Committee   Following submission of a state's report to the secretariat, the state will normally join the queue of states whose reports are awaiting consideration. When the report is scheduled for consideration (normally one to two sessions ahead), the Committee designates one of its members to be the main country rapporteur. The country rapporteur assumes special responsibility with respect to the country report she has been assigned, including presenting her preliminary impressions of an initial report to the Committee in closed session before the discussion with the state, as well as taking the major role in drafting the concluding comments on that state's report.[74] In the case of periodic reports, the country rapporteur sends this analysis to the pre-session working group so it can incorporate her concerns in the list of questions and issues sent to the state party prior to its presentation.[75] The country rapporteur is obviously an important person for non-governmental organizations to contact and provide with information well before the session at which their country's report is to be considered. Unfortunately, unlike a number of the other treaty bodies, the Committee has not agreed that the identities of country rapporteurs be made public; this makes the task of national NGOs trying to gain effective access to the Committee more difficult that it would otherwise be.

   The procedure adopted by the Committee for the review of initial reports and second reports is largely similar, though with a few minor differences. In the case of initial reports, the first formal stage[76] in the consideration of the report is the hearing before the Committee, at which the state representative will introduce the report – often at excessive length. This will be followed by general comments on the report by the country rapporteur and questions by other Committee members, article by article. State representatives may respond to these questions on the spot, return at a subsequent meeting to provide answers, or undertake to provide information in writing. This will depend on the nature of the questions, the expertise present in the delegation and the opportunities for the delegation to obtain information from home. The Committee emphasizes that the delegation be both of sufficiently high status to show that the government takes the Convention and the reporting procedure seriously, while insisting that the delegation should, so far as possible, comprise members who have real expertise in the areas covered by the Convention so as to ensure that there will be an informed discussion with the Committee.

Following the conclusion of the meetings with the state party, the responsible country rapporteur will draft concluding comments, in which the discussion between the Committee and the state representatives is reflected; these will be adopted by the Committee at the end of its session and then made available to the state party and the public. The practice of adopting concluding comments is only a few years old in CEDAW and the Committee has taken a few years to decide finally on the form of these observations and the procedure to be adopted.

In the case of second and later reports, a working group of the Committee has from mid-1999 met for one week at the end of the session preceding the one for which the review is scheduled.[77] The group compiles written questions based on questions provided by the country rapporteur and other members, as well as from specialized agencies and NGOs.[78] This is then sent to the state party before the meeting at which the report is to be discussed, and forms the basis of discussion at the meeting (although further questions are permitted). The question and answer session follows a pattern similar to that adopted for initial reports, and the Committee adopts concluding comments in the same way.

The review of a state's report by the Committee is not intended to be a judicial or quasi-judicial process in which the extent of the state's compliance with the provisions of the Convention is determined by the Committee. Rather, it is an occasion on which the state can identify the progress it has made, and the obstacles that face it, in implementing the Convention, and discuss these with the Committee, in what has become known in UN jargon as a 'constructive dialogue'. While this term underlines that the process is not intended to be a (quasi-)judicial procedure, on the other hand this does not mean that the Committee's consideration of a state report involves an uncritical and mutually congratulatory discussion of the state report. Individual committee members, and indeed the Committee as a whole, may be critical of either the technical limitations of a state report (for example, failure to comply with the Committee's guidelines, thus depriving the Committee of the information on which to basis its evaluation of progress made in the country concerned), or the substantive position in the country as revealed in the report (and also frequently more clearly in non-governmental reports). Both in individual comments and in the Committee's collective concluding comments on a report, extremely critical assessments have been made, although the Committee seeks to express a balanced view.

In adopting its concluding comments on a state, the Committee has decided to follow the structure used by a number of the other treaty bodies.[79] This standard format consists of an introduction, a section on positive aspects (organized in the order of the articles of the Convention), a section 'on factors and difficulties affecting the implementation of the Convention', and a final section that identifies principal areas of concern and also contains concrete suggestions and recommendations in response to the problems identified by the Committee.

The concluding comments are an important document, since they encapsulate the Committee's view of the priority areas for action in the implementation of the Convention in the country concerned, as well as providing detailed recommendations for action. It is this document which NGOs at the national level can use to lobby governments, legislatures and other decision-makers to adopt the changes recommended by the Committee. Unfortunately, concluding comments have been of variable quality, depending on the independent information available to the Committee, and the skill and commitment of the persons primarily involved in drafting them. It is in the interest of the Committee that these concluding comments be as well-honed as possible, since they are critical to ensuring that the reporting procedure has an impact at the national level.

The role of NGOs in the reporting procedure The Convention accords non-governmental organizations no formal role in the review of the reports of states: it provides that this review is to be carried out on the basis of material contained in the state reports and also, perhaps, information supplied by the specialized agencies of the United Nations.[80] Thus, representatives of NGOs are not permitted to speak at meetings at which the Committee is considering a state report, nor are documents submitted to the Committee translated and circulated as official documents.

Nevertheless, NGOs have always played an important role in supporting the work of the Committee,[81] in particular by providing it with information from national groups that supplements (and in many cases contradicts) the information provided by governments. Members of the Committee have, with few exceptions, been receptive to NGO information and have drawn on it in their analysis of state reports and questioning of state representatives. In recent years the Committee has begun to recognize the importance of NGO input by taking steps to facilitate NGO access, for example by asking the secretariat to arrange briefings for Committee members by NGOs from countries whose reports are to be reviewed,[82] and by encouraging NGOs to contribute to general thematic discussions or to provide information relevant to draft general recommendations being considered by the Committee.[83] Most recently, the Committee has decided that NGOs should be invited to provide information to and participate in the Committee's pre-sessional working group,[84] and in January 1999 the

Committee for the first time invited NGOs to address it early in its session in relation to those countries whose reports were being reviewed at that session.

Experience shows that the most effective NGO use of hearings before a treaty body occurs when the occasion of reporting forms part of an ongoing national strategy of which the international aspect forms but a part.[85] In deciding whether or not to commit resources to following the reporting procedure in any given case, a national NGO will have to assess whether the time, effort and money involved justify its doing so.[86] Obviously the strategies adopted will depend on the situation of each country, but it is important that, wherever possible, the use of the international procedures be integrated into the national efforts to ensure the realization of women's rights.[87]

The General Recommendations of the Committee

Under Article 21 of the Convention CEDAW has the power to make 'suggestions and general recommendations' to states parties.[88] Since the early 1990s CEDAW has begun to use its power to make general recommendations to elaborate its understanding of particular articles of the Convention, or of how the Convention applies to thematic issues (such as violence against women). The use of this power in such a way is an important development in the work of CEDAW[89] (which in this respect has followed the lead of the Human Rights Committee and the Committee on Economic, Social and Cultural Rights). Formally, the *General Recommendations* are not binding interpretations of the Convention, but are considered as influential interpretations of it.[90] The more recent *General Recommendations* of the Committee and its future ones[91] are likely to provide useful material to support arguments based on the Convention in political as well as legal contexts.

As of mid-1999 the Committee had adopted 24 *General Recommendations*.[92] While a number of the earlier *General Recommendations* are rather short and of somewhat limited utility, in 1992 the Committee began to adopt more detailed recommendations. The three most detailed *General Recommendations* adopted to date are *General Recommendation 19* (1992) dealing with violence against women, *General Recommendation 21* (1994) dealing with equality in marriage and the family,[93] and *General Recommendation 23* (1997) dealing with women in political and public life.[94] Each of these *General Recommendations* sets out in detail the Committee's understanding of the meaning of articles of the Convention and makes detailed recommendations to states parties about the steps that need to be taken in order to fulfil their obligations under the treaty.

Although as a formal matter of international law these general recommendations are not binding on states parties, nevertheless they are considered as particularly persuasive interpretations of it; they have been invoked before courts and tribunals,[95] though less frequently than the *General Comments* of the Human Rights Committee, which have been less frequently relied on before courts, both in jurisdictions in which the ICCPR has been incorporated (such as Hong Kong[96] and Japan)[97] and in jurisdictions in which it has not (such as Australia).

A complaints procedure for the Convention One of the results of the activism promoting the acceptance of women's rights as human rights and the participation of many women's human rights activists in the various world conferences held in the 1990s was the resuscitation of the proposal that an individual complaints procedure under the Convention be adopted, similar to those existing under the Optional Protocol to the ICCPR and other treaties.[98]

Following expressions of support for the idea at the Vienna World Conference on Human Rights in 1993, NGOs, supportive governments and foundations and CEDAW took up the issue. The International Human Rights Law Group organized an expert seminar in Maastricht in late 1994 to prepare a preliminary draft of an optional protocol. The Maastricht draft,[99] which proposed both an individual complaint procedure and an inquiry procedure, drew on existing models as well as containing a number of innovative elements, and has been extremely influential in framing the discussions within CEDAW and the CSW.

Following the Maastricht meeting, CEDAW examined the issue in detail in early 1995, adopting *Suggestion No. 7*,[100] in which the Committee set out the elements which it considered should be included in any optional protocol. While this document essentially endorsed the content of the Maastricht draft, it was CEDAW's *Suggestion* that formed the focus of comments by governments and discussion in the CSW when the Commission took the matter up.

In 1995 the CSW decided merely to invite comments on CEDAW's *Suggestion No. 7* and to take the matter up in 1996. At its 1996 session an open-ended working group of the Commission discussed the feasibility of a protocol and a number of the more important issues, on the basis of government and NGO comments.[101] At this stage there was no draft before the Commission, and following the general discussion the Commission decided to consider the matter further at its 1997 session, on the basis of additional views submitted by governments and NGOs.[102]

Finally, at the 1997 session of the Commission the working group of the Commission moved from its general discussion to discussion of a draft text,[103] which had been prepared by the chairperson of the working group.[104] The working group completed a first reading of the draft and deferred consideration of the amended draft[105] to a further meeting of the working group at the 1998 Commission.[106] Further negotiations took place in the working group at the March 1998[107] and March 1999[108] sessions of the Commission. The Commission finally adopted the draft protocol on 12 March 1999,[109] and its adoption by the General Assembly was anticipated for December 1999.

The draft optional protocol contains both an individual complaints procedure (similar to the First Optional Protocol to the ICCPR), which will permit individuals who allege that they are victims of a violation of the rights in the Convention to complain to the Committee,[110] and an inquiry procedure empowering the Committee to conduct an inquiry into a situation in a state party where it appears that grave or systematic violations of the Convention are occurring or have occurred.[111] A state that becomes party to the optional protocol must accept the individual complaints procedure, but has the right to opt out of the inquiry procedure.[112] The protocol will enter into force three months after it has received ten ratifications or accessions.[113] Reservations to the protocol are expressly prohibited.[114]

The original draft in large part followed the ICCPR model so far as the individual complaints procedure was concerned (and Article 20 of the Torture Convention in relation to the inquiry procedure), though with some efforts to strengthen and consolidate the practice under that instrument. The most contentious issue during the negotiations was the question of who could bring complaints, in particular whether non-governmental organizations could bring complaints on their own behalf and on behalf of others without their express consent. Other contentious issues included the inquiry procedure generally, the status of the Committee's views, the permissibility of reservations to the protocol, the power to request interim measures, and the justiciability of the obligations under the Convention.[115] The negotiations on the protocol saw most of the innovative elements in the original draft removed or whittled down, and the final product looks very much like the existing communications procedures, with some innovation.

The protocol was entered into force upon the receipt of ten ratifications in December 2000, after its adoption by the General Assembly in December 1999. In view of the considerable NGO involvement in the development of the instrument, it seems likely that NGOs will be keen to use the procedure once it is operative. This entry into force of the protocol will mean that the Committee will have further demands on its limited resources, but also the opportunity to develop a solid jurisprudence of the Convention based on individual cases.

Using the Convention at the National Level

Although the status of the Convention as an international legal commitment and the international dimensions of the reporting process are important, in the final analysis it is the implementation of the Convention's guarantees at the national level that is critical. While the strategies for achieving this goal will vary and may not even involve explicit reference to or use of the Convention, there are a number of ways in which the Convention can be invoked in order to advance women's equality at the national level.

There have been many instances in which the Convention and its jurisprudence have been invoked in support of efforts to enact or amend laws to advance the goals of the Convention and the position of women. In many countries the actual or pending ratification of the Convention has brought about legislative reform, in order to bring national law into conformity with the Convention's requirements.[116] In some countries the Convention has been invoked to persuade courts when applying existing law to do so by reference to the standards of the Convention.[117] The following discussion refers to some examples that illustrate the role that the Convention can play in informing the formulation of legislation and its interpretation.[118]

The Convention as a Resource for Legal Change

The Australian Sex Discrimination Act 1984 and protection against sexual harassment in employment   Under Australia's federal constitution, modelled in this respect on the United States Constitution, the federal parliament has limited legislative powers. Those powers are less extensive than the powers enjoyed by the United States Congress and, when Australia ratified the CEDAW Convention in 1984, the federal government was faced with the need to legislate against discrimination in many areas that did not, as such, fall explicitly under its enumerated legislative powers. Prior to the ratification of the Convention, the parliament was not able, for example, to enact a law prohibiting sexual harassment in employment nationwide.

However, with the ratification of the Convention, the parliament was then able to draw on its power to legislate with respect to 'external affairs', a power that has been held broad enough to permit the federal legislature to implement treaty obligations binding on Australia.[119] The parliament enacted the Sex Discrimination Act 1984 (Cth), which contained a provision which explicitly prohibited sexual harassment in employment; so far as sexual harassment of women was concerned, the provision was applicable nationwide. The constitutional validity of the section in this respect was based on the view that sexual discrimination against women was a form of discrimination against women as defined in the Convention and that, therefore, the legislation was clearly within federal legislative power.

In *Aldridge* v. *Booth*[120] the provision was challenged as being beyond the power of the Commonwealth, on the ground that sexual harassment was not a form of discrimination against women as defined in the Convention. The court rejected the challenge, holding that Article 11 of the Convention imposed a very clear obligation on Australia to eliminate sex discrimination in employment, and that sexual harassment was a form of sex discrimination within the meaning of the Convention.[121] Accordingly, the exercise of the legislative power was based firmly on the Convention and the provision was constitutionally valid.[122]

Legislative initiatives in Hong Kong and the proposed extension of the Convention to Hong Kong Another example of the impetus that actual or pending ratification of the Convention can have on the enactment of domestic legislation comes from Hong Kong.[123] From the second half of the 1980s (and even before then) women's groups and others had been pushing for the extension of the Convention to Hong Kong, as well as for the repeal or amendment of laws that are discriminatory against women. The activism of the late 1980s and early 1990s was particularly intense, putting sufficient pressure on the Hong Kong government to agree in principle that the Convention should be extended to Hong Kong and to seek approval for that extension from the Chinese government through the Sino–British Joint Liaison Group (the Convention was applied to Hong Kong with effect from 14 October 1996).

One of the ways in which the proposed extension of the Convention added momentum to the campaign for legislation prohibiting discrimination by private as well as by public actors was the government's recognition that a good-faith reading of the Convention's obligations meant that it would have to enact domestic legislation prohibiting discrimination against women in a wide range of activities. Previously the administration had claimed that its existing treaty obligations did not require it to enact such legislation, and that the Hong Kong Bill of Rights Ordinance[124] had in any event discharged any obligations binding on the government and public authorities not to discriminate on the basis of sex.

In mid-1995 the Hong Kong Legislature enacted the Sex Discrimination Ordinance.[125] The Ordinance was modelled closely on the United Kingdom's Sex Discrimination Act, consistent with the Hong Kong government's tendency to adopt British models in many areas of law reform. Unfortunately, the Hong Kong adaptation of the British model did not include the important overlay that the sex discrimination law of the European Communities has brought to UK law, and Hong Kong's draft Bill included provisions that had been superseded by European law, even if not yet actually removed from the Sex Discrimination Act itself. In addition to this imperfect copy of the UK law on sex discrimination, the Hong Kong government proposed a lengthy list of exceptions and exemptions (the government itself was the primary beneficiary of many of these).

When the government's bill came to be considered by the Legislative Council, it came in for strong criticism from many women's groups and others who considered that the bill was defective. Critics invoked international standards to support their calls for the strengthening of the bill by removing various exceptions and expanding its limited coverage in a number of areas (for example, in relation to its coverage of marital status discrimination, which was confined to the areas of employment and education). Among the benchmarks against which the bill was measured was the CEDAW Convention, with critics claiming that the enactment of the bill in the form proposed by the government would mean that, once the Convention had been extended to Hong Kong, there would already be a failure to implement its provisions, since the Sex Discrimination Ordinance would fall short of the standards required by the Convention.

Although this criticism had some impact, the government was adamant in sticking to most of the exemptions it had written into the bill. Nevertheless, as a result of the criticism, the scope of the bill's protection against discrimination on the grounds of marital status was broadened to cover more than discrimination in employment and education, an expansion that was clearly consistent with giving effect to the Convention's requirements to eliminate discrimination against women 'irrespective of their marital status'.[126] Similarly, the government accepted proposals to include explicit reference to 'hostile environment' sexual harassment in the field of employment,[127] and to provide that provisions taken to redress previous discrimination would not constitute discrimination within the meaning of the Ordinance, neither of these provisions appearing in the UK model. The latter, permitting the temporary special measures expressly provided for in Article 4 of the Convention, was justified by reference to the Convention, as well as on other grounds.

A more direct attempt to incorporate the Convention's standards into the Sex Discrimination Ordinance (which was, after all, intended to be legislation implementing a number of provisions of that treaty) was made by legislator Anna Wu Hung-yuk. In July 1994 Ms Wu had introduced into the Legislative Council a comprehensive Equal Opportunities Bill,[128] a move that had stimulated the government to introduce legislation of its own in the field of sex discrimination. Wu's bill explicitly provided that a court, when interpreting the legislation, should have reference to a number of international treaties and instruments (including the CEDAW Convention), most of which were applicable to Hong Kong and which the legislation was intended to implement in part.[129] Wu's bill was delayed and subsequently reformulated after the government introduced its own Sex Discrimination Bill, which was weaker than Wu's bill.

Accordingly, Wu proposed a number of amendments to the government's Sex Discrimination Bill that were intended to strengthen it and to bring it into line with applicable international standards (in particular the International Covenant on Civil and Political Rights as applied to Hong Kong and the CEDAW Convention, which the government had by then announced would be extended to Hong Kong). One of the amendments she proposed was a provision that provided an explicit reference to the provisions of the CEDAW Convention along the lines of the provision in her own Equal Opportunities Bill. As one of the government's purposes in introducing the bill was to permit extension of the Convention to Hong Kong, Wu argued that it was entirely appropriate that the bill should be interpreted in accordance with the Convention, and that in any event this was merely spelling out what was an established rule of statutory interpretation (that a statute enacted in order to implement a treaty should be interpreted consistently with the terms of the treaty).[130] The government, however, opposed this amendment, and was eventually able to muster enough votes to defeat the amendment when the bill was finally voted on.

Although it is a well-established rule of interpretation in common law jurisdictions (as well as in many civil law jurisdictions) that the legislature is presumed, in the absence of clear words, not to have legislated inconsistently with its international obligations and that an implementing statute should be read so far as possible to give effect to the treaty it implements, the addition of an explicit reference to the relevant treaty may in practice direct the attention of those interpreting the statute to its international source. Unfortunately, one cannot assume that courts and advocates will always be aware of the international origin of a statute, without a clear signpost in the direction of an international law standard.[131] Notwithstanding the defeat of the attempts to remove most of the exceptions and exemptions in the Sex Discrimination Ordinance, international standards will continue to play a role in the evolution and interpretation of the Ordinance; further efforts to amend the Ordinance to bring it into line with international standards will continue to be made.

The Hong Kong experience is just one example of how advocates of equality can invoke international standards in order to support legislative initiatives.[132] While the calls to implement the international obligations fully have not been successful in a number of important instances, the recourse to international standards has lent those claims additional legitimacy and has put additional pressure on a government which was unlikely to have moved at all unless pushed.

Using the Convention in the courts[133] In many countries ratification of a Convention may make it possible to invoke the Convention before the national courts and tribunals. The extent to which the Convention may be relied on depends on rules governing the relationship between international law and national law under the legal system of the state, the extent of national law covering the issue, and the receptivity of courts to arguments grounded in international law.[134]

Where the Convention forms part of national law In many countries (especially civil law countries) ratified conventions form part of national law and may override conflicting national laws. The exact relationship between rules of international law and national provisions ranges from giving treaty provisions supra-constitutional status (as in the Netherlands in certain cases),[135] constitutional status, superior status to all national laws, or superior status to all earlier national laws. In these cases, where the provisions of national law or administrative practices are inconsistent with a guarantee under the Convention, it may be possible to invoke the provisions of the Convention directly.

This may, of course, depend on whether the courts consider that the relevant provision (or the Convention as a whole) is directly applicable or self-executing, or whether the provision in question needs further implementing legislation and therefore cannot be relied on directly before the court. Although many of the Convention's obligations are couched in such terms as 'states parties shall take all appropriate measures', many of the provisions are in classically justiciable terms and even these more broadly worded guarantees can be viewed as justiciable in important respects.[136]

Despite the many countries in which treaties do form part of national law, there appear to have been relatively few cases in which the Convention has been invoked (although there have been more cases in which the non-discrimination provision of the International Covenant on Civil and Political Rights has been invoked as part of national law).

Where the Convention does not form part of national law The position in nearly all Commonwealth and common law countries (as well as many other countries) is in formal terms fairly similar: unincorporated treaties may not generally be relied on before domestic courts directly to found a cause of action, but they may nevertheless have an indirect impact on the interpretation and application of law. The presumption that the legislature does not intend to legislate in a manner that is inconsistent with international law is well-accepted in most common law and civil law jurisdictions, and has as its corollary a principle of statutory interpretation – of uncertain practical importance – that statutes should be interpreted in a manner consistent with international law.[137] International treaties and customary international law are also recognized as relevant sources for the development of the common law. Examples of how unincorporated treaties have been used by courts include:[138]

- as an aid to constitutional or statutory interpretation, either generally or in order to resolve an 'ambiguity';[139]
- as a relevant consideration to be taken into account in the exercise of an administrative discretion by a decision-maker (and thus subject to judicial review);[140]
- as giving rise to a *legitimate expectation* that the provisions of the treaty will be applied by a decision-maker unless a hearing is given to the person affected;[141]
- as a factor that may be taken into consideration in the development of the common law, where the common law is unclear;[142] and
- as a factor that may be taken into account when identifying the demands of public policy.[143]

Cases in which the Convention has been relied on or cited The Convention has been cited to and by courts in an increasing number of cases in recent years. These cases include instances in which the Convention is an authoritative national rule and determinative of the outcome of a case (sometimes in conjunction with other constitutional or statutory provisions), a relevant source to be taken into account in the interpretation of a constitutional or statutory provision, or a statement of values relevant to the decision-making process, as well as cases in which it may be cited simply as background material without any apparent significant impact on the decision.

For example, the Convention, along with other human rights instruments, has been relied on in a number of cases to interpret constitutional guarantees of equality.[144] One well-known example is the Botswanan case of *Dow* v. *Attorney General of Botswana* in which Unity Dow, a Botswanan citizen, successfully challenged the provisions of Botswana's nationality law, which did not permit a Botswanan woman married to a non-Botswanan national to pass on her citizenship to the children of the marriage.[145]

In *Ephrahim* v. *Pastory*[146] the High Court of Tanzania relied on the Convention (as well as on the ICCPR and the African Charter on Human and Peoples' Rights)[147] in interpreting the Bill of Rights contained in the Tanzanian Constitution. The court held that the guarantee of equality contained in the Bill of Rights overrode the customary law rules that prevented women from selling clan land, while permitting men to do so (subject to the condition that any other clan member could repurchase the land from a purchaser).

In a Nepalese case, *Dhungana and another* v. *Government of Nepal*,[148] which also involved property and inheritance rights, a challenge was made to the Nepali law that provided that, while a son was entitled to a partition share of his father's property at birth, a daughter was entitled to obtain a share only when she reached the age of 35 and was still unmarried. Under Nepali law ratified treaties form part of the law of Nepal and an action was brought challenging this law on the ground that it violated both the guarantee of equality in the Constitution and Article 15 of the CEDAW Convention.[149] The court appeared to consider that there was a violation of these guarantees, but was reluctant to declare the law unconstitutional with immediate effect. The court eventually ordered the government to 'introduce an appropriate Bill to Parliament within one year ... by making necessary consultations as to this matter with the recognised Women's Organisations, sociologists, the concerned social organisations and lawyers ... and by studying and considering also the legal provisions made in other countries in this regard'.[150] This was one of a number of cases brought to challenge sex discriminatory laws in reliance on the Convention; in each case the court referred the matter to the government with an order to introduce conforming legislation within a year.

The Supreme Court of India has referred to the Convention in a number of cases in recent years.[151] One important case in which it has relied on the Convention and given effect to it in a most direct manner is *Vishaka* v. *State of Rajasthan*.[152] That case arose out of an alleged gang rape and the failure of officials to investigate complaints of rape (the women who were raped were state employees). A writ was lodged with the Supreme Court requesting it to direct the state to form a Committee to frame guidelines for the prevention of sexual harassment and abuse of women. The terms proposed to the court by counsel for the petitioners were in part drawn directly from certain passages in CEDAW's *General Recommendation 19* dealing with violence against women. While the decision of the court was based on a number of guarantees of fundamental rights under the Con- stitution of India[153] and the court's jurisdiction under Article 32 of the Constitution to enforce fundamental rights, the court referred to Article 11 of the Convention and to *General Recommendation 19*. It commented:[154]

In the absence of domestic law occupying the field, to formulate effective measures to check the evil of sexual harassment of working women at all workplaces, the contents of international conventions and norms are significant for the purpose of the interpretation of the guarantee of gender equality, the right to work with human dignity in arts 14, 15, 19(1)(g) and 21 of the Constitution and the safeguards against sexual harassment implicit therein. Any international convention not inconsistent with the fundamental rights and in harmony with its spirit must be read into these provisions to enlarge the meaning and content thereof, to promote the object of the constitutional guarantee.

The court then went on to quote from the Convention and from the *General Recommendation* to inform its interpretation of the constitutional guarantees; the guidelines and norms laid down by the court in an order agreed between the parties also drew directly on those instruments.[155] This is one of the few cases in which the Committee's *General Recommendations* have been cited.[156]

An imaginative use of the Convention has been made in India in an attempt to get the Indian government to give full effect to the spirit of the Convention in the area of personal laws. When India ratified the Convention in 1993, it entered a declaration in these terms:

> With regard to articles 5(a) and 16(1) of the Convention on the Elimination of All Forms of Discrimination Against Women, the Government of the Republic of India declares that it shall abide by and ensure these provisions in conformity with its policy of non-interference in the personal affairs of any Community without its initiative and consent.

As much inequality in India is the direct result of systems of personal law governing matters of family status and rights, this declaration was viewed by activists in India as essentially a reservation that undermined the seriousness of India's commitment to the principles of the Convention. The government apparently took no steps to determine what views the communities involved had on this issue or on repealing discriminatory personal laws. Accordingly, an action was commenced in the Supreme Court of India by the Women's Action Research and Legal Action for Women (WARLAW). In that action, brought in the court's public interest litigation jurisdiction, the petitioners sought an order from the court directing the government of India to show what steps it had taken to ascertain the views of the Hindu community on whether it was appropriate to repeal discriminatory personal laws with a view to ensuring equality for women.[157] The case is still pending.[158]

The Convention was also invoked in a challenge before the Constitutional Court of Guatemala[159] to various provisions of the Guatemalan penal code relating to adultery and concubinage, which treated women and men differently. The petitioners invoked both the equality guarantees of the Guatemalan Constitution and international treaties to which Guatemala was party (including the CEDAW Convention, the American Convention on Human Rights[160] and the Inter-American Convention on Violence against Women).[161] The court held the articles unconstitutional, reasoning that to hold the impugned articles valid would not only render nugatory the constitutional mandate to eradicate inequality but would also represent a failure by Guatemala to fulfil its obligations under the conventions mentioned above, which according to Article 46 of the Guatemalan Constitution prevailed over the provisions of the Penal Code.[162] The Convention has also been invoked in a number of Australian cases. For example, the federal Sex Discrimination Commissioner has intervened in cases before industrial courts in order to present arguments based on the CEDAW Convention and its implementing legislation.[163] The Convention has also been relied on to support a refusal to disclose documents containing complaints of sexual harassment, which would have permitted the respondent to identify the persons who had lodged those complaints.[164] In a case involving a dispute between two divorced parents over the surname by which their child should be known,[165] Warnick J referred to the provisions of Article 16 (1)(g),[166] noting that by the incorporation of this guarantee into national law by the Sex Discrimination Act 1984, the legislature had 'demonstrated a commitment to equal rights to husbands and wives in the choice of a family name, at least for themselves'.[167] Warnick J continued:[168]

> 31. I do not see that the Act affects the discharge of this court's judicial responsibilities, but in the absence of argument do not express a concluded view. Even should the Act have application in this case, I cannot see that it would impinge upon my decision-making process, which must be to weigh those factors bearing upon the best interests of the child, except insofar as the Act might require me not to give preference to the position of one party as against the other, on the basis that one party has an exclusive or more significant parental right in relation to choice of the child's surname, than does the other party.
>
> 32. In this regard I note sub-paragraph (d) of Article 16 of the Convention provides for measures to ensure: 'the same rights and responsibilities as parents, irrespective of their marital status, in matters relating to their children; in all cases the interests of the children shall be paramount'.

Two contrasting Australian cases from the industrial law field show clearly the difference that taking account of the relevant international standards can make to the outcome of a case. Both concerned provisions in union rules intended to ensure that there were some women members on the executive bodies of unions or their branches. In *Re Australian Journalists' Association*[169] the Commission refused to permit a change to the rules of the Australian Journalists' Association designed to ensure that there was at least one-third representation of women members on the Association's governing body. Boulton J found that the provision was discriminatory and did not fall within section 33 of the Sex Discrimination Act, which permitted measures to be taken which are intended to ensure equality of opportunity.[170] Boulton J held that women had the same opportunity formally to stand for election and that therefore the section did not apply.

Had the judge looked to Article 4 of the CEDAW Convention (which section 33 was intended to reflect), it is difficult to see how he could have come to any conclusion other than one holding the measure was a permissible temporary special measure and therefore not unlawful. The union subsequently applied for and was granted an exemption under the legislation. In its decision granting the exemption the Human Rights and Equal Opportunity Commission stated that it did not necessarily agree with the interpretation of Boulton J.[171]

In a later decision of the Australian Industrial Commission, the Commission considered a similar issue and, after considering Article 4 of the Convention and other international cases dealing with the concept of discrimination, took the view – albeit somewhat tentatively – that a union rule providing that each union branch has to have at least one female vice-president was covered by section 33 of the Sex Discrimination Act.[172]

A decision of the Constitutional Chamber of the Supreme Court of Justice of Costa Rica also relied on the Convention in an analogous case.[173] The court upheld a challenge to the failure of the executive government to include any women in the list of candidates forwarded to the legislature for appointment to the Board of Directors of the Monitoring Body for Public Services (Junta Directiva de la Autoridad Reguladora de los Servicios Públicos), a body that monitors government's functioning in regards to its public services such as public transport, hospitals, schools, water and services. The court took the view that both the guarantees of equality under national law and the obligation embodied in Article 7 of the Convention to take appropriate measures to ensure that women enjoyed equality in public life meant that the government had to take active steps to achieve this goal – and this included nominating a similar number of women and men to public posts (assuming that there were sufficient qualified candidates of each sex). The court ordered the government to ensure that future nominations contained a representative number of women.

In some cases the Convention and CEDAW's work may provide little more than background for the courts.[174] For example, in *Ruka* v. *Department of Social Welfare*,[175] the appellant had been convicted of welfare fraud for claiming benefits available only to persons who were not married or who were not living in a relationship in the nature of marriage. Ruka had been living with a man in a relationship in which she suffered frequent beatings and rape; her partner made no financial contribution to the household. The appellant succeeded in her appeal against the conviction, a majority of the court concluding that there was no relationship in the nature of marriage because of the lack of financial interdependence, and (in the view of one judge) also because of the lack of mental and emotional commitment by her to the relationship as she suffered from battered women's syndrome.

The counsel who appeared as *amicus curiae* submitted a brief making extensive reference to the CEDAW Convention, CEDAW's *General Recommendation 19* and other international instruments relating to violence against women, as well as general human rights instruments in support of her case.[176] However, only one judge, Thomas J, referred to this material, noting[177]

> the extensive work being undertaken at an international level to ensure that violence towards women is recognised as a major barrier to women achieving fundamental human rights and freedoms ... While the importance of this work [CEDAW's work, among other sources] is recognised, it is not necessary to traverse the reports in this judgment. It is sufficient to acknowledge that they emphasise the disastrous effects of violence against women and the extensive impact which it has on the basic rights of women.

While not every invocation of the Convention or other human rights treaty in a domestic court necessarily wins the day,[178] reliance on the Convention, in conjunction with other human rights instruments and constitutional or statutory guarantees of equality, can assist in advancing a case before domestic courts.

The extent of utilization of unincorporated treaties depends largely on the approach adopted by the judiciary: a judiciary that is prepared to be open to international influences and to draw on international jurisprudence has some scope for doing so in most common law systems. The task is probably easier where the judge is interpreting a constitutional or statutory Bill of Rights (in which there may be similar or identical guarantees to those contained in treaties by which the state is bound or which form part of customary international law). This is the case for the vast majority of Commonwealth countries that became independent after the Second World War; many of these countries have constitutions that trace their parentage to the European Convention on Human Rights.[179] This makes reference to international jurisprudence under the European Convention (and the ICCPR) particularly easy to justify in formal terms, if any justification is needed. For those countries that have accepted the competence of the Human Rights Committee under the First Optional Protocol to the ICCPR to consider individual complaints, the relevance of international case law is even more immediate.[180]

In recent years a number of Commonwealth courts (especially those in Southern Africa) have energetically embraced international jurisprudence in the interpretation of national constitutional guarantees, including treaties to which the state concerned is not a party as well as those by which it is bound.[181] There are, of course, a number of reasons why judges may wish to be cautious in drawing too enthusiastically on treaties that have not been incorporated as part of domestic law, even though they are binding on the state as a matter of international law. Justice Michael Kirby (now of the High Court of Australia) has identified a number of matters that may influence judges to take a less expansive approach to the use of treaty norms.[182] They include the fact that the ratification of a treaty is generally an executive act, which may or may not reflect the views of the populace or the parliament; or, in federal states, concern that the federal government may use the power to ratify treaties (and associated legislative power to implement them) to expand federal power at the expense of the power of the states.[183] Other concerns are that the process of judicial development of the law may divert attention from the more open and democratic adoption of such norms by way of statutory or constitutional bills of rights, suspicion about the composition and competence of international bodies, and a concern that the drive towards international conformity not lead to a neglect of the relevant national and local social and historical context.[184]

Political and Other Uses of the Convention

The standards of the Convention and the commitment that a government evinces through its ratification of the Convention (often minimal but rarely empty) have been utilized by non-governmental groups at national and local levels in a multitude of ways. Quite apart from the opportunities that the reporting process may present, the Convention provides an independent framework for assessing the situation of women in the community and the steps that may be needed to improve it. In addition to the lobbying and litigation strategies referred to above, the Convention has been utilized in education programmes, in empowering grassroots women, in legal literacy programmes, as a resource for teaching and research, and in other strategies.[185]

A particular striking example of making the Convention part of regional and local policy-making and activism is the *Paulista Convention on the*

Elimination of All Forms of Discrimination against Women.[186] This document was adopted as the result of a strategy initiated by women's and community groups in São Paulo State, Brazil.[187] These groups took the CEDAW Convention as the basis of negotiations entered into with governments, the purpose of which was to persuade governments to express support for the general principles of equality for women contained in the Convention but also to commit themselves to taking specific concrete actions to give effect to those principles and the provisions of the Convention. The strategy proceeded from initial research on the situation of women to education about the Convention and women's human rights, then to the holding of seminars with the community and local government institutions in which the principles of the Convention were compared with women's material condition and the prevailing law and practice.[188]

Conclusion

The discussion above shows that there are many ways in which the Convention on the Elimination of All Forms of Discrimination against Women can be called on by those seeking to advance the enjoyment of equality by women. Whether as an international treaty utilized at the international level, or in domestic courts and legislatures, or as a tool for lobbying education and activism, an imaginative and informed use of the Convention tailored to the national and local circumstances and combined with other relevant strategies can contribute in meaningful ways to the struggle for gender equality.

Notes

Andrew Byrnes is Professor of Law, Australian National University, and was formerly Associate Professor and Director, Centre for Comparative and Public Law, Faculty of Law, University of Hong Kong. This chapter consists in large part of a revised version of material presented at the First to Fourth Postgraduate Courses on Human Rights of Women organized by the World University Service Austria in Austria and Uganda from 1992 to 1996. In the preparation of those lectures and of this chapter the following colleagues have provided considerable assistance for which I would like to thank them: Dorota Gierycz of the United Nations Division for the Advancement of Women, Marsha Freeman and Sharon Ladin (formerly of the International Women's Rights Action Watch), Shanthi Dairiam of the International Women's Rights Watch (Asia-Pacific), and Jane Connors (formerly of the University of London and now of the UN Division for the Advancement of Women). I would also like to thank the organizers of the course (Wolfgang Benedek, Dorothea Gaudart, Dorota Gierycz and Manfred Nowak) for giving me the opportunity to participate in it, and the many participants in the courses for the opportunity to learn from them; and to express my appreciation to Gerd Oberleitner, of the Institute of International Law and International Relations, University of Graz, for his efficiency and patience throughout the project. This chapter is based in part on research made possible by grants from the Hong Kong Research Grants Council and the University of Hong Kong's Committee on Research and Conference Grants.

1.   GA Res 34/180, 1249 UNTS 13, Document 69 in United Nations, *The United Nations and the Advancement of Women 1945–1996*, United Nations Blue Books Series, Vol. 6 (New York: United Nations, rev. edn 1996) (hereinafter *UN and Women*). Two recent book-length commentaries on the Convention are Lars Adam Rehof, *Guide to the Travaux Préparatoires of the United Nations Convention on the Elimination of All Forms of Discrimination against Women* (Dordrecht: Martinus Nijhoff, 1993) (hereinafter Rehof), and Japanese Association of International Women's Rights, *Commentary on the Convention on the Elimination of All Forms of Discrimination against Women* (Bunkyo: Japanese Association of International Women's Rights, 1995) (hereinafter *JAIWR Commentary*). See also Maria Isabel Plata and Maria Yanuzova, *Los Derechos Humanos y La Convención Sobre La Eliminación de Todas Las Formas de Discriminación contra La Mujer* (Bogotá: Profamilia, 1988). For a discussion of the process leading to the adoption of the Convention, see Noreen Burrows, 'The 1979 Convention on the Elimination of All Forms of Discrimination against Women' (1985), *Netherlands International Law Review* 419–57; Arvonne Fraser, 'The Convention on the Elimination of All Forms of Discrimination against Women (The Women's Convention)' in Anne Winslow (ed.), *Women, Politics and the United Nations* (Westport, CT and London: Greenwood Press, 1995) 77–94; and Yasuko Yamashita, 'The drafting of the Convention on the Elimination of All Forms of Discrimination against Women' in *JAIWR Commentary*, 9–16. For a detailed bibliography on the Convention and related matters, see Rebecca J. Cook and Valerie L. Oosterveld, 'A select bibliography of women's human rights' (1995), 44 *American University Law Review* 1429. This bibliography is updated and made available on-line through the Internet by the Laskin Law Library at the University of Toronto. The URL is http:// www.law. utoronto.ca/pubs/h_rghts.htm. See also the website of the International Women's Rights Project, Center for Feminist Research, York University, which contains a bibliography: http://www.web.net/~marilou/resources.htm

2.   See generally Hilkka Pietilä and Jeanne Vickers, *Making Women Matter: The Role of the United Nations* (London and New Jersey: Zed Books, 3rd edn 1996), 117–32; Boutros Boutros Ghali, 'Introduction' in *UN and Women*, 3–74; Katerina Tomasevski, *Women and Human Rights* (London and New Jersey: Zed Books, 1993), 98–106; Natalie Kaufman Hevener, *International Law and the Status of Women* (Boulder, CO: Westview, 1983) (discussing instruments adopted from 1945); See also Betty G. Elder, 'The rights of women: their status in international law' (1986) 25 *Crime and Social Justice* 1, and Anne M. Trebilcock, 'Sex discrimination' in Rudolf Bernhardt (gen. ed.), *Encyclopedia of Public International Law* (Max Planck Institute for Comparative Public Law and International Law), Vol. 8, 476 (Amsterdam: North-Holland, 1985).

3.   GA Res 2263 (XXII), adopted on 7 November 1967, Document 36 in *UN and Women*.

4.   *Multilateral Treaties Deposited with the Secretary-General* (New York: United Nations) (hereinafter *Multilateral Treaties*), as available on http://www.un.org/Depts/ Treaty on 17 January 2002.

5.   The Convention's explicit application to discrimination in the field of private life as well as public life (as in the International Convention on the Elimination of All Forms of Racial Discrimination), its requirement in Article 5 that states must eliminate traditional and stereotyped notions of the roles of the sexes, and Article 14's explicit concern with rural women are innovative provisions.

6.   See, e.g., Marsha Freeman, 'Women, development and justice: using the Inter-

national Convention on Women's Rights', in Joanna Kerr (ed.), *Ours by Right: Women's Rights as Human Rights* (London: Zed Books and the North–South Institute, 1993) (hereinafter *Ours by Right*), 93.

7. Many states have entered reservations to the Convention limiting their obligations in quite fundamental ways, either by general reservations or by reservations in relation to specific articles. See discussion at text accompanying footnotes 36–44.

8. For a legal analysis of the different types of obligations under the Convention see Andrew Byrnes and Jane Connors, 'Enforcing the human rights of women: a complaints procedure for the Convention on the Elimination of All Forms of Discrimination against Women?', (1996) 21(3) *Brooklyn Journal of International Law* 679, 707–32, and Rebecca J. Cook, 'State accountability under the Convention on the Elimination of All Forms of Discrimination against Women', in Rebecca J. Cook (ed.), *The Human Rights of Women: National and International Perspectives* (Philadelphia: University of Pennsylvania Press, 1994) (hereinafter *Human Rights of Women*) 228.

9. See in particular Rehof and *JAIWR Commentary*.

10. Although it should be noted that the obligation to eliminate discrimination by the state is more strongly expressed in Article 2 than in relation to private discrimination ('to take all appropriate measures to eliminate').

11. Article 21 provides for reference of a dispute over the interpretation of the Convention to the International Court of Justice, a provision to which many states parties have entered reservations and which has never been used.

12. See the discussion accompanying notes 98–115.

13. 1155 UNTS 331.

14. Article 4 of the Vienna Convention stipulates that its provisions apply 'only to treaties which are concluded by States after the entry into force of the present Convention with regard to such States'. The Vienna Convention entered into force on 27 January 1980; the CEDAW Convention was adopted by the General Assembly on 18 December 1979.

15. *Article 31*: 1. A treaty shall be interpreted in good faith in accordance with the ordinary meaning to be given to the terms of the treaty in their context and in the light of its object and purpose.

2. The context for the purpose of the interpretation of a treaty shall comprise, in addition to the text, including its preamble and annexes:

(a) any agreement relating to the treaty which was made between all the parties in connexion with the conclusion of the treaty;

(b) any instrument which was made by one or more parties in connexion with the conclusion of the treaty and accepted by the other parties as an instrument related to the treaty.

3. There shall be taken into account, together with the context:

(a) any subsequent agreement between the parties regarding the interpretation of the treaty or the application of its provisions;

(b) any subsequent practice in the application of the treaty which establishes the agreement of the parties regarding its interpretation;

(c) any relevant rules of international law applicable in the relations between the parties.

4. A special meaning shall be given to a term if it is established that the parties so intended.

Article 32: Recourse may be had to supplementary means of interpretation, including the preparatory work of the treaty and the circumstances of its conclusion, in order to confirm the meaning resulting from the application of Article 31, or to determine the meaning when the interpretation according to Article 31:

(a) leaves the meaning ambiguous or obscure; or

(b) leads to a result which is manifestly absurd or unreasonable.

16. See discussion at text accompanying footnotes 88–97.

17. See Byrnes and Connors, supra note 8. See also *Quilter* v. *Attorney-General* [1998] 1 NZLR 523, at 531, per Thomas J (New Zealand Court of Appeal).

18. In a number of instances the Human Rights Committee has received fairly prompt objections to views it has expressed in its *General Comments*. The most recent relates to its *General Comment No. 24 (52)* dealing with reservations to the ICCPR: *Report of the Human Rights Committee in 1995*, UN-Doc. A/50/40 (1995), Annex V, at 124. This attracted objections from the United Kingdom, the United States and France: see Byrnes and Connors, supra note 8, 739–40.

19. See, e.g., the references to a number of national and international sources by the Australian Industrial Relations Commission in examining Article 4 of the Convention and the national legislation giving effect to it: *Re Municipal Officers' Association of Australia: Approval of Submission of Amalgamation to Ballot* (1991) EOC ¶92–344 (1991) 12 *International Labour Law Reports* 57. See also the discussion of the same article by the Advocate General in the context of the Equal Treatment Directive: *Marschall* v. *Land Nordrhein-Westfalen*, Case C-409/95 (1998) IRLR 40, 44–5.

20. Reproduced in UN-Doc. HRI/GEN/1/Rev. 3 (1997), at 2–54.

21. 999 UNTS 171.

22. Reproduced in UN-Doc. HRI/GEN/1/Rev. 3 (1997), at 55–99.

23. 993 UNTS 3.

24. Convention concerning Equal Remuneration for Men and Women Workers for Work of Equal Value 1951, 165 UNTS 304.

25. Discrimination (Employment and Occupation) Convention 1958, 362 UNTS 31.

26. Convention of Belém do Pará, 33 ILM 1534 (entered into force on 5 March 1995).

27. During the drafting of the Convention, proposals were put forward that the Convention cover discrimination on the basis of sex, but these did not prevail: see Rehof, supra note 1, 45–7.

28. 660 UNTS 195.

29. The Human Rights Committee has interpreted the guarantees against discrimination contained in the International Covenant on Civil and Political Rights in similar terms: see *General Comment 18 (37)* (1989), UN-Doc. CCPR/C/21/Rev. 3 (1997), 26.

30. Although the wording of Article 1 is not as precise as it might be to achieve this effect (a 'neutral practice' is arguably not one 'made on the basis of sex'), it is clear from the object of the Convention and its drafting history, as well as the practice under the Convention and other similarly worded treaty provisions, that indirect or disparate impact discrimination is covered by Article 1.

31. See Rachel Rosenbloom, 'Introduction' in Rachel Rosenbloom (ed.), *Unspoken Rules: Sexual Orientation and Women's Human Rights* (San Francisco: International Gay and Lesbian Human Rights Commission, 1995) ix, xiv–xxi.

32. See, e.g., *Toonen* v. *Australia*, in which the Human Rights Committee appeared to accept that Tasmanian laws that made criminal homosexual acts between consenting

adult men in private were, in addition to being a violation of the right to privacy under Article 17 of the ICCPR, also a violation of the prohibition against discrimination on the basis of 'sex' under Article 26: Communication No. 488/1992, in *Report of the Human Rights Committee in 1994*, UN-Doc. A/49/40, Vol. II, Annex IX.EE (1994). But see *Quilter* v. *Attorney-General* (1998) 1 NZLR 523 (New Zealand Court of Appeal) (discussion of whether refusal to permit same-sex marriage amounts to discrimination on the basis of sex). See also the opinion of Advocate-General Elmer in *Grant* v. *South-West Trains Ltd*, European Court of Justice, Case C-249/96, (1998) ICR 449 (1998) All ER (EC) 193 (expressing the view that discrimination on the ground of sexual orientation by denying benefits to same-sex partners was discrimination on the basis of sex within the meaning of the Equal Treatment Directive). However, the Court did not share this view: (1998) ICR at 476–80, paras 24–51. See generally Robert Wintemute, *Sexual Orientation and Human Rights* (Oxford: Clarendon Press, 1995) 124–9 and Eric Heinze, *Sexual Orientation: A Human Right* (Dordrecht: Martinus Nijhoff, 1995).

33. Cf. Theodor Meron, *Human Rights Law-Making in the United Nations* (Oxford: Clarendon Press, 1986), 60–3, who argues, based largely on the United States case law, that this extension into the private sector is inappropriate. For a riposte, see Arati Rao, 'Right in the home: feminist theoretical perspectives on international human rights' (1993), 1 *National Law School Journal (Special Issue on Feminism and Law)*, 63, 69–71.

34. CEDAW, *General Recommendation 19* (1992), UN-Doc. HRI/GEN/1/Rev.3, at 128.

35. See, e.g., Catherine Tully, *A Feminist Analysis of the Prohibition Against Sex Discrimination in International Law: The Convention on the Elimination of All Forms of Discrimination against Women*, LLM dissertation, Dalhousie University, September 1998; Hilary Charlesworth, 'What are Women's International Human Rights' in *Human Rights of Women*, supra note 8, 58, 64–5.

36. See Rebecca J. Cook, 'Reservations to the Convention on the Elimination of All Forms of Discrimination against Women' (1990), 30 *Virginia Journal of International Law* 643; Belinda Clark, 'The Vienna Convention reservations regime and the Convention on Discrimination against Women' (1991), 85 *American Journal of International Law* 281 (1991); Liesbeth Lijnzaad, *Reservations to UN-Human Rights Treaties: Ratify and Ruin?* (Dordrecht: Martinus Nijhoff, 1995) 298–370; and Christine Chinkin, 'Reservations and objections to the Convention on the Elimination of All Forms of Discrimination against Women', in J. P. Gardner (ed.), *Human Rights as General Norms and a State's Right to Opt Out – Reservations and Objections to Human Rights Conventions* (London: British Institute of International and Comparative Law, 1997), 64.

37. For example, when it ratified the Convention, New Zealand reserved 'the right, to the extent the Convention is inconsistent with the provisions of the Convention concerning the Employment of Women on Underground Work in Mines of All Kinds (ILO Convention No. 45) which was ratified by the Government of New Zealand on 29 March 1938, to apply the provisions of the latter'. Following denunciation of ILO Convention No. 45 by New Zealand on 23 June 1987, it withdrew the reservation.

38. Vienna Convention on the Law of Treaties, Article 19.

39. *Multilateral treaties*, supra note 4. Among other countries making such reservations with reference to Islam are Bangladesh, Egypt, Iraq, Kuwait, Libya and Malaysia. Other countries where Islam is an official or widespread religion have ratified without reservation or with reservations that are more restricted in scope. See generally Jane Connors, 'The Women's Convention in the Muslim world' in Mai Yamani (ed.), *Feminism*

and Islam: Legal and Literary Perspectives (New York: New York University Press, 1996), 351.

40. There have also been moves at the international level to generate support for a reference to the International Court of Justice of the question of reservations to the Convention, but these have not proceeded very far and do not seem likely to do so. See resolution 1995/26 of the Sub-Commission on Prevention of Discrimination and Protection of Minorities, in which the Sub-Commission requested the Secretary-General to obtain the views of CEDAW and the Commission on the Status of Women on the question 'whether it would be desirable to have an advisory opinion on the value and legal effect of reservations concerning the Convention'. For a summary of the response from the Division for the Advancement of Women, which did not explicitly address the question of whether the Committee thought the reference of the matter to the International Court would be desirable or not, see UN-Doc. E/CN.4/Sub.2/1996/20 (11 June 1996). The International Law Commission has also been studying the question of reservations generally and in relation to human rights treaties, and in 1998 the Sub-Commission once again took up the issue of reservations to human rights treaties: see generally *Reservations to Human Rights Treaties, Working Paper submitted by Ms Françoise Hampson pursuant to Sub-Commission decision 1998/113*, UN-Doc. E/CN.4/Sub.2/1999/28.

41. An example of the objections lodged by states parties against broad-ranging reservations is the objection made by Norway in relation to the reservations entered by the Maldives upon accession:

> In the view of the Government of Norway, a reservation by which a State Party limits its responsibilities under the Convention by invoking general principles of internal law may create doubts about the commitments of the reserving State to the object and purpose of the Convention and, moreover, contribute to undermine the basis of international treaty law. It is in the common interest of States that treaties to which they have chosen to become parties also are respected, as to their object and purpose, by all parties. Furthermore, under well established international treaty law, a State is not permitted to invoke internal law as justification for its failure to perform its treaty obligations. For these reasons, the Government of Norway objects to Maldives reservations.
>
> The Government of Norway does not consider this objection to constitute an obstacle to the entry into force of the above-stated Convention between the Kingdom of Norway and the Republic of Maldives.
>
> States have also objected to reservations made to specific provisions, especially where they concern central articles such as Articles 2, 15 and 16 of the Convention.

42. GA Resolution 44/25, Annex (1989).

43. See, for example, the comments of the Committee at its 17th session (1997) on Israel's maintenance of its reservations and on Bangladesh's decision to withdraw some of its reservations: *Report of the Committee on the Elimination of Discrimination against Women (sixteenth and seventeenth sessions)* (hereinafter *CEDAW 1997 Report*), UN-Doc. A/52/38/Rev.1 (1997), at 90 (para. 157) and 119 (para. 424).

44. *Report of the Committee on the Elimination of Discrimination against Women on its Thirteenth Session*, UN-Doc. A/49/38 (1994) at 13 (hereinafter *CEDAW 1994 Report*). These views are now incorporated in the Committee's guidelines for the content of states parties' reports: *Guidelines for the Preparation of Reports by States Parties*, UN-Doc. CEDAW/C/7/Rev.3 (1996), para. 9..

45. *Report of the Committee on the Elimination of Discrimination against Women (eigh-*

teenth and nineteenth sessions), UN-Doc. A/53/38/Rev.1, Part Two, at 47–50, paras 1–25 (1998) (hereinafter *CEDAW 1998 Report*).

46. For one example, see the case commenced against the government of India in relation to the Indian reservations to the Convention relating to personal laws described in Rani Jethmalani, 'WARLAW's Petition in the Supreme Court of India at New Delhi (Civil Original Jurisdiction) Writ Petition (Civil) No. 684 of 1994 in Rani Jethmalani (ed.), *Kali's Yug: Empowerment, Law and Dowry Deaths* (New Delhi: Har-Anand Publications, 1995) 107–19 (hereinafter *Kali's Yug*).

47. Earlier discussions of the work of the Committee include Roberta Jacobson, 'The Committee on the Elimination of Discrimination against Women' in Philip Alston (ed.), *The United Nations and Human Rights: A Critical Appraisal* (Oxford: Clarendon Press, 1992) 444, and Andrew Byrnes, 'The "other" human rights treaty body: the work of the Committee on the Elimination of Discrimination against Women' (1989), 14 *Yale Journal of International Law* 1. See also Andrew Byrnes, 'The Committee on the Elimination of Discrimination against Women' in Philip Alston (ed.), *The United Nations and Human Rights: A Critical Appraisal* (Oxford: Clarendon Press, 2nd edn 2002) (hereinafter Byrnes).

48. 660 UNTS 195, Articles 8–16.

49. 999 UNTS 171, Articles 28–45.

50. Article 17. On the background to the decision to establish an expert committee rather than adopt some other form of supervisory mechanism, see Burrows, supra note 1, 452–7.

51. Article 17. The requirement is similar for the Human Rights Committee: ICCPR, Article 31 (2).

52. Article 21.

53. Article 22.

54. See Byrnes, supra note 47.

55. For a description of the various activities of the Committee up to 1995, see *Report by the Committee on the Elimination of Discrimination against Women*, Fourth World Conference on Women, UN-Doc. A/CONF.177/7 (1995) (hereinafter *CEDAW World Conference Report*).

56. The reports of the Committee on the work of its sessions are contained in the report of the Committee to the General Assembly, issued as a supplement (generally Supplement No. 38) to the Official Records of the General Assembly, and are obtainable in the official languages of the United Nations from the Division for the Advancement of Women, United Nations, New York. Documents from the earlier sessions of the Committee are to be found in United Nations, *The Work of CEDAW: Reports of the Committee on the Elimination of Discrimination against Women (CEDAW), Volume 1 (1982–1985)* (New York: United Nations, 1989), UN Sales No. E.89.IV.4, and United Nations, *The Work of CEDAW: Reports of the Committee on the Elimination of Discrimination against Women (CEDAW), Volume 2 (1986–1987)* (New York: United Nations, 1990), UN Sales No. E.90.IV.4. For a review of the work of the Committee up to the Beijing Fourth World Conference on Women, see *Report of the Committee on the Elimination of Discrimination against Women (CEDAW) on the progress achieved in the implementation of the Convention*, UN-Doc. CEDAW/C/1995/7 (1995), reproduced as Document 115 in *The United Nations and the Advancement of Women 1945–1995*, United Nations Blue Books Series, Vol. 6 (New York: United Nations, 1995), at 511 (this document is not reproduced in the revised edition of *UN and Women*, supra note 1). Many recent documents of the Committee and information about the Committee and its members can be found on the

website of the Division for the Advancement of Women: http:// www.un.org/ womenwatch/daw/cedaw

57. UN-Doc. A/RES/50/202 (1995). See *Report of the Secretary-General to the General Assembly on the Convention on the Elimination of All Forms of Discrimination against Women, including the text of the proposed amendment to article 20 of the Convention*, UN-Doc. A/50/346 (1995), extracts from which appear as Document 123 in *UN and Women*, supra note 1, at 612.

58. See generally Office of the High Commissioner for Human Rights, United Nations Institute for Training and Research and United Nations Staff College Project, *Manual on Human Rights Reporting under Six Major Human Rights Instruments* (New York: United Nations, 2nd edn 1997) (hereinafter *UN Reporting Manual*).

59. Article 18. The Committee has requested that in general states parties should submit their second reports four years after their initial reports and every four years thereafter: *General Recommendation 1 (fifth session, 1986)*, UN-Doc. HRI/GEN/1/Rev. 3 (1997), at 117; *General Recommendation 2 (sixth session, 1987)*, ibid. On a small number of occasions the Committee has, on an exceptional basis, requested reports from states where there appear to be gross violations of women's rights (including Croatia, Bosnia and Herzegovina, Rwanda, Federal Republic of Yugoslavia [Serbia and Montenegro] and Zaire (now the Democratic Republic of the Congo): see *CEDAW 1997 Report*, supra note 43, paras 344–51 and Annex IV.E.

60. For an overview of the procedure, see Michael O'Flaherty, *Human Rights and the UN: Practice before the Treaty Bodies* (London: Sweet & Maxwell, 1996) 123–38.

61. Committee on Economic, Social and Cultural Rights, *General Comment No. 1* (1989), UN-Doc. HRI/GEN/1/Rev.3, at 56, E/1989/22, Annex III.

62. UN-Doc. HRI/CORE/1, reproduced in International Women's Rights Action Watch and the Commonwealth Secretariat, *Assessing the Status of Women: A Guide to Reporting under the Convention on the Elimination of All Forms of Discrimination against Women* (2nd edn 1996) (hereinafter *Assessing the Status of Women*), Annex B, at 58.

63. UN-Doc. CEDAW/C/7/Rev.3 (1996). These combine and update the separate *Guidelines* which dealt with initial and periodic reports respectively (reproduced in *Assessing the Status of Women*, supra note 62, Annex C, at 59).

64. A detailed guide to reporting under the Convention which provides an article by article list of questions based on the CEDAW's questions and *General Recommendations* is *Assessing the Status of Women*, supra note 62. See also the manual prepared by the United Nations: *UN Reporting Manual*, supra note 58, 305–66.

65. The figures are based on information contained in *Report of the Committee on the Elimination of Discrimination against Women in 2001*, UN-Doc. A/56/38, Annex VIII.

66. Most of the states whose initial reports are more than five years overdue are developing countries, primarily in Africa, Asia and the Caribbean; many of them are small states.

67. See Anne Bayefsky, 'Making the human rights treaties work', in Louis Henkin and John Lawrence Hargrove (eds), *Human Rights: An Agenda for the Next Century* (Washington, DC: American Society of International Law, 1994) 229, at 233–4; International Law Association Committee on International Human Rights Law and Practice, *First Report of the Committee*, in International Law Association, *Report of the Sixty-Seventh Conference, Helsinki, 1996* (London: International Law Association, 1996) (authored by Anne Bayefsky), 336, at 339.

68. Decision 16/III, *CEDAW 1997 Report*, supra note 43, at 1.

69. As of 10 May 1999, over half the reports awaiting consideration by the Committee were combined reports: *Status of the Submission of Reports by States Parties under Article 18 of the Convention, Report of the Secretary-General*, UN-Doc. CEDAW/C/1999/II/2, Annex II (1999).

70. See *Ways and Means of Expediting the Work of the Committee, Report by the Secretariat*, UN-Doc. CEDAW/C/1999/II/4, paras 5–7 (1999).

71. Ibid. at paras 11–16.

72. Ibid. at para. 14.

73. The delay between the submission of the report to the CEDAW and its consideration by the Committee – which for those reports considered at the 1997 sessions of the Committee was, for most countries, in the order of two and a half to three years in the case of both initial and subsequent reports.

74. See supra note 70 at para. 355.

75. Two other members are also assigned the responsibility of preparing questions on that country for the pre-session working group: *CEDAW 1998 Report*, supra note 45, para. 436.

76. Following the Committee's decision to encourage country-specific briefings of the Committee by NGOs outside formal meetings, to permit NGOs to participate in pre-sessional working groups (and possibly meetings of the Committee), and the existing practice of briefing Committee members, much will already have happened before the formal proceedings commence.

77. Prior to June 1999, the questions on periodic reports were prepared by a pre-sessional working group of the Committee, meeting just before the session at which the reports were to be considered. In 1998 the Committee decided that the pre-sessional working group would from 1999 be held at the conclusion of each session. The object of the change was to give states time to provide written answers to the Committee's questions on their reports (and thus avoid the need to spend hours of meeting time reading out answers): Suggestion 16/2, *CEDAW 1997 Report*, supra note 43, at 2; *CEDAW 1998 Report*, supra note 45, Suggestion 18/I, and para. 437.

78. In 1998 the Committee decided to permit these bodies and groups to provide country-specific information to the pre-sessional working group at its meetings: *CEDAW 1998 Report*, supra note 45, Decision 18/I.

79. Decision 16/I, *CEDAW 1997 Report*, supra note 43, at 1. For the latest statement in relation to structure and content of concluding comments see *CEDAW 1998 Report*, supra note 45, at 80–1, paras 395–7 (1998).

80. Article 20 provides that the Committee is to meet 'in order to consider the reports submitted under Article 18 of the Convention', while Article 21 empowers the Committee to make 'suggestions and general recommendations based on the examination of reports and information received from states parties'. Article 22 entitles the specialized agencies to submit reports to the Committee 'on the implementation of the Convention in areas falling within the scope of their activities'.

81. Of particular importance has been the International Women's Rights Action Watch (IWRAW), which has supported the general work of the Committee, as well as providing it with country-specific information. However, many national groups have provided the Committee with information since the early years of the Committee, and interest on the part of both international and national NGOs has been increasing in recent years. See Jane Connors, 'NGOs and the human rights of women at the United Nations' in Peter Willetts (ed.), *'The Conscience of the World': The Influence of Non-*

Governmental Organisations in the UN System (London: Hurst and Co., 1996) 147, at 163–5.

82. Decision 16/II, *CEDAW 1997 Report*, supra note 43, at 1.

83. Ibid. at para. 480 (procedure for the adoption of general recommendations).

84. See supra note 78.

85. For examples of the use of hearings before the Committee on the Elimination on Discrimination against Women to attract international attention to issues see International Women's Rights Action Watch, *Report of the Colloquium of the International Women's Rights Action Watch and the Committee on the Elimination of Discrimination against Women, New York, 13–14 January 1996* (1996); Ilana Landsberg-Lewis (ed.), *Bringing Equality Home: Implementing the Convention on the Elimination of All Forms of Discrimination against Women* (New York: United Nations Development Fund for Women [UNIFEM], 1999), available on-line http://www.unifem.undp.org/cedaw/indexen.htm. For examples of experiences before other treaty bodies in particular cases, see Ursula Kilkelly, 'The UN Committee on the Rights of the Child – an evaluation in the light of recent UK experience', (1996), 8 *Child and Family Law Quarterly*, 105 and Michael O'Flaherty, 'The reporting obligation under Article 40 of the International Covenant on Civil and Political Rights: lessons to be learned (1994), 16 *Human Rights Quarterly* 515 (1994); and Andrew Byrnes, 'The uses and abuses of the reporting procedure under UN human rights treaties: Hong Kong between two systems', in Alston and Crawford, supra note 47.

86. See generally Andrew Byrnes, 'Using international human rights procedures to advance the human rights of women', in Kelly Askin and Dorean Koenig (eds), *Women and International Human Rights Law*, Vol. 2 (Transnational Publishers, 1999) and Women, Law & Development International and Human Rights Watch Women's Rights Project, *Women's Human Rights Step by Step: A Practical Guide to Using International Human Rights Law and Procedure to Defend Women's Human Rights* (1997). For an example, see Moana Erickson and Andrew Byrnes, 'Hong Kong and the Convention on the Elimination of All Forms of Discrimination against Women', *Hong Kong Law Journal* 350.

87. Issues of women's human rights may be pursued not just under the CEDAW Convention but under all of the other treaties, in particular the two Covenants. Since a state will report under each of the treaties only once every few years, it may be necessary to take advantage of a hearing before one of the treaty committees other than CEDAW to raise the same issues. One may also be able to lodge complaints under those treaties.

88. In 1988 CEDAW decided that, as a general rule, 'general recommendations' should be directed to the states parties, while 'suggestions' would normally be addressed to the Economic and Social Council and other bodies in the United Nations system: see Byrnes, supra note 47, at 42–5.

89. In 1997 the Committee decided on a procedure for the adoption of general recommendations (which replaces the rather *ad hoc* approach adopted previously). The three-stage procedure involves (a) a general thematic discussion at an open meeting of the Committee, at which specialized agencies and NGOs could have input; (b) the preparation of an initial draft, to be discussed by a working group of the Committee, leading to the preparation of a revised draft; and (c) the consideration of the revised draft and adoption of the general recommendation by the plenary Committee: *CEDAW 1997 Report*, supra note 43, at para. 480.

90. See Byrnes and Connors, supra note 8, at 766–7.

91. Following the adoption of the general recommendation on Article 12, the Committee confirmed its previous plans to formulate general recommendations on Articles 4 and 2: *Report of the Committee on the Elimination of Discrimination against Women (Twentieth session)*, UN-Doc. A/54/38 (Part I), at 44, para. 433 (1999) (hereinafter *CEDAW 1999 Report [Part I]*).

92. The text of these *General Recommendations* appears at UN-Doc. HRI/GEN1/ Rev.3, at 117–57 and *CEDAW 1999 Report (Part I)*, supra note 91, at 5, paras 1–29 and on-line at http://www.wun.org/womenwatch/daw/cedaw (as well as various other websites), and *General Recommendations 1–22* appear in *Assessing the Status of Women*, supra note 63, Annex E.

93. UN-Doc. HRI/GEN/1/Rev.3, at 135.

94. Ibid. at 145.

95. See, e.g., *Quilter* v. *Attorney-General* [1998] 1 NZLR 523, at 553, per Thomas J (New Zealand Court of Appeal) (referring to *General Recommendation 21*); and *Vishaka* v. *State of Rajasthan* AIR 1997 SC 3011, at 3015 (1998) 3 BHRC 261 (Supreme Court of India) (citing *General Recommendation 19* in relation to sexual harassment).

96. See generally Andrew Byrnes, 'And some have bills of rights thrust upon them: the experience of Hong Kong's bill of rights', in Philip Alston (ed.), *Promoting Human Rights through Bills of Rights: Comparative Perspectives* (Oxford: Clarendon Press, 1999), Chapter 9.

97. See generally Yuji Iwasawa, 'The domestic impact of acts of international organizations relating to human rights', in Alston and Crawford, supra note 47 and Yuji Iwasawa, 'The impact of international human rights law on Japanese law – the third reformation for Japanese women' (1991), 34 *Japanese Annual of International Law* 21, at 26–36 (hereinafter *The Third Reformation*).

98. For the history and content of the draft optional protocol, see generally Byrnes and Connors, supra note 8; Aloisia Wörgetter, 'The draft optional protocol to the Convention on the Elimination of All Forms of Discrimination against Women' (1997), 2 *Austrian Review of International and European Law* 261; Andrew Byrnes, 'Slow and steady wins the race? The development of an optional protocol to the Women's Convention' in *Proceedings of the 91st Annual Meeting of the American Society of International Law* (1997) 383; Ursula O'Hare, 'Ending the "Ghettoisation": The right of individual petition to the Women's Convention' (1997) 5 *Web Journal of Current Legal Issues*; and Elizabeth Evatt, 'The right to individual petition: assessing its operation before the Human Rights Committee and its future application to the Women's Convention on Discrimination', *Proceedings of the 89th Annual Meeting of the American Society of International Law* 227 (1995). See also http://www.un.org/womenwatch/daw/cedaw/protocol/optional.htm

99. For the text of the Maastricht draft, see Byrnes and Connors, supra note 8, at 784–97; (1995) 44 *American University Law Review* at 1419; and (1995) 13(1) *Netherlands Quarterly of Human Rights* 85. For a detailed discussion of the contents of the Maastricht draft, see Byrnes and Connors, supra note 8.

100. Committee on the Elimination of Discrimination against Women, *Suggestion No. 7, Elements for an Optional Protocol to the Convention on the Elimination of All Forms of Discrimination against Women, Report of the Committee on the Elimination of Discrimination against Women (fourteenth session)*, UN-Doc. A/50/38 (1995), at 8.

101. See *Report of the Open-ended Working Group on the Elaboration of a Draft Optional Protocol to the Convention on the Elimination of All Forms of Discrimination against Women,*

Commission on the Status of Women, Report on the Fortieth session (11–22 March 1996), UN-Doc. E/1996/26, Annex III (1996).

102. For a summary of the additional views, see UN-Doc. E/CN.6/1997/5 (18 February 1997).

103. UN-Doc. E/CN.6/1997/WG/L.1 (10 March 1997). A member of CEDAW, Justice Silvia Cartwright of New Zealand, attended the working group's meetings as a resource person. For her views of the negotiations, see Silvia Cartwright, 'Rights and remedies: the drafting of an optional protocol to the Convention on the Elimination of All Forms of Discrimination against Women' (1998) 9(2) *Otago Law Review* 239.

104. Ms Aloisia Wörgetter of Austria.

105. *Revised Draft Optional Protocol, Commission on the Status of Women, Report on the Forty-first Session*, UN-Doc. E/1997/27 (1996), Annex III.

106. For a review of the discussions, see *Report of the Open-ended Working Group on the Elaboration of a Draft Optional Protocol to the Convention on the Elimination of All Forms of Discrimination against Women, Commission on the Status of Women, Report on the Forty-first Session*, UN-Doc. E/1997/27 (1997), Annex III.

107. For a review of the 1998 discussions, see *Chairperson's Summary of Views Expressed and Comments Made by Delegations During Negotiations on the Optional Protocol to the Convention on the Elimination of All Forms of Discrimination against Women*, in *Report of the Open-ended Working Group on the Elaboration of a Draft Optional Protocol to the Convention on the Elimination of All Forms of Discrimination against Women*, Commission on the Status of Women, *Report on the Forty-second Session (2–13 March 1998)*, UN-Doc. E/1998/27, Annex II, Appendix II (1998). For the text that emerged, see *Revised Draft Optional Protocol 1998*, ibid. at Annex II, Appendix I. See Andrew Byrnes, 'An effective individual complaint mechanism in an international human rights context', in Anne F. Bayefsky (ed.), *On the Future of the UN Human Rights Treaty System* (Dordrecht: Kluwer, 2000).

108. For the report of the working group, see *Report of the Open-ended Working Group on the Elaboration of a Draft Optional Protocol to the Convention on the Elimination of All Forms of Discrimination against Women*, Commission on the Status of Women, *Report on the Forty-third Session (1–12 March and 1 April 1999)*, UN-Doc. E/1999/27, Annex II (1999).

109. For the text of the protocol as adopted by the Commission, see Commission on the Status of Women, *Report on the Forty-third Session (1–12 March and 1 April 1999)*, UN-Doc. E/1999/27, at 1 (1999), 38 ILM 763, (1999) 17(2) *Netherlands Quarterly of Human Rights* 213, and on-line at http://www.un.org/womenwatch/daw/cedaw/protocol/adopted.htm

110. Art. 2.

111. Art. 8.

112. Art. 10.

113. Art. 16.

114. Art. 17.

115. See Byrnes, 'Slow and steady wins the race?', supra note 98, at 382.

116. One such example is the passage of the Japanese Equal Employment Opportunity Act following Japan's ratification of the Convention. For others, see Landsberg-Lewis, *Bringing Equality Home*, supra note 85.

117. With regard to the invocation of international standards before courts, in common

law countries there are many more cases in which other human rights treaties are invoked, especially the International Covenant on Civil and Political Rights and, in the United Kingdom, the European Convention on Human Rights.

118.   The following discussion draws on material that first appeared in Andrew Byrnes, 'Pie in the sky or food on the table? The utility of international guarantees of equality for advancing the human rights of women' in *Sino-British Seminar on Women and the Law* (Beijing: Law Department Peking University and Cultural and Education Section, British Embassy, 1997) 57–77.

119.   *Commonwealth v. Tasmania* (the Tasmanian Dam case) (1983) 158 CLR 1 (High Court of Australia) ('holding that the power of the Commonwealth Parliament to legislate with respect to … external affairs' permitted the parliament to enact legislation implementing Australia's treaty obligations).

120.   (1988) EOC ¶92-222, 80 ALR 1.

121.   That the court's conclusion was correct in terms of the Convention can been seen from CEDAW's view as expressed in its *General Recommendation 19 (1992)*, UN-Doc. HRI/GEN/1/Rev.3, at 128, paras 17–18, in which the Committee makes clear its view that sexual harassment is a violation of Article 11 of the Convention and is a form of gender-specific violence.

122.   (1988) EOC ¶92-222, at 77,093. The Court also rejected an argument that legislation applying only to sexual harassment against women was inconsistent with Article 15 (1) of the Convention, which provides that 'States Parties shall accord to women equality with men before the law' (1988) EOC ¶92-222, at 77,095.

123.   For an excellent survey of the political and legal developments leading to the enactment of Hong Kong's sex discrimination legislation, see Carole Petersen, 'Equality as a human right: the development of anti-discrimination law in Hong Kong' (1996) 34 *Columbia Journal of Transnational Law* 335.

124.   The Bill of Rights package consisted of the Hong Kong Bill of Rights Ordinance (Cap 383) – (1991) 30 *ILM* 1310 – and article VII(3) of the Hong Kong Letters Patent, subsequently renumbered as art VII(5) of the Letters Patent. These instruments are reproduced in Andrew Byrnes and Johannes Chan (eds), *Public Law and Human Rights: A Hong Kong Sourcebook*, 20–1, 215–29 (Butterworths, Singapore, 1993); Johannes Chan and Yash Ghai (eds), *The Hong Kong Bill of Rights: A Comparative Perspective*, Appendixes 1 and 2, 525–40 (Butterworths, Singapore, 1993); and (1991) 1 *HKPLR* liv–lxviii.

125.   Sex Discrimination Ordinance (Cap 480), *Hong Kong Government Gazette, Legal Supplement No. 1*, 21 July 1995, A1627. The Ordinance entered into force in late 1996.

126.   See the definition of 'discrimination' in Article 1 of the Convention.

127.   On the sexual harassment provisions of the draft and final versions of the legislation, see Harriet Samuels, 'Upholding the dignity of Hong Kong women: legal responses to sexual harassment' (1995) 4(2) *Asia Pacific Law Review* 90.

128.   Equal Opportunities Bill 1994, *Hong Kong Government Gazette, Legal Supplement No. 3*, 1 July 1994, C991. This bill was also accompanied by a bill to establish a human rights commission to implement the discrimination legislation and other human rights guarantees. Since this bill would have involved the outlay of public money, the governor's consent was required for its introduction into the Legislative Council; that consent was not given. The text of the draft Human Rights and Equal Opportunities Bill appears in George Edwards and Andrew Byrnes (eds), *Hong Kong's Bill of Rights 1991–94 and Beyond* (Hong Kong, Faculty of Law University of Hong Kong, 1995), Appendix, 83–140.

129. Clause 7 of the Equal Opportunities Bill 1994 provided:

Relevance of international instruments

(1) In interpreting this Ordinance, regard shall be had to the fact that a principal purpose of this Ordinance is to give effect to international obligations applicable to Hong Kong.

(2) In interpreting the provisions of this Ordinance, an interpretation which gives effect to international obligations applicable to Hong Kong is to be preferred to any other interpretation, so far as the provisions of the Ordinance permit such a construction.

(3) Subject to subsection (2), in interpreting the provisions of this Ordinance, an interpretation which is consistent with the standards contained in the international instruments referred to in section 2(f) and (g) is to be preferred to any other interpretation, so far as the provisions of the Ordinance permit such a construction.

Clause 2 provided that the objects of the Bill were:

(e) to give effect to obligations applicable to Hong Kong under international treaties to take appropriate steps, including legislative measures, to eliminate discrimination, in particular obligations under the International Convention on the Elimination of All Forms of Racial Discrimination, the International Covenant on Civil and Political Rights and the International Covenant on Economic, Social and Cultural Rights, as applied to Hong Kong;

(f) to give effect to the standards contained in the Convention on the Elimination of All Forms of Discrimination against Women, as adopted by the General Assembly of the United Nations on 19 December 1979; and

(g) to give effect to relevant provisions of the United Nations Declaration on the Rights of Disabled Persons, the United Nations Declaration on the Rights of Mentally Retarded Persons, and the International Labour Organization Recommendations No. 90 on Equal Remuneration for Men and Women Workers for Work of Equal Value, No. 111 on Discrimination in Occupation and Employment and No. 165 on the Rights of Workers with Family Responsibilities.

130. A rule explicitly accepted in Hong Kong in relation to the Hong Kong Bill of Rights Ordinance as constituting 'a well-established principle of common law': see *R* v. *Sin Yau-ming* (1991) 1 HKPLR 88, at 105 per Silke VP (Hong Kong Court of Appeal).

131. The question of the use of international standards in the interpretation of domestic legislation is not merely a matter of academic interest; the consideration or failure to consider a relevant standard can have important practical consequences for the interpretation of a statutory provision. For example, under the Hong Kong Sex Discrimination Ordinance, protection is provided against discrimination in employment, including in the terms and conditions of employment. One of the critical issues in the field of employment is that of equal pay. However, there is an important difference between equal pay for equal work, and equal pay for work of equal value. The latter concept seeks to address, among other matters, sex-segregated workforces and the devaluation of the work that women do in comparison with that done by men, and is likely to be of greater utility than the guarantee of equal pay for equal work. The issue that is very likely to arise under the Hong Kong statute is whether the Ordinance's prohibition of discrimination in terms and conditions of employment guarantees merely equal pay for equal work, or whether it goes further, guaranteeing equal pay for work of equal value. Had the amendments requiring interpretation in accordance with the CEDAW Convention been adopted, the answer would have been relatively clear, since Article 11 of the Convention clearly requires equal pay for work of equal value. See also CEDAW's *General Recommendation 13* (1989) UN-Doc. HRI/GEN/1/Rev.3, at 123, reproduced in *Assessing the Status of Women*, supra note 63, at 67. The danger is, however, that in the

absence of such an explicit reference, the Hong Kong judiciary, for whom sex discrimination legislation is largely a new field, may be inclined to construe the provision more restrictively. Indeed, they might even be encouraged to do so by the fact that an amendment linking the provision to the Convention's standard of equal pay for work of equal value was rejected. The end result would then be a failure to comply with the Article 11 (1) of the Convention. For a discussion of the issue, see Adam Mayes, 'Missing pieces of the jig-saw puzzle: the right to equal pay under the Sex Discrimination Ordinance', paper presented at Conference on Hong Kong Equal Opportunities Law in International and Comparative Perspective, Hong Kong, 10–12 November 1997.

132. Advocates have invoked not just the Convention but also other international obligations, in particular those under the International Covenant on Civil and Political Rights and the International Covenant on Economic, Social and Cultural Rights, both of which have applied to Hong Kong since 1976. Women's groups and human rights groups have utilized the occasion of submission of reports to the relevant supervisory bodies to raise these issues and to draw support from the conclusions of these bodies on the extent to which guarantees of equality have been implemented in Hong Kong. For example, in November 1994, the Committee on Economic, Social and Cultural Rights criticized the lack of legislation in Hong Kong in relation to sex discrimination, as well as various exceptions contained in the government's Sex Discrimination Bill. Similarly, in October 1995 the Human Rights Committee criticized the exceptions and exemptions contained in the Sex Discrimination Ordinance.

133. The following discussion draws on material which appears in Andrew Byrnes, 'Human rights instruments relating specifically to women, with particular emphasis on the Convention on the Elimination of All Forms of Discrimination against Women', in Andrew Byrnes, Jane Connors and Lum Bik (eds), *Advancing the Human Rights of Women: Using International Instruments in Domestic Litigation: Papers and Statements from the Asia/South Pacific Regional Judicial Colloquium, Hong Kong 20–22 May 1996* (London: Commonwealth Secretariat, 1997) (hereinafter *Hong Kong Colloquium*), 39.

134. See generally Benedetto Conforti and Francesco Francioni (eds), *Enforcing International Human Rights in Domestic Courts* (Dordrecht: Kluwer Law International, 1997) and Francis G. Jacobs and Shelley Roberts (eds), *The Effect of Treaties in Domestic Law* (London: Sweet & Maxwell, 1987). For a useful review in relation to the CEDAW Convention, see 'Enforceability of the Convention in domestic legal systems', *Ways and Means of Expediting the Work of the Committee, Report by the Secretariat*, UN-Doc. CEDAW/C/1999/II/4, Annex III (1999).

135. See Henry G. Schermers, 'Netherlands' in Jacobs and Roberts, supra note 134, 109.

136. For a detailed discussion of the question of the justiciability of the provisions of the Convention in the context of an individual complaints procedure, see Byrnes and Connors, supra note 8, at 707–34.

137. The issue can be complicated somewhat in relation to treaties. As a strictly logical proposition it might be maintained that in general a legislature can be presumed to have legislated consistently only with treaties that were in force for the state concerned (or at least in contemplation) at the time when the statute was passed.

138. For an endorsement by Commonwealth judges of this position and the possibilities of drawing on international treaties (including the CEDAW Convention), see *Victoria Falls Declaration of Principles for Promoting the Human Rights of Women* (1994) and *Conclusions of the Asia/South Pacific Judicial Colloquium for Senior Judges on the Domestic Application of International Human Rights Norms Relevant to Women's Human*

Rights, in *Hong Kong Colloquium*, supra note 133, at 3–8. These statements built on the declarations of previous Commonwealth judicial colloquia relating to the use of international human rights norms generally at the national level: see P. N. Bhagwati, 'Creating a judicial culture to promote the enforcement of women's human rights' in ibid. at 20–1. See also J. Cartwright in *Northern Regional Health Authority* v. *Human Rights Commission* (1997) 4 HRNZ 37, at 57–8 (NZ High Court).

139. See, for example, *Attorney-General of Botswana* v. *Unity Dow* [1991] LRC (Const) 574 (High Court of Botswana); [1992] LRC (Const) 623 (Court of Appeal of Botswana) (consideration of various international instruments in deciding whether constitutional guarantee of equality included discrimination based on sex).

140. See, for example, *R* v. *Director of Immigration, ex parte Simon Yin Xiang-jiang* (1994) 4 HKPLR 264 (Hong Kong Court of Appeal) (existence of treaty obligation not to expel a stateless person except on grounds of national security or public morals should be taken into account by decision-maker considering whether to expel such a person on other grounds), citing *Tavita* v. *Minister of Immigration* [1994] NZAR 116 (New Zealand Court of Appeal).

141. *Teoh* v. *Minister for Immigration and Ethnic Affairs* (1994) 128 ALR 353 (High Court of Australia) (relevance of guarantees in the Children's Convention to decision to deport a parent).

142. *Rantzen* v. *Mirror Newspapers* [1994] QB 670 (English Court of Appeal) (guarantee of freedom of expression and its relation to applicable standard for review of jury awards in defamation cases).

143. See, for example, *Canada Trust Co* v. *Ontario Human Rights Commission* (1990) 69 DLR (4th) 321 (Ontario Court of Appeal) (international treaties on non-discrimination, including the CEDAW Convention taken into account in determining whether a sexist, racist and classist charitable trust was against public policy).

144. For a discussion of a number of the African cases, see Marsha Freeman, 'Law, and land at the local level: claiming women's human rights in domestic legal systems' (1994) 16 *Human Rights Quarterly* 559.

145. (1992) LRC (Const) 623 (Court of Appeal), on appeal from (1991) LRC (Const) 574 (High Court)

146. (1990) LRC (Const) 757 (High Court of Tanzania).

147. OAU Doc CAB/LEG/67/3/Rev.5, reprinted in (1982) 21 *ILM* 58.

148. *Dhungana and another* v. *Government of Nepal*, Supreme Court of Nepal, Writ No. 3392 of 1993, 2 August 1995. I am grateful to Ms Sapana Pradhan Malla, of Development Law Associates, Kathmandu, counsel in the case, for providing me with an English translation of the judgment.

149. Article 15 provides, in part, that:

1. States Parties shall accord to women equality with men before the law.
2. States Parties shall accord to women, in civil matters, a legal capacity identical to that of men and the same opportunities to exercise that capacity. In particular, they shall give women equal rights to conclude contracts and to administer property and shall treat them equally in all stages of procedure in courts and tribunals.
3. States Parties agree that all contracts and all other private instruments of any kind with a legal effect which is directed at restricting the legal capacity of women shall be deemed null and void.

150. *Dhungana and another* v. *Government of Nepal*, supra note 148, at p. 17.

151. See, e.g., *Madhu Kishwar* v. *State of Bihar*, AIR 1996 SC 1864. The case involved

a challenge to sex discriminatory inheritance rights under customary law. The court cited extensively from the Convention and noted that 'article 2(e) of CEDAW enjoins this Court to breath life into the dry bones of the Constitution ... to prevent gender discrimination and to effectuate right to life including empowerment of economic, social and cultural rights'. See also *Gaurav Jain* v. *Union of India*, AIR 1997 SC 3021 (citing, among other international instruments, the CEDAW Convention and the Convention on the Rights of the Child).

152. AIR 1997 SC 3011, (1998) 3 *BHRC* 261.

153. The court placed primary emphasis on the guarantees of the right to equality, the right to life and the right to liberty; however, it also noted the relevance of the right to practise any profession or to carry on an occupation, and the right to just and humane conditions of work.

154. AIR at 3013–14, 3 *BHRC* at 264.

155. AIR at 3015–16, *BHRC* at 267–8.

156. See also *Quilter* v. *Quilter* [1998] 1 NZLR 523, at 553 (1997) 4 HRNZ 170 (per Thomas J) where reference was made to CEDAW's *General Recommendation 21*, as part of a general discussion of the nature of the 'family' protected by international law and the guarantees of equality of spouses within marriage.

157. See Rani Jethmalani, 'WARLAW's petition in the Supreme Court of India at New Delhi (Civil Original Jurisdiction) Writ Petition (Civil) No. 684 of 1994' in *Kali's Yug*, supra note 46. See generally Rani Jethmalani, 'Social action litigation in India' in ibid. at 21–35.

158. I am grateful to Ms Rani Jethmalani of WARLAW, counsel in the case, for information about it.

159. Case No. 936-95, Constitutional Court of Guatemala, judgment of 6 March 1996. I am grateful to Ms Elizabeth Abi-Mershed for providing me with a copy of this decision.

160. 1144 UNTS 123.

161. Case No. 936-95, supra note 159, at 2. Article 46 of the Constitution of Guatemala provides that in relation to human rights, international treaties and conventions to which Guatemala is a party prevail over internal law which is inconsistent with the provisions of those treaties.

162. Ibid. at 7. See also the decision of the Constitutional Court of Colombia, in which it considered Article 11 of the Convention in relation to a claim of unlawful and unconstitutional employment discrimination against a female pilot who was unable to undertake flying duties due to treatment for reproductive health difficulties: Case No. T-341/94, 27 July 1994. I am grateful to Ms Adriana de la Espriella for providing me with a copy of this judgment.

163. See, for example, Quentin Bryce, 'The Convention at work: submission to the Industrial Relations Commission in support of the ACTU test case on parental leave', in *Ten Years of the Convention on the Elimination of All Forms of Discrimination against Women*, Occasional Paper from the Sex Discrimination Commissioner, No. 4 (Sydney: Human Rights and Equal Opportunity Commission, 1990).

164. *Re Robert Southern and Department of Education, Employment and Training, Australian Administrative Appeals Tribunal* (1993) EOC ¶92-491. The Tribunal held:

27. It is not only a matter of public interest and importance to maintain a workable sexual harassment complaints and elimination system, it is a fulfilment of the legal responsibilities of any agency under the Act. The Act itself is a fulfilment of

Australia's obligations under the Convention on the Elimination of All Forms of Discrimination against Women, as appears in s 3(a) of the Sex Discrimination Act. These are substantial public interest considerations. It is important, in my view, that complainants or potential complainants be assured of confidentiality when they invoke the mechanism established by their employing agency to complain of sexual harassment. They should be free to withdraw formal complaints without proceeding to a formal hearing (at which of course some of the matters alleged must be made known to the alleged offender) without fear that their identity or the substance of their complaint would be made public. It is in the public interest, not only that justified complaints be treated sensitively and in confidence, but also that other complaints, which may or may not be justified, may be withdrawn without fear of recrimination. To facilitate a different result would be to cause a substantial adverse effect on the management of personnel.

165. *In the marriage of Mahony and McKenzie* (1993) ¶FLC 92-408, (1993) 16 Fam LR 83 (Family Court of Australia).

166. Article 16 (1)(g) provides: 'States Parties shall take all appropriate measures to eliminate discrimination against women in all matters relating to marriage and family relations and in particular shall ensure, on a basis of equality of men and women: ... (g) The same personal rights as husband and wife, including the right to choose a family name, a profession and an occupation.'

167. (1993) ¶FLC 92-408 at p. 80, 185 (Warnick J). However, see also the later decision of the same judge in *Fooks* v. *McCarthy* (1994) ¶FLC 92-450, in which he stressed that in such cases the paramount consideration was the welfare of the child rather than giving effect to the principle of equal status of the spouses by mandating the use of hyphenated family names where each parent wished the child to bear his or her family name.

168. (1993) ¶FLC 92-408 at 80, 185.

169. (1988) EOC ¶92-224.

170. Section 33 provides: 'Nothing in Division 1 or 2 renders it unlawful to do an act a purpose of which is to ensure that persons of a particular sex or marital status or persons who are pregnant have equal opportunities with other persons in circumstances in relation to which provision is made by this Act.'

171. *Re an application for an exemption by the Australian Journalists' Association* (1988) EOC ¶92-236, at 77, 209.

172. *Re Municipal Officers' Association of Australia: Approval of Submission of Amalgamation to Ballot* (1991) EOC ¶92-344, (1991) 12 *International Labour Law Reports* 57.

173. Vote Nos 716–98, Supreme Court of Justice of Costa Rica, 6 February 1998, *Boletín de la Sala Constitucional de la Corte Suprema de Justcia*, No. 59, April 1998, 10. I am grateful to Ms Alda Facio for providing me with information about this case.

174. See, e.g., *Coburn* v. *Human Rights Commission* [1994] NZLR 323, 328 (New Zealand High Court); *Chan* v. *Canada* (1995) 128 DLR (4th) 213, 248 (Supreme Court of Canada), per La Forest J; *Brink* v. *Kitshoff NO*, 1996 (4) SA 197, 214–15 (South African Constitutional Court); *Re B and B: Family Law Reform Act 1995* (1997) FLC ¶92-755 (Full Court of the Family Court of Australia). The Convention has also often been cited in asylum cases, in which the applicant is relying on gender discrimination in the country from which she has fled to bring herself within the definition of 'refugee' in the 1951 Refugee Convention. See, e.g., the discussion of the New Zealand experience in this regard in Rodger P. G. Haines, 'Gender-based persecution: New Zealand jurisprudence', *International Journal of Refugee Law, Special Issue – Autumn 1997, UNHCR Symposium*

on Gender-based Persecution, 129, 141–2. For two Australian examples, see Refugee Review Tribunal, Case N97/19046, 16 October 1997 (reference to the initial report submitted under the Convention by Nigeria in support of a claim for asylum status based on claimant's fear that her daughter and she would be subjected to female circumcision, if returned to Nigeria); and Refugee Review Tribunal, Case N95/07780, 4 September 1997, available on http://www.austlii.edu.au (reference to Convention and other instruments in context of claim for refugee status based on fear of violence from husband and the likely failure of the Indonesian authorities to provide redress in particular case).

175. (1997) NZAR 15, [1997] 1 NZLR 154 (New Zealand Court of Appeal).

176. 'Submissions of amicus curiae', *Ruka* v. *The Queen*, CA No. 45/96, Court of Appeal Wellington.

177. (1997) NZAR at 32 (1997) 1 NZLR at 171.

178. See Yuji Iwasawa, *The Third Reformation*, supra note 97, at 56–61, who describes a number of cases in which Japanese courts appear to have gone out of their way not to apply the clear language of the Convention.

179. See the classic statement of Lord Wilberforce in *Minister of Home Affairs and Another* v. *Fisher* [1980] AC 319, at 328–30; (1979) 44 WIR 107 (Privy Council).

180. Cf. the views of Brennan J of the High Court of Australia in *Mabo* v. *Queensland (No 2)* (1995) 175 CLR 1, at 42: 'The opening up of the international remedies to individuals pursuant to Australia's accession to the Optional Protocol to the International Covenant on Civil and Political Rights brings to bear on the common law the powerful influence of the Covenant and the international standards it imposes.'

181. See, e.g., *Attorney-General of Botswana* v. *Unity Dow* (1991) LRC (Const) 574 (High Court of Botswana); (1992) LRC (Const) 623 (Court of Appeal of Botswana); *State* v. *Ncube*, 1990 (4) SA 151 (Supreme Court of Zimbabwe); *In re Corporal Punishment*, 1991 (3) SA 76 (Namibian Supreme Court); *Rattigan* v. *Chief Immigration Officer of Zimbabwe* (1994) 103 ILR 224, (1994) 1 LRC 343, 1995(2) SA 182 (Supreme Court of Zimbabwe). See generally John Dugard, 'The role of treaty-based human rights standards in domestic law: the Southern African experience', in Alston and Crawford, supra note 47.

182. See Michael Kirby, 'The role of international standards in Australian courts', in Philip Alston and Madelaine Chiam (eds), *Treaty-Making and Australia* (Sydney: Federation Press, 1995), 81.

183. Ibid. at 86–7.

184. Ibid. at 87–8.

185. See, e.g., *The Women's Convention and CEDAW: Opportunities and Challenges in Light of Beijing, A Colloquium of the International Women's Rights Action Watch and the Committee on the Elimination of Discrimination against Women*, New York, 13–14 January 1996, at 16–19 ('NGOs and the Convention: action and reaction with the work of the Committee'), and *Report of the Seminar on the Human Rights of Women and Children: Challenges and Opportunities for NGOs in Monitoring the Implementation of the Convention on the Rights of the Child and the Convention on the Elimination of All Forms of Discrimination against Women*, New York, 21–22 January 1998. See also International Women's Rights Watch Asia-Pacific and Initiatives: Women in Development, *The Convention on the Elimination of All Forms of Discrimination against Women – An Orientation: A Report of Workshops Held in India* (July 1995) at 48–55, and International Women's Rights Action Watch, *The Women's Convention in Africa, Papers Presented at the African Regional Preparatory Meeting for Beijing*, Dakar, Senegal, November 1994 (1996) (contains papers

detailing the use made by national NGOs of the Convention). For on-line materials, see also the International Women's Rights Project, www.yorku.ca/iwrp.

186. *Paulista Convention on the Elimination of All Forms of Discrimination against Women* (*Convencão Paulista Sobre a Eliminação de Todas as Formas de Discriminação contra a Mulher*), mimeo, International Women's Rights Action Watch translation of the Portuguese original.

187. See Margareta Arilha, 'The Convention in São Paulo, Brazil: women's human rights at the local level', paper presented at the International Women's Rights Action Watch conference, Vienna, 14 January 1993. See also Silvia Pimentel, 'Special challenges confronting Latin American women' in *Ours by Right*, supra note 6, 27, at 31.

188. The final outcome of the process was the *Paulista Convention*. As of 1993 some 12 per cent of the municipalities of the state (representing some 45 per cent of the then population of 31.2 million) had signed the Convention: Arilha, supra note 187, at 3.

6

Women and Humanitarian Law

Françoise Hampson

Any discussion of women and humanitarian law involves a consideration of women and war. This at once presents us with conflicting images of considerable mythological power. There is the strand of female fighters from the Amazons, through Boadicea who took on and at first defeated the Romans, and Joan of Arc to the more recent female belligerent political leaders – Golda Meir, Indira Gandhi, Sirimavo Bandaranaike and Margaret Thatcher. Against that is the image of the woman left behind – Penelope waiting for the return of her warrior husband. This suggests the female as vulnerable, passive and in need of protection. Further along that spectrum is the woman as pacifist, in the name of allegedly female characteristics such as nurture, caring and wholeness. The Greenham Common encampment seemed to strike a particular chord not merely in the UK. During the Cold War, the decision was taken to deploy US Cruise missiles in the UK. Women set up a tented village by the perimeter fence of the base, much to the annoyance of local villagers, who thought them dirty and politically suspect. The protest was organized by and for women. Many women elsewhere in the UK were challenged by the knowledge of what was going on at Greenham Common. It challenged them as women. And that happened while Margaret Thatcher was prime minister.

Cutting across this variety of archetypal images from women as warriors to women as earth-mothers is the feminist question. Feminist critiques of the law as a gender-neutral process or system, led notably by Catherine MacKinnon in the USA, eventually reached international law in the early 1990s. Hilary Charlesworth, Christine Chinkin and Shelley Wright, all working from Australia, challenged the alleged neutrality of international law, both in terms of its organizational structure and in terms of its normative structure. If there is any area of international law of which such an analysis holds good, it might be expected to be the institutions for dealing with and the rules applicable to the conduct of fighting. Within the international community, the regulation of the use of force is the apex of the responsibilities of the Security Council. The nature and vocabulary of Security Council discourse appears intended to be ambiguous, to cloud issues, to dictate the terms rather than to seek solutions. In the games of power politics, one may be forgiven for thinking that sustainable solutions that meet the needs of the human race come second to not losing face. The very structure of international law, mediated as it is through states, means that the needs of the human race come second to *raisons d'état*.

I shall look at women and the nature of organized conflict before considering the law on the resort to armed force. That is a completely separate body of law from the rules that apply to the conduct of hostilities. In looking at that second body of rules, I shall be looking both at the extent to which the rules treat women as a separate group, whether as combatants or civilians, and also at the assumptions built into the law, as reflected both by the rules themselves and by the vocabulary in which they are expressed. Then, at the end, I shall look at the legal framework for attempts to bring assistance or relief to women victims of conflict. I shall not deal as such with refugee law. There is obviously an overlap between humanitarian law and refugee law. In the process of looking at these substantive issues, I shall try to consider whether there is anything to the feminist critique of international law and, if so, what.

Women and the Nature of Organized Conflict

Women, conflict and foreign policy When something recognizable as an organized conflict erupts somewhere, it becomes a foreign policy problem for other states. The significance of the problem depends on factors such as: (a) proximity to the territory; (b) strategic value of the territory or its resources; and (c) the likely impact on adjacent states. What role do women have in determining the response of the international community to the conflict? I would suggest that the role of women is the same as that of men. It depends on their position. If they are in foreign ministries, their freedom of manoeuvre will be restricted by all the constraints that appear to beset such institutions. They need to consider the response of their allies or states in the region with which they have special relationships. If we are talking about the influence of women citizens on foreign policy, then it would seem to be neither more nor less than male citizens, where both have the vote on equal terms and are represented in institutions which articulate the response of the 'public', such as the media and the legislature. What would be interesting would be to discover whether that influence would be exercised in a different way or direction from that of male citizens. I suspect that there is more likely to be such a difference in the case of the citizenry generally than in the case of professionals, who seem to acquire a blanket uniform, irrespective of gender. The reaction of the citizenry is not itself unaffected by other influences, notably that of the media. If the news of the conflict is accompanied by images of refugees or the victims of massacres, this may affect the form of the response.

Women seem traditionally to have organized around domestic issues within a country or relief/development issues overseas. I have in mind the work of volunteers raising funds for organizations such as the Red Cross or Save the Children Fund. In my experience, it is much easier to interest women in the work of the Federation of Red Cross and Red Crescent Societies than in the work of the International Committee of the Red Cross, which takes place during hostilities. Men, on the other hand, are readily interested in that. If that empirical observation contains some truth, it may be that women choose not to be involved in the response to the conflict itself, even though they may seek to assist in responding to the consequences of conflict. It may be the case that women get involved in the promotion of peace and of disarmament and in medical and relief activities but not in the conflict itself.

The public/private dichotomy One of the explanations offered for the limited role of women in certain spheres is that those areas are seen as public concerns whereas women's interests concern the domestic or private sphere. There is a problem with the nature of this analysis. There is a risk that, rather than characterizing the sphere in the abstract and then testing it against the facts, a sphere will be defined by reference to whether women participate in it. If they do, it will be defined as private. If not, it will be characterized as public. That would be to make the dichotomy a self-fulfilling prophecy.

Provided one handles the dichotomy with caution, it does seem to contain or to lead to some useful insights. If the private includes the day-to-day incidents of living, that would suggest that women inhabit a sphere in which food, warmth and shelter are key concerns. The affairs of state as such or the conduct of conflict would not generally come into the same sphere. That seems to be confirmed by my observations of the areas of interest of Red Cross members.

The danger lies not in the division itself but in the failure to recognize the degree to which the public impacts on the private sphere – fighting will inevitably cause deaths, casualties and material destruction in the domestic sphere – and the possible devaluing of the private sphere. Public organizations may be involved in providing private sphere help to alleviate the consequences of conflict. It would be interesting to compare the perception of men and women as to the relative significance of the roles of, say, UN peacekeepers and the UNHCR.

The role of the state It was suggested earlier that diplomats may be hermaphrodites on account of the uniform thrown over them by their role. In so far as success depends on conforming to certain ideals and notions as to the role of a diplomat, it may be that traditional diplomatic values are ones commonly associated with men.

The nature of the foreign policy process and the degree to which it is state-centric or mediated through the state may have a distorting effect on what is done. Attempts to transcend such limitations, such as the Earth Summit or the Vienna Conference on Human Rights, have not been successful in those terms. The democratization of the UN, for example, would require some mechanisms for the involvement or participation of individuals or groups, independent of the state. While that has been suggested, by Brian Urquhart among others, I see no sign of any advance in that direction. At the regional level, I know of only one directly elected regional assembly – the European Parliament – and that has very limited powers. The response to a conflict situation will therefore be mediated through the state and state institutions. In the case of the state involved, the barriers of sovereignty and non-intervention will be raised.

Women and the armed forces One needs to guard against two competing tendencies when considering the role of women in the armed forces. The first is to assume that they have never had a fighting role and the second is to overstate the numbers in the past actually involved in fighting. The occasional woman was a member of the armed forces in the not too distant past, often disguised as a man. Some rose to positions of some prominence. Nevertheless, it is clear that fighting was essentially the province of men. In the nineteenth century, women acquired a role as nurses in and after the Crimea. In the two world wars, women played certain support roles but ones that made them targets of enemy action. Women became munitions workers to liberate men for fighting. The munitions factories were targets. Individual women also played roles of great heroism in resistance movements (such as Violet Szabo, the subject of the film *Carve her Name with Pride*). I mention that to show that women have been in positions of danger where they were engaged in offensive action against the enemy but they were, generally, not part of organized fighting units. In relation to the regular armed forces, women did work not only as nurses but as secretaries, ambulance drivers and suchlike. There were separate female military organizations such as the WRNS and the WRAF in the UK.

That has changed significantly in certain armed forces in the past 20 years, as illustrated by Kate Muir's book *Arms and the Woman*. It should be emphasized that it overwhelmingly deals with the armed forces of Western Europe and North America. Women have been given access to an ever wider range of jobs within the armed forces. Some forces stop short of allowing them to be front-line troops but the conflict in the Gulf showed that that does not stop them from becoming casualties. A female US pilot was killed, and one of the US prisoners of war was a woman.

Why should a woman want to join the regular armed forces? I would suggest both for the same reasons as a man and separate reasons. In many countries, it offers a way of acquiring education, a profession and social mobility. They do not expect to have to fight but recognize that they may be called upon to do so. The element that is missing for women is the attraction of a macho physical environment. Are women suited to participation in all roles in the armed forces? My answer would be no. Where a particular function requires a certain muscle-to-body-weight ratio, women will not be able to perform the task. That is not a reason for reducing the job specifications. More controversially, I believe that the non-physical elements that make platoons work suggest that you may be able to have male and female platoons but they should not be mixed. The starting point should be what is the function that X is supposed to perform. If it can be performed by a woman, my second question is in what conditions does the group perform that function. Only in the case of front-line platoons would I argue that the function of the group as a group transcends that of the individual.

Women and irregular armed forces Irregular armed forces come in all shapes and sizes. I would suggest that one needs to distinguish between three types of irregular forces:

- forces fighting for independence or liberation from a colonial power, an occupier or apartheid;
- forces fighting for a particular political vision of society; and
- forces simply fighting for power as an end in itself.

It would be interesting to see research conducted on the role of women in all three types of fighting forces. I do not know of such comparative research. My impression – I put it no higher than that – is that women are to be found playing important roles in the first two types of forces but are much more rarely found in the last. Where women do play a part in a liberation struggle, it is not often in the numbers that would reflect their numbers in society but those who are involved may play very significant roles, militarily and politically. In the case of Eritrea it has been reported that one-third of the fighting forces were female. Charlesworth, Chinkin and Wright suggest that there is a tension between fighting for national liberation and fighting for the liberation of women and that those who saw the former as a way of achieving the latter have been disappointed.

Women and pacifism One movement in which women have been more prominent over the past century is the pacifist movement. What is striking here is that not only are some women actively involved, but those who do not usually join groups or take part in demonstrations seem to respond to the message. It seems as though there is a sympathetic, non-activist constituency in which women may feature disproportionately. In so far as they are passive supporters of an anti-war stance, this would appear to reinforce the stereotype of women as passive and reactive creatures who do not get involved in the public sphere. This is clearly not true of the Greenham Common women to whom I referred at the start. There, opposition specifically to nuclear weapons, a concern with disarmament and women finding a voice as women made for a heady cocktail. It must be remembered, however, that there are also groups of women who, if not militaristic, do come together to support the role of armed forces.

The Right to Resort to Armed Force

Let us now turn to consider the law relating to the use of armed force, looking first at the rules on the resort to armed force.

Prevention The objects of the UN Charter include the maintenance of international peace and security and the prevention of conflict. War in the technical legal sense is precluded under the Charter. A state may only defend itself, which presupposes an unlawful attack, and may only do so until the Security Council takes the necessary action to deal with the source of the threat. The UN Charter is premised on a system of collective security. Over and above that, the UN is supposed to be about the prevention of conflict. In every conceivable respect – economically, politically, morally – prevention is better than cure. The Charter requires that parties settle their disputes peacefully and provides for mediation and conciliation. Why then has not only the UN but the international system generally been so appallingly bad at preventing the outbreak of foreseeable conflicts? The human rights constituency, for example, had sent out warning signals for a couple of years before the tragedy that erupted in Rwanda. What did the OAU or the UN do about it? Commentators sent out increasingly urgent warnings about the situation in the former Yugoslavia. The OSCE, which has special mechanisms supposedly designed for conflict prevention, sent in monitors when the flames had already broken out. Why is the international community unwilling or unable to act to prevent conflict? I would suggest that several factors are involved. First, the prevention of conflict requires the positive pursuit of policies based on values that avoid the causes of conflict. This would require the pursuit of social and economic justice within and between states. This has implications for the international economic system. The argument against the effective insistence on policies pursuing such goals is the usual one – state sovereignty. There is also the unwillingness of the 'haves' to cope with the scale of change necessary to help the 'have nots'. A second factor is the ostrich-like tendency of individuals, groups and states to think that a situation will go away if they ignore it. Third, there is the short-termism that prevents decision-makers from seeing that it is in their own interest to prevent the outbreak of conflict and, fourth, there is the attempt by the state to keep out external interference in the name of sovereignty. This last is a respectable legal argument and one heard with sympathy by states who would react in the same way in the same situation. The state thinks it can handle the situation itself – i.e. achieve the result it wants.

In addition to these factors, one must bear in mind the limitations in the institutions charged with dealing with such situations. The paralysis of the Cold War in the Security Council may be at an end but this does not, of itself, free up institutional structures. No state is going to give *carte blanche* authority to an institution to act swiftly and effectively without giving the state the opportunity to determine what it perceives to be its interest. Effective prevention entails having the means to act swiftly. I see no evidence that states are willing to transfer this authority to international bodies with an independent power of action. The only sign of actual forward movement is within the OSCE, where it is recognized that certain decisions can be taken by consensus minus one, which prevents a single state exercising a power of veto.

The feminist analysis suggest that this paralysis of institutions and the insistence of states on maintaining the illusion of sovereignty is somehow linked to the inadequate participation of women and to the failure of the international system to pay sufficient attention to issues of concern to women. I think that an equally plausible explanation may be found in the nature of bureaucratic structures. If women were to articulate what are perceived as being their concerns, how would they make them effective without creating a cooperative institutional framework? There seem to me to be too many variables in the different world proposed by the feminist agenda for one to be able to say with any confidence that it would avoid the current difficulties or avoid creating new ones.

The resort to armed force   In the case of inter-state conflict, the rules assume an aggressor and a victim of aggression. As already explained, the state is entitled to resort to armed force in self-defence. UN practice suggests that this includes self-defence not only against an actual armed attack but also against an imminent armed attack, on condition that it is overwhelmingly clear that the attack is both certain and imminent. In reserving the right of self-defence, Article 51 of the UN Charter describes it as an inherent right, which suggests that it derives its existence and its scope from outside the Charter, in other words from customary international law, subject only to such limitations as may have been introduced by the Charter. On that basis, states may respond with a proportionate response to armed attacks against them. The formula used in the exchange of diplomatic correspondence between US Secretary of State Webster and British Ambassador Fox in the *Caroline* incident in the nineteenth century still seems to represent the customary law position.[1] The limitation introduced by the Charter is that the right exists until the Security Council has taken the action necessary to maintain international peace and security. The Charter does not say who determines whether such action has been taken or what criterion should be applied.

Article 51 clearly leaves open the possibility of a unilateral response. In addition, of course, the UN may act collectively to undo an act of aggression. The Charter envisaged the formation of a UN standing army, but that has not occurred. Nothing in the Charter precludes the UN from authorizing member states to take collective action, either in the name of the UN or as a UN-authorized coalition. The latter is what happened in the case of the Gulf conflict. It was not a UN operation but a UN-authorized operation. The combined force was not an alliance but a coalition. One may call into question the motives for the operation – certain individuals have suggested that the fate of Bosnia-Herzegovina would have been very different if it had had oil – but the law looks not at motive in this context but merely at legal justification.

So far, I have only considered the classic case of an inter-state armed conflict. The law also addresses other forms of the use of force. In these other cases, the forces of State A are involved in an extra-territorial operation. In the first situation, State A may have been asked to provide assistance to State B in dealing with an insurrection. In the second situation, State A may have been asked to provide assistance to State B in dealing with assistance being provided by State C to the insurgents. Under customary law, it appeared to be permissible for one state to assist another where either the latter was subject to an armed attack by another state or in dealing with insurgents. Restrictions may have developed on the general principle where the so-called insurgents were fighting against a colonial power in the name of self-determination. The ICJ in the Nicaragua Case appears to have reaffirmed the general principle as far as insurgents are concerned but not so far as third state assistance to rebels is concerned. The provision of material assistance by State C to rebels in State B does not justify State A in launching an attack against State C, even though A can attack the rebels in B and State B might be justified in launching an attack, in the name of self-defence, against State C. Clearly much depends on the threshold of assistance. At what point does material assistance become intervention – the supply of weapons, logistics, training or military advisers? The danger of the state claiming to be intervening upon request is that of establishing that a body competent to ask for help did in fact ask for it (such as the USSR in Afghanistan and the USA in Grenada).

Intervention to assist rebels is clearly unlawful, with the possible exception of rebels fighting in the name of self-determination, and has the effect of setting the scene for a confrontation between the two states, since they are on opposing sides (such as India's support for the nascent Bangladesh against Pakistan).

I have suggested that there is some doubt in relation to conflicts in the name of self-determination. Certain General Assembly resolutions, which do not themselves as such have the status of international law but whose contents may reflect customary international law, suggest that certain groups have the right to seek self-determination, if necessary by force. General Assembly Resolution 2625 goes further in saying that it is unlawful to assist a state opposing self-determination and implying that it is lawful to render assistance to those fighting on the other side. While such a position may have been tenable when self-determination was, in practice, confined to colonies and non-self-governing territories, the position is much more problematic now that other groups have seized on the self-determination label and are using it as a justification for claims to secession.

International law does not as such recognize a right to revolt, but it does appear to recognize that some conditions make revolt more likely, and when the fighting reaches certain proportions, the law of neutrality implies that states may or must take note of the facts. The preamble of the Universal Declaration on Human Rights, for example, recognizes that a systematic denial of human rights may lead to revolt.

Is there then a right to intervene to assist those facing widespread and severe persecution, what is commonly called humanitarian intervention? It might appear paradoxical if states in the UN Charter committed themselves to upholding human rights but could do nothing when a state fundamentally violated its own obligations in that regard. It is necessary to distinguish unilateral humanitarian intervention and collective humanitarian intervention in the name of the UN. The proponents of a right of individual humanitarian intervention have argued that it is not inconsistent with the UN Charter, because it is not directed against the territorial integrity of a state and because it is in furtherance of one of the purposes of the UN, the promotion of human rights. They also suggest that it would be intolerable to stand by and watch while people were massacred because the international community could not agree on action. Those opposed to humanitarian intervention argue that it is inherently dangerous because the state will have other reasons for intervening. The protection of human rights is only an excuse. There should be no exception to the prohibition on the unilateral use of force except in self-defence.

The practice of the UN suggests that where the human rights situation in a state is extremely serious, and where the intervention is limited in scope and time, then not too much fuss will be made. The best example is the Tanzanian invasion of Uganda, which helped oust Idi Amin. Nevertheless, individual humanitarian intervention was generally frowned upon.

Collective humanitarian intervention by the UN is clearly consistent with the Charter. Until the end of the Cold War it could not happen because of the veto power of the Big Five. The difficulty at present is that the UN seems to be trying to exercise this function without having laid down the necessary intellectual foundations, or the necessary military organizational capabilities. The circumstances in which the UN should or should not exercise such a function and how they should carry it out were not thought through, and we are paying the price now.

The rules on the resort to armed force do not seem to have any particular role for women. General issues that arise across the board include the way in which the rules are formulated and the underlying assumptions. Chinkin would argue that the content and form of the rules reflects the assumptions of a state-centred system, which means one which pays inadequate regard to women's concerns.

The Rules Applicable to the Conduct of Conflict (*Ius in Bello*) in International Conflicts

Two streams There are two streams in the law of armed conflicts. There are rules that regulate the conduct of the actual hostilities, sometimes called the law of the Hague. That is what we are dealing with here. Later, we will deal with the other stream, which deals with the protection of the victims of conflict, which is often called the law of Geneva. In looking at the rules applicable to the conduct of fighting, or the means and methods of warfare, I shall look at the rules on targeting and the rules on weapon use. The content of the rules should be considered separately from the language in which they are expressed.

Let me start by saying a few words on what I described as the Hague stream of law. The earliest rules on the conduct of hostilities – and they go back to Sun Zu over 2,000 years ago – were in fact the rules that regulated the fighting between the fighting parties. Until recently, with the exception of medieval sieges and some types of civil war, war was fought in defined spaces, almost by appointment. Civilians were not around. You didn't need much in the way of rules on targeting. One can hardly complain that rules that were evolved at a very different time should show the preoccupations of their time. In those days, fighters were overwhelmingly male. The great underlying impulses behind the rules (and it must be remembered that until the nineteenth century the majority of states were European, and they were the ones making international law) were the Judaeo-Christian 'just war' tradition, with its emphasis, at least in theory and when fighting other Christians, on proportionality and the avoidance of unnecessary suffering, and secular, aristocratic notions of chivalry and honour. It may be that the impulse for the other stream of law, Geneva law, showed some of the intellectual, philosophical and moral under-pinnings of the Hague law. It must also be remembered, however, that in the nineteenth century the term 'victims' was not loaded with the disabling pejorative connotations with which it is treated in some quarters today.

We must not only remember that the language in which a rule is expressed is often a reflection of its historical origin, but must also remember an inherent characteristic of law, or a characteristic I would regard as inherent. Law is necessarily about labelling things, making dis-tinctions, drawing boundary lines and compartmentalizing. The feminist lawyers appear not to challenge that but rather to call into question the criteria or compartments used. I issue that warning because there is a danger that any objections to the substantive content of a rule are objections to the fact of making distinctions. If that is the basis of the objection, I do not see how you can have anything that could be claimed to be a legal system.

Means and methods of warfare   Restrictions are put on the conduct of hostilities in two ways – by restricting the targets that can be attacked and by limiting the weapons that can be used. I shall deal with these in turn.

Targeting   The Declaration of St Petersburg made it clear in the preamble that the only lawful objective in fighting was to weaken the military forces of the enemy. This is a reflection of the customary law requirement usually known as the 'principle of distinction'. Fighters must distinguish between military objectives, which can be the lawful target of attack, and others. More recently, this approach has found expression in the 1977 Protocols to the Geneva Conventions. It is important that the implications of the approach adopted should be understood. The Protocol in Article 52 defines a military objective. There is no competing definition of a civilian objective. Rather that is defined negatively – it is not a military objective. That means that you cannot say of an object that it is either a military or a civilian objective, giving you a choice between the two. You must ask only whether it is a military objective. If it satisfies the test in the definition, which is a threshold requirement rather than a balancing one, then it is a military objective and can be attacked, even if it also serves a civilian function. There is no special category for dual-use targets but there is a presumption, in the case of buildings usually used for civilian purposes, such as schools. If, in the circumstances, that object comes within the definition of a military objective, then the presumption is rebutted and the object can be attacked. The one advantage of the definition of military objective is that it has to be applied to every potential target individually. There is no such thing as a class of legitimate targets. Clearly, in practice, military installations are in effect a class of target; therefore each will satisfy the test of a military objective. Where the principle will make a difference is in the case of, for example, bridges, where the need to establish that each one is, on the facts, a military objective may be an indirect way of recognizing dual use.

Having been identified as such, military objectives can be the target of attack. Other things cannot be. The other provisions in the Protocol on targeting are, in effect, no more than an elaboration of the general principle. So civilians and the civilian population cannot be targeted, and neither can civilian property. There are specific rules prohibiting attacks against cultural property, against objects essential to the survival of the civilian population – such as foodstuffs, growing crops and water – against installations containing forces that would be dangerous if they escaped (such as dams and dykes) and attacks likely to cause long-term environmental damage. Furthermore, such attacks are not ever permitted by way of reprisal where the enemy has itself launched such unlawful attacks.

The principle of distinction, while a good start, would not protect the civilian population from very much. After all, it does not make military sense to target the civilian population. To win, a force has to defeat the armed forces of the enemy. Attacks directed against the civilian population represent a waste of firepower and effort.

A second principle enters into play that, potentially, has more impact on the protection of civilians. That is the principle of proportionality. This must be distinguished from proportionality in the *ius ad bellum*, the resort to armed force. The requirement of proportionality means that an object cannot be targeted or an attack against a military objective launched if it is likely to result in disproportionate casualties among civilians in relation to the military advantage anticipated from the operation. This raises a number of questions. First, is there a positive requirement of proportionality, or is it rather that casualties must not be disproportionate? The second would be a higher threshold and, in effect, would only prohibit a wanton disregard for the civilian population. Second, proportionality requires a balance to be struck but it is between not only two different things but two different types of things. How does one assess the balance? Third, on a slightly more positive note, it would seem that the formula as articulated in Protocol I requires commanders to consider the effects of their actions. If so, this addresses Walzer's objection to the application of the doctrine of double effect, familiar to theologians and moral philosophers. Under that doctrine, as traditionally formulated, you must seek only the good result and that good result must outweigh the negative consequences but there is no positive obligation to consider the negative consequences and to do your best to minimize them. Walzer, writing in relation to the war in Vietnam, wanted to reformulate the doctrine so as to make it necessary to consider those negative consequences. The formula used in Protocol I has done that. The fourth implication of the proportionality principle needs to be considered carefully because it reveals a difference between human rights law and the law of armed conflict, and the language in which it is expressed often grates on civilians – men and women alike. A large number of dead civilians is not necessarily a violation of the laws of war. Under human rights law, which concerns the civil liability of the state, you might argue that the state's obligation to protect the right to life means that a large number of dead civilians is *prima facie* evidence of a breach of the obligation. Under the law of armed conflicts, however, you would need to ask were the civilians targeted, and, if not, whether the attack was disproportionate. In other words, the law of armed conflicts recognizes that in an armed conflict civilians will be killed and their deaths will not necessarily be unlawful. Expressed in those terms, it seems obvious. What really makes people uncomfortable is describing such deaths as 'collateral casualties'. The choice of phrase changes them from men, women and children into objects. Furthermore, 'collateral' implies something peripheral, not central. It seems to minimize them, while dehumanizing them. This presumably represents an attempt by the military to keep such deaths at arm's-length. It may be that they need to speak in these terms on account of their humanity. If that is the reason then, in my eyes, that reduces them. I am more impressed by someone who carries out an action he/she believes to be right while acknowledging honestly the negative consequences than by a person who avoids facing those consequences by using depersonalized language. I would suggest that this is mainly a problem for pilots, commanders and military press men. The soldier on the ground confronted with the evidence of his own eyes has to cope with his reaction to dead civilians.

Finally, it can be seen that to evaluate proportionality one needs to know how an objective was attacked. The first question is 'was it a military objective?' If not, the attack was unlawful. It is only after it has been decided that it is a military objective that the second principle comes into play. At that stage you need to ask with what weapon the target is to be attacked. To attack a specific structure within a built-up area with B52 bombers or Scud missiles is likely to lead to a high rate of casualties in the surrounding area. That would not be the case with an isolated target. To attack the structure with a Cruise missile, however, might reduce the number of casualties to a legally acceptable level.

That leads on naturally to a consideration of the rules on weapon use. Before turning to that, however, I should like to make one final point about targeting. Women are often, rightly or wrongly, seen as having more awareness of inter-generational environmental issues. That was, for example, a common theme running through the objections of the Greenham Common women to the deployment of Cruise missiles. To what extent are long-term environmental considerations relevant to the conduct of war? That covers a very wide range of possible scenarios. There is the release of noxious substances – from the obvious case of nuclear or bacteriological weapons, which are inherently dangerous, to substances whose inappropriate release can cause harm (such as oil). Then there is the detritus of war – not only unexploded sub-munitions and rusting equipment abandoned where it ceased to be operational, but also the contemporary plague of abandoned minefields. The indiscriminate use of mines in unmarked minefields represents a long-term and very serious problem in countries such as Angola, Iraq, Somalia and Cambodia. It prevents or makes very dangerous the return of refugees. It causes serious dislocation in food production and causes massive social and economic problems in what are often subsistence economies. There are three relevant legal rules and an additional text specifically on the use of landmines. So, is the problem lack of respect for the law or inadequate rules? I would suggest both. While it looks as though the Iraqi attacks on Kuwaiti oil fields were illegal and the majority of problems with landmines arise from their unlawful use, I would argue that the rules on targeting and on weapon use fail to take adequately into account the cumulative and the long-term impact of certain types of attack. The old Hague law of 1907 prohibits wanton destruction. While that should be sufficient to deal with the case of the Kuwaiti oil fields, the threshold is very high. There is a convention on the use of the environment as such as a weapon of war (such as the introduction of chemicals into the atmosphere to make it rain), but that is not really the issue here. A much bigger problem is the impact on the environment of actions not designed to manipulate the environment. The 1977 Protocols prohibit attacks that will result in widespread, long-term and severe damage to the environment. The requirements are cumulative and the threshold is high. It could be argued that the illegal use of mines could come within this prohibition. The problem there is the existence of a special text dealing specifically with landmines – Protocol II to the 1980 Conventional Weapons Convention – which does not address the environmental issue as such. The Protocol has been revised to make more rigorous the criteria that must be satisfied in order for any use of anti-personnel mines to be lawful. Furthermore, a group of states led the way in formulating a treaty adopted in Ottawa in late 1997, which commits ratifying states to a ban on the use, manufacture or stockpiling of anti-personnel mines. What is striking is the apparent inability of the military to take into account the long-term social and economic consequences of their actions. Their line seems to be: 'We do not want to have to fight but sometimes have to do so. Landmines are a militarily useful weapon to channel the enemy or delay the enemy.' The experience of NGOs suggests that when serving officers are confronted with the after-effects of the indiscriminate use of mines in countries such as Cambodia, they get a real shock and become strong supporters of the campaign to ban the use of anti-personnel mines. This suggests a certain lack of moral imagination on the part of armed forces. Such a lack of imagination may be necessary if they are to fight at all. But, in that case, it is up to some other part of the military machine to take on board the long-term effects of their actions and to create rules that will mitigate those effects when applied by those without the imagination to work it out for themselves.

Weapon use   Turning back to the question of weapon use generally, there are three basic principles. One of them shows its origin in codes of chivalry and honour. The first principle is that it is unlawful to use a weapon that causes unnecessary suffering or superfluous injury. This applies not just to non-combatants but to the combatants themselves. The rule is found both in customary law and in treaty law. Quite apart from the odd notion that some suffering is by implication necessary, what does this mean? It means that combatants can kill one another but there are certain types of injury that they cannot inflict on one another – those injuries that are very difficult to treat or render death inevitable. The classic example is 'dum-dum' bullets, which fragment on impact, so that there is a small entry wound but a huge cavity is created inside and the bullet does not exit. Low-velocity ammunition and 'tumbling bullets' may nowadays give rise to similar injuries. At first sight it seems extraordinary that you can kill but not cause certain injuries. There is a parallel in human rights law. In certain circumstances the state can lawfully use lethal force, but the prohibition of torture, inhuman and degrading treatment is absolute.

While the prohibition of the use of 'dum-dum' bullets seems objectively justifiable, there are some very interesting other applications of the principle. The use of lethal gas, at least the first resort to lethal gas, is unlawful. That could be based on the second principle, the prohibition of the use of indiscriminate weapons, because it is very hard to control its spread. But another basis on which exception is taken to its use is that it is invisible. It is, in a sense, a secret weapon. There are analogies with poison and poisoned arrows. Their use is prohibited under customary law, apparently on the basis that it is unfair to use a secret weapon. This has a whiff of the concept of honour about it.

Even more striking are the recent discussions on the use of laser weapons. The Gulf War showed that, as target designators, laser beams have a useful role to play in directing bombs and helping precision targeting. There is a problem if lasers are used in order to blind. If they contact the naked eye, that may be their effect. Research has shown that the higher the level of battlefield stress, the shorter period of time for which forces are effective. One of the elements in battlefield stress is the fear of being maimed, not killed. Soldiers fear maiming more than they fear death. If you remember that they are predominantly young, male and in an environment dominated by physical activity, that may be easier to understand. Maiming, in the view of soldiers, includes blinding. It would be interesting to know whether female soldiers react in the same way as male soldiers to the fear of being maimed.

I mentioned earlier the issue of secret weapons and the impression that they are seen as representing, in some sense, cheating. That sense is also to be found in customary and treaty law on ruses of war and perfidy. These represent tactics rather than weapon use. A ruse of war is something designed to mislead the enemy. It is legitimate. Perfidy, on the other hand, is to claim the protection of an international protected symbol and then to abuse that protection and to gain an advantage over the enemy by that abuse. An example would be to drive a vehicle marked in the proper way with a red cross and then to open fire from the vehicle. The enemy would have believed that he was not free to attack the vehicle because it was transporting the wounded and sick. The rule can be analysed in two ways. First, it is like the children's game 'tag' where there is a sign for suspending the chase. In that sense, the rule is based on notions of fair play. It also serves the very practical purpose of reinforcing the protection to be given to certain symbols. Once one side starts abusing a symbol, the other party is likely to assume that it is always abusing it. Those being protected by the symbol are the ones who will suffer.

The second general principle regarding weapon use is that the use of an indiscriminate weapon is unlawful. This is closely related to the targeting rule on attacks likely to cause disproportionate civilian casualties. This principle is one reason for the prohibition of the use of gas. It would also apply to the use of B52s and Scud missiles against specific targets. That would represent the unlawful use of a potentially lawful weapon. Similarly, for some states landmines are lawful weapons that may be used unlawfully if they are used indiscriminately. It could be argued that the prohibition of the use of weapons that cause long-term and widespread and severe environmental damage is a specific sub-head of the prohibition of the use of indiscriminate weapons.

The third principle is that weapons may be subject to specific treaty bans. This may overlap with the other two principles in that it is easier to ban a weapon by treaty where it violates some other principle. In addition to the treaty bans already mentioned, such as the 1899 Hague Declaration on Dum-Dum Bullets, the 1925 Geneva Gas Protocol and the 1980 UN Conventional Weapons Convention, one should also add that certain areas of the globe are by treaty nuclear-free zones. In so far as it is possible to envisage a discriminate use of nuclear weapons that would only cause injury to combatants and would not cause severe environmental damage, the treaty ban is a useful supplement to the other two principles.

We cannot leave the question of weapon use without some comment on what was perceived to be a gender difference on the response to the television coverage of the Gulf War. Certain commentators suggested that men got hooked on the technology and the vocabulary. They were fascinated by the equipment, by smart bombs and by the mechanics of the fighting. They readily took to using phrases such as 'collateral casualties', which had the effect of distancing them from the realization that they were talking about dead civilians, people like themselves. If members of the armed forces need to distance themselves from the consequences of their actions, at least at the time, that is not true of civilians. If a conflict is being fought in our name, it seems to me that we have a responsibility to be fully aware of the implications. The commentators suggested that women were much less interested in the technology and were more aware of the civilian casualties.

So far, we have considered the rules on the conduct of hostilities as they are presented in customary and treaty law. They are not discriminatory in the sense that gender simply does not appear to be relevant. That is understandable, in so far as historically the overwhelmingly majority of fighters were male. That is to neglect, however, women serving with armed forces but not in a combatant role, and the more recent development of the use of women in a combat role.

Women as fighters In regular armed forces, women play an increasingly important role as combatants on two counts. First, there are now more of them and in a greater variety of roles. Second, technological development means that it is not only frontline forces who are vulnerable. In the past women were often excluded from roles by reference to whether they were frontline functions. The purpose of that criterion was to afford women protection. The effectiveness of that protective criterion has been reduced at the same time as women have challenged their exclusion from combat roles.

The presence of women makes a difference to the running of the armed forces in the field – or is thought to do so – in relation to such issues as hygiene and sanitary facilities. I would suggest that equally if not more problematic is the role of women as mothers. In the Gulf War, there were photographs in newspapers of American servicewomen having to leave babies only three or four weeks old. Some of them seem to have experienced that as more of a problem than the army authorities, who expected them to behave like any other serviceman. It would be interesting to know whether in fact there is a difference of perception and experience here. It may be that women are seen by the authorities as only posing a problem in the field, whereas the big problem for women may be going into the field at all – at least in the case of new mothers – rather than the conditions when they get there.

Fundamental issues are raised by certain objective differences. It is generally true that women do not have the strength-to-weight ratio of men because their musculature is different. Some jobs can be done by two men or three women. The first reaction is that strength is not a key factor in all jobs – but does that not mean privileging women if they are not exposed to the full range of tasks a man would have to fulfil? Second, one could keep the same standards of physical fitness, recognizing that very few women would make the grade. But would it not be more disruptive to have the odd woman scattered here and there, rather than a certain proportion throughout the armed forces? Third, what about the argument that women are entitled to serve their country in that way, if they want to do so? In other words, it is up to the armed forces to arrange matters so that they can do so. That is a late twentieth-century argument that clashes with the earlier notion that men joined the armed forces to protect women and children at home. Throughout humanitarian law, there is a tension between the principle of women as objects of protection and the unrecognized principle of women as having the right to participate.

In the case of irregular armed forces, this is seen as posing much less of a problem, but I suspect that that is merely because women are free to volunteer. There is no need for policies on equality of access or the provision of special facilities simply on account of the practical distinction between regular and irregular armed forces. In both the recent and more distant past women have played an important role in irregular forces. In the case of conflicts to secure liberation from colonial rule, there was a certain tension for women participants. On the one hand, their participation appeared to reinforce claims for equality or to be evidence that it was achieved. On the other hand, those who came into power after independence often sought to reinforce the constraints of what were patriarchal societies. This was but another form of the problem that had affected Western European women after the two world wars. During those conflicts, they had been able to assume roles not previously open to them to liberate men to fight. Once the war was over, they were expected to go back meekly to the kitchen stove. It is instructive to look at changes in the right of women to vote and the dates of such changes. They often followed the evidence that women could undertake jobs not previously undertaken and accompanied their return to the home.

Women have also served as non-combatant members of armed forces. This has included roles such as drivers, messengers and secretaries. This indicates clearly that the problem was not seen in terms of the presence of women in armed forces. Where they are perceived as causing a problem is if they are to be fully integrated, rather than serving as discrete units attached to other parts of the forces and, second, if they are to be allowed to engage in combat.

One field in which women have played a key role for over a century is that of nursing. This did not pose the usual challenge for the armed forces since, as we shall see, the medical function is a protected one. Since the wounded and sick are protected from attack, those caring for them are also protected. This includes both doctors and nurses. At first, there was discrimination in the exercise of the medical function in that doctors were male and nurses female. That was a reflection of the situation in medicine generally and was not confined to the armed forces. While nowadays that would be seen as discrimination, it is not clear that that was how it was perceived at the time when Florence Nightingale first organized nurses for the Crimea. They may rather have been seen as two separate functions – doctoring and nursing – rather than one function. The existence of female military nurses is evidence that women were not seen as in need of protection from all contact with the battlefield. It was not that warfare did not involve them. It was rather that they should not be involved in fighting but could be involved in a caring role. This represented a significant development in so far as it represented a recognition that women were part of the community whose lives were affected by the existence of conflict.

Protection of victims of conflict – women and victims of conflict

The Geneva Conventions of 1949 are sometimes referred to as Conventions for the Protection of Victims of War. In fact, the official name of each Convention depends on the group being protected.

Geneva Convention I deals with wounded and sick, Geneva Convention II with the wounded, sick and shipwrecked, Geneva Convention III with Prisoners of War (POWs) and Geneva Convention IV with civilians in the power of the enemy, either because they are in occupied territory or because they are in a state with which their home state is fighting. What these groups have in common is:

- vulnerability;
- they are in the hands of the enemy; and
- they currently pose no military threat to the enemy, even if, in the case of former combatants, they did previously.

It is therefore clear that the word victim carries or was intended to carry no pejorative or disabling connotations. Indeed, it was intended rather to convey the need and the obligation for protection. Before criticizing the language of the Conventions, one should remember when they were drafted and what they are designed to do. They are designed to provide rules for the conduct of armed forces in dealing with particular groups. The armed forces may well be used to the notion of the protection of civilians. In many cases, they may think they are fighting to protect their own civilians. In that case, it may make psychological sense to make reference to that familiar concept when trying to influence their behaviour towards those of the enemy in their control.

Terminology – disabling Feminists and criminologists nowadays take exception to the use of the term 'victims'. They see it as suggesting a passive response to a situation. In that sense, it is a disabling idea. It defines the person by reference to the experience, with the emphasis on the experience. That event is something that happened at the instance of the perpetrator. To speak of a 'victim' is therefore seen as putting the emphasis on the perpetrator rather than on the survivor of the event. In view of the warning about the way in which the term is used in the context of the law of armed conflicts, it is not enough to look at the vocabulary used. Rather one must examine the substantive rules to see whether they treat women as passive objects or whether they recognize the fullness of their personality. The first question is whether women are treated as a group apart from other members of the class in which they find themselves.

Women as a separate group because they are women – POWs While women as fighters are treated by the law no differently from other fighters, what happens upon capture? Are they treated in the same way as male ex-fighters? If any distinction is drawn between the two groups, on what is it based? If one is looking for something like a 'control group' – that is to say another discrete group of ex-fighters whose separate treatment, if any, one might want to compare with that of female ex-fighters – such a group is captured child soldiers. The legal status of a captured ex-fighter is the same for both sexes. If the fighter qualifies for combatant status as defined in the Regulations annexed to Hague Convention IV, he or she is entitled to prisoner of war status. That is usually a highly desirable status because it means that you cannot be prosecuted for the fact of having fought but only for any war crimes you may have committed during the hostilities. The fact of your capture will be made known to your own side and you should be allowed to send communications of a strictly personal nature to your family, so that they at least know that you are alive. The ICRC should have access to POW camps, which is one of the ways of ensuring respect for the rules. The third Geneva Convention of 1949 lays down the most detailed rules for the treatment of POWs, covering everything from day-to-day living to disciplinary measures, particularly in the event of escape and recapture and repatriation. There are three issues we need to consider in relation to the treatment of female POWs: (i) whether there are any provisions specific to women; (ii) whether there are issues or considerations likely to be of particular concern to women that are not addressed at all or addressed in a fashion more suitable for men; and (iii) whether there are rules that seem to show a particularly male frame of reference, including notions of chivalry and fair play.

Specific rules relating to women The specific rules relating to women take two forms. They may treat them as separate but equal, as under Article 25 on the standard to obtain in places where POWs are quartered or accommodated, which provides that: 'In any camps in which women prisoners of war, as well as men, are accommodated, separate dormitories shall be provided for them.' The other type of rule treats women as being in need of special measures of protection or respect (for example, Article 14 provides that 'women shall be treated with all the regard due to their sex and shall in all cases benefit by treatment as favourable as that granted to men'). While the general provision on hygiene and sanitation provides for separate lavatories for women (Article 29), the provisions on medical care for POWs make no special reference to women. Geneva Convention I, which deals with wounded and sick fighters, provides that women shall be treated with all consideration due to their sex – which is not very specific. There is a similar provision in Geneva Convention II, which deals with the wounded, sick and shipwrecked. The general provision on POW labour requires the detaining power to take into account the age and sex of the prisoner as well as other attributes, but none of the detailed provisions specifically refers to women. There is no mention in Geneva Convention

III of the possibility that a woman may be pregnant. The other provisions of Geneva Convention III that refer to women follow this model. That is to say that the rule is to be found in the general provision, rather than its specific elaboration, and is designed to ensure either equal treatment as compared to women in the forces of the Detaining Power or men or, alternatively, provides for the separation of women from men particularly with regard to sleeping arrangements and sanitation. This suggests that either women or the conjunction of men and women is seen as some sort of threat to discipline and good order. Even if this is based on experience, and to that extent objectively justifiable, it seems to suggest an acceptance of male imposed patterns of conduct, rather than any attempt specifically to restrain that conduct. The provisions in question are:

- Article 88, which provides that a woman POW shall not be awarded a more severe punishment in disciplinary proceedings than a male or female member of the armed forces of the detaining power;
- Article 97, which provides that women POWs undergoing disciplinary punishment shall be confined in separate quarters from male POWs and shall be under the immediate supervision of women; and
- Article 108, which contains a similar provision in relation to those women serving a sentence imposed by a court. One interesting point is that only those detained other than merely as POWs must be under the supervision of women. There is no such requirement in the case of those simply detained as a POW.

I will look in a moment at the question of whether issues of specific concern to women are addressed, but there is one provision to which I would like to draw your attention. In this case, it has been recognized that there is a need for a specific institution, but it has not been recognized that there may be a need for separate female representation or participation. Under Articles 79–81, where there are POWs but no officers, POWs are to elect representatives whose job is to represent them before the military authorities, Protecting Powers, the ICRC, and so on. Where there are officers, it is assumed that they do the job! There is no separate provision for female representation. There are clearly two competing arguments here. Either having female representatives would be a form of discrimination, which the Conventions seek to avoid, and would ghettoize certain concerns by having them labelled women's issues when an issue affecting specifically women ought nevertheless to be a concern of men. Or, alternatively, women's concerns will in practice be downgraded or not heard at all unless they can participate and be represented in their own right. This is the one area that leaps out at me where it seems to me they have failed to treat women as a separate group when it would be reasonable to do so. The

Convention may be a child of its time but this position was not changed with the conclusion of the 1977 Protocols. Protocol I did, however, make one innovation. Protocol I has the advantage of dealing with situations in which all four Geneva Conventions apply. In other words, it does not have to address wounded and sick women, shipwrecked women, female POWs and so on. It can address the issue of women across the board. There is indeed such a provision. Article 76 of Protocol I focuses on two specific attributes of women – their vulnerability to attack taking a sexual form, and women as mothers. It is a classic case of the two great female stereo-types: woman as Eve or the Virgin Mary. Article 76 provides that women shall be the object of special respect and shall be protected in particular against rape, forced prostitution and any other form of indecent assault. Paragraph 2 requires that detained pregnant women or mothers having dependent infants shall have their cases considered with utmost priority (why not male civilians with dependent children?) and Paragraph 3 requires parties not to carry out the death penalty on such women and to avoid even pronouncing the death penalty. Article 76 does not as such address women as fighters or POWs, except in so far as they are pregnant or have dependent children. It is not clear whether the mothers in question are assumed to have the dependent children with them in detention.

We have dealt with women as ex-fighters and have seen that one of the dangers in labelling people as 'victims' is that it makes them into objects. So, before looking at the rules on women as civilians, which at least implies that they are human, is there any evidence that women are seen as objects and seen through the eyes of male non-objects?

Women as protected objects There is one body of law that does seem to treat women as objects, and frail vessels at that, but that is hardly surprising given its age. The fourth Hague Convention of 1907 has Regulations annexed to it concerning the conduct of war on land. The Nuremberg Tribunal held that the Regulations represent customary law. Section III deals with belligerent occupation and with military authority over the territory of the hostile state. One should remember not only the time when the Convention was concluded but also that it is specifically directed at the armed forces – at that time, men. Nevertheless Article 46 of the Regulations now has a strange ring to it: 'Family honor and rights, the lives of persons and private property ... must be respected.' What is meant by family honour? I would suggest that what is meant is that a man must not be dishonoured by having his mother, sister or daughter raped or sexually assaulted. Not only is this to deny that women may have their own sense of honour (unless they are included) but it is to see them merely as a possible source of dishonour. I find this way of addressing the protection of the occupied civilian population odd, even given the date of the Convention. It does, after all, prohibit pillage, and the phrase 'rape and pillage' is common enough in the English language. But instead the issue is seen as one of family honour. I suggested earlier that some of the provisions of the Geneva Conventions may also appear to be based on the notion of women as objects.

Women as civilians We have already seen that civilians are to be protected from attack, including by their own forces. Here we are dealing with the protection of civilians as 'victims' of the conflict, that is to say in the hands of the enemy – either in occupied territory or in the land territory of the enemy. So what we are looking for here is evidence as to whether women are singled out as a group among such civilians and, if so, the nature of the special provisions affecting women. There are rules on the treatment of enemy civilians in the Regulations Annexed to the fourth Hague Convention of 1907, the fourth Geneva Convention and Protocol I of 1977.

The only provision relating to women in the Hague Convention is the one already mentioned about family honour. The main thrust of the Convention is the administration of the territory. It sets limits on the authority of the occupying power to change the law in the territory and to take property.

The principal text on the protection of civilians is the fourth Geneva Convention. There are first general provisions (Articles 1–12). Then there is a brief section dealing mainly with medical matters, which covers the civilian population generally, both civilians in the hands of the enemy and civilians generally (Articles 13–26). Then there is a section which covers both occupied territories and civilians in the hands of the enemy but not civilians generally (Articles 27–34). Then Articles 35–46 deal with civilian aliens in the territory of a party to the conflict. Articles 47–78 deal with occupied territories. There are then detailed provisions on internment, which apply both in occupied territories and to aliens in the hands of a party to the conflict (Articles 79–135). Then a brief section deals with information and tracing (Articles 136–41). The rest of the Convention deals with the execution of the provisions of the Convention.

The provisions dealing with women are, by and large, similar to those dealing with female POWs, but there are one or two interesting differences. First of all, there is a provision in the section on medical measures for the protection of all civilians. Not surprisingly, they deal with otherwise healthy women only if they are pregnant or the mothers of children under seven. If the women are injured or sick they are covered as such. I can see the need for special provision for healthy pregnant women. The further extension for mothers of children under seven seems rather to be designed to protect the children.

Generally speaking, the protection of women is addressed by means of a sentence inserted into a general provision. The exception is a very specific provision in sections on detention and internment. So, for example, all protected persons must be respected (Article 27). That includes respect for their person, their honour and family rights. They are to be protected against acts of violence or threats of them. Within that context, the honour of women is to be respected and they are to be protected against rape, enforced prostitution and indecent assault. I shall come back to the issue of rape in war later. Equally, women are not to be discriminated against. These general provisions on protection apply both to aliens in the territory of a party to the conflict and in occupied territory.

Again, in both cases, there is not only special protection for expectant women and the mothers of children under seven but, in the case of occupied territories, such women may benefit from preferential treatment. In other words, there are both non-discrimination provisions to protect all women against adverse treatment and the possibility of preferential treatment for one group of them.

Where women are detained or sentenced in occupied territories, they cannot receive a discriminatory penalty. They are to be confined in separate quarters and under the direct supervision of women (Article 76). In the case of internment, women on their own are to be accommodated in separate places of internment, not merely separate quarters. Where, as an exceptional and temporary measure, it is necessary to accommodate women not members of a family unit in the same place as men, then under Article 85 it is obligatory to provide separate sleeping quarters. In the case of internment in occupied territories, members of the same family are to be accommodated together and where possible to be given accommodation separate from other internees.

One provision that has no parallel in the third Convention on POWs is the requirement that female internees can be searched only by women. I cannot explain why it should not be in the third Convention. It may be that they did not think about it, rather than any objection to a requirement to have female guards in POW camps. That possibility is reinforced by the extraordinary way in which the provision appears in the fourth Geneva Convention. It is a sentence inserted into a long Article (97) on the personal property and financial resources of internees!

The primary responsibility for the enforcement of the Conventions is that of the national jurisdiction of the alleged offender. 'Grave breaches' of the Geneva Conventions, however, are made crimes of universal jurisdiction. Not only may other states prosecute but they are under an obligation to seek out and try alleged offenders in their jurisdiction. 'Grave breaches' are defined in each Convention by reference to the group protected by the particular Convention. An unlawful act is not a 'grave breach' merely because it is done to a woman. Nevertheless, the enforcement provision has the potential to protect women if states in fact honoured their obligation to prosecute. Under the fourth Geneva Convention grave breaches are wilful killings, torture or inhuman treatment, wilfully causing great suffering or serious injury to body or health, taking of hostages and extensive destruction and appropriation of property, not justified by military necessity and carried out unlawfully and wantonly.

Women as mothers Women as mothers benefit from special measures of protection, particularly in the case of civilians, at least where they are expectant mothers or mothers of children under seven. That suggests that it is a derivative protection – like the measures of protection for medical personnel who are protected because of their medical function in relation to the wounded and sick, who are the real objects of protection. Just as doctors and nurses are not protected as such, neither are mothers.

We have seen that civilians generally benefit from protection against both the effects of the hostilities and also when in the power of the opposing forces, but what about experience in practice? The majority of recent conflicts have been internal or non-international, and the detailed body of rules I have been considering has not been applicable as such. I will come back to internal conflicts later. There have been some conflicts of mixed or ambiguous status, such as Afghanistan and the former Yugoslavia. The pattern in those conflicts seems to be no different from that in internal conflicts. Indubitably international conflicts in recent times include the Iran–Iraq war, the conflict in the Falklands/Malvinas Islands, the conflict over Kuwait and that between Armenia and Azerbaijan. The Falklands/Malvinas conflict was unusual because of the very limited number of female combatants and civilians generally. The Iran–Iraq war was essentially a frontline operation apart from the war of the cities. The Kuwait conflict was unusual in a variety of respects, including the time available for planning and the number of female combatants. The conflict between Armenia and Azerbaijan is international by accident of history. The fourth Geneva Convention is also applicable to the Israeli occupation of the Occupied Territories and Gaza Strip.

It seems to me that, looking at the treatment of women in those situations, one can say that they figure disproportionately among the internally displaced and refugees. Since among that population, which consists overwhelmingly of the elderly, children and women, women are the most likely to be capable of doing things, the responsibility for keeping going falls largely on them. Where one is better able to assess the attitude of the fighting parties either to the women or to respect for the law is where the parties have dealings with women, rather than simply leaving them to fend for themselves.

Many recent conflicts have been marked by indiscriminate attacks, attacks against civilian targets and other breaches of the rules on the conduct of hostilities. In so far as all civilians suffer, women are not being singled out but they are the ones who will have to pick up the pieces. The Yugoslav conflict provides an unusually broad range of evidence. One of the objects of at least one of the fighting groups has been to secure the displacement of the population. This meant dealing with both men and women. Generally it seems that the 'ethnic cleansing' process involved the rounding up of the population, splitting the men from the women and children, detaining the men but holding the women only until arrangements were made to take them to places from which they could reach territory controlled by the other side. The interesting question is why did they split the men from the women? I don't know if there is a single answer. In so far as the men had fought, they would want to stop them rejoining the fighting. If they had not fought, there was still a risk that they would be mobilized. But that could apply to women of fighting age. They may have been held to provide something to exchange for their own captured fighters. Or, given the apparent pattern of ill-treatment in places such as the Red House in Omarska, some may have been detained to enable one group to eliminate community leaders from among the other group. But community leaders were not all male in the former Yugoslavia. For example, the wife of the Bosnian Muslim mayor of one town was herself the head of the hospital.

I do not want to give the impression that women were not detained. Some were held for relatively brief periods in fairly primitive conditions where they were not held for any purpose other than rounding them up and moving them on. In such situations, it is of course easy for people to target individual females, but whether you will suffer such an attack is arbitrary. The fear of arbitrary attack may be as difficult to cope with, in different ways, as the certainty of attack. Once a large number of women is known to be in one place they become vulnerable to attacks of opportunity. In addition, in some cases, small groups of women were held for longer periods in what were essentially male detention centres. They were sometimes kept separate, as in the case of the group of about twenty-four women held in Omarska. The object of their detention appears to have been rape. They included a female lawyer and a policewoman, which raises the possibility that women in prominent community roles were being targeted. The detention of that group was ancillary to the broader purpose of Omarska. In other cases, there have been allegations that women have been held for the specific purpose of rape (as in the partisans' hall in Foca). What these situations do show is that, perhaps instinctively, fighters do treat male and female civilians differently. Leaving aside the case of detention for sexual purposes, the instinct of the fighters at the very moment of rounding up the population seems to have been to separate them. It may be that this is a universal reaction, but one that is not usually tested because normally there are very few civilian men around and the object is not usually the displacement of the population. Generally speaking, women appear to suffer the same fate as other civilians but are left with the responsibility of dealing with the resultant situation.

Women and rape I should now like to turn to the very controversial issue of women and rape in war. The conflict in Bosnia-Herzegovina has focused attention on the question, first on account of the alleged scale of rape and second because it has been alleged that rape, and in some cases consequent pregnancy, has been used as a weapon of war. The issue of rape in war, however, is as old as war itself. It is clearly a highly emotive issue and before going any further we need to be clear about some distinctions.

First, what is 'rape'? The definition of rape will tell you whether it can only be performed by a male and whether it can only be done to a female. But surely the thing that repels people about rape is first the violence, second the lack of consent, third the violation of one's physical integrity. If that is the case, surely men can be raped too. Second, there is the related issue of whether rape is a sexual act or essentially a violent act. Traditional explanations of high levels of rape in war often suggest it is the result of sexual frustration and/or high adrenaline levels after combat. More recent work from the viewpoint of women survivors is that they experience the act as violent rather than sexual. Third, there is the question of whether the incidence of rape does go up in war and, if so, why. That is linked to the fourth, more general question, which is currently being considered by researchers in the USA: are armed forces in some way environments in which men are predisposed to rape, not just in war? Finally there is the question that in some parts of the feminist movement is seen as so shocking – is rape the worst that can happen to you? Is indiscriminate shelling resulting in the deaths of civilians not at least as unpleasant, even if some of the casualties are male? Or again – and this possibility will arise with more frequency the more women there are in armed forces – what about other forms of torture, designed to break your will or individuality? I have been told that women combatants contemplating capture put rape some way down their list of possible horrors.

Cutting across these universal general issues are culturally specific ones.

Does rape have differing consequences in different societies? If so, what are they and do they depend on factors such as whether the rape is known about, or is it enough that it happened? On the basis of my experience fact-finding, I would suggest that there is a wide range of response among women to rape. Some are made angry, some are humiliated, but it is not something that any woman can simply shrug off. When one talks of what rape means in a particular society, often one means not the reaction of the survivors but the reaction of those around them, notably, in patriarchical societies, their fathers and brothers. I have been told that some raped Afghan women killed themselves because their fathers could not live with the shame of not having been able to protect them.

The fact that rape may have particular implications in particular societies is linked to the fact that rape may have a quite specific implication in different conflicts. There seem to be at least three different types of conflict from this standpoint. There is first traditional rape – whatever gives rise to that. I don't have enough information to know whether that would apply to the rapes committed by Iraqis in Kuwait. Then there are situations in which the fighters despise the people they are fighting. This may be reflected in their vocabulary, as when US servicemen described the Vietnamese as 'mere gooks'. This contempt may have been the product of ignorance. That seems to have affected the attitude of the American servicemen to rape. Finally, within a society where there are actual or alleged ethnic or racial differences, rape of a member of the other group is an assertion of power and subjection to power.

Women, rape and pregnancy One thing that distinguishes male rape and female rape is the risk of pregnancy. This must affect the response of the survivor. It eliminates the response of privacy unless abortion is readily available and acceptable. It has been alleged that, in the Yugoslav conflict, pregnancy has been used as a weapon of war. It has been said that some of those who were detained to be raped were told that they would be held until they were too advanced in pregnancy to obtain an abortion. I have seen no reliable testimony to support this. Furthermore, it is inherently implausible. If a child born to a Bosnian Muslim woman by a Bosnian Serb father is brought up by its mother, how will this help the Serb ascendancy? The birth of children conceived by rape poses a challenge to the society and raises fundamental issues of public policy. Should the woman be encouraged to keep the child or should she be encouraged to give up the child for adoption? In Western Europe there is currently – these things seem to be a matter of fashion – almost a presumption against adoption in any circumstances. Rape babies born in Yugoslavia have called this into question. Is the child not bound some day to know the story of its conception? Does this suggest the need for in-country adoption or adoption outside the country? What about those cultures in which adoption is uncommon? One of the most heartening things in post-conflict Kuwait is that, even while they were treating the Palestinians despicably, Kuwaiti families were adopting rape babies born to Kuwaiti women, even though there was no real tradition of adoption. What happened to babies born to Filipina and Indian rape survivors I do not know.

What does the law say about rape in conflict? One of the most dangerous reactions to the allegations of systematic rape in Yugoslavia was the outraged response of women's groups, 'Rape ought to be a war crime.' That implies that it is not one. In that case, it would violate fundamental principles of law to try someone for rape in that conflict. In fact, rape is against the criminal law of every jurisdiction I have ever heard of. In some cases, they may call it aggravated assault to include both male and female rape. Second, rape in war is a breach of the Hague Conventions and Geneva Conventions and Protocols. It may or may not be referred to as rape but the type of conduct involved is unlawful. That does not mean that every rape in a territory where war is going on is necessarily a war crime. It will be a crime under domestic law, but in order to be a war crime it must be somehow linked to the conflict. In the case of a soldier under orders, his commanders have failed to ensure that their forces respect the fourth Hague Convention. That does not give rise to universal jurisdiction. Under the Geneva Conventions and Protocols, the rape of POWs or foreign civilians may be not only a war crime but a grave breach if done wilfully and on a wide scale. There are also principles of command responsibility, which would enable the trial of commanders or camp commandants who failed to prevent or stop what they ought to have known was going on.

There is no problem with the law as such. Where there is a problem is with its enforcement. The investigation and prosecution of rape has not been handled with the urgency and seriousness that the offence itself would require. An example is to be found in the book *Casualties of War* (Lang 1989), based on a true episode in the Vietnamese conflict. The authorities do not say that rape is not wrong. They do not, however, act in such a fashion as to make it clear to their forces that it is taken seriously. That is but an extreme form of the response to sexual harassment evidenced by the Tailhook Convention episode, which has caused such repercussions in the US forces.

The Ad Hoc War Crimes Tribunals for the former Yugoslavia and Rwanda are taking the issue of rape and sexual assault very seriously. Certain of the indictments include specific charges arising out of such alleged activities. It will be interesting to see how the two Tribunals handle those charges, particularly given evidentiary problems in trials so long after the event and the difficult issue of protecting victims while ensuring a fair trial for the accused. The answer may not lie in international trials, which inevitably could only try the isolated offender. His colleagues may think he was merely unlucky. The answer lies in the attitude to rape taken by national armed forces. That involves the society in question more generally. The question of how to help the survivors of rape raises the broader question of assistance to the victims of conflict.

Women and assistance to the victims of conflict We have seen that women feature prominently among the displaced and refugees. We have also seen that the burden of caring for the elderly and children falls disproportionately on them. This suggests that those providing assistance are going to come into considerable contact with women. You might therefore expect them to have learned from experience – particularly the permanent organizations, whether IGOs or NGOs – and to have developed mechanisms for consulting women to identify the needs in a particular situation, rather than simply imposing their view of the needs. There will obviously be a significant overlap in their respective analyses of needs, but one area of possible divergence is assistance in organizing grassroots organizations.

IGOs and assistance Certain IGOs focus specifically on a particular group. UNICEF, for example, deals with children and UNHCR with refugees. It has taken some time, but IGOs are beginning to recognize the need to consider the role of women in the particular situation and to foster policies that will empower rather than disable them. The more they can work through the population in need, the better equipped that group will be to return to normal life and the greater the chances of avoiding relief dependency.

It is not just a matter of physical or material independence. To a significant extent, the mental health of a displaced population depends on the maintenance of as normal a pattern of life as possible. That job falls predominantly on women. While the need is recognized, the implementation in practice often leaves a lot to be desired. When you look at the situation of refugee women, you will discover that insufficient attention has been paid to the need to protect them from the local population and their fellow refugees in the layout of refugee camps. If there were proper channels of communication instituted with women as a group, and if the IGOs listened to what they were saying, a more prompt and effective response to the needs could be provided.

Certain IGOs are concerned not with the provision of relief but with monitoring a situation. Human rights monitoring, for example, may be taking place. This could involve thematic rapporteurs, a special rapporteur or, in the field of humanitarian law, an *ad hoc* Commission of Experts as appointed for the former Yugoslavia and, more recently, Rwanda. There, one must consider the extent to which they address violations of the rights of women and whether they are equipped to do so, at the most basic level. This may mean female investigators for allegations of rape. It is also interesting to consider the composition of such groups. How many of the rapporteurs are women? In the case of the Commission of Experts for the former Yugoslavia, the Commission, as originally appointed, consisted of five men. Following the resignation of one member and the death of another, two female replacements were appointed, but that was long after the allegations of widespread rape had surfaced. This issue must be kept in perspective. The real crisis is usually the lack of adequate resources and the problem of getting any investigators into the field. The UN fact-finding mechanisms have limited experience in the field of humanitarian law. They tend, for example, to seize on the names of people who may be available, rather than identifying the areas of expertise needed. Nevertheless, I would suggest that the necessary lessons might be learned more swiftly if the fact-finders collaborated or sought the advice of CEDAW.

Foreign NGOs NGOs come in an almost infinite variety of shapes and forms. Some are well established, have gathered considerable expertise in their fields and in fact act as, in a sense, the agents for governmental and intergovernmental relief initiatives. Other NGOs come together on account of the particular crisis and are often no more than a few individuals keen to do something to help. In other cases, NGOs may have a specific constituency such as women or children. Again, their work would be done more effectively if they empowered women and worked through organized women's groups. This is no more than an impression, but I have the sense that development NGOs have developed more policy guidelines in this area than relief NGOs. If this is true, it may be explained by their long-term perspective. It would be interesting to compare the effectiveness of relief programmes in situations of conflict as between situations in which development work has been going on and women have been used as an organizing channel for the work on the one hand and situations in which there is no such background on the other. It should be remembered that the levels of health and of agricultural development have been shown to depend significantly on the literacy rate of women.

Grassroots NGOs The empowerment of women requires assistance to be given them to organize at grassroots level. To impose such a structure from outside would destroy the object of the exercise. It has to be a bottom-up experience, but the evolution of such mechanisms can be assisted.

An interesting example of such a development has occurred in the former Yugoslavia. There appears to have been no organized self-help infrastructure of grassroots women's groups before the conflict. There was only the start of an as yet small women's movement. The need to help, in particular, rape survivors provided the momentum of some local grassroots organizing. This was materially helped by the involvement of women's groups from countries with greater experience of self-help and grassroots groups. Again, this must be handled sensitively. The object is not to impose a European or American solution. It is to give women a voice to enable them to articulate their needs and then to help them meet them in a way that empowers and does not disable the women. While progress is being made, I would suggest that all initiatives in situations of conflict should look at the measures adopted in the development field to mobilize the energy and initiative of local women and should try to adapt such measures to the conflict situation.

Non-international Conflicts

The rules I considered under the Hague and Geneva Conventions and Protocols apply in international armed conflicts. This does not mean that there are no rules in non-international conflicts, but the rules are much less specific and detailed and they encounter rather different problems of enforcement. The only provisions of humanitarian treaty law that apply to non-international conflicts are Article 3, common to all four of the Geneva Conventions, and Protocol II of 1977, if it has been ratified by the state in question. In addition, there may be rules of customary law that are relevant.

On the face of them, the rules do not address the conduct of the fighting but merely proscribe acts of violence against non-combatants. The prohibition of violence to life and person could, however, be said to imply both the principle of distinction and that of proportionality, both of which probably feature as part of customary law. In addition, common Article 3 prohibits outrages upon personal dignity, in particular humiliating and degrading treatment. Protocol II amplifies this by a general provision on humane treatment (Article 4.1) and by repeating the prohibition of outrages upon personal dignity and elaborating the list to include not only humiliating and degrading treatment but also rape, enforced prostitution and any form of indecent assault and threats to commit any of those acts. It is not clear whether these represent an addition, in which case they are only binding on states which ratify, or merely a clarification of the scope of terms already used in common Article 3. The most fundamental provisions on internment in Geneva Convention IV have been made applicable in non-international conflicts by Protocol II, including the provision on the accommodation of families as a unit and the need for separate accommodation for men and women not in family units.

I said that there are special problems of enforcement in the case of the rules in non-international conflicts. First, there are no specific provisions on enforcement as such, merely on dissemination. Second, the state authorities tend to have an ambivalent attitude. They are frightened to do anything that might imply any form of recognition for what, in their eyes, are 'rebels'. That is why, for example, the non-governmental fighter does not have the status of a combatant and of a POW upon capture in non-international conflicts. The state claims the right to try the fighter for fighting against the state. There are both legal and practical difficulties in binding the non-governmental fighters. Legally, how can they be bound by the provisions of a treaty to which they are not a party? The traditional answer is that the state's ratification of the Geneva Convention binds the entire population, either directly or as a result of incorporation. Article 3 speaks of the parties to a conflict not of an international character. Therefore Article 3 binds the non-governmental forces as well as those of the state. Following the decision of the International Criminal Tribunal for the former Yugoslavia in the Tadic case, it would appear that war crimes can be committed in a non-international conflict and that individual acts in violation of common Article 3 may be crimes of universal jurisdiction and, as such, be triable before the domestic criminal courts of any state willing to act and recognizing such a basis of jurisdiction. Practically the rebels may be ignorant of the legal requirements and may, at least in the case of positive obligations, have difficulties in meeting them. This does not explain the prevalence of violations of rules prohibiting certain conduct. This problem needs to be addressed by a combination of measures including an effective international system of enforcement, incentives for the 'rebels' to conform to the law and practical assistance in meeting their obligations without the assisting entities being drawn into the conflict. To evaluate the significance of any improvement that could be achieved, one only needs to consider the proportion of recent conflicts that have been of a non-international character.

Non-derogable Human Rights Law

Some human rights texts, notably the International Covenant on Civil and Political Rights, permit a state to modify the scope of its obligations in times of national emergency. The most significant features of such provisions are first that it is ultimately for the monitoring body to determine whether there is a situation in which the state may derogate, second that there are some rights from which no derogation is possible, and third that, even in relation to those rights in relation to which derogation is possible, the government must show that the measures taken were actually necessary. Measures in derogation of human rights obligations must also be consistent with the state's other obligations in international law. The state's obligations include the Geneva Conventions, that have achieved near universal ratification. They may include the Protocols if the state has ratified them. The applicability of non-derogable human rights law is most likely to be of significance in the case of monitoring mechanisms that include a right of individual petition.

In addition, some other human rights mechanisms may be involved in situations of conflict. They include thematic rapporteurs such as those on torture and arbitrary and summary executions. A special rapporteur may also be appointed for the country in question. The rapporteurs report to the Commission on Human Rights, which means there is political input into the monitoring. This is a mixed blessing. On the positive side, it means there is state support for doing something, if a special rapporteur is appointed. On the negative side, it may prevent the appointment of a special rapporteur. A recent complication, which has only been used in the case of the former Yugoslavia and Rwanda, has been the appointment by the secretary-general, in the name of the Security Council, of a Commission of Experts to report specifically on war crimes. This gives rise to problems of overlapping jurisdiction, and the danger of the duplication of effort. If there is to be any question of the criminal prosecution of those allegedly responsible for war crimes, a different type of evidence from that applicable in human rights cases is needed. I would suggest that where a Commission of Experts is appointed, it should take the lead and be given the bulk of the resources because its evidence could be used by the special rapporteur, whereas the converse is not necessarily true.

Future Developments

The Fourth World Conference on Women in Beijing in 1995 identified as an area of concern women and armed conflict. As part of the follow-up, the UN Division for the Advancement of Women examined the issue and the results were considered at the 1998 session of the Commission on the Status of Women. In addition, any follow-up to the Machel Study on the Impact of Conflict on Children, presented to the UN secretary-general in 1996, may have implications for women in conflict situations.

Conclusions

So to what conclusions does our examination of women and humanitarian law lead us? First, the processes that lead to, or fail to prevent, the outbreak of conflict do not provide for the separate participation of women. It is not clear whether such participation would make a difference to the incidences of conflict or whether they are the result of the processes themselves, rather than the fact that men are disproportionately represented in them.

In the area specifically of humanitarian law – the *ius in bello* – there is very limited provision dealing specifically with women as such, except in the case of special measures of protection for expectant and nursing mothers and in the case of female detainees. With one specific exception, I do not see this as a problem, because women are combatants or civilians first and women second and get protection by virtue of that status. In other words, in most instances a woman does not need separate protection from that afforded others with the same status. The exception is in the case of POWs and internees. Women are accommodated separately from men, either women together or in family units. I would suggest that the committees for POWs and internees should contain separate representation for these groups. Not only may the circumstances of the women be different and outside the knowledge of a male representative, but that is a context in which the law itself sees gender as relevant. Apart from that, I do not see why the law itself on the conduct of hostilities or the protection of victims should single out women.

Where there does need to be a recognition of a special role of women is in the administration or carrying out of relief operations. The need to 'pick up the pieces' arises from the situation or conflict, and not from the law itself. The problem with the law is not the norms themselves but their non-enforcement. In attempting to keep to a minimum the dislocation of war, women have a key role to play. They are casualties but are also in a position to help articulate and meet the needs of their communities. International relief organizations should recognize the need to avoid creating dependency and work through local community groups. This will actually make the relief effort more effective. To this end, they must assist those in need to organize themselves. Grassroots or 'bottom-up' organizations are most likely to achieve the desired result. A disproportionate number of those with whom the relief organization will need to work are able-bodied female civilians. The development of grassroots organizations among them is likely to lead to the empowerment of women, and may give them a more significant voice in the affairs of their community after the end of the conflict.

I would suggest, therefore, that humanitarian law is not the problem. The lack of respect for humanitarian law is part of the problem but not the whole of it. The problem is war itself. Ways need to be found of preventing the outbreak of conflict. Women have an important contribution to make in that sphere. They should be making it now, in the home, in the workplace, in their local community and in national life. That would be the biggest contribution women could make to humanitarian law.

Note

1. In 1837 a group of Canadian insurrectionists rebelled against their British colonial overseers. US President Martin Van Buren's administration took a neutral position, but US sympathizers in New York sent the US steamboat *Caroline* with military supplies for the insurrectionists. On 29 December 1837 British troops set fire to the *Caroline*, which overturned and went over Niagara Falls. US Secretary of State Daniel Webster wrote to British Ambassador Henry Fox to express concern over the necessity of the British response. He asked Fox for justification that the acts were not 'unreasonable or excessive'; the right of self-defence was not questioned in principle.

Bibliography

Charlesworth, Hilary and Christine Chinkin (2000) *The Boundaries of International Law*, Manchester: Manchester University Press.

Lang, Daniel (1989) *Casualties of War*, New York: Pocket Books.

MacKinnon, Catherine (1991) *Towards a Feminist Theory of the State*, Cambridge, MA: Harvard University Press.

Muir, Kate (1993) *Arms and the Woman*, London: Coronet Books.

Wright, Shelley (2001) *International Human Rights, Decolonisation and Globalisation*, London: Routledge.

7

The European System of Protection of Human Rights and Human Rights of Women

Wolfgang Benedek

The European system of human rights of today is the result of a long historical process during which human rights were first protected as citizen rights and minority rights on the national level. A regional system of protection of human rights was developed in Europe only after the Second World War in the framework of the Council of Europe, which was founded in 1949. One of the first priorities of the Council was to draft a Human Rights Charter, which took the form of the Convention for the Protection of Human Rights and Fundamental Freedoms, which was signed on 4 November 1950 and entered into force in 1953.

A major driving force for the elaboration of this human rights instrument was the experience of the Second World War and the determination of the member states of the Council of Europe, which numbered only 15 at that time, to prevent future wars and atrocities through cooperation based on the principles of the rule of law, human rights and fundamental freedoms and pluralist democracy as enshrined in the Statute of the Council of Europe.[1] The principle of democracy is considered as being part of the European heritage.[2] It appears in the limitation clauses for Arts 8–11 of the European Convention, according to which the rights guaranteed, i.e. the rights to private and family life, to freedom of thought, conscience and religion, to freedoms of expression and of assembly and association can only be subjected to limitations, which, inter alia, 'are prescribed by law and are necessary in a democratic society'.

Post-war Europe was characterized by a division between democratic market-economy states associated in the Council of Europe and the socialist Eastern European countries characterized by communism and planned economies. The relationship between the two groups of states with antagonistic political and economic systems was characterized by the Cold War from 1948 to 1989. During this time, the membership of the Council of Europe grew to about 23, in particular through the accession of the South

European states including Turkey. In 1989, a new era of self-determination in Europe started.[3] The Soviet Union was dissolved and replaced by Russia and the Commonwealth of Independent States (CIS), and the Federal Republic of Yugoslavia was dissolved into five successor states. The two German states reunited and Czechoslovakia separated into the Czech and Slovak Republics. Most of the successor states of the Soviet Union and Yugoslavia as well as all Eastern European states applied for membership in the Council of Europe, which was obligatorily connected with membership in the European Convention on Human Rights, its additional protocols and the other major European human rights treaties. As a result, the membership of the Council of Europe grew to 43 (2001), including Russia.

However, there are altogether three regional systems of human rights in Europe. Besides the Council of Europe there is also the Organization for Security and Cooperation in Europe (presently 55 members), which started as the Conference on Security and Cooperation in Europe in 1975 as an effort of creating a common framework of cooperation for all states in Europe, as well as the United States and Canada. From the beginning, it also included a strong component on human rights, which is still relevant today, in particular for those Eastern European states that have not yet been able to join the Council of Europe.

In 1957, a more limited group of countries formed the European Economic Community, now called the European Union. The European Union also places particular emphasis on human rights in the work of its bodies and in its policies. Both the Council of Europe and the European Union have a particular focus on issues of equality and non-discrimination. Before this is elaborated in the following, a short overview about the main legal instruments of the Council of Europe will be provided.

The Main Elements of the Human Rights System of the Council of Europe

The main elements of the system of protection of human rights by the Council of Europe consist in the European Convention on Human Rights and its additional protocols, the European Social Charter with its amendments, the European Convention for the Prevention of Torture and Inhuman or Degrading Treatment or Punishment and the European Framework Convention for the Protection of National Minorities.[4] In addition, there is a number of declarations and recommendations ranging from the issue of intolerance to violence against women. Issues of equality and non-discrimination have been dealt with mainly under the European Convention, the Social Charter and the promotional activities of the Council of Europe.

The European Convention on Human Rights (1950)

The rights protected The European Convention focuses mainly on civil and political rights and has been developed in a very particular way. It started in 1950 with a rather limited catalogue of rights, which were complemented by so far eleven additional protocols. However, part of these protocols deal with improvements of the procedure of human rights protection.

The Convention itself contains a number of basic rights such as the right to life, the prohibition of torture, slavery and forced labour, the right to freedom and security, the right to fair trial, the right to private and family life, to freedom of thought, religion and conscience and of expression and information, to the right to assembly and association and to the right to marry and found a family. Further rights, such as the right to property, the right to education, the right to free elections by secret ballot and the right to freedom of movement and residence were incorporated in the additional protocols. In this way, additional protocol No. 6 on the abolition of the death penalty has also become part of the general European system of human rights, although this process took some time.

All the rights contained in the European Convention and its additional protocols are formulated as universal human rights. That means that they are rights not just of Europeans but of every person who lives or temporarily resides in one of the member states of the Council of Europe, including foreigners.

The procedure of human rights protection The European Convention provides for individual and state complaints. There have been several state complaints under the European system, in particular against Turkey. There is regularly a very high number of individual complaints, which in 2000 amounted to 10,486, of which only 10–20% were accepted.

Since November 1998, the Council of Europe has had a new system of protection of the rights enshrined in the European Convention on Human Rights. The European Commission on Human Rights and the European Court on Human Rights were replaced by one single body, the permanent European Court on Human Rights, which presently (2001) consists of 43 judges corresponding to the number of member states.

As in the past, it can receive complaints from both individuals and states as well as non-governmental organizations, which, however, have to demonstrate that they have been the victim of a violation. In addition, the complainant has to show that he or she has been violated in one of the rights guaranteed under the Convention, that he or she has exhausted all legal remedies available domestically, and that the last decision on the national level does not date back for more than six months. Every complaint is reviewed for its admissibility by a committee of three judges. The cases are dealt with by chambers of seven judges, which include a judge from the country concerned. In exceptional cases, when fundamental issues or changes of interpretations are at stake, a Grand Chamber of 17 judges can hear the case. This might coincide with the exceptional cases where an appeal is granted. However, in order to accelerate the procedure, no appeal is foreseen in 'normal' cases. The Court may also decide on a compensation for the victim. Its decision is final and binding in international law. The Committee of Ministers of the Council of Europe is supervising the execution of the judgments of the Court. As in the past, efforts are made to reach a friendly settlement prior to the decision of the Court. In cases of urgency, the Court may also undertake 'provisional measures', for instance against the deportation of foreigners to a country where they risk torture or the death penalty.

The European Social Charter (1961) The European Social Charter was adopted in 1961 in order to protect economic and social rights. The membership of this instrument is optional. In 2001, 24 European states have become members.

Rights protected There are 19 different economic and social rights protected under the European Social Charter of 1961. However, to facilitate accession, members were allowed to make a certain selection of rights by which they would like to be bound, with the result that not all members are bound by the same rights. The basic idea is the gradual development of economic and social rights which is also reflected in the procedure. In 1988, an additional protocol was adopted, which contains four additional rights, *inter alia*, 'the right to equal opportunities and equal treatment in matters of employment and occupation without discrimination on grounds of sex'. Further rights were added and consolidated into a revised version of the Social Charter.[5]

Procedure of protection The European Social Charter in the past only provided for a reporting system. State reports are reviewed by a committee of independent experts, the conclusions of which are considered by a governmental committee of the Council of Europe. To strengthen the central mechanism, a procedure of collective complaints was introduced by an additional protocol. The complaints are reviewed by the Committee of Independent Experts. The supervision of the implementation of recommendations made is again the responsibility of the Committee of Ministers, which addresses its recommendations to member states.

The European Convention on the Prevention of Torture and Inhuman or Degrading Treatment or Punishment (1987) This Convention is based on Article 3 of the European Convention on the Prohibition of Torture. It does not state any additional rights, but put in place an original system of visits to places of detention by members of the European Committee for the Prevention of Torture. These visits can take place any time without further authorization and can cover any place of detention. The main purpose is the prevention of violations of Article 3 ECHR. The Committee draws up a report on its findings, which is submitted to the respective government for comment. The final report may be published with the agreement of the government concerned, and this has become the general rule. Through a protocol, the Convention was also opened to non-member states of the Council of Europe.[6]

The European Framework Convention for the Protection of National Minorities (1995) This Convention was adopted as a response to the newly increasing minority problems in Europe after 1989 resulting from the dissolution of the Soviet Union and Yugoslavia in particular. It protects a number of rights of members of national minorities, such as the right to effective equality in economic, social, political and cultural life, equality before the law and equal protection by the law. The state has to promote conditions for minorities to maintain and develop their culture and identity and provide protection in cases of assimilation against their will. However, its enforcement mechanism is limited to a reporting system and the review of these reports by an advisory committee of experts.[7]

Additional texts There are a number of pertinent declarations and other texts adopted by the Council of Europe on various issues of importance in the field of human rights, in particular the Declaration Regarding Intolerance of 1981, the Declaration on Freedom of Expression and Information of 1982, the Declaration on Equality of Women and Men of 1988 and the Declaration on Policies for Combating Violence against Women in a Democratic Europe of 1993. These declarations contain guiding principles for the policies of the Council of Europe and its member states. The Council of Europe also serves as a framework for the elaboration of conventions (so far more than 160), for example the European Convention on Recognition and Enforcement of Decisions concerning Custody of Children of 1980. The Committee of Ministers of the Council of Europe has adopted a number of recommendations pertaining to the issue of equality and family life.[8]

Related Activities of the Council of Europe and its partners Besides its activities on protection of human rights proper, the Council of Europe pursues a number of activities in the field of equality, the media and human rights education, and so on. Whereas until the 1990s the Council of Europe focused more on the protection of human rights, since 1989, when a number of new European states with little experience of human rights and the rule of law joined the Council of Europe, the Council reacted by expanding its advisory services. Various activities were launched in the field of human rights education, the establishment of national institutions for the promotion of human rights was encouraged, and studies were undertaken on various problems such as prison conditions, police behaviour or the situation of immigrants. Cooperation with NGOs and with the media was further developed. New bodies were established, such as the European Commission against Racism and Intolerance, set up by the Vienna Summit of the Council of Europe in 1993 to implement the Plan of Action to Combat Racism, Xenophobia, Anti-Semitism and Intolerance – issues that, unfortunately, gained greater prominence in Europe in the 1990s. Examples of other issues addressed by the Council of Europe are trafficking in women and forced prostitution.

Equality and Non-discrimination in the System of the Council of Europe

The history of human rights is also a history of limitations of human rights. The Declaration on the Rights of Man and Citizen of 1789 in the context of the French Revolution was followed in 1791 by a Declaration of the Rights of Woman and Citizen by Olympe de Gouges,[9] which can be considered one of the first efforts at drawing attention to the human rights of women. It should also be noted that the European Convention on Human Rights of 1950 still contained several so-called 'colonial clauses', such as Article 63 para. 1, according to which the extension of the Convention was possible to the territories for whose international relations the contracting parties were responsible, which had to be done by a specific notification. According to Art. 63 para. 3 the provisions of the Convention should be applied to such territories however with due regard to 'local requirements', which opened the way for the introduction of double standards.

Finally, Art. 63 para. 4 provided for the possibility of a declaration on the acceptance of a right to petition of individuals of those territories. It has to be noted, however, that the right to individual complaints in Art. 25 of the European Convention was made dependent on the acceptance by the respective state. However, in the 1980s all member states had given their agreement. The newly acceding states in the 1990s had to accept the right to individual complaints as well as the competence of the European Court of Human Rights as a condition of membership. The new system introduced on the basis of the 11th protocol in 1998 finally contained the right of the individual to make a complaint to the European Court of Human Rights as a constituent element.

Provisions on equality in the European Convention on Human Rights

There are various provisions in the European Convention that are of particular relevance for the issue of equality and non-discrimination. Art. 14 contains a general prohibition of discrimination regarding all rights and liberties recognized by the convention, which includes any discrimination on the basis of sex, race, colour, language, religion and so on. In cases of differentiation, the principle of proportionality has to be observed. Art. 8 protects the private and family life. This provision has been developed considerably by the practice of the bodies of the European System of Human Rights, i.e. the former European Commission of Human Rights and the European Court of Human Rights.

Art. 12 contains the right to marry and to found a family. This right is conditioned by a reference to national laws, which regulate the exercise of this right. Of particular relevance is Art. 5 of the 7th Add. Prot. of 1984, according to which spouses enjoy equal rights and responsibilities of a private law character as to the marriage, during marriage and in the event of dissolution as to between themselves and in their relations to their children.

The European standards have been developed and clarified through a number of cases. Regarding Art. 8 on protection of private and family life several cases dealt with the absence of a legal divorce in Ireland. In *Airey* v. *Ireland* (1979), the Irish government refused legal aid to a woman wishing to obtain judicial separation from her violent husband. The Court held that Art. 8 did not merely compel the state to abstain from arbitrary interference, but that there might also be positive obligations inherent in an effective respect for private and family life. The Court also found a violation of the right to fair trial. In the case *Marckx* v. *Belgium*, again in 1979, a mother and her natural child challenged Belgian laws for requiring a mother to take specific action to give her child legal status as her daughter and for excluding such a child from full legal status *vis-à-vis* other members of the family. The Court found a violation of the right to family under Art. 8, because a state has to determine its domestic legal system in such a manner that those concerned can lead a normal family life. In this respect, no difference should be allowed between the treatment of legal children and children born out of wedlock. In the cases *Dudgeon* v. *United Kingdom* (1981) and *Norris* v. *Ireland* (1988) the Court found that a prohibition by a state of homosexual acts between adults over the age of 21 did constitute an unjustifiable interference with the right to respect for private life under Art. 8.

The right to family life was also upheld by the Court against restrictive immigration laws in force in the United Kingdom (*Abdulaziz, Cabales and Balkandali* v. *United Kingdom*, 1985), which allowed foreign women, but not foreign men, to come to the UK to be reunited with their partner. Equality was considered to be more important than the protection of the labour market. In another case (*Berrehab* v. *Netherlands*, 1988), the Court found that a Moroccan father who had married and divorced in the Netherlands, but maintained close contacts with his very young daughter and contributed to her material support, could not be deported without a violation of Art. 8.

In 'Open Door and Dublin Well Woman' the interdiction of the Irish Courts of Dissemination of information on possibilities of abortion abroad was found as violating the right to information and expression in Art. 10. The infringement of the Irish law was not considered proportional to the infringement of the right, which was held to be more important.

With regard to the right to marry and the equality of spouses, the Commission found that states cannot prohibit prisoners from marrying but can prohibit married prisoners from living together (*Draper* v. *United Kingdom*, 1980, *Hamer* v. *United Kingdom*, 1979). With regard to the right to marry, the Court in *F* v. *Switzerland* (1987) held that the temporary prohibition of remarriage of a man who had been married and divorced three times within 18 years and wished to marry again did constitute a violation of the right to marry under Article 12.[10]

Promotional activities on equality   Until 1979, the work of the Council of Europe in the field of equality,[11] which focused on improving the legal status of women and their employment situation, was largely carried out on an *ad hoc* basis. For example, the European Social Charter of 1961 contained a number of specific rights for women like the right to equal remuneration of male and female workers, protection of mothers and working women, and so on.

In 1979, the Council of Europe set up a committee of experts with the task of promoting equality on the basis of an action plan for the promotion of equality between women and men. Among the issues studied was the situation of women in politics, equality and education, and violence against women. Some rights missing in the European Social Charter concerning the equal treatment in general and equal opportunities and treatment for workers of both sexes with family responsibilities were included in an additional protocol to the European Social Charter in 1988.

In 1988 again, the Committee of Ministers adopted the Declaration on Equality of Women and Men, which emphasized that equality was a principle of human rights and that 'sex-related discrimination in various fields constitutes impediments to the recognition, enjoyment and exercise of human rights and fundamental freedoms'.[12]

The preamble of the declaration by the Committee of Ministers on Equality of Women and Men of 1988 recognizes persisting inequalities and discriminations. It expresses the commitment to the principle of equality of women and men as a *sine qua non* of democracy and an imperative of social justice. It contains a number of detailed commitments such as participation and access to all levels of civil service, education, professions, information, and so on. In 1989, on the occasion of its fortieth year of existence, the Council of Europe commissioned a comprehensive study on equality between women and men in Europe, in which after a general overview on different forms of equality an analysis was provided regarding the incorporation of international provisions on equality into the legal systems of member states and of positive action, including cases of reverse discrimination.[13]

Again in 1989, the Committee on Equality was transferred from the field of social and economic affairs to the human rights field, which signals the growing awareness of women's rights as a human rights issue. In 1992, the European Committee for Equality between Women and Men was given the rank of a Steering Committee.[14] The Committee undertook to work out the fundamental human right of women and men to equality in an additional protocol to the European Convention on Human Rights, which, however, so far has not been adopted although the Parliamentary Assembly of the Council of Europe took a vote of recommendation in 1994.[15]

The Steering Committee for Equality established a 'European Observatory on Equality between Women and Men' and organized several workshops and conferences. The Committee also dealt with the precarious position of women in the countries of Central and Eastern Europe during the economic transformation.[16]

Within the Secretariat of the Council of Europe positive discrimination (affirmative action) was introduced into the staff rules by giving 'preference to the under-represented sex'. The Council of Europe publishes a yearly report on promotional measures within its own Secretariat.

Further to the recognition of women's rights as human rights the Committee focused on equality and democracy, on all forms of violence against women, and on the right to free choice in matters of reproduction and lifestyles. In 1995 a conference on 'Equality and Democracy' was organized by the Council of Europe as a contribution to the Beijing Conference, which emphasized the free choice of maternity as a democratic value. In this context, it was recognized that 'promotion of effective equality between women and men is synonymous with the promotion of human rights and pluralist democracy'.[17]

The Human Rights System of the Organization for Security and Co-operation in Europe (OSCE)

The former Conference on Security and Cooperation in Europe (CSCE), renamed OSCE in 1994, is basically a security organization with a strong emphasis on human rights. Its 55 members span an area from Vancouver to Vladivostok. There is no legal statute of the organization, which was not given international legal personality, and most of its human rights declarations and recommendations are of a soft law nature, starting from the Helsinki Declaration of 1975. However, this was largely compensated for by the development of a very successful monitoring mechanism of regular follow-up conferences. The 'Helsinki Process' had an important role in opening a space of cooperation during the East–West conflict in Europe. After the end of the Cold War the Paris Charter for a New Europe of November 1980 paved the way for a new era of cooperation in Europe. The headquarters of the OSCE, which is a regional organization according to Chapter VIII of the UN Charter, is based in Vienna, Prague and Warsaw. It is headed by a secretary-general, whose seat is in Vienna. Its main focus is on prevention and mediation, fact-finding and peace-keeping.[18]

Human dimension Among the ten principles of the Helsinki Declaration is one devoted to respect for human rights and fundamental freedoms, including freedom of thought, conscience, religion and belief. The 'human dimension' has become a major field of activity for the OSCE. Accordingly, cooperation in the humanitarian field is one of its priorities. For example, when the OSCE is conducting field missions, as in the case of Bosnia-Herzegovina or Kosovo, human rights officers are deployed all over the country in order to monitor and report on the human rights situation.

Human Rights Mechanisms and Institutions Regular conferences monitor the performance of member states with regard to human rights. Special conferences and meetings are organized on the human dimension in particular. A 'special mechanism on emergency consultations' has been set up to deal with major human rights violations in member states, and institutions have been established to take care of particular issues. However, there are practically no sanctions, except suspension of the membership rights, as happened in the case of Yugoslavia in 1992.

The main body of the OSCE is the OSCE Council, which has a chairman-in-office rotating every twelve months. There is also a Parliamentary Assembly. The OSCE has an Office for Democratic Institutions and Human Rights (ODIHR), which is located in Warsaw and promotes democratic elections, election monitoring, practical support to democratic institutions and human rights. It also helps strengthen civil society and the rule of law.[19] In 1996, a Representative for Freedom of the Media was established in Vienna to monitor compliance with the freedom of the expression and the right to independent and pluralistic media. Special attention is given to the rights of minorities in Europe, for which purpose a High Commissioner on National Minorities was established in 1992. His role of identifying and seeking early resolution of ethnic tensions is mainly conciliatory and promotional. While the OSCE institutions deal with individual cases only in field missions, they focus on addressing human rights situations in member states.

Equality Although equality and non-discrimination issues have been included in the standards adopted by the CSCE since 1975, gender issues started to figure more prominently on the agenda of the OSCE since 1998. A 'Focal Point on Gender Issues' and a 'Gender Mainstreaming and Human Rights of Women Advisor' were created in the ODIHR to increase gender awareness and mainstreaming. Research projects and workshops are organized to promote women's participation in politics, in conflict resolution and post-conflict rehabilitation and to strengthen observance of their human rights. Gender issues are also included in the OSCE training programme for new mission staff.[20]

The European Union and Human Rights

The development of a human rights policy of the European Union

Although the Treaty on the European Economic Community (EEC) of 1957 did not contain any provisions on human rights, the European Court of Justice as the Court of the EEC developed a jurisdiction based on human rights of individuals as derived from the 'common constitutional traditions of member states' and international treaties ratified by them, in particular the European Convention on Human Rights. Among the rights considered as general principles of community law are the right to property, freedom of association and religion, the principle of equality, the protection of the family, and so on.

The political organs of the EEC, which later became the European Community (EC) and the European Union (EU), i.e. the European Parliament, the European Commission and the European Council (the representation of the EU governments, which is the main political organ of the EU, to be distinguished from the Council of Europe) increasingly developed a human rights policy, first for the conduct of trade and foreign relations of the EU and then also for the internal relations.

As a basis, a number of declarations and provisions on human rights were adopted, from the joint declaration of the European Parliament, the Council and the Commission on respect for human rights and fundamental freedoms in the exercise of their powers in 1977 to Articles 6 and 7 in the Treaty on the European Union as revised in Amsterdam, which states that the Union is based on the principles of freedom, democracy, respect for human rights and fundamental freedoms and the rule of law, with particular emphasis on the European Convention of 1950 and provides for a procedure of sanctions against any member found in serious violation of these principles.

The European Parliament has been instrumental in shaping the human rights policy of the EU through a number of resolutions and measures, in particular two regular reports, one on the situation of human rights in the world, the other on the situation of human rights in the European Union. On the request of the European Parliament, so-called human rights clauses have to be included in all agreements of the European Union with third states according to which the respect for human rights is considered an 'essential element' of these agreements, the violation of which can lead to the suspension of rights under the agreements.[21]

The human rights policy of the European Community/Union was elaborated in particular in the framework of its development cooperation policy. Accordingly, Art. V of the Lomé Convention of 1990 contained a human rights clause and Art. 177 para. 2 of the EC Treaty emphasizes that the policy of the Community in the field of development cooperation contributes to the objectives of strengthening democracy and the rule of law as well as human rights and fundamental freedoms. To stimulate such policies by developing states, various positive measures are foreseen, whereas violations of fundamental human rights, according to the principle of conditionality, can result in sanctions, such as the suspension of rights.[22]

In reaction to growing problems, the EU put particular emphasis on activities against racism and xenophobia. For this purpose, new legal provisions were included in the Treaty on the European Community and a European Monitoring Centre on Racism and Xenophobia was established in Vienna in 1997. The following year, a 'Plan of Action against Racism' was adopted, which foresees a number of legal and promotional measures.

Through the Treaty of Amsterdam, which entered into force in 1999, several provisions on equality were introduced into the EC Treaty. Art. 2 now includes 'equal treatment of men and women' among the tasks of the EC and in Art. 3 para. 2 it is specifically provided that in all its activities the Community will work towards the elimination of inequalities and the promotion of equality of men and women ('mainstreaming clause').

Furthermore, a new article (Art. 13) on measures against discrimination was added to the EC Treaty, according to which the Council of the European Union can take measures to fight against discrimination based on sex, race, ethnic origin, religion or conscience, disability, age or sexual orientation, which will allow the European Union to increase its activities in this field.

The European Union and equality The different organs of the European Community/Union have dealt with numerous issues related to equality and non-discrimination. The European Parliament took up issues such as violence against women, forced prostitution or conditions of employment. For example, in the sector of employment a five-year-programme called 'New Opportunities for Women' (NOW) was started in 1994 by the European Commission.

The European Court of Justice dealt with a number of economic and social equality cases – equal pay for equal work, access to certain professions, such as the police, the issue of night work of women and positive legal measures aimed at equal treatment of women at their workplace.[23] Of particular interest here are the legislative acts of the EU to promote equality and two recent judgments of the European Court of Justice in this context.

A new provision in the Treaty on the European Community, Art. 141 on 'equal payment for men and women', provides that member states will apply the principle of equal pay for equal work without any discrimination based on sex. Measures are to be adopted to provide equality of opportunity. In order to establish the full equality of men and women at work, the principle of equal treatment does not prevent member states from maintaining and deciding on specific advantages to facilitate the recruitment of the under-represented sex or to prevent or balance disadvantages in the professional career.

Since the 1970s, different directives have been adopted in this field – for example, on equality of treatment of women regarding access to employment, promotion and equal working conditions.[24] In the 1980s, different recommendations by the Council were adopted on the promotion of equal opportunities,[25] which included 'suitable general and specific measures' to counter discrimination against women and facilitate positive measures in recruitment.

In two recent cases, the European Court of Justice has tried to clarify the proper understanding of the provisions of the Directive of 1976 regarding national legislation for promoting equality. In the case of Kalanke (1995), the equal treatment law of the Land of Bremen in Germany provided that until a certain quota of women was employed in the public service women had to be given preference in cases of equal qualification.

The Court found that national provisions, which foresaw an automatic and unconditional preference for women in recruitment of promotions, were themselves discriminatory since they constituted cases of reverse discrimination. However, to apply principles of equal representation of women in individual cases was considered justified. This led to numerous critical reactions.

In the Marschall case (1997), regarding a provision of the Civil Service Act of the Land of North-Rhine Westphalia in Germany, the law permitted the preferential treatment of women in recruitment 'unless grounds associated with the person of the other candidate prevail'. The Court recognized the existence of structural inequalities in the promotion of women, which can be remedied by giving preference to the under-represented sex. However, it specified that there had to be a procedure in which male applicants with equal qualifications were given an objective assessment of all relevant criteria and were selected if this assessment was in their favour (so-called 'saving clause'). Therefore, priority can be given to women only if one or several of the criteria that must not have a discriminatory effect against women are not in favour of the male candidate. Accordingly, women can be promoted only after a proper procedure in which all criteria in question are examined. Consequently, laws that give preference to women as the under-represented sex to promote equality are not generally in contradiction with the law of the European Union if they contain a saving clause that meets the conditions set out by the Council.[26] In this context, according to an amendment of the Austrian Constitution of 1998, the federal government, the provinces and the local authorities commit themselves to the equal treatment of women and men in actual fact and to positive measures intended to guarantee equal treatment of women and men, above all by eliminating existing inequalities.[27]

Comparison between the European System and the African System of Human Rights

Framework and contents   It is obvious that the European and the African systems are the result of a different historical experience and tradition and do respond to a different political, economic and cultural environment. In a way, the African system is the modern one in that the African Charter on Human and Peoples' Rights does incorporate all three dimensions of human rights – civil and political rights, economic, social and cultural rights and rights of solidarity or peoples' rights in one single legal framework. The African system was shaped after the Universal Declaration of Human Rights of 1948 and the subsequent UN covenants, i.e. the UN Bill of Rights, and did not take as an example the European Convention of

Human Rights of 1950 as did the American Convention on Human Rights of 1969. From the beginning, the African Charter put much larger emphasis on the promotion of human rights as part of the tasks of the African Commission on Human and Peoples' Rights, whereas the European system developed the promotional aspect only after 1989, when it had to absorb a number of Eastern European states.

Although the African system is more comprehensive with regard to the rights covered, these rights are often not spelt out in much detail and the African Commission is only slowly developing the necessary practice in order to make those rights more specific. Furthermore, the limitation clauses on the rights are much wider, and important elements of the European limitation clauses such as what is 'necessary in a democratic society' are missing.[28]

The African system so far has seen the preparation of only one additional protocol on substantive rights, that on women's rights, which, however, still has not been completed and opened for ratification. There are no special instruments regarding the prevention of torture or the protection of minorities. With regard to minorities, the Charter speaks only of the rights of peoples and does not deal with minority protection as such.

Enforcement Another major difference is in the enforcement system. It took the African Commission a number of years until it established a policy of larger transparency and publicity, and the procedure for dealing with individual communications is not highly developed. The findings of the Commission, mostly reached after a long time, lack a proper enforcement mechanism.[29] After a discussion of several years a protocol on an African Court of Human and Peoples' Rights has been adopted in the framework of the OAU and opened for ratification.[30] It will not replace the Commission but will provide an additional body, which, like the European Court, will have the advantage of being able to make enforceable decisions and also decide on compensation. However, the main limitation might be funding.[31] The African Commission has not found it possible to get the necessary funding for its activities and it might therefore be even more difficult to obtain the funding for the second body to work side by side with the Commission. The disadvantages of the former European system of very long periods until a case is finally decided can also be expected for the African system. However, at the time it was considered too radical to replace the Commission by the Court, and in addition the various promotional functions of the Commission could hardly be taken over by the Court.

Protection and promotion of human rights of women in Europe and in Africa A comparison of the legal instruments of protection and promotion of human rights of women in Europe and in Africa shows that there are also great differences.[32] The African Charter as the younger instrument does have a provision on women's rights, whereas the European Convention so far lacks any particular provisions, and its planned additional protocol on equality has not yet materialized.

Art. 18 para. 3 of the African Charter provides that 'the state shall ensure the elimination of every discrimination of women and also ensure the protection of the rights of the woman and the child as stipulated in international declarations and conventions'. This is a potentially very far-reaching provision as it allows the Commission to interpret the rights of women under the African Charter on the basis of the UN Convention on the Elimination of All Forms of Discrimination against Women of 1979 and its subsequent practice. This remarkable provision is a special case of Art. 60 of the African Charter on 'applicable principles', according to which the Commission 'shall draw inspiration, *inter alia*, from the Universal Declaration of Human Rights and other instruments adopted by the United Nations in the field of human and peoples' rights'.

However, it seems that little use has been made of this provision and its potential by African women themselves, as there have hardly been any cases brought to the Commission.[33] Instead, in 1994 African women's NGOs decided to work on drafting a protocol to the African Charter in order to have women's issues dealt with in a more comprehensive way. In 2000, the protocol was still under consideration.[34] The danger of this approach is that it may lead to delays in implementing the human rights of women and give the impression that those rights are guaranteed only in the additional protocol, which states may take a long time to ratify. However, the Commission is already in a position to reach largely the same result by an interpretation of the African Charter that makes full use of its interpretative powers as specified in Art. 18 para 3.[35] In order to allow the Commission to do so, women's NGOs should bring well-prepared cases to the African Commission. In addition, the African Commission, with the assistance of interested organizations and donors, could make more use of its promotional mandate to study the implementation of human rights of women in the different national legislations, analyse existing discriminations and prepare proposals of how to eliminate them. The consideration of state reports provides another opportunity for systematically inquiring into the respect for human rights of women in the countries reviewed.

Conclusions

Taking into account the historical and cultural differences, the European system of human rights and European efforts towards the promotion of equality and non-discrimination of women are worth studying as they can provide valuable lessons for the protection and promotion of human rights of women in Africa. The problems faced by women in gaining full equality are largely the same worldwide, as can be seen at the different world conferences on women. Women can benefit from learning from each other and the various regional systems can also draw important lessons from an exchange of their respective experiences.[36] The European experience has a longer tradition and is therefore more comprehensive, while the African practice is often very innovative and has to face even greater challenges.

Notes

Wolfgang Benedek is Professor of International Law and International Organizations, University of Graz, Austria.

1. See Art. 3 of the Statute of the Council of Europe.

2. See Council of Europe, *Human Rights, a continuing challenge for the Council of Europe*, Council of Europe Press 1995, 76 et seq.

3. Konrad Ginther and Hubert Isak (Hrsg.), *Selbstbestimmung in Europa?* Böhlau Verlag, Vienna 1991.

4. See *Human Rights Today*, European legal texts, Council of Europe, Strasburg 1999.

5. See Council of Europe, *European Social Charter – Collected Texts*, Strasburg 1997; Lenia Samuel, *Fundamental Social Rights: Case Law of the European Social Charter*, Council of Europe Publishing, Strasburg 1997; Council of Europe, *Women in the Working World*, Strasburg, 1995.

6. See Malcolm D. Evans and Rod Morgan, *Preventing Torture: A Study of the European Convention for the Prevention of Torture and Inhuman and Degrading Treatment or Punishment*, Oxford University Press, New York, 1998; Rod Morgan and Malcolm D. Evans, *Protecting Prisoners: The Standards of the European Committee for the Prevention of Torture in Context*, Oxford University Press, New York, 1999; Renate Kicker, 'The European Committee for the Prevention of Torture (CPT) developing European human rights law?', in Wolfgang Benedek, Hubert Isak and Renate Kicker (eds), *Development and Developing International and European Law, Essays in Honour of Konrad Ginther*, Peter Lang, Frankfurt 1999, 595–610.

7. See *Framework Convention for the Protection of National Minorities – Collected Texts*, Council of Europe, Strasburg 1999; see also Gerd Oberleitner, 'Monitoring minority rights under the Council of Europe's framework convention', in P. Cumper and S. Wheatley (eds), *Minority Rights in the 'New' Europe*, Kluwer Law International, London 1999, 71–88.

8. See, for example, Recommendation No. R (98) 14 of the Committee of Ministers to Member States on Gender Mainstreaming and Recommendation No. R (98) 8 of the Committee of Ministers to Member States on Children's Participation in Family and Social Life.

9. See the text in Katarina Tomasevski, *Women and Human Rights*, Zed Books, London 1993, 3–7.

10. See Donna Gomien, *Short Guide to the European Convention on Human Rights*, Council of Europe, 2nd edn, Strasburg 1998; D. Gomien, D. Harris and L. Zwaak; *Law and Practice of the European Convention on Human Rights and the European Social Charter*, Council of Europe, Strasburg 1996; and M. Buquicchio-De Boer, *Equality between the Sexes and the European Convention on Human Rights*, Council of Europe, Strasburg 1995.

11. See Council of Europe, *Council of Europe Action in the Field of Equality between Women and Men*, Doc. EG (2000) 1, Strasburg 2001.

12. See the Council of Europe Declaration on Equality of Women and Men of 1988, in Human Rights in International Law, Council of Europe Press 1992, 275-277.

13. Equality between Women and Men, Positive Action and the Constitutional and Legislative Hindrences to its Implementation in the Member States of the Council of Europe, by Eliane Vogel-Polsky, Council of Europe, Strasburg 1989.

14. See Council of Europe, the Steering Committee for Equality between Women and Men (CDEG), Doc. EG (99) 2, Strasburg 1999.

15. See Recommendation 1229 (1994) of the Parliamentary Assembly.

16. See Council of Europe, Guaranteeing Freedom of Choice in Matters of Repro- duction, Sexuality and Lifestyles in Europe: Trends and Developments, Proceedings, Tallinn, November 1997, Strasburg 1999; Council of Europe, Gender Mainstreaming, Strasburg 1998; Council of Europe, Promoting Equality: A Common Issue for Men and Women, Proceedings, Strasburg 1998; Council of Europe, National Machinery to Promote Equality between Women and Men in Central and Eastern European Countries, Proceedings, International Workshop Ljubljana 1994, Strasburg 1998 and Council of Europe, The Strategies, Role and Functions of NGOs Working for the Promotion of Equality between Women and Men, Proceedings, Strasburg 1997.

17. See the preparatory document of the Council of Europe for the World Conference on Women in Beijing 1995, in *Equality and Democracy: Utopia or Challenge?* (Proceedings, Beijing and Strasburg 1995), Council of Europe 1996.

18. See *OSCE Handbook*, Vienna 1999 and A. Bloed (ed.), *The Conference on Security and Cooperation in Europe: Analysis and Basic Documents 1972–1993*, Martinus Nijhoff, 1993; A Bloed (ed.), *The Conference on Security and Cooperation in Europe: Analysis and Basic Documents 1993–1995*, Martinus Nijhoff, 1997.

19. See A. F. Glover, 'Opinion: the human dimension of the Organization on Security and Cooperation in Europe – the ODIHR in Warsaw', *European Human Rights Law Review*, Issue 6/1997, 553–65.

20. See OSCE website: http://www.osce.org.

21. See Daniela Napoli, 'The European Union's Foreign Policy and Human Rights', in Nannette A. Neuwahl and Allan Rosas (eds), *The European Union and Human Rights*, Kluwer Law International, London 1995, 297–312.

22. See Wolfgang Benedek, 'Die Bedeutung der Menschenrechte in der EU', in *Journal für Entwicklungspolitik* 1/1994, 13–31; Wolfgang Benedek, 'Menschenrechte und Entwicklung am Beispiel der EU', in A. Liebmann und W. Amon (Hg.), *Umwelt, Friede und Entwicklung*, Vienna, 145–56 and Christian Pippan, 'Positive Maßnahmen als Aspekt der Demokratieförderung in der Entwicklungszusammenarbeit der EU', in *Journal für Entwicklungspolitik*, 4/1998, 439–64.

23. See L. Betten and D. Mac Deritt (eds), *The Protection of Fundamental Social Rights in the European Union*, Kluwer Law International, London 1996.

24. See Council Directive 207/76 on the Equal Treatment of Women and Men regarding access to employment, vocational training, etc.

25. See Council Recommendation 635/84 on the Promotion of Positive Measures for Women.

26. See legal rule of priority for women in the promotion in sectors of the public service containing a 'saving clause' not precluded by the 1976 Equal Treatment Directive (Marschall case), *Human Rights Law Journal*, Vol. 19 (1998), 2–4, 114–16.

27. See Anna Sporrer, 'The legislative basis for positive action in Europe', in *The Promotion of Women in the Public Service of the Member States and Institutions of the European Union*, European Union Conference in Vienna 1998, EC-DG V (Austrian) Federal Ministry for Women's Issues and Consumer Protection, Vienna 1999, 10–23. This book contains a valuable overview of the legal practice on equality in EU states.

28. See Oji Umozurike, *The African Charter on Human and Peoples' Rights*, Kluwer Law International, London 1998; Wolfgang Benedek, 'The African human rights system', in Catarina Krause and Allan Rosas (eds), *Development Cooperation and Processes Towards Democracy*, Helsinki 1991, 43–50; Catarina Krause and Allan Rosas (eds), 'The African Charter and Commission on Human and Peoples' Rights, how to make it more effective', *Netherlands Quarterly of Human Rights*, Vol. 11 (1993) 1, 25–44.

29. See Rachel Murray, 'Serious or massive violations under the African Charter on Human and Peoples' Rights: a comparison with the inter-American and European mechanisms', in *Netherlands Quarterly of Human Rights*, Vol. 17 (1999) 2, 109–33.

30. See *Protocol to the African Charter on Human and Peoples' Rights on the Establishment of an African Court on Human and Peoples' Rights*, OAU/LEG/MIN/AFCHPR/PROT (I), rev. 2, adopted in June 1998. It needs the ratification of 15 states to come into force.

31. See Makau Mutua, 'The African Human Rights Court: a two-legged stool?', *Human Rights Quarterly*, Vol. 21 (1999) 2, 342–63.

32. See Wolfgang Benedek, 'The role of international law in the protection and promotion of human rights of women in Africa', in *The Review of the African Commission on Human and Peoples' Rights*, Vol. 5 (1995), 1–2, 21–34.

33. See the Annual Reports of the African Commission on Human and Peoples' Rights, which list the cases in annex.

34. See Rachel Murray, *The African Commission on Human and Peoples' Rights and International Law*, Oxford (Hart) 2000.

35. Cf. Wolfgang Benedek, supra note 32, 31 et seq.

36. Such exchanges have taken place in the past. See Wolfgang Benedek/Wolfgang Heinz (eds), 'Regional systems of human rights protection in Africa, America and Europe', Third Afro-Americo-European Conference, Strasburg 1992, Friedrich Naumann Foundation, Brussels 1992.

Part II

African Experiences

8

Introduction to the African System of Protection of Human Rights and the Draft Protocol

Henry Onoria

The African Charter on Human and Peoples' Rights[1] had its origin in concerns about human rights on the continent on the part of the Organization of African Unity.[2] The Charter represents the continent's efforts to provide for a regional mechanism for the protection of human (and peoples') rights in the same mould as the systems that were conceived in Europe in 1950 and the Americas in 1969. Some scholars, however, argue that it is a product of the 'geopolitical realities' of the decade preceding its inception in 1981, of wanton violations of human rights by dictatorial regimes and the 'human rights rhetoric' that underpinned the foreign policy of Western donor states.[3] This criticism was perhaps well-founded given that in 1981 a large number of the governments that agreed to the final version of the Charter in Banjul were far from democratic.[4]

The African Charter is nevertheless to be contrasted with its European and American predecessors in the manner of its 'conceptualization' of rights (and duties) as well as its 'enforcement' mechanisms (at least as initially conceived in 1981 until the late 1990s). The Charter is premised upon what its framers perceived as a characteristic feature of the African societal set-up: a communitarian unit in which the status of the individual is defined within the family, society and state.[5] The relationship between the individual and community underpins certain facets of the normative regime regarding rights under the Charter. First, the inspiring norms are the 'traditions and values' borne out and reflected in 'African civilization'.[6] Second, the rights are paralleled by 'duties' that are owed by the individual to the communitarian units.[7] Third, the rights accrue to both the individual and 'peoples' – though the latter might similarly reflect the collective in a community, it is more evident that the notion of peoples' rights in the Charter is a continium of a rubric of 'self-determination' rights originally conceived during the period of decolonization.[8] Apart from this, the conception of the enforcement mechanisms under the Charter makes it distinct from the European and American systems – for in its initial lack of a Court, which is a major feature of these other systems, the Charter in putting in place only the African Commision on Human and Peoples' Rights (coupled with the nature of its mandate) reflected the 'conciliatory' approach to the resolution of issues characteristic of most traditional African societies. This has turned out to be a major weakness of the Charter system of protection, which has since necessitated the setting up of an African Court on Human and Peoples' Rights.[9]

The Banjul Charter has yet to be blessed with an engaging jurisprudence that has become the main strength of the European and American human rights systems. So it remains to be seen how the organs of the Charter will address these jurisprudential and philosophical facets of its normative sources. It is notable that the Charter calls on the African Commission on Human and Peoples' Rights to consider 'African practices ... customs generally accepted as law, general principles of law recognised by African states'[10] as subsidiary sources. The presumption is that the Commission (and the Court) is expected to make reference to traditional practices and customs that are common to African societies, and are 'consistent with international norms on human and peoples' rights'. Presently, municipal courts are playing a leading role in the invocation of 'traditions' and 'customs' in respect of not only relationships within society but also the protection of human rights. Thus a Mauritius court referred to a custom on land ownership rights,[11] and a South African court to the age-old *ubuntu* concept of 'humanness' common to the Bantu peoples to construe the death penalty as a violation of the right to life.[12] In the latter instance, the South African Supreme Court was able to explore the intricacies of the *communitarian* and *reconciliatory* set-up that reflects traditional African society. On the other hand, the municipal courts have themselves found, in the philosophical content of the Charter provisions, the guiding spirit of society. This was the more apparent in the instance of the Tanzanian Court of Appeal, which referred to the Charter provisions on 'duties' as a corollary to the rights that an individual claimed to be entitled to.[13] The court drew a link between the Banjul Charter and the Tanzanian Constitution:

> the Constitution recognised and guaranteed not only basic human rights, but also basic human duties. This was symbolic and significant, expressing a constitutionally-recognised co-existence of the individual human being and society, as well as the co-existence of rights and duties of the individual and society ... This view was supported by the principles under-lying the African Charter on Human and Peoples' Rights ... which Tanzania signed in 1982 and ratified in 1984, and account of which should therefore be taken

in interpreting the Bill of Rights and Duties introduced into the Constitution of Tanzania in 1985.[14]

Since the major concern of this course is the human rights of women, this cannot be done without first understanding the implications of this philosophical premise of the Charter. Women in Africa have largely remained trapped in communitarian structures steeped in tradition, and it is this subject that is to be addressed next.

Women's Rights under the African Charter on Human and Peoples' Rights

The Banjul Charter is perhaps further distinct from the other regional systems for the protection of human rights in that it has a specific provision that addresses the rights of women. This is apart from the commonplace provisions on the 'right to equality' and 'freedom from discrimination'[15] that adorn most international and regional human rights treaties[16] – these remain but the starting premise of any discourse on gender relations and rights of women.[17] With specific regard to human rights of women, the Charter provides that: 'The State shall ensure the elimination of every discrimination against women and also ensure the protection of the rights of the woman and the child as stipulated in international declarations and conventions.'[18]

The provision has been regarded as being too general, without any substantiation on the rights of women, with the most scathing attack being that '[t]he Banjul Charter has placed the rights of women in a "legal coma"'.[19] Furthermore, the criticism may be levelled upon the fact that rights of women are addressed with those of children in the same breath – while women and children have always been perennial victims of violations of human rights in a conflict-ridden continent, it brings to mind the undesirable connotation of equating the former with the latter. On the other hand, the Charter is seen as providing a starting point for the protection of women's rights.[20]

While the Banjul Charter does not have the specificity on women's rights contained in the Convention on the Elimination of All Forms of Discrimination against Women,[21] it can form the basis for having states account for the status of women and protection of their rights within their *national legal orders*. Article 18, paragraph (3) is specific as regards the protection of the human rights of women to the extent that it places *responsibility* on states to 'eliminate discrimination' and 'protect their rights'. This *responsibility* in effect enjoins African states to undertake positive steps to ensure that their national laws and policies seek or result in the attainment of these two primary goals. To this end, it is to be noted that protection of women's rights under the Charter is envisaged in terms of the fact of their stipulation in international declarations and conventions, and this would include CEDAW. Thus states that are party to the Charter and the various conventions on women's rights would have to undertake the entire rubric of 'protection' called for in those conventions. This seems to have been the position that was taken by the Botswana Supreme Court in *Attorney-General* v. *Unity Dow*, when it made reference to both the Banjul Charter and CEDAW, both of which Botswana was a party to [22] – this was nothwithstanding the fact that neither had been domesticated in its municipal law.[23] Because the Charter organs are to draw inspiration from 'instruments adopted by the United Nations and by African countries in the field of human and peoples' rights ...',[24] the Commission would be expected to make reference to the *forms* of protection envisaged under, for instance, CEDAW to determine whether a particular state was giving effect to Article 18, paragraph (3).

Perhaps the more problematic aspect of the protection of human rights of women under the Charter is the 'contextualization'. Article 18, paragraph (3) is placed within the context of the 'family' and 'traditional values' in paragraphs (1) and (2). There may seem manifest a conflict in the perceived role of the state in this regard which is to protect the 'family as the custodian of traditional values' at the same time as ensuring the protection of 'rights of the woman'. The operative word here is *manifest*, given the fact that the major violations of rights of women occur within the private realm of family relations, or, for that matter, its wider forms of clan, caste or tribe. Further, the suppression of women's rights often occurs under the cloud of tradition, custom and cultural values. An early criticism of the 'family' provisions of the Charter in this respect was voiced by Makau wa Mutua in his remarks that:

> The Charter tolerates, confirms and supports repressive structures of social and political ordering. A particular problematic issue concerns its 'family' provisions, especially their gender implications. Article 18 of the Charter provides, inter alia, that the 'family shall be the natural unit and basis of society' and shall be assisted by the State as the 'custodian of morals and traditional values' ... Among other things, this language seeks to entrench the oppressive family structure, complete with its exploitation and marginal-isation of women in the public and so-called private spheres.[25]

The family unit remains the most repressive of rights of women (and girl children) in the African societies. Within this unit, women suffer battery, rape, and inequality as regards education opportunities and rights of inheritance, to mention but a few instances. When an English judge refused to recognize a subsisting relationship as a marriage in colonial Kenya early in the century,[26] the African scholars were up in arms over what they saw as his ignorance in the ways of the African. But his denunciation of what he viewed as treating the woman as a 'chattel' would find a place in modern discourse on rights of women. No wonder a Zimbabwean woman was willing to go to prison for arson in burning up her father-in-law's hut rather than agree to his sexual demands on her on the grounds that while his son was away, he had a duty to look after his son's 'property', or a Ugandan woman sought to challenge her arrest for elopement on account that she had married a man other than the brother of her late husband as being in violation of her constitutionally granted rights.[27] In these instances the family unit was backed up by tradition and custom, and the former was indeed purporting to act as the 'custodian' of the latter.

What is significant in this respect is how states and the courts have responded to this 'manifest' conflict in the Charter provisions – for their attitude may ultimately guide the Charter organs in event of a communication bearing on 'rights of women' and an age-old 'tradition' or 'custom'. Invariably, as noted above, Charter organs will be expected to draw inspiration from traditions and customs that are *consistent with international norms on human and peoples' rights*.[28] Further, since the rule on exhaustion of local remedies is a feature of the Charter's enforcement regime, it is inevitable that it is at the point of the national courts that the tussle between rights of women and tradition will and is to be felt. Thus, apart from deferring to the 'non-discrimination' provisions of the Charter, the Botswana Supreme Court disallowed the argument about 'traditions' of a 'patriarchal society' that denied lineage (and in effect citizenship) via the mother.[29] In effect, the court was willing to discard a tradition that was in violation of the rights of women[30] and uphold the principle of non-discrimination. In a more recent saga, in Uganda, an age-old tradition associated with the cultural institution of the Kabakaship in Buganda was the cause of an uproar. According to this custom, a young virgin girl called 'Nakku' was to be given to the Kabaka as a 'ceremonial wife' – the particular girl chosen turned out to be 14 years old.[31] While the matter did not end up before the courts, it posed the potential problem of the conflict between 'tradition' and 'women's (or girl child's) rights' even within the domestic setting, where the Constitution recognizes the 'right to practise culture' but also disavows customs that offend the dignity and rights of women.[32]

Significant developments have taken place towards a more comprehensive legal regime for the protection of human rights of women. The result has been a draft protocol to the Banjul Charter on Women's Rights[33] – the draft protocol elaborates on the provisions of Articles 2 and 18 of the Charter,[34] and is an impressive catalogue of various rights ranging from dignity and physical security, domestic relations, political rights, economic and welfarist rights, health and reproductive rights. The rights contained in the draft protocol are in certain respects elaborative of existing rights under the Banjul Charter in their application to women. For the present purposes, it may be necessary to comment on certain aspects of the draft protocol.

a) First, it reiterates the *responsibility* stipulated in Article 18, paragraph (3) for states parties to take *positive action* in areas where discrimination against women continues to exist *in law and in fact*, as well as take in effect 'affirmative' action.[35]

b) Second, the preservation of African values (customs, traditions, etc.) must accord with the principles of 'equality and dignity of women',[36] with measures to be taken to protect women from the harmful effects of cultural (or religious) practices.[37] In effect, incidents such as those referred to above would be in violation of the dignity and rights of women.

c) Third, the violations that occur in the 'private sphere' of the family, clan, or tribal setting are dealt with under the right to physical security, which embraces matters such as rape, trafficking and commercial exploitation and female genital mutilation.[38] This is further backed up by specific provisions relating to marriage and widowhood[39]– the instance of the tradition of 'wife inheritance' is actually contemplated under the draft protocol.[40] Related aspects to this aspect of dignity of women are the provisions on measures to prohibit all forms of 'violence against women'[41] and 'reproductive rights',[42] construed along Articles 4 and 16 of the Bajul Charter respectively.

d) Fourth, the rights of women are to embrace the civil and political rights,[43] economic and social welfare rights[44] in conformity with Articles 13 and 15 of the Banjul Charter respectively. Related are the rights to education and training,[45] and to adequate housing.[46]

e) Fifth, the rights of women are construed within the realm of the peoples' rights of *peace* (and in effect, their protection as one of the primarily vulnerable groups in armed conflict situations), *environmental management*, and *development* (in terms of access to land, credit, etc.).[47]

It is yet to be seen whether any modifications will be made to the draft protocol for any substantive critique of its provisions. As it stands, the protocol promises to be as good an elaborative document as CEDAW for the protection of women's rights.

Mechanisms for the Protection of Rights under the African Charter on Human and Peoples' Rights

The primary mechanism for the promotion and protection of human rights under the Charter is the African Commission on Human and Peoples' Rights[48] which was established in 1987. In recent years, the most prominent aspect of the Commission has been its promotional function[49] – the Commission has carried out promotional activities in the form of research, workshops and seminars with respect to the human rights situation on the continent. The Commission's primary role of 'protection' in respect of dealing with human rights violations has not got off the ground in a serious way[50] – in effect, there is no profound jurisprudence in this regard that parallels its European and American counterparts. In the light of this weakness, the idea of an African Court on Human and Peoples' Rights was mooted in 1992,[51] culminating in a protocol for its establishment in 1998.[52] It is yet to be seen how successful this new organ will be in light of the shortcomings and problems that hampered the Commission.

The 'protection' under the Charter is not dissimilar from that of the European and American systems. The Charter envisages communications on allegations of human rights violations from the state parties[53] and other entities (in this regard, individuals and NGOs).[54] Invariably, the usual matters are called into play. First, the claim can only be presented against a state that is a party to the Charter.[55] Second, a claim may be brought before the Commission only after the *exhaustion of local remedies*.[56] As noted above, the tension between the protection of women's rights and dictates of tradition is likely to occur at the first instance before the national courts. It is only inevitable that the present jurisprudence on this subject has come from the domestic fora.[57] Third, it must relate to the human and peoples' rights under the Charter. So a claim pertaining to the violations of the human rights of women would be properly brought before the Commission under the various articles of the Charter – Articles 2, 3 and 18 (3). The prominent rights that have been dealt with by the African Commission, as of 1996, have been those regarding 'fair trial' under Articles 7 and 26 of the Charter.[58] Apart from the non-exhaustion of local remedies, certain of the communications have been regarded as 'incoherent' and the complaints as 'vague' – this has been the case with respect to a claim of 'torture' against Kenya,[59] and a claim of 'self-determination' by Katanga 'people' against Zaire.[60]

Domestication of the African Charter on Human and Peoples' Rights

The Banjul Charter invariably begs the question of its status before the *domestic legal order* of its states parties. Furthermore, it also brings to mind its invocation or referral before the *domestic courts* of those states. The fate of the protection of human rights of women under the Charter is to an extent dependent on this factor. In any event, Article 18, paragraph (3), in placing obligation on a state to ensure the elimination of discrimination against women, must enjoin the state to carry out legislative measures to bring this about. It is on this basis that the argument may be made that the failure to domesticate provisions of the Charter would itself, as regards women's rights, be construed as a failure to ensure the protection envisaged under Article 18 – in effect, even violations of rights that occur in the 'private sphere' would be imputable to the state. On the other hand, it may be debated whether the existence of legislation or constitutional provisions securing and protecting women's rights amounts to domesticating Article 18 of the Charter. The more practical aspect of domestication of the Charter is the passing of an enabling legislation by the state party's legislature – this would then enable an aggrieved individual to rely on the Charter obligations before national courts (and other judicial organs), or for the courts to refer to such obligations in their decisions.

The record of domestication of the Charter among the states parties has been rather unimpressive. In a seminar organized in Banjul-Gambia in October 1992, the African Commission noted that 'few African States which [had] ratified the Charter [had] incorporated it into their domestic systems'.[61] Further, and more significantly, in the face of the pathetic state of incorporation,

> [t]he Seminar called upon the judiciary in African States, when rendering decisions in domestic courts, to have regard to international human rights norms and regional human rights instruments. It was stressed that such instruments were a useful aid to interpretation of domestic legislation, as well as the wealth of international jurisprudence which exists on human rights matters.[62]

The domestic courts have in fact been proactive as regards the obligations entered into by states under the Banjul Charter. Invariably, due to the non-domestication of the Charter, the courts have adopted a number of stances such as (i) provisions of the Charter being an aid to interpretation of national legislation; (ii) presumption of consistency of domestic legislation with international obligations; and (iii) duty of the courts to ensure respect by the state of its international obligations.[63] In two cases, the courts have referred to the Charter for purposes of stressing the obligations with respect to protection of rights of women, specifically where acts complained of were discriminatory – in the Unity Dow case in Botswana[64] and the Longwe case in Zambia.[65] In fact, the latter case involved discrimination on the part of Intercontinental Hotels, and not by an agency of the state – the reference to the Charter in the circumstances is quite innovative as regards dealing with violations of women's rights by 'private entities'.

Concluding Remarks

The Banjul Charter has shown itself capable of being a mechanism for the protection of rights of women. The draft Protocol to the Charter on the Rights of Women is a welcome instrument to provide for greater articulation of Article 18, paragraph (3). As to the practical realization of equality and non-discrimination of women in gender relations in Africa, the tension between 'tradition' and 'rights' will have to be tackled, alongside holding the states to their obligations of putting in place 'measures' for its realization – where the articulation in international instruments is a much easier task to accomplish, the protection of women's rights in practice remains problematic.[66]

Notes

This chapter reflects the substance of the lectures given during the Sixth Postgraduate Course on Human Rights of Women held at Fairway Hotel, Kampala, Uganda, 23–24 August 1999. Henry Onoria is Lecturer, Department of Public and Comparative Law, Faculty of Law, Makerere University.

1. *African Charter on Human and Peoples' Rights*, OAU Doc. CAB/LEG/75/3, rev. 5, 1981 (hereinafter Banjul Charter).

2. See C. Nwankwo, 'The OAU and human rights' (1993) 4(3) *Journal of Democracy* 50; E. C. Welch, Jr, 'The OAU and Human Rights', in Y. El-Ayouty (ed.), *The Organisation of African Unity after Thirty Years*, (Westport: Praeger Publishers, 1994) 53.

3. Makau wa Mutua, 'The African human rights system in a comparative perspective: the need for urgent reformulation' (1992) 44 *Nairobi Law Monthly* 27: 27.

4. The apparent ommission of reference to 'will of the people' as the basis of government is notable in the Charter. While paras (1) and (2) of Article 13 of the Charter are similar to paras (1) and (2) of Article 22 of the Universal Declaration of Human Rights, the equivalent of para. (3) in the latter is lacking in the Charter. Furthermore, the clawback clauses in the Charter are seen to reinforce 'undemocratic' tendencies: Makau wa Mutua, ibid., at 28.

5. See Keba Mbaye, 'African Charter on Human and Peoples' Rights', an introduction to the conference on *Implementation of Human Rights in Africa* (Nariobi, Kenya, 2–4 December 1985).

6. Banjul Charter, preambular para. 5; Arts 17 (3), 18 (2), 29 (7) and 61.

7. Ibid., Arts 27–9.

8. Ibid., Arts 19–24. The peoples rights in question are: (a) equality of all peoples; (b) existence and self-determination; (c) disposal of natural resources; (d) development; (e) peace; and (f) environment.

9. Protocol for the Establishment of the African Court on Human and Peoples' Rights, 1998.

10. Banjul Charter, Art. 61.

11. *La Compagnie Sucrière de bel Ombre Ltee* v. *Government of Mauritius* [1995] 3 LRC 494.

12. *State* v. *Makwayane* [1995] 1 LRC 269.

13. *DPP* v. *Pete* [1991] LRC (Const) 553. In this particular intance, the right claimed was in respect of 'bail'.

14. Ibid., pp. 554, 565. The Court of Appeal referred to the preamble of the Charter: ibid., at 565–6.

15. Banjul Charter, Arts 2 and 3.

16. See, for instance, Universal Declaration on Human Rights, 1948, Arts 1, 2 and 7.

17. For a general overview of the concepts as regards the Banjul Charter: P. Nnaemeka-Agu, 'Discrimination and the African Charter on Human and Peoples Rights' (1993) 19(4) *Comm. L. Bull.* 1670. In one instance where a national court made reference to the Charter as regards non-discrimination, it did so with regard to the provision on the 'basis of sex' rather than 'protection of rights of women': *Longwe* v. *Intercontinental Hotels* [1993] 4 LRC 221, p. 223 (Zambia).

18. Banjul Charter, Art. 18(3).

19. W. Benedek and W Heinz (eds), *Regional Systems of Human Rights in Africa, America and Europe: Proceedings of the Conference* (1992) 17 (remarks by Khadija Elmadmad).

20. L. Kois, 'Article 18 of the African Charter on Human and Peoples' Rights: a progressive approach to women's human rights' (1996) 3(2) *EAJP&HR* 103.

21. Convention on the Elimination of All Forms of Discrimination against Women, 18 Dec. 1979 (hereinafter CEDAW).

22. *Attorney-General* v. *Unity Dow* [1992] LRC (Const) 623 (Botswana). A central facet of the argument before the Court was that the non-reference to 'sex' in provisions of the Citizenship Act in effect permitted inequality and discrimination in the treatment of women.

23. The Court took the view that the reference to the Charter (and other conventions) would ensure that Botswana honoured its international obligations.

24. Banjul Charter, Art. 60.

25. Makau wa Mutua, supra, note 3, at 28.

26. *Rex* v. *Amkeyo* [1917] KLR 14.

27. *Maliam Adekur & Another* v. *Joshua Opaja & Another*, Constitutional Petition No. 1/1997. The applicant was, in challenging the custom of 'wife-inheritance', relying on the provisions of Article 33 (1), (4) and (6) of the 1995 Constitution of the Republic of Uganda. The petition itself was dismissed for its having been brought against the wrong (second) defendant.

28. Banjul Charter, Art. 61.

29. Unity Dow case, supra, note 22, at p. 586.

30. For comparative purposes, the Papua New Guinea Supreme Court ruled that an age-old tradition of 'blood-marriage', where a young girl was given to a family whose member had been killed by a member of the girl's family, was in violation of the 'rights of the girl-child': *State* v. *Kunle* [1991] PNG.

31. For a criticism of the 'Nakku' tradition: see e.g. P. Luganda, 'This culture treats the woman as a chattel to satisfy ritual values and treats her as sub-human', *The New Vision*, 6 April 1999, 19.

32. See: Constitution of the Republic of Uganda, 1995, Arts 37 and 33 (6) respectively.

33. Draft Protocol to the African Charter on Women's Rights, report of the second meeting of the Working Group, Dakar, Senegal, 14–15 June 1999. The Dakar draft protocol has since undergone amendments: Draft Protocol to the African Charter on Women's Rights, report of third meeting of the Working Group, Kigali, Rwanda, 30–31 October 1999, annex.

34. Draft Protocol, ibid., preamble, paras 2 and 3; Art. 1.

35. Ibid., Art. 4.

36. Ibid., Arts 2, 4(a).

37. Ibid, Arts 4(b), 5(e), 19(2) and (3).

38. Ibid., Art. 5. The rights are construed along the provisions of Arts 4 and 5 of the Banjul Charter.

39. Ibid., Arts 7–9.

40. Ibid., Art. 9(3). Reference is to be made to the instance of the case of *Maliam Adekur*, supra, note 27.

41. Ibid., Art. 13.

42. Ibid., Art. 16.

43. Ibid., Art. 11.

44. Ibid., Art. 15.

45. Ibid., Art. 14. This is in conformity with Art. 17 of the Banjul Charter.

46. Ibid., Art. 18.

47. Ibid., Arts 12, 20 and 21 respectively. See Arts 21–4 of the Banjul Charter.

48. Banjul Charter, Art. 30.

49. Ibid., Art. 45 (1).

50. Ibid., Arts 45 (2), 47, 50, 56.

51. See African Commission on Human and Peoples' Rights, 'National Implementation of the African Charter on Human and Peoples' Rights', seminar held in Banjul, Gambia, 26–30 October 1992, reported in (1993) 19(1) *Comm. L. Bull.* 312. In December 1995, a draft Protocol was adopted as drafted by government legal experts: 'Government legal experts meeting on the question of an African Court on Human and Peoples' Rights', 6–12 September 1995, Cape Town, South Africa, reported in (1994) 20(2) *Comm. L. Bull.* 652.

52. Supra, note 9.

53. Banjul Charter, Art. 47.

54. Ibid., Arts 55–6.

55. *Kenya Human Rights Commission* v. *Kenya*, AfCHPR Commn. No. 135/94, session of 26 March–4 April 1996 (1996) 10(2) *Interrights Bulletin* 62 – the communication was originally held inadmissible as Kenya was not then a party to the Charter, but was resubmitted after it became a party.

56. Banjul Charter, Art. 56 (5). For communications dismissed for non-exhaustion, see e.g. *Kenya Human Rights Commission*, ibid; *Haye* v. *The Gambia*, AfCHPR Commn. No. 90/93, session of 2–11 October 1995 (1996) 10(1) *Interrights Bulletin* 14.

57. See supra, notes 22 and 23 and accompanying text.

58. See e.g. *Constitutional Rights Project (in respect of Akamu, Adega & Others)* v. *Nigeria*, AfCHPR Commn. No. 60/91, session of 2–11 October 1995 (1996) 10(1) *Interrights Bulletin* 18; *Civil Liberties Organisation* v. *Nigeria*, AfCHPR Commn. No. 129/94, sess. of 26 March–4 April 1996 (1996) 10(2) *Interrights Bulletin* 65.

59. *Njoka* v. *Kenya*, AfCHPR Commn. No. 142/94, session of 2–11 Oct. 1995 (1996) 10(1) *Interrights Bulletin* 34.

60. *Katangese People's Congress* v. *Zaire*, AfCHPR Commn. No. 75/92. The Commission took the view that no concrete evidence was given of violations of 'human' and 'peoples" rights.

61. 'National Implementation of the African Charter' seminar, supra, note 51, at 312. The object of the seminar was to 'explore means by which incorporation of the Charter into African domestic legal systems could be encouraged': ibid.

62. Ibid.

63. See, e.g., Pete case, supra, note 13, at 565–6 (rights and duties); Makwayane case, supra, note 12, at 383 (right to life, freedom from torture); *Kauesa* v. *Minister for Home Affairs & Others* [1994] 2 LRC 263, 302–3, 306 (non-discrimination). In the case of *Nemi & Others* v. *State* [1994] 1 LRC 376, 385–6, the court applied the Charter provision by the fact that Nigeria had domesticated the Charter through an Act of Parliament.

64. Unity Dow case, supra, note 22.

65. Longwe case, supra, note 14, p. 223.

66. For an appraisal of the status and rights of women in Kenya, Tanzania, and Zimbabwe, see: M. A. Freeman, 'Measuring equality: a comparative perspective on women's legal capacity and constitutional rights in five Commonwealth countries' (1990) 16(4) *Comm. L. Bull.* 1418. Modern constitutions in some countries do contain specific provisions on 'women's rights': e.g. Constitution of the Republic of Uganda, Arts 31–3 (this is apart from provisions granting access to public office at local and national level).

9

Women's Rights under Islam

Khadija Elmadmad

Today, women's rights are a world problem as their rights are violated all over the globe. In a letter addressed to the secretary-general of the UN, the Sudanese Fatima Ibrahim, president of the International Democratic Federation of Women[1] and publisher of the Magazine *Women's Voice*, wrote in April 1992: 'Injustice towards women and children all over the world constitutes a failure of democracy and a violation of the principle of justice and of human rights.'[2]

This situation concerns all women in the world in general and Muslim women in particular. In fact, the case of Muslim women is not different from that of women in general, but it is specific. Today, the legal rights and obligations of women under Islam are a vital issue where emotional judgements play a big part and where thoughtful discussion is taking place. In the present Muslim world, there is a great discrepancy between theory and reality, and between national and international laws.

Conceptually, the terms 'human rights', 'women' and 'Islam' have something in common: their ambiguity and plurality of meanings and contextual variation according to culture, usage and geographical location. Human rights could be defined as the rights that guarantee the respect of human dignity. As social concepts they are based on a need for liberty, justice and equality. As ideas, they are relevant to all societies and civilizations, depending on the rights given to individual men and women. But as a legal international concept, they appeared only in the twentieth century and were codified first in the Universal Declaration of Human Rights of 1948. They are now embodied in various national, regional and international laws.[3]

The term 'woman' applies generally to the feminine sex, a female as opposed to a male. A woman is generally opposed to a girl child. Thus the definition of a 'woman' will depend on the definition given to a 'child'. There is no universal consensus on the definition of a 'child' and in some cases the concept of a 'woman' includes that of a child. In Islamic theory, a female becomes a woman when she starts menstruating, generally around ten to twelve years; according to Western standards, at this age she is still a child.

A child is generally opposed to an adult. However, the international standards are not clear on the age when a child attains maturity and there is no exact or fixed international definition of a child. The 1986 international Convention on the Rights of the Child stipulates in its Article 1 that the age limit of childhood is 18 in general, unless the national legislation stipulates a lower age.[4] Article 2/2 of the same Convention declares that: 'each state is free to apply the convention according to its national definition of a child'. In addition, there is no unique legal age of reaching manhood or womanhood (that is, majority) in international practice. There is a majority for penal responsibility (generally 16 years),[5] a majority to take part in armed conflicts (generally 15),[6] a minimum age for access to work (14 to 18),[7] a minimum age to agree to sexual relations.[8]

The term 'Islam' comes from the Arabic verb *aslama*, which means to submit. In the context of the Islamic religion, the word Islam is used in conjunction with two meanings that merge into one another: surrender to God (an inner action) and profession of Islam, that is to say adherence to the message of Prophet Muhammad.[9] The word is also connected with the Arabic concept of *Assalaam*, that is, peace. It denotes that Islam is a way to achieve peace, notably at the personal level. Islam is a religion (*din*) and a way of life (*dunia*). It deals with relations between individuals and God and concerns the relations between Muslims and their relation with their political leaders.

In Western language, it has become customary to speak of Islam to mean the whole body of Muslim people (countries and states), in their socio-cultural as well as religious spheres.[10] This has replaced in the twenty-first century the words 'Mohammedanism' and 'Islamism'.[11] Both of the terms used to mean a religion and a socio-political area. It is in this similar meaning that modern Arabic uses sometimes the word Islam. This includes all the Islamic states gathered in the Organization of the Islamic Conference (OIC) and the Muslim minorities living in the non-Muslim states.[12] Islam is found all over the world, although it is mostly confined to Asia and Africa. There are more than 750 million Muslims in the world and there are some 17 states that declare their adherence to Islamic law in their constitutions.[13]

Muslim women represent approximately half of the international Muslim world. These women live in different situations. When dealing with women in Islam, it is important to distinguish between married/non-married (bachelor, divorced and widowed) and Muslim/non-Muslim women married to Muslim men. The rights of each of these women differ according to their legal and social status.

Human Rights in Islam: Specificity versus Universality

The problem of the universality and specificity of human rights is quite important, especially when dealing with women's rights. This was one of main topics of the United Nations Vienna Conference of Human Rights (14–19 June 1993).[14] Most Muslim countries are Muslim today mainly by their Islamic laws relating to women and the family. Few Muslim states have ratified the international human rights instruments on the rights of women. Very often their refusal to adhere to the universal stipulation relating to women is justified by the Islamic specificity. The few Muslim states that ratified these instruments (mainly Muslim African states) did so with many reservations. Most of these reservations refer to the Islamic law and culture, while in so many other situations and laws Islam is completely absent in these states.[15]

Some defenders of Muslim women's rights have called for a universal human rights cultural legitimacy for all women (Muslim or non-Muslim).[16] Thus Professor An-Na'im is opposed to cultural relativism in human rights and suggests that a cross-cultural analysis of these rights should be undertaken, taking into consideration human dignity. 'Despite the initial lack or inadequacy of concern with universal cultural legitimacy during the formulation and adoption of international standards of human rights, and despite the inadequacy of subsequent efforts to supplement that initial deficiency, those standards remain to be improved rather than abandoned.'[17] He adds that it is not too late to correct the situation in the Muslim world by undertaking cross-cultural work to provide the necessary internal legitimacy for human rights standards: 'The inherent dignity and integrity of the human person, taken as the fundamental underlying value of all human rights, can be extended beyond barriers of sex, race, religion and so on through the principle of reciprocity – namely, that one should concede to others what one claims for oneself.'[18]

When dealing with Islam, one should distinguish between Islamic theory and practice. Islamic theory means the Islamic commands and laws as included in the main Islamic sources: the Koran and the Sunna (the words and acts of the prophet as reported in the books of *Al-Hadith* by Muslim specialists).[19] Despite the division of Islam in the Shia and Sunni sects and the existence of some orthodox and non-orthodox Islamic schools, this division relates mostly to political Islam and remains minor as to the general principles of the Islamic religion and laws.[20] Consequently, women's rights in Islam should be the same all over the Muslim world in theory, but in practice there are many 'Islams' when it comes to women's rights. This can be explained in terms of the different ways the Islamic sects and schools have been interpreting the Koranic stipulations concerning women.

The Situation of Women in Pre-Islamic Arabia

To understand the Islamic rules on women, one should link them with the situation of women in pre-Islamic Arabia and even elsewhere at that time. In most ancient societies from Greece to India, the situation of women was not glorious, but the situation of women in pre-Islamic Arabia was objectively more oppressive. In the *jahilya*, the pre-Islamic era, Arab women were generally considered as goods and were put in the same market as slaves. Within families, they were not allowed to think or speak freely. They could not choose their husbands or keep their dowries. Even the right to life of the newly born female child depended on her father's will and his decision to bury her alive or not to do so. *Waadou al-banat* (female infanticide) was a very common practice among the Arabs of *jahilya*. Women in many Arabian communities had no rights to inheritance and could not participate in the political life of their communities.[21]

Islam brought many innovations and rights for women. But Islam has a universal mission, and is not directed only towards Arab women. In some other parts of the world (though very few), women's rights were not violated as in the pre-Islamic society. For example, in pre-Islamic North Africa, Berber women were considered as equal to men. In some situations, they were even superior to men. Al-Khahina was a well-known Berber political woman leader in North Africa. Her real name was Dhya, and she was called Al-Khahina (the fortune-teller) by the Arabs during their invasion of the area and their fight for the Islamization of the region as they were surprised to see a woman commanding the army. Al-Khahina led the Imazignen tribes and died fighting against the Muslims.

> They are surprised to see a woman lead her community.
> They veil their wives to get a better price for them.
> The most beautiful woman for them
> Is not else than a product for sale.
> She should not be seen from a short distance at all
> She should not speak, she should not be listened to.[22]

Today, the Khahina of North Africa is quite different, and her future seems uncertain. For example, the destiny of the Algerian Khahina is in the hands of some armed groups who, in the name of Islam, are deciding what her rights should be.

Women's Rights in International Law and Islamic Theory

At the international level many documents were issued to assert and protect women's rights. These documents are universal and regional, general and specific.[23] But few Muslim states have adhered to the international stipulations on the rights of women.

The main international instruments on women's rights Among the universal instruments one can quote the UN Charter. This legal document represented in 1946 a turning point in the development of the defence of human rights. It deals with both men and women (Preamble, Art. 1/3, Art. 8). In 1946, a special Commission on Women was created in the UN in order to advance their rights and in 1948, the Universal Declaration on Human Rights was adopted by the General Assembly. This Declaration is generally considered as the first step in the direction of an effective protection of human rights and includes the first international definition of the principle of equal rights.[24]

The United Nations Covenant on Political and Civil Rights of 1966 can be considered as an international codification of human rights and equal rights. It stipulates equal treatment of women and non-discrimination between sexes (Arts 2/2 and 3). The 1966 Covenant on Economic and Cultural Rights also declares equality between men and women.[25]

Among the specific instruments on the rights of women, we can quote the 1952 Convention on the Political Rights of Women, which places women on an equal footing with men in the field of politics, guaranteeing for women the same active and passive voting rights (Arts 1/2) and equal access to public office and all public functions (Art. 3). The 1957 Convention on the Nationality of Married Women places the obligation on contracting states to ensure that neither marriage nor dissolution of marriage between nationals and aliens nor a change in the nationality of the husband during the marriage can *ipso facto* have an effect on the wife's nationality (Art. 1/2). The 1962 Convention on Consent to Marriage, Minimum Age for Marriage and Registration of Marriages represents another universal instrument protecting women's rights. In addition, many of the ILO Conventions relate to equal rights between men and women, such as Convention No. 100 concerning equal remuneration for men and women workers for work of equal value, Convention No. 111 on the elimination of discrimination with respect to employment and occupation, or Convention No. 122, which calls for particular regard for the situation of women in employment policy measures.

However, one of the most significant international achievements in the field of women's rights is without doubt the Convention on the Abolition of All Kinds of Discrimination against Women of 19 December 1979. The proposal to elaborate a Convention of this kind goes back to 1972, when the Commission on the Status of Women took concrete steps to implement the principles contained in the Declaration on Discrimination against Women.[26] This Convention was a great success for women and was signed by some Muslim states: Bangladesh, Egypt, Indonesia, Iraq, Jordan, Libya, Mali, Morocco, Tunisia, Turkey and Yemen.[27]

From the point of view of international law, the Convention represents a unique achievement concerning the rights of women at the universal level. But there is no international procedure for an effective enforcement of the rights provided for in most of these Conventions. It is exclusively a matter for sovereign states to decide how to comply with the international obligations, and not many Muslim states seem to do so.

Women's rights in Islamic theory with reference to universal fundamental human rights Islam has its own concern with human rights. It stresses the need to respect human beings' dignity, both men and women. It is said, thus, in the Koran: 'We have bestowed blessings on Adam's children and carried them by land and sea. We have provided them with good things and exalted them above many of Our creatures.'[28] Some verses deal with the creation of both men and women and state that the first woman was part of the first man on earth: 'Creators of the heavens and the earth, He (God) has given you wives from among yourselves and cattle, male and female.'[29] The fundamental role played by the woman within the family is fully recognized in Islam and there is no difference between men and women, except for their acts: 'Men (meaning human beings), we have created you from a male and a female, and made you into nations and tribes that you might get to know one another. The noblest of you in Allah's sight is the most righteous of you.'[30] Very often, Islam refers to the three fundamental international human rights: equality, liberty and justice. But these rights are sometimes absolute and sometimes not. In addition, in Islam, rights are generally accompanied by duties. The right of a man to inherit (in some situations) twice the share of a woman entails, for example, the duty of a permanent maintenance of women by men whatever a woman's financial situation. The chapter on women in the Koran is a good summary of women's rights in Islam.[31] Equality between men and women is not always absolute. Islam recognizes some differences between the rights of both sexes and a kind of male superiority.

Absolute equality Absolute equality is recognized when dealing with some specific rights. For example, before God men and women are absolutely equal, as it is said in the Koran: 'Men, we have created you from a male and a female, and made you into nations and tribes that you might get to know one another. The noblest of you in Allah's sight is the most righteous of you. Allah is wise and Allah is knowing.'[32] Everyone (men and women) receives retribution from God according to his or her deeds. God says in this respect: 'There are degrees for all according to their deeds. So that Allah may duly requite them for their works. They shall not be wronged.'[33]

The right to life is also an absolute right for both men and women and the killing of any human being is forbidden, except through the process of law: 'Whoever killed a human being, except as a punishment for murder or for sedition in the earth, should be looked upon as though he had killed all mankind; and that whoever saved a human life should be regarded as though he had saved all mankind.'[34] Preserving a human life is for Islam the equivalent of preserving all humanity. The *Qasas* law philosophy (life for life, eye for eye and tooth for tooth) is intended to preserve life for all human creatures, even for the foetus. That is why abortion is forbidden in many cases.

In Islam, equality is guaranteed between men and women before their children, who should owe them the same obedience and should show kindness to both of them: 'If either or both of them attain old age with you, show them no sign of impatience, nor rebuke them; but speak to them kind words. Treat them with humility and tenderness and say: "Lord be merciful to them. They nursed me when I was an infant."'[35] Prophet Mohammed even spoke of a superior rank of mother over fathers when he said: 'Paradise is under the feet of mothers.'

The right to education is also a right of both sexes. It is a duty for men and women to seek knowledge. The Koran says on this: 'Lord, increase my knowledge.'[36] In Islam, intellectuals are liked by God (Surat the creation, v. 28). Education is a duty and parents should educate both their male and female children. Learned men and women should spread knowledge, as those who know and keep knowledge for themselves will be punished. According to Abu Daoud, the Prophet Muhammad said: 'Any educated person who keeps her knowledge for herself will wear in the other life a burning muzzle.'[37]

The right to own and keep property is also absolute for both sexes in Islam. This right should be respected and no one is allowed to violate it.[38] Chopping off the hands of thieves is the sanction Islam reserves for those who do not respect this right. However, this right can be sometimes restricted for both sexes if the individual property owned by a person is much more important than what the person needs, especially if the members of the same family live in total misery. Rich Muslims should take care of the poor members of their family. In addition, in some situations, the right to property can be restricted by the community for public interest.[39] Freedom of property for women is assorted (as it is the case for men) by the obligation of *zakaat* or alms, a kind of a tax given to the needy persons annually.

Non-equal rights between men and women Equality between Muslim men and women is not always absolute in Islam. In certain cases men have more rights than women, and the contrary also happens, but very rarely. Muslim scholars speak of equity instead of equality between sexes. Some Koranic stipulations deal clearly with men's superiority over women: 'Men have authority over women because Allah has made the ones superior to the others, and because they spend their wealth to maintain them. Good women are obedient.'[40] In inheritance women do not have the same share as men: 'A male shall inherit twice as much as a female. If there be more than two girls, they shall have two-thirds of the inheritance; but if there be one only, she shall inherit half.'[41] A woman cannot separate from a man without his consent, while he can repudiate her easily.[42] According to many Islamic schools she cannot marry without a tutor. Polygamy is permitted in Islam. It is said in the Koran: 'If you fear that you cannot treat orphans with fairness, then you may marry such women as seem good to you: two, three, or four of them. But if you fear that you cannot do justice, marry one only or those you possess. This will make it easier for you to avoid injustice.'[43] But this permission is very conditional and polygamy is almost forbidden if we refer to the following verse of the same chapter: 'In no way you can treat your wives in a just manner even though you may wish to do that. Do not set yourself altogether against any of them, leaving her, as it were in suspense.'[44]

Inequality between men and women in Islam can be found in other fields: after separation or death of a husband, a woman cannot marry immediately and has to wait for a fixed waiting period (*Iddah*), and as a witness she has not legally the same rights as a man. In work, she does not have the same rights to legal, religious or political jobs. Justifications are generally found for each of these inequalities: the superior physical condition of men, a woman's sensitivity and so on. However, in some specific situations, women have also more rights than men. For example, guardianship is automatically given to the mother unless she relinquishes this right to the father. Moreover, mothers are more honoured in Islam than fathers: 'Fear Allah, in whose name you plead with one another and honour the mothers who bore you.'[45]

Liberty of women in Islam Women are sometimes absolutely free, but it is not always the case. Islam has called for freedom for all human beings, who all have the same origin: 'You are the descendants of Adam and Adam comes from earth.'[46] Islam has recommended abandoning slavery (for both men and women) and has encouraged its abolition: 'The penalty for a broken oath is the feeding of ten needy men with such food that you normally offer or the freeing of one slave.'[47] Other verses encourage also the abolition of slavery. For an involuntary killing, it is recommended to free a slave (Surat of Women, v. 92). To forgive those who have sworn not to have any more relations with a woman and have changed their mind, it is also recommended to free a slave: 'Those who divorce their wives by *Zihar* and afterwards retract their words shall free a slave before they touch each other again.'[48] Al-Khalifa Omar Ibn Al Khattab, the second Islamic leader after the Prophet Muhammad, frequently repeated that human beings are born free and no one should enslave them.

Marriage in Islam is normally entered into by a contract of offer and acceptance by the mutual consent of the two parties: the bride and the bridegroom. Women should not be obliged, generally, to marry against their will. If a woman has been obliged to marry, she is allowed to ask for divorce.[49]

Liberty in Islam is conditional in some cases. Tolerance and liberty of opinion are sometimes absolute but not always. For example, in religious matters, one should be tolerant and accept other people's ideas as no one is obliged to adopt Islam: 'There shall be no compulsion in religion.'[50] Women are not entitled to total freedom. In specific situations, their liberty is limited. Abortion, sexual relations out of marriage, changing religion after having accepted Islam or marring a non-Muslim are considered to be anti-Islamic actions.

The right to dress freely represents a very important question in the Islamic world. The question of the veil is very sensitive in Muslim culture, notably now with the development of fundamentalist movements within the Muslim communities. The interpretation of the few verses reserved to this question in the Koran varies from one Islamic school to another and from one country to another. Concerning the veil, it is said in the Koran: 'Say to the believing women to turn their chastity; to cover their adornment, except such as are normally displayed; to draw their veil to their bosoms and not to reveal their finery except for their husbands, their fathers, their husbands' fathers, their sons, their step-sons, their brothers, their brothers' sons, their sisters' sons, their women servants, the women they possess, male attendants lacking in natural vigour, and children who have no knowledge of sex. And let them not stamp their feet in walking so as to reveal their hidden trinkets.'[51] Referring to this verse, various practices relating to women's customs have developed in the Muslim world. A liberal interpretation has given birth to the wearing of modern clothes, and conservative interpretations resulted in covering women from their heads to their feet. Today in some countries, notably in Iran, Algeria, Sudan or the Gulf States, a special way of veiling women is imposed and women have no right to dress freely.

Justice as a right of women in Islam Justice is very important in Islam. Islam is against injustice, dictatorship and tyranny for all human beings, regardless of their sex. In verse 279 of the Chapter of the Cow, God instructs believers not to wrong anyone. Many of God's names in Islam mean justice (*al-haqq*). A *hadith* states that God likes 'just persons'.[52] He even understands the revenge of a person who has endured injustice: 'Those who avenge themselves when wronged incur no guilt. But great is the guilt of those who oppress their fellow men and conduct themselves with wickedness and injustice. These shall be sternly punished.'[53] Men and women are equal before law, though in other fields there exists a kind of inequality between the two sexes: 'Women shall with justice have rights similar to those exercised against them, although men have a status above women.'[54] Islam calls for the respect of women and kindness towards women within the family. It said in the Koran that God 'gave you wives from among yourselves, that you might live in tranquillity with them and put love and kindness in your hearts'.[55] These are some of the rights granted to women in Islam, but Islam does not give an organized code of women's rights as do the present international instruments relating to the human rights of women.

Muslim States' Attitude towards the Question of Women's Rights

The diversity of interpretations of the Islamic commands and the various Muslim practices concerning women are more important in the Islamic world than in any other fields. When considering women's rights, one is confronted by 'many Islams'. The Turkish, the Indonesian or the Tunisian laws on women are completely different from the Sudanese, the Saudi, the Iranian or the Moroccan ones. Muslim states have rarely adhered to the international universal standards on the rights of women or incorporated them in their national laws. Islamic documents relating to human rights are mainly draft documents and most of them refer to the Sharia (Islamic law) without giving a clear meaning to this law. Most domestic laws on the right of women refer also to Islam with different interpretations of the Islamic stipulations.

Women's rights in the Islamic regional documents There are no regional binding Islamic conventions on human rights, but there are some draft texts in the Muslim and in the Arab worlds.

Documents issued in the Muslim world There are few regional Islamic draft instruments on human rights. Among these instruments, one can mention the Islamic Universal Declaration on Human Rights of 19

September 1981, which was issued by the Islamic Council in London. This declaration stipulates in Article XIX the right to marry according to religion, to establish a family and to be respected by the other partner. This Article declares that: 'women and men should share obligations and responsibility according to their sex' and that 'no one should be married against his/her will'.[56]

However, Article XX speaks only of the rights of married women and seems to ignore those who are unmarried. The rights of a married woman are: to live in the house of her husband, to have enough means to live at the same level as her husband and to receive after divorce during the period of *iddah* an amount of money for subsistence and for taking care of her children. This right exists whether she earns money or not. A woman has the right to demand *khul* (dissolution of marriage by abandoning some of her rights) and has also the right to ask for divorce by courts of justice. She is entitled to inherit from her husband, parents or other persons according to Islamic law. Her husband or ex-husband should keep her secrets and she has the right of confidentiality, but is required also to keep confidentiality *vis-à-vis* her husband's secrets. In August 1990, the Organization of the Islamic Conference issued in Cairo a Declaration on Human Rights.[57] It stipulates in Article I that: 'All men are equal in terms of basic human dignity and basic obligations and responsibilities, without any discrimination on the grounds of race, colour, language, sex ... '. Article 4 declares: 'a) woman is equal to man in human dignity, and has rights to enjoy as well duties to perform; she has her own civil entity and financial independence, and right to retain her name and lineage. b) the husband is responsible for the support and welfare of the family.' Article 19 adds: 'All individuals are equal before the law.'

Instruments issued in the Arab world For a long time, the Arab League has been working on a draft Convention on Human Rights in the Arab World, but no consensus seems to have been reached on this draft.

However, a Charter on Human and Peoples' Rights in the Arab World was prepared by a group of experts at the International Institute of Higher Studies in Criminal Sciences, Siracusa, in 1987 and was proposed for adoption by the Arab states. This Charter stipulates freedom of movement (Art. 8), equality before the law and before the courts (Arts 11 and 12), and the right to have a family (14), but there is no specific article on women's rights, although there is an article relating to disabled persons. This might be explained either by the fact that the topic of women's rights is a sensitive one among the Arabs or by the fact that there is not a common view about it in the region. The Arab Labour Organization (a special organization within the Arab League) issued in 1955 an Arab charter on labour and in 1967 a treaty on levels of work. Both of these documents deal with women workers' rights in the region.[58] Other stipulations of other regional instruments can also apply to some Muslim women, such as Article 18 of the African Charter on Human and Peoples' Rights of 1981.[59]

Present laws and practices relating to women in the Islamic world
In practice, women's rights vary from one Muslim state to another and from one region to another. Some examples of some Arab domestic laws on women will be mentioned, but an emphasis will put on the Moroccan legislation.

Women's rights in some selected Arab countries Although the Arab world seems to form one region, laws and practices concerning women's rights vary a lot from one Arab state to another. In Libya, for example, Articles III and V of the Constitution grant women equality in political rights, and no Libyan law forbids women from participating in political activities. Libyan law does not establish a difference between men and women in terms of economic rights, social security or the right to work. Women in Libya are entitled to ask for separation from their husbands for some specific reasons (notably long absence from home, illness or no maintenance).

In Lebanon, women's rights differ according to the confessional group they belong to and to the personal status they are governed by. But the Constitution proclaims equality between men and women. Men give their nationality to the children but women can also do so in the case of an illegitimate child. Women married to Lebanese men become nationals after one year of marriage. A woman is considered an adult at the age of 18. But to engage in commerce, women need their husband's permission. Polygamy is permitted when it is necessary and according to the personal status referred to and the stipulations of the marriage contract. In penal law, if a wife has been murdered to safeguard the husband's honour, the murderer sanction is lightened. In the case of adultery, a woman's punishment is more severe than that of a man.[60]

In Syria, polygamy is permitted on the condition that a man can support all his wives. As for dowry, the Syrian law accepts a minimum or even no dowry, if the woman accepts this. Maintenance is a duty of a man according to his economic situation. There is a possibility of repudiation (unilateral separation) of a woman by her husband, but he should pay an indemnity when the divorced wife is poor. Marriage cannot be contracted for a girl who is under 18 (17 for a boy), and needs her consent. A woman can marry herself if there is no opposition from her tutor. Maintenance should be paid for a divorced woman taking care of her children. In civil matters, a woman is free to conduct transactions at the age of 18 without any authorization. This applies to Muslim women; other religions are governed by their own personal status.[61]

In Sudan, from 1956 to 1985, all the previous constitutional texts guaranteed a kind of equality between men and women.[62] For example, Article 38 of the 1973 Constitution proclaims an absolute equality of men and women before duties and for rights. Because of this, Sudanese women were given many rights under the early government of Numeiry, such as equality in getting jobs or social security. In 1960, an active Commission of Women was created with the aim to fight for the freedom to travel abroad without the need for permission from the husband or tutor. In addition, according to the 1957 Law on Nationality, women could give their nationality to their husbands. With the introduction of Sharia Law in Sudan, women have seen some of their equal rights disappear, notably the rights to free movement, liberty of dress or equality with men in courts. The Islamic law introduced by Numeiry in the 1970s (and confirmed by Al-Bachir's government in the 1990s) allowed that a woman could be forced to marry if prostitution was feared.[63] A girl child can thus be married at the age of ten if she presents signs of not having good conduct.[64]

In Saudi Arabia, the only law that applies to women is the Sharia (interpretation of the Islamic sources). This law refers to the Hanbalite school, the most conservative Sunni school. The Saudi government does not recognize human rights as they have been universally proclaimed and opposes any movement that refers to them. In the beginning of May 1993 a group of six Saudi intellectuals decided to create a non-governmental national Human Rights Commission for protecting human rights and receiving claims relating to human rights violation according to the international standards. They issued a note concerning this commission, which was signed by over ten thousand people all over the country. But the Supreme Committee of Muslim Scholars (*Ulamaa*) issued a declaration (taken by consensus) condemning this Human Rights Commission and proclaiming it illegal. The Islamic Scholars' Committee declared: 'This Human Rights Commission is illegal and cannot work in Saudi Arabia as this country is ruled by God's law and there are many courts in the country controlling the respect of Sharia Law.'[65]

On 10 May 1993, during its fortieth meeting, the Islamic Scholars' Committee expressed 'its shock and surprise following the act of those who considered themselves as the protectors of human rights in the country and the publicity they made of this event in the foreign media'.[66] As a reaction to the adherence of the members of the Human Rights Commission to the universal standards on human rights, the Saudi government issued a decision to dismiss five of them from their functions in the government and to bar them from practising law in the country. In addition, 400 people were then jailed, including the press representative of the commission, M. Mohammed Abdallah Al-Masaari. The Arab Organization of Human Rights has protested against the Saudi behaviour with the founding members of the commission.

Women's rights in Morocco In Morocco, women's rights were first codified in 1957 in the *Moudouyyana*, the Moroccan code of personal status.[67] This code was based on Islamic law and did not proclaim equal rights between men and women. A lot of criticism was addressed to this *Moudouyyana* and some draft reforms were proposed. But it is especially from 1980 on that this criticism became acute. Following this, King Hassan II decided to take the matter into his hands. Referring to a *Hadith* of the Prophet Muhammad, he asserted: 'Women are equal to men as far as their rights are concerned.'[68] In a speech on 8 September 1992, the king declared that he would personally deal with women's problems in Morocco and added that it was high time 'to render justice to the other half of the Moroccan population'. He then contacted most of the Moroccan women's organizations and formed a commission to discuss the problem of women's rights.[69] The King promised to render justice to women by applying 'the tolerant dimension of Sharia Law'.[70] He decided then to review the *Moudouyyana*, and many *ulema* (Muslim scholars), experts and representatives of women's organizations were associated with this work.

The king received a delegation of women and discussed with them the possibilities of reforming the code of personal status. These proposals were submitted to some Islamic scholars and intellectuals and the result was reported to the women's delegation.[71] One may ask what was the rationale for the new law on Moroccan women. Many factors could explain the king's decision. First, in 1991 the king created a National Council of Human Rights with the aim of studying the general situation of human rights in Morocco and offering a set of proposals for change. Second, the new developments at the international level concerning women's rights had to be acknowledged by national legislation. Third, problems were created by applying the Moroccan law on personal status to nationals living abroad. In Europe, notably, many Moroccan women, after having applied for European citizenship and got it, wanted to be governed by the law of their country of residence instead of the law of their country of origin. Fourth was the selective way used in applying the Islamic law of personal status in European countries. In France, for example, some rules of the *Moudouyyanna* are not accepted, such as polygamy, repudiation or the non-maintenance of wives by their ex-husbands after divorce.[72]

Reforming the law concerning women was not an easy task. Women's rights are a taboo topic in the Arab and Muslim worlds generally and in Morocco specifically. When the new draft law was ready, the king received the women's committee to discuss the problem of reforming the law on personal status and submitted to them the proposed reforms. He gave them a summary of the proposed amendments and declared that his intention was to demonstrate that there is equality between men and women in Islam.[73] He deplored the violations of women's rights and the abusive way in which Islamic law was used by Moroccan men inside and outside Morocco. These amendments relate to some important points of the law: child custody, repudiation and divorce, polygamy and so on. He also proposed the creation of a family council to advise families on their internal problems.[74]

The new revised code was made public on 10 September 1993.[75] The main changes introduced consist in authorizing polygamy only by a decision of the *Qadi* (the Muslim judge) while there was no control on it before,[76] in requiring for any divorce or repudiation that the two partners should be present before the judge, in diminishing the role of the tutor (a woman can marry now without a guardian in some specific situations), in granting children's custody to the husband also (a husband had no right to the custody of the children before), in creating the family council which will play the role of the counsellor for the families and will help them solve their problems, etc.[77] By this reform, the mother becomes, for the first time, the legal tutor for her children after the husband's death. But she acts under the supervision of the judge. In addition, the father can always nominate a male tutor while he is still alive. In short, the reform has abolished the humiliating aspect of tutelage and the only tutor is now the father. But even the father has only a moral role and cannot oblige his daughter to marry against her will. The woman should agree to marry by signing the marriage contract and polygamy is restricted.

Despite these changes, many problems are still present when dealing with women's rights in Morocco, such as the absence of registering marriages and divorces (which might allow polygamous marriages without authorization from the judge). Moreover, the judges specializing in personal status matters are not modern judges: they still refer to traditional methods and have no authority to punish those who do not respect the new law or refuse to come before them. Repudiation still exists. What is new is that repudiation is now done in the presence of the wife and that if the husband repudiates his wife unjustly this will be taken into consideration by the judge, who will increase the amount of money given to the wife as her maintenance (*Nafaqa*). But after separation, all the work of a repudiated woman and the time she spent serving her husband and any physical accident of this wife during her life with her husband are not taken into consideration. Under the new Moroccan law, unilateral repudiation is always possible and no material security is guaranteed for an unemployed wife after divorce, while under the Algerian, Jordanian, Syrian or Egyptian laws wives receive an indemnity in the case of an abusive repudiation.

These new limited reforms are not followed by sanctions guaranteeing their implementation. As such, they will not be effective unless sanctions against their violation exist. In May 1993, in an interview with the French journalist Anne Sinclair for her programme '7/7', King Hassan II affirmed that equality between men and women would be guaranteed in Morocco and promised that women would no longer be absent from politics, as this does not contradict the main sources of Islam: the Koran and Sunna.[78] He declared that it was high time to make women participate in the affairs of the country. He notably said that nothing forbids a woman from being a minister and that women are generally hard workers and rarely corrupted.

The Situation of Muslim Women Today

Recent developments in the world and the failure of ideologies have given rise to fundamentalist ideas all over the world and notably in the Muslim world.[79] The fundamentalist movements in the Islamic world demand veiling women and not allowing them to work, to leave the house or to seek education. In short, these movements want to consider women as minors. Their attacks on women's liberation movements in the Muslim world are so aggressive that few of these movements have succeeded in confronting them. Some of these Islamist movements have their own fundamentalist women's movements: in 1933, Hassan Al-Banna, the famous Egyptian leader of the Muslim Brothers, created a women's movement called the 'Muslim Sisters'.[80] The future for women living both inside and outside the Muslim world is unknown. This future is more frightening now than ever before. Muslim women are being attacked by Muslims and non-Muslims: the attacks on Muslims in Bosnia and violation of their human rights were mainly attacks on Muslim women and children.

Algeria gives a symbolic example of the dramatic situation of Muslim women today. Many of them have been killed after having been raped in the name of Islam.[81] Each armed terrorist faction has its own understanding of Islam and chooses the law to adopt. Muslim terrorists interpret Islam as they want and behave with women according to the interpretation they give to Islam. The present situation of Algerian women is worse than in a declared war: in a war, one can identify clearly one's enemies but it is not possible to do so in Algeria now. The enemy could be a neighbour or a cousin. Many Algerian women were raped and killed by relatives. Sometimes the raped women know their aggressors but refuse to go to courts and testify against their aggressor in order not to be killed afterwards. Barbaric acts against women are often justified by Islam, by *Mutaa* marriage.[82] There are many stories of women who have experienced sexual violence in Algeria. A young girl of 20 was raped in front of her mother, who was chained to a tree so that she could see her daughter being raped. After this, they were killed, although both of them were practising Muslims and invoked God until the last moment. Another woman describes her ordeal: 'They took me from home in front of my father and put me in a lorry. I was taken to a place I can never describe. It was night and we found ourselves in a forest. They took me to a dark place where there was an old woman. Some hours later, three men came to me and raped me one after the other. I was a virgin. The old woman near me was crying silently. One of them beat her and they left. I stayed there for three days, then they took me back home. My father rejected me and I had to go and live with a cousin.'[83]

One can note the confusing way in which Islam is being used today. Terrorists mix Islamic rules, schools and sects. For example, in Algeria, a Sunni (or orthodox) country, terrorists have imported some of the Shia (unorthodox Iranian Islam). They have, for example, banned the mixing of women with men and have used temporary or *Mutaa* marriage. By introducing and misusing *Mutaa* marriage (never practised before in Algeria), some Algerian terrorists are treating women as objects in the name of Islam.

Conclusion

On the whole, the Muslim world has failed to do justice to womanhood and many Muslim women's rights are not guaranteed according to the international standards of human rights. Like the majority of women in the world, women under Islam are subject to inequalities in the political, social, economic and cultural fields. After the fall of the Berlin Wall, the new world order continues to be the order of men. Despite its imperfections, communism was an ideology in favour of the advancement of the rights of women. This advancement has been, in a large measure, undermined by the dismantling of the communist world.

Structural inequalities between the two sexes exist largely in Muslim societies because of a narrow interpretation of Islam, of introducing some non-Islamic rules or practices in Muslim communities, such as female genital mutilation, and the manner in which Muslim societies have evolved. Today, most Muslim states tend to encourage attachment to Islamic law only when women and family matters are concerned and to forget about other Islamic laws and practices.[84] These states are Muslim only by their law on personal status and by all their Islamic laws relating to women.

Muslim women are not protected according to human rights standards. Dominating women and invoking cultural specificity is very often the only way for Muslims to assert their identity in a world where all the social and cultural specificities are disappearing. The most problematic reason for the violation of women's human rights is, without doubt, the slow pace at which men's traditional conceptions on women change and the confusion in the way equality between the two sexes is understood in the Islamic world. It is due also to the lack of specialized international institutions for the protection of human rights and women's rights in the Muslim world.

We believe that the situation is unlikely to change in the future. One may wonder whether, at least, a partial solution to this question cannot be seen in the decision of several Muslim states to become parties to the contracting parties. Generally, the violations of women's rights is linked more with democracy than with religion. Under a dictatorship, women are more exploited. Most dictators in the world enacted or intend to enact legislation in order to submit women to the sole will of men.[85]

Islam is a religion that can adapt with the social evolution of the Muslim societies. Muslim thinking and methods should therefore be reviewed. There are conditions for this revision: 1) it should be free from any psychological, historical or Western pressures; 2) its main objective should be to correct the present situation, to be self-critical and to seek to find alternatives; and 3) it should especially be logical, realistic, acceptable and applicable in the present time.[86]

Notes

1. Fatima was the first Arab, African and Third World woman to occupy this function 46 years after the creation of this federation.

2. From Fatima Ibrahim, president of the Women's International Democratic Federation, to Mr Boutros Boutros-Ghali, United Nations, London, 12/2/1992 (in Arabic); personal translation.

3. For more details on the concept of human rights see Karel Vasak (ed.), *The International Dimensions of Human Rights*, UNESCO, Paris 1982.

4. For a very detailed analysis on the lack of a consensus at the international level concerning a fixed maximum age for childhood, see Eric Sottas and Ester Bron, 'Exactions et enfants', *Bulletin de l'Organisation Mondiale contre la Torture SOS/Torture*, No. 39-40-41, June 1993, 9–12.

5. See Art. 4/1 of the Convention on the Rights of the Child. Generally when a child is under 16, he/she is considered as a minor and cannot be considered responsible as an adult. There are, however, some exceptions to the rules in some countries, such as Iran or Afghanistan.

6. Art. 38/2 of the Child Convention.

7. Art. 32 of the Convention on the Child does not give a fixed age, but insists on

the protection of children against dangerous work. For this age one can refer to the ILO conventions, where this age varies between 14 and 18.

8. Art. 34 of the Convention on the Rights of the Child does not fix a minimum age, and this age varies according to domestic laws and to cultures. The minimum age generally agreed on is 15.

9. See *Encyclopedia of Islam*, new edn, E. J. Brill, Leiden, The Netherlands 1978, Vol. IV, pp. 171–7.

10. Ibid., p. 173.

11. It is said in the Muslim holy book, the Koran, that Islam aims to be the best religion (Chapter on the Table, verse 3, Chapter of Imran family, verse 110).

12. The Organization of the Islamic Conference was established in 1971 following a summit meeting of Muslim heads of states at Rabat (Morocco) in 1969 and the Islamic Foreign Ministers' Conference in Jeddah in March 1970, and in Karachi in 1970. This organization includes at present some 50 states. For more details on this Organization, see *The Middle East and North Africa 1990*, thirty-sixth edition, Europa Publication Limited, London 1989, pp. 254–5.

13. See Mohammed Sharif Bassiouni (in Arabic), 'Sources of Islamic Sharia and the protection of human rights in Islamic penal law', in *Human Rights: Practical Studies on the Arab World*, Dar Al-Ilm Lil Mallayin, Beirut 1989, p. 17.

14. See World Conference on Human Rights: The Vienna Declaration and Programme of Action, United Nations, June 1993.

15. For more details on the ratification of the international human rights treaties and conventions, see J. B. Marie, 'International instruments relating to human rights: classification and status of ratification as for 1 January 1994', in *Human Rights Law Journal*, Vol. 15, No. 1–2, pp. 51–67.

16. See Abdullahi Ahmed An-Na'im, 'Problems of universal cultural legitimacy for human rights' in A. A. An-Na'im and Francis Deng, *Human Rights in Africa*, Brookings Institution, Washington 1990, pp. 331 66.

17. Ibid., p. 366.

18. Ibid., p. 367.

19. The most known book of *Hadith* is *Sahih Al-Bukhari*.

20. In the Sunni doctrine there are four well-known schools, and in the Shia doctrine, there are as many as twelve schools.

21. See Huyam Khawam (in Arabic) 'Women's rights in the Arab national laws', in Sherif Bassiouni Mohammad Said Addaqqaq, *Human Rights: Practical Studies in the Arab World*, Dar Al-Ilm lil Malayin, Beirut 1989, p. 417.

22. See Noureddine Saadi, *La femme et la loi en Algérie*, Editions Le Fennec, Casablanca 1991, p. 11.

23. See Jack Greenberg, 'Race, sex and religious discrimination', in Theodor Meron (ed.), *Human Rights in International Law: Legal Policies and Issues*, Clarendon Press, Oxford 1984, Vol. II, pp. 307–43.

24. The Declaration was accepted without any vote against it and with only two abstentions: from Saudi Arabia and South Africa.

25. See Maria Berger's course, *The Status of Women*, International Institute of Human Rights, Collection of Lectures, Sixteenth Session (1–26 July 1985).

26. This declaration was made in Resolution 2263 (XXII) adopted by the General

Assembly on 7 November 1967. The work begun on the Convention in 1974 was given further impetus by the fact that the General Assembly proclaimed 1975–85 United Nations Decade for Women with the slogan 'Equality, development and peace' within which a world action plan was to be conducted for guaranteeing full equality of rights with men and the elimination of the longstanding barriers for women.

27. These ratifications were done with many reservations.

28. Koran, Surat Al-Isra (the Night Journey), v. 70, in *The Qoran, an English Translation of the Qoran*, checked and revised by Mahmud Y. Zayid, Dar Al-Choura, Beirut 1980.

29. Surat Al Shura (the Counsel), v. 10.

30. Surat of Al-Hujurat (the Chambers), v. 13.

31. This chapter was the object of three workshops.

32. Surat Al-Hujurat (Chapter of the Chambers), v. 17.

33. Surat Al-Ahqaf, v. 19.

34. Surat Al-Maida (Chapter of the Table), v. 32.

35. Surat Al-Isra (The Night Journey), v. 23.

36. Surat Taha, v. 114.

37. Quoted in the article 'Islam et droits de l'homme', in the weekly *Magazine of the Maghreb*, No. 127, 3rd year, p. 7 (personal translation).

38. See ibid., p. 7.

39. Ibid., p. 7.

40. Surat Al-Baqara (Chapter of the Cow), v. 34.

41. Surat Al-Nisaa (Chapter of Women), v. 10.

42. See Surat Attalaq (Chapter on Repudiation), the topic of workshop II.

43. Chapter on Women, v. 2.

44. Chapter on Women, v. 129.

45. Chapter on Women, v. 1.

46. According to Iman Al-Bukhari, quoted in the article supra note 37.

47. Surat Al-Maida (the Table), v. 89.

48. Surat Al-Mujadal (Chapter of She who Pleaded), v. 3.

49. See Huyam Khawwam, *Women's Rights in Arab National Laws*, p. 418.

50. Surat of the Cow, v. 256.

51. Surat Al-Nur (the Light), v. 31.

52. Supra note 37, p. 7.

53. Surat Al-Shura (the Counsel), v. 41.

54. Surat Al-Baqara (the Cow), v. 228.

55. Surat Al-Rum (the Greeks), v. 20.

56. Personal translation.

57. Res. No. 49/19.

58. For the text of this convention see Arab League (in Arabic), *Texts of Treaties and Conventions*, Tunis 1985, pp. 312–15.

59. See for more details on this question, in French, see Khadija Elmadmad, 'Les droits de la femme dans la Charte Africaine des Droits de l'Homme et des Peuples',

Afrique 2000: Revue africaine de politique internationale, Publications de l'Institut Pan-africain des Relations Internationales à Bruxelles, Trimestriel No. 14, July/August/September 1993, pp. 21–37.

60. See ibid., p. 424.

61. Ibid., pp. 424 et seq.

62. See for more details, Siham Samir Awad, 'Women's rights in Sudan', in M. S. Bassiouni et al., *Human Rights: Practical Studies in the Arab World*, Vol. 3, op. cit., pp. 427–33.

63. Regulation No. 54 of 1970 and No. 35.

64. Ibid., p. 433.

65. See *Asharq Al Awsat*, the international daily newspaper of the Arabs, No. 5280 of 13/5/1993, p. 1.

66. Ibid., p. 1; see for the text of the Declaration of the Islamic Scholars' Committee (in Arabic), *Asharq Al Awsat*, the international daily newspaper of the Arabs, No. 5281 of 14/5/1993, p. 1.

67. See Aberrazak Moulay R'Chid, *La femme et la Loi au Maroc*, Collection dirigée par Fatima Mernissi, Editions Le fennec, Casablanca 1991.

68. See the newspaper *Le Matin du Sahara et du Mahgreb*, No. 8158 of 20 May 1993, p. 1.

69. Ibid., p. 1.

70. Ibid., p. 1.

71. See newspaper *Le Matin du Sahara* of 2/5/1993, pp. 1 and 3.

72. Declaration of Professor Moulay R'Chid, a Moroccan specialist in women's questions; see the Moroccan newspaper *Al Bayane* of 13/5/1993, p. 6.

73. See the Moroccan daily newspaper *Le Matin du Sahara* of 20/5/1993, p. 3.

74. Ibid., p. 3.

75. See Code du Statut Personnel et des Successions: mis à jour conformément aux dernières modifications introduites par dahir portant loi No. 1-93-347 du 10 septembre 1993, Librairie Al Wahda Al Arabia, Casablanca, 1993.

76. This rule exists already in some other Muslim states: in Syria and Iraq. In Morocco, it was proposed for the text of 1957 but not accepted and was included in the two reform proposals of 1979 and 1981.

77. For a detailed study of the reform, see Round Table on Reforming the *Moudouyanna* in Morocco, in the Moroccan daily newspaper *Al Bayane* of 13/5/1993, pp. 6–7.

78. See for the text of this interview the Moroccan newspaper *Le Matin du Sahara et du Maghreb* of 17/5/1993, pp. 1, 2 and 4.

79. See (in Arabic), Sanaa Al-Misri, *Khalfa Al-Hijaab: Mawqifo al-Jamaato Al-Islamiya min Qadiyati Al-Maraati* (Beyond the Veil: The Attitude of the Islamic Grouping towards Women), Sinaa Publications, Cairo 1989.

80. See ibid., p. 35.

81. See Souad Benhaddad, 'Ils violent au nom de Dieu', *Marie Claire*, No. 510, February 1995, pp. 74–8.

82. *Mutaa* marriage is a practice that is exclusively Shi'ite. It consists in establishing a contract between a man and a woman for a limited period of time: one week, one

month, one year, etc. It has been encouraged by the present Iranian government to legalize extramarital sexual practices. It does not exist in the Sunni countries, such as North Africa.

83. Souad Benhaddad mentioned these two cases in her article 'Ils violent au nom de Dieu', supra note 81.

84. This factor was to some extent facilitated by colonial influence.

85. See N. Saadi, *La femme et la loi en Algérie*, supra note 22, pp. 18–19.

86. Taha Jabri Al Alwani, *Pour une stratégie culturelle islamique*, Institut International de la Pensée Islamique, trans. Rachid Messaoudi, London, 1990, p. 14.

Bibliography

Human rights and women under Islam

Ahmed, Leila, *Women and Gender in Islam: Historical Roots of Modern Debate*, Yale University Press, New Haven, CT and London, 1992.

Al-Acha Gahassan, Mohammed, *Le statut inférieur de la femme en Islam*, L'Harmattan, Paris, 1987.

— Adelkhah, Fariba, *La révolution sous le voile: femmes islamiques d'Iran*, Khartala, Paris, 1991.

Al-Hibri Azizah (ed.), *Women in Islam*, Pergamon Press, Oxford, 1982.

An-Na'im Abdullahi, Ahmed, *Towards an Islamic Reformation: Civil Liberties, Human Rights and International Law*, New York, Syracuse University Press, 1990.

An-Na'im Adullahi, Ahmed and Francis M. Deng, *Human Rights in Africa: Cross-Cultural Perspectives*, Brookings Institution, Washington, DC, 1990.

Atkins, Susan and Brenda Hoggett, *Women and the Law*, New York, Blackwell, New York, 1984.

Azari, Farah (ed.), *Women of Iran: The Conflict with Fundamentalist Islam*, Ithaca Press, London, 1983.

Bani Sadr avec la collaboration de Laurent Chabry, *Le Coran et les droits de l'homme*, Maisonneuve & Larose, Paris, 1989.

Chérif Chamari, Alya, *La femme et la loi en Tunisie*, Editions Le fennec, Casablanca, 1991.

Collection dirigée par Fatima Mernissi, *Femmes partagées famille-travail*, Editions Le fennec, Casablanca, 1988.

— *Portraits de femmes*, Editions Le fennec, Casablanca, 1987.

Dhina, Amar, *Femmes illustres en Islam*, Entreprise nationale du livre, Algeria, 1991.

Dwyer, Daisly Hilse, *Images and Self-images: Male and Female in Morocco*, Columbia University Press, New York, 1978.

El-Khayat-Bennai, Ghita, *Le monde arabe au féminin*, L'Harmattan, Paris, 1985.

— *Les Maghreb des femmes: les femmes dans l'U.M.A.*, Editions Eddif, Casablanca, 1992.

El-Saadawi, Nawal, *The Hidden Face of Eve: Women in the Arab World*, Zed Books, London, 1980.

Fahmy, Mansour, *La condition de la femme dans l'Islam*, Allia, Paris, 1990.

Gaudio, Attilio, *La Révolution des femmes en Islam*, Julliard, Paris, 1957.

Gaudio, Attilio et R. Pelletier *Femmes d'Islam ou le sexe interdit*, Denoel, Paris, 1980.

Goodwin, Jan, *Price of Honour: Muslim Women Lift the Veil of Silence on the Islamic World*, Little, Brown, London, 1994.

Haddad, Tahar, *Notre femme: la législation islamique et la société*, Maison tunisienne d'Edition, Tunis, 1978.

Kandiyoti, Deniz, *Women, Islam and the State*, Macmillan, London, 1991.

Khushalani, Yougindra, *Dignity and Honour of Women as a Basic and Fundamental Human Rights*, Martinus Nijhof, The Hague, 1982.

Mernissi, Fatima, *Beyond the Veil: Male, Female Dynamics in Muslim Society*, Al-Saqi Books, London, 1985.

— *Sexe, idéologie, Islam*, Editions Maghrébines, Vols I and II, Casablanca, 1985.

— *L'amour dans les pays musulmans*, Editions Maghrébines, Casablanca, 1986.

— *Sultanes oubliées: femmes chefs d'Etat en Islam*, Albin Michel, Paris, 1990.

Minai, Naila, *Women in Islam: Tradition and Transition in the Middle East*, London, 1981.

— M'rabet, Fadéla, *La femme algérienne suivie de les algériennes*, Maspero, Paris 1969.

Naamane-Guessous, Soumaya, *Au-delà de toute pudeur: la sexualité féminine au Maroc*, Soden, Casablanca, 1987.

Nasir, J. J., *The Status of Women under Islamic Law and under Modern Islamic Legislation*, Graham and Trotman, London, 1990.

Saadi, Noureddine, *La femme et la loi en Algérie*, Editions Le fennec, Casablanca, 1991.

Sebti, Lahrichi Fadéla, *Vivre musulmane au Maroc: Guide des droits et obligations*, LGDJ, Paris 1985.

Souriau, Christine, *Femmes et politique autour de la Méditerranée*, L'Harmattan, Paris, 1980.

Tibi, Aida, *A Study of Al-Ma'afiri's Biographies of Famous Women in Early Islam*, Oxford University Press, Oxford, 1974.

Utas, Bo (ed.), *Women in Islamic Societies: Social Attitudes and Historical Perspectives*, Atlantic Highlands Humanities Press, Scandinavian Institute of Asian Studies, 1983.

Wazir, Jahan Karim, *Women and Culture: Between Malay 'Adat' and Islam*, Westview Press, San Francisco, 1992.

Woodsmall, Ruth Frances, *Women in the Changing Islamic System*, Bilma Publishing House, Delhi, 1983.

Zayid, Y. Mahmud, *The Quran: An English Translation of the Meaning of the Quran*, Dar Al-Choura, Beirut, 1980.

Articles and special publications

Abdelkrim-Chikh, Rabia, 'Les femmes exogènes: entre la loi de Dieu et les droits de l'homme', *Annuaire de l'Afrique du Nord*, Vol. 27, 1988, pp. 235–54.

Afshari, Reza, 'An essay on Islamic cultural relativism in the discourse of human rights', *Human Rights Quarterly*, Vol. 12, No. 2, May 1990, pp. 235–76.

Belhassen, Souhayr, 'Femmes tunisiennes islamistes', *Annuaire de l'Afrique du Nord*, Vol. 18, 1979, pp. 77–94.

Elmadmad, Khadija, 'Les droits de la femme dans la Charte Africaine des Droits de l'Homme et des Peuples', *Afrique 2000, Revue africaine de politique internationale*, Brussels, Trimestriel No. 14, August–September 1993, pp. 21–38.

Fekkar, Yamina, 'La femme, son corps et l'Islam: questions et contradictions suscitées par le vécu quotidien en Algérie', *Annuaire de l'Afrique du Nord*, Vol. 18, 1979, pp. 135–46.

Ibrahim, Fatima Ahmed (president of the Women's International Democratic Federation), 'An Outcry', The Print and Publishing Centre, London, January 1992.

Malik, Maqbul Ilahi, 'The concept of human rights in Islamic jurisprudence', *Human Rights Quarterly*, Vol. 3, No. 3, Summer 1981, pp. 56–67.

Mathurin, Mair Lucile, 'Women: a decade is time enough', *Human Rights Quarterly*, Vol. 8, No. 2, 1986, pp. 583–93.

Tibi, Bassam, 'Islamic Law/Shari'a, human rights, universal morality and international relations', *Human Rights Quarterly*, Vol. 16, No. 2, 1994, pp. 277–89.

UNESCO, *Report by the Directory-General Concerning the Revision of All Basic Texts with a View to the Use of Gender-Neutral Terminology and Wording*, CL/3320, May 1993.

Welch, C. E., 'Human rights and African women: a comparison of protection under two major treaties', *Human Rights Quarterly*, Vol. 15, No. 3, August 1993.

Islamic law in general
Books

Abdur, Rahim, *The Principles of Muhammadan Jurisprudence According to the Hanafi, Maliki, Shafii and Hanbali Schools*, Hyperion Press, Westport, CT, 1981.

Al-Azmeh, Aziz (ed.), *Islamic Law: Social and Historical Contexts*, Routledge, London and New York, 1988.

Ameer Ali, Sayed, *Mohammedan Law: Compiled from Authorities in the Original Arabic*, Himalayan Books, New Delhi, 1988.

Amin, *Sayed Hassan, Islamic Law in the Contemporary World: Introduction, Glossary and Bibliography*, Royston, Glasgow, 1985.

Amin, S. H., *Islamic Law: Social Contexts*, Croom Helm, London, 1987.

Anderson, J. N. D., *Islamic Law in the Modern World*, Greenwood Press, Westport, CT, 1975.

Anderson, Jerome N. D. and Norman Coulson, *Islamic Law in Contemporary Cultural Change*, Munchen Verlag Karl Albert, Freiburg, 1967.

Anderson, Norman, *Law Reform in the Muslim World*, Athlone Press, London, 1976.

Bassiouni, Cherif M. (ed.), *The Islamic Criminal Justice System*, Oceana Publications, London, Rome and New York, 1982.

Bhatia, H. S. (ed.), *Studies in Islamic Law, Religion and Society*, Deep & Deep Publications, New Delhi, 1989.

Burton, John, *The Sources of Islamic Law: Islamic Theories of Abrogation*, Edinburgh University Press, Edinburgh, 1990.

Coulson, N. J., *History of Islamic Law*, Edinburgh, 1964.

Doi, Abdur Rahman, *Shari'ah: The Islamic Law*, Ta Ha Publishers, London, 1984.

El-Alami, Daoud S., *The Marriage Contract in Islamic Law in the Shari'ah and Personal Status Laws of Egypt and Morocco*, Graham & Trotman, London, 1992.

Hamidullah, Mohammed, *Le Prophète de l'Islam*, Editions de l'Association des Etudiants Islamiques en France (AEIF), Paris, 1989.

Heer, Nicholas (ed.), *Islamic Law and Jurisprudence*, University of Washington Press, Washington, DC, 1990.

Holkinson, Keith, *Muslim Family Law: A Source Book*, Croom Helm, London, 1984.

Hooker, M. B., *Islamic Law in South-East Asia*, Oxford University Press, Oxford, 1984.

Khadduri, M., *The Islamic Law of Nations: Shaybani's Siyar*, Johns Hopkins University Press, Baltimore, MD, 1966.

Khadduri, Majid and Herbert J. Liebesny (eds), *Law in the Middle East*, AMS Press, New York, 1955.

Khan, Muhammad Zafrullah, *Islam and Human Rights*, Islamic International Publication Limited, Raqeen Press, Islamabad and Surrey (UK), 1988.

Liebesney, Herbert J., *The Law of the Near & Middle East*, State University of New York Press, Albany, 1975.

Mallat, Chibli and Jane Connors, *Islamic Family Law*, Graham & Trotman, London, 1990.

Nasir, Jamal, *The Islamic Law of Personal Status*, Graham & Trotman, London, 1986.

Powers, David S., *Studies in Qur'an and Hadith: The Formation of the Islamic Law of Inheritance*, Berkeley, University of California Press, 1986.

Rosen, Lawrence, *The Anthropology of Justice: Law as a Culture in Islamic Society*, Cambridge, 1989.

Schacht, Joseph, *The Origins of Muhammadan Jurisprudence*, Clarendon Press, Oxford, 1979.

— *Introduction to Islamic Law*, Oxford, Clarendon Press, 1984.

Shaukatali, Zeenat, *Marriage and Divorce in Islam: An Appraisal*, Jaico Publishing House, Bombay, Delhi, Bangalore, Calarta, Hyderabad, Madras, 1987.

Shukri, Ahmed, *Muhammadan Law of Marriage and Divorce*, AMS Press, New York, 1966.

Siddiqi, Muhammad Iqbal, *The Penal Law of Islam*, Kazi Publications, Lahore, Pakistan, 1979.

Vesey-Fitzgerald, S., *Muhammadan Law: An Abridgement According to its Various Schools*, Scienta Verlag Aalem, London, 1979.

Waddy, Charis, *The Muslim Mind*, Grosvenor, London, 1990.

Weeramantry, C. G., *Islamic Jurisprudence: An International Perspective*, Macmillan Press, London, 1988.

Journals and reviews

For different issues on the topic, consult, among others:

Encyclopaedia of Islam
International Journal of Middle East Studies
Journal of Islamic and Comparative Law
Journal of African Law
Islam and the Modern Age
Islamic Quarterly
Islamic Studies
Revue des études islamiques
Studia Islamica
The Muslim World

10

Women, Culture and Human Rights: Female Genital Mutilation, Polygamy and Bride Price

Esther M. Kisaakye

Globally, it is now recognized that women's rights are human rights. This was acknowledged by the world leaders in 1993 at the World Conference on Human Rights and reaffirmed by the world community in subsequent conferences held in Cairo, Copenhagen and Beijing.

Given this global recognition, and provisions in international human rights instruments, which entrench and guarantee the equality of sexes, equal and full dignity of the person; non-discrimination on the basis of sex; and freedom from cruel, inhuman and degrading treatment,[1] it could be expected that women can now enjoy their human rights. In practice, this is not so, and particularly in sub-Saharan Africa, where the enjoyment of women's human rights remains elusive for the majority of African women. The situation is further compounded by low literacy levels, a lack of properly articulated legal rights, and recognition of customary law that give legal basis for some discriminatory practices.

The cultural and traditional practices that violate women's human rights are many and include early marriage of young girls, forced marriage, female genital mutilation, polygamy, bride price, widow inheritance, widowhood rites, the *trocosi* system (female religious slavery), wife sharing, husband sharing, killing of twins and albinos, food taboos for women, honour killings, land/property acquisition and ownership rules, human sacrifice and witchcraft, male/boy preference and wife replacement.

However, there is glaring absence of national legislation outlawing cultural practices, as political commitment to outlaw these practices has also been lukewarm. Many African governments have not put women's rights high on their agenda, despite their being signatories to international human rights instruments. In addition, the few efforts to outlaw or otherwise eradicate some of these practices have often been confronted with resistance from not only the community but in some cases also from women who are the victims of these practices. The participation of women in practices that violate their rights can be explained by their socialization, which leads them to accept the status quo, or their fear of becoming outcasts in their communities, as well as the fact that many of these practices are embedded in the value systems of the respective communities.

Culture has often been cited as a key single obstacle to the enjoyment of women's human rights, and the major reason underlying this resistance from the communities. It has thus become increasingly clear and important for human rights activists who are working towards the realization of women's rights, especially in Africa, to recognize this on-going tension between women's human rights and culture and to understand the relationship between the two. It is only by doing so that appropriate interventions to target their eradication will be put in place.

This chapter explores the difficult question of how African governments and the whole international community can ensure that women enjoy their full human rights without becoming outcasts in their communities. It focuses on three institutions: female genital mutilation, polygamy and bride price, which are so entrenched in many African societies and are discussed for illustrative purposes only, to highlight the difficulty and challenge ahead for achieving women's enjoyment of their rights. By focusing on these three institutions, we hope to demonstrate that culture still remains one of the greatest constraints on the enjoyment of women's human rights in Africa and that it continues to pose a real challenge not only for women who are members of these communities but also for all those governments and individuals who are committed to the realization of full respect for women's human rights.

We shall examine the prevalence of each practice, the justification/reasons advanced for each practice and how it affects the enjoyment of women's human rights. We shall also examine the international and regional human rights instruments with respect to each practice and highlight how the practices violate women's rights. Finally, we shall examine the global and national strategies for combating such practices and also explore the way forward for finding a balance that will ensure women's enjoyment of their human rights.

Female Genital Mutilation

Female genital mutilation (FGM) is the collective name given to several different practices that involve the cutting of female genitals.[2] Another more embracing definition, which was adopted by the WHO, UNICEF and UNFPA in 1997, defines FGM as comprising 'all procedures involving partial or total removal of the external female genitalia or other injury to the female genital organs whether for cultural or other non-therapeutic reasons'.[3]

There are two main types of FGM: clitoridectomy and infibulation. Clitoridectomy involves an operation where one or more parts of the external genitals are removed. It may include partial or total removal of the clitoris or the removal of the clitoris and the labia minora.[4] It is estimated that approximately 85 per cent of the women who undergo FGM go through this type and experience complications of a physical, sexual and psychological nature.[5]

Infibulation involves an operation where the clitoris is removed, the whole of the labia minora is cut off and then the surface is stitched together.[6] For this kind of practice, the girl's legs are tied together for weeks, to ensure that the vaginal opening is completely closed off. A small opening is left for purposes of passing urine and menstrual blood.[7] Complications associated with infibulation are more severe. The women's vagina has to be reopened every time she gives birth and restitched after childbirth. In some communities, she may also be opened for the purposes of sexual intercourse, depending on whether she can dilate or not.[8] While it is estimated that 15 per cent of all the women who undergo FGM undergo this type,[9] the figure is based on the global prevalence rates. Prevalence rates on a national basis can be quite high, such as in Sudan, Somalia and Djibouti, where 80–90 per cent of FGM is of the infibulation type.[10]

It should be noted, however, that under each of the major classifications mentioned above, there are variations in the actual practices and extent of genital mutilation. The World Health Organization, which has been taking a keen interest in this practice since the mid-1980s, has classified these procedures into four types, being:

- excision of the prepuce, with or without excision of part or all of the clitoris;
- excision of the clitoris with partial or total excision of the labia minora;
- excision of part or all of the external genitalia and stitching/narrowing of the vaginal opening (infibulation); and
- other unclassified practices, such as picking, piercing or incision of the clitoris and/or labia, stretching of the clitoris and or labia, cauterization by burning of the clitoris and surrounding tissues, introcision, scraping (angurya cuts) or cutting (gishuri cuts) of the vagina or surrounding tissues, and introduction of corrosive substances or herbs into the vagina.[11]

The prevalence of female genital mutilation Female genital mutilation is widely practised in Africa in at least 28 countries.[12] The actual numbers of women who have undergone FGM are not known, due to the silence that surrounded the practice for a long time, and the fact that the issue did not receive international attention until the 1980s. However, by 1998, it was estimated that 136,797,440 women and girls in Africa had undergone one form or another of FGM.[13]

Estimated country prevalence rates range from as high as 98 per cent in Djibouti to 5 per cent in Uganda and the Democratic Republic of Congo.[14] Countries with an estimated prevalence rate of 70 per cent and above include Egypt, Mali, Somalia, Sudan, Togo, Burkina Faso, Eritrea, Ethiopia, Gambia and Sierra Leone. Prevalence rates are expressed in percentages of the total female population and may not necessarily bring out the entire picture. For example, Nigeria's estimated prevalence rate is 40 per cent, but expressed in numbers this translates into 25,601,200 women as compared to Sierra Leone with an estimated prevalence rate of 90 per cent, which amounts to 2,167,200.[15] FGM is, however, not only an African problem. It is also practised in other parts of the world, such as the Arab world, Asia and in Europe by African immigrants, although on a much smaller scale.[16]

The victims of this practice are women and children. In many of the communities, the age of mutilation varies from an infant of a few weeks old to young girls of tender age, and to adolescents who are undergoing initiation rites. Indeed, it is globally estimated that 2 million girls a year or 6,000 girls per day are at the risk of undergoing FGM.[17] In Somalia, where the prevalence rate of FGM ranges between 95 per cent and 98 per cent, out of which 90 per cent is of the infibulation type, FGM is usually performed on girls of between seven and ten years.[18] In Gambia, FGM is performed on young girls between two and fourteen years, during the school holidays.[19] If the girl develops any complications after the procedure, they are often attributed to witchcraft and other supernatural powers.[20]

One of the questions that has continued to puzzle human rights advocates and researchers in this field is the contradiction posed by the fact that the centuries-old practice of FGM, which results in great risks and damages the women's sexuality, is seemingly perpetuated by women against fellow women. Traditionally the FGM procedure was performed by women, a role either inherited or learned from a relative.[21] In the Gambia, the procedure is performed by a woman, the Ngasimba, who is highly respected and believed to possess supernatural powers.

In some communities, performing this role brings respect to women who originate from poor families and ethnic groups that are otherwise regarded as inferior. For these traditional circumcisers, the role bestows on them respect and control in their communities, which in turn makes them look upon themselves as the custodians of their culture. For example, in Sierra Leone, circumcisers are highly respected women leaders who control the traditional secret societies, and are seen as priestesses.[22] With the advent of Western civilization, medically trained midwives and nurses joined the traditional circumcisers to perform this role, usually charging a fee. For example, in Sudan and Gambia income derived from FGM is far higher than the regular income of midwives and nurses, making it a lucrative business.

Reasons advanced for practising FGM Some of the reasons advanced by communities for practising FGM are:

- to initiate the woman into womanhood and the tribe;
- to reduce the woman's sexual urge;
- to protect the baby and to prevent maternal and infant mortality;
- to prevent the death of the woman, by removing the clitoris, which is believed in some communities to be poisonous;
- to preserve virginity; and
- to prevent promiscuity, sexual deviance and excessive arousal.[23]

A survey of 400 women carried out in Sierra Leone in 1985 found that 369 women had undergone FGM and gave the following reasons: tradition (257), societal acceptance (105), religion (51), increasing chances of marriage (12), preservation of virginity (11), female hygiene (10), prevention of promiscuity (6), enhancement of fertility (3) to please husband (2) and to maintain good health (1).[24] The reasons can be classified in four major categories: cultural subordination, religious obligation, morality and health.[25] Many of these reasons are also surrounded in myths that are deeply entrenched among women and ensure their compliance. For example, it is believed in some communities that if you do not go through the practice, you may not have children or you may cause the death of your husband. In Burkina Faso, a woman was reported to have been forcefully circumcised by excision when she was about five months pregnant because neighbours were afraid that her offspring might be killed.[26] It has been urged that there is a relationship between polygamy and FGM, arising from the need to suppress women's sexual desires.

Although the harmful effects of FGM are well documented, eradication of this practice has proved difficult. In many of the communities practising FGM, proponents have argued that the practice is so deeply imbedded in the value system of the communities that its abolition is likely to be seen as an attack on the age-old respected cultural practices and beliefs of the communities.

Resistance to reform has come from the communities practising FGM as well as the women members of the same communities. For example, in 1988, in response to a campaign to eradicate the practice by the Inter-African Committee for the Eradication of Harmful Traditional Practices, the District Council of Kapchorwa passed a Resolution making FGM compulsory for every Sabiny girl of 14 years and above or else she would be considered a social outcast.[27] Studies undertaken in the concerned communities in several countries indicate that FGM was supported by women of all age ranges,[28] and that females were more often likely to support the continuation of FGM than males. For example in Ethiopia, a survey undertaken by the Inter-African Committee (IAC) found that 30 per cent of women interviewed were in favour as opposed to 23 per cent of men.[29] In another study undertaken in Kenya in 1991, 65 per cent of women supported the practice.[30] In Togo, a study undertaken found that 12 per cent of women of 15 years and above had undergone the practice, with the Central Region most affected. However, 90.4 per cent of women polled supported the abolition of the practice.[31] The cultural significance of FGM can be seen in the following ways.

In some of the communities where FGM is practised, it is intended, among other reasons, to initiate the girl into womanhood, which also declares her readiness for marriage. In many African tribes, marriage continues to be the role envisaged for every woman. Therefore, the possibility of failure to get married because of one's inadequacy is a matter that has serious implications, not only for the girl/woman's status but also for her family. For example, traditionally among the Sabiny of Uganda, a woman who had not undergone FGM was considered a girl, and could not get married to a Sabiny man.[32] In addition, she could not carry out important functions such as milking cows, collecting cow-dung from anybody's kraal for smearing a house and climbing into a granary to collect seeds. She was also not allowed to fetch water, grind grains or do anything before her circumcised counterparts, or to attend the circumcision ceremonies of others. Similarly in Ethiopia and Ghana, in the communities that practised FGM, undergoing the procedure was seen as a precondition for marriage.

Apart from the initiation of the girl, there is also the issue of identity of the individual. Since FGM is usually carried out at a particular time of the year, and involves many young girls in the same age group, there is the fear of losing the psychological, moral and material benefits of 'belonging', if one fails to undergo FGM. In the context of sub-Saharan Africa, where we have high illiteracy levels among other things and of course strong cultural ties and rules, this fear of ostracization and limited choices available to women all make women more susceptible to FGM.

FGM as a violation of women's human rights In spite of the justification advanced for FGM and the resistance to change from communities practising FGM, it poses a very serious violation of women's human rights in several ways. FGM violates women's right to equality,[33] non-discrimination on the basis of sex and the right to life and health, and also constitutes an arbitrary intrusion into one's privacy. Women also have a right to equal protection under the law and therefore the failure of the governments to enact protective laws is a breach of their rights. States parties are under obligation to take or adopt legislative and other appropriate measures to give effect to these rights.

FGM also violates children's right to life, survival and development, which are protected under the Convention of the Rights of the Child (CRC).[34] The fact that the practice is done without their consent further aggravates the violation. The same Convention also enjoins states parties to take all appropriate measures with a view to abolishing practices prejudicial to the health of children.[35] Governments' failure to protect children from FGM, which is performed in the majority of case without their consent, therefore amounts to a violation of the Convention.

Action against FGM   Although it has not been possible so far to eradicate the practice of FGM, some interventions have been put in place by various governments. These interventions range from constitutional protections to legislative interventions specifically against FGM, to educational programmes intended to change or modify the attitudes, beliefs and practices of the communities practising FGM.

Constitutional protections   The independence and post-independence constitutions of countries where FGM is practised did not prohibit discrimination on the basis of sex. This created a loophole in the legal framework for challenging discriminatory practices such as FGM. However, many of the African countries have since revised their constitutions to prohibit sexual discrimination as well as harmful cultural practices affecting women. Such countries include Ethiopia, Ghana and Uganda.[36] Although constitutional provisions have not been enough in the past to protect women's rights, they are nevertheless an important first step in the process of combating these practices.

Legislative interventions   The role of legislation in fighting FGM has been a subject of controversy, given an apparent failure of early legislative interventions in countries such as Sudan. However, in the 1990s, Ghana, Burkina Faso, Togo and Côte d'Ivoire adopted the legislative option to fight this practice. Ghana passed a law against FGM in 1994. In 1998, a male practitioner who had performed the practice on five girls ranging between 15 and 18 years was sentenced to five years' imprisonment with hard labour. The court rejected the accused's defence that he had performed the practice after consulting a traditional soothsayer, who attributed the death of his two sons to his failure to continue the family tradition of performing FGM.[37] Burkina Faso also passed a law that criminalized FGM and imposed a punishment for practitioners ranging from six months to three years if the victim survives and five to ten years if the victim dies. In 1997, a number of practitioners were convicted for illegally performing FGM. They received up to five months in prison and a fine of US$91. As a result of the conviction, the traditional practitioners stopped performing FGM and changed to male circumcision. In addition, a National Anti-Excision Committee (CNLPE) was formed by a Presidential Decree, among others things in order to sensitize the police.[38] Côte d'Ivoire also passed a law against FGM in 1996. Togo was the third ECOWAS member to ban FGM, in 1998. Excisors can be imprisoned for between two and ten years and fined US$200–2,000. Excisors and those who aid its performance are covered.

One of the arguments frequently cited against legislative interventions is that they may drive the practice underground instead of eliminating it. The argument gains validity especially where no other complementary efforts to educate the communities to promote attitude change have been undertaken. However, the role of legislation in tackling practices that violate women's human rights should not be underestimated. Given the power relations in patriarchal communities of sub-Saharan Africa, where women are subordinated to their male counterparts and their cultures, the law offers one powerful tool for those who wish to resist or contest these practices to do so, while at the same time sending a powerful message from the government that these practices will not be tolerated. Indeed, governments, which are states parties to the CEDAW and CRC Conventions, are obliged to take all appropriate measures to eliminate discrimination, to abolish/modify existing laws and customs that discriminate against women and to modify social and cultural patterns to eliminate prejudices based on stereotyped roles and positions of men and women.[39]

Given the constitutional and legislative provisions now in place in several countries, the roles of police and the judiciary are going to be crucial. African judges will need to follow the example of their European counterparts such as France, where a court rejected the defence of culture and sentenced the woman who carried out FGM to an eight-year jail sentence and the mother of the child to a two-year sentence.[40] Enforcing the law will send a strong signal to the practitioners and in the long run deter them from performing FGM, especially on children.

Promoting attitude change in the communities Some measure of success has also been recorded by interventions that have involved/targeted attitude change in the communities. Such interventions have focused on working with the community to eliminate mutilation, while retaining the other coming of age ceremonies through a procedure commonly referred to as alternative rights of passage. These alternative ceremonies ensure that the initiation of the girl into womanhood is carried out. 'Alternative coming of age ceremonies are a viable solution to the eradication of FGM, especially in communities where the practice is carried out during the adolescent years and traditional initiation ceremonies used to be the norm.'[41] Such interventions have been supported by other parallel measures that provide information about the health hazards of FGM and also support girls' formal education. Success in these interventions has been recorded among the Sabiny community of Uganda through the UNFPA-supported REACH programme, in Kenya and in some communities in Egypt. For example, in Kenya, the Programme for Appropriate Technology in Health (PATH) was designed in consultation with the community. It excludes cutting of the genitalia but mimics the traditional coming of age seclusion, information-giving and final celebration. The programme incorporates the initiates' seclusion week, where the girls are kept in the house and instructed on all aspects of family life. The actual ceremony involves feasting, gift-giving and handing out of graduation certificates. The programme has been reported to have been successful – starting with twelve families in 1996 in one village and increasing in one year to 200 families in three Divisions and eleven different locations. Three hundred girls had graduated from the programme.[42] Findings of a baseline survey in seven Districts undertaken by the Mandeleo Ya Wanawake Organization (MYWO) indicate that girls appreciated being part of the initiation ceremonies, which included imparting traditional wisdom, gifts, food, merrymaking and gaining respect, maturity and peer recognition.[43]

Education Increasing educational opportunities for girls in FGM-practising communities is another intervention that can have positive results in fighting FGM. Formal education seems to have a direct correlation with discontinuation of FGM. Education empowers an individual with knowledge and analysis, which in the long run increase the choices beyond the marriage option.

Polygamy

Polygamy covers the practice of polygyny and polyandry, which refer to a system of marriage where a man can be married concurrently to more than one woman and a woman being concurrently married to more than one man, respectively. This section focuses on the practice of polygamy as practised by men, as the latter, though reported in some communities in

Africa, has been phased out. This practice, viewed from the preceding discussion on female genital mutilation, does not at first seem to have serious human rights implications for women. Indeed, many people, for example in Uganda, have questioned what is wrong with polygamy whenever this issue comes up for debate. However, the practice, like FGM, has subtle but fundamental effects on the enjoyment of women's human rights. Yet its eradication is still as elusive as ever.[44]

Prevalence While the prevalence of polygamy across Africa has not been exhaustively documented, it is a fact that it is widely practised in African countries and to a lesser extent in Islamic countries. However, a 1995 survey of eight anglophone countries established prevalence rates in at least four countries, based on the national demographic statistics.[45] In Ghana, approximately 28 per cent of currently married women (including nearly 40 per cent of married women in their forties) were in polygamous unions.[46] In Kenya, 19.5 per cent of all married women were in polygamous unions,[47] while in Nigeria, women married in polygamous unions constituted 42.6 per cent.[48] Lastly, in Zimbabwe, one in five married Zimbabwean women were in polygamous marriages and the average union was found to consist of 2.3 wives per man.[49]

The legal basis for the practice of polygamy The legal basis for the practice of polygamy is customary law and Islam. Most of the polygamous marriages contracted under customary law are in most cases not registered, although such a requirement is usually imposed by law. In many countries, polygamy assumes either of the following forms *de jure* polygamy, and *de facto* polygamy. While the former applies to marriages that are expressly permitted under the law to be polygamous or potentially polygamous, the latter applies to a common practice where men who are otherwise married under a monogamous form of marriage enter and maintain a permanent or semi-permanent relationship, which is usually acknowledged as a 'marriage' by friends and acquaintances and the entire neighbourhood where the woman resides.

Justification for the practice of polygamy The arguments usually advanced for the practice can be categorized into four areas. The first one is the religious argument, which argues that Islam permits a Muslim man to marry up to four wives, provided the husband fulfils the conditions in the Koran. Proponents of this agreement perceive any attempt to regulate the practice as an unjustified attack on their rights to practise their religion. The second argument is the cultural argument, which is that polygamy is natural to Africa and is deeply entrenched in African society. Underlying this argument is the notion that monogamy is a Western value and its 'imposition' on Africa would be an attempt to impose these values on the African community. But it should be noted that despite the reported prevalence of polygamy, the majority of men in polygamy-practising communities may not necessarily be polygamous. Early studies of two indigenous communities in Uganda found only 32.6 per cent of men in polygamous marriages in one community, while in the other, most men were found to have only one wife.[50] The third argument is the polygamy by choice argument, which is erroneously premised on the fact that parties in polygamous unions have a right to a marriage of their choice. The last argument usually made in support of polygamy is that it benefits both society and women, in reducing the incidence of prostitution and ensuring that 'surplus' women and widows in society also get an opportunity to marry or remarry and also to be relieved of some of the burden of marital chores. Many of these arguments, when carefully analysed against the international and regional human rights instruments, are not valid, as demonstrated in the following section.

Polygamy and the rights of women Polygamy violates several recognized women's rights. First of all, it violates the fundamental right to equality of all persons and non-discrimination, which are recognized in the national constitutions,[51] and international and regional human rights instruments.[52] By giving an exclusive right to the man to marry up to four wives in Islam and an unlimited number of wives under customary law, the right of women to equality in such marriages is violated. The discrimination is further aggravated by the fact that many legal regimes that permit polygamy do not grant a right to a wife to divorce a husband who has married a second wife. On the contrary, the legal regimes provide for very stringent laws on adultery, particularly for married women, and entitle a husband to divorce the wife, even after a single incident of adultery. For example, in Uganda, prior to the 1995 Constitution, a husband could petition for divorce under s. 5 of the Divorce Act on the grounds of his wife's adultery and also claim for damages and costs against the man who committed adultery with his wife. In addition, the wife and the co-adulterer would be liable for criminal prosecution for adultery under s. 150A of the Penal Code. The wife, on the other hand, had to couple the grounds of adultery with additional grounds such as cruelty or desertion for two or more years and the husband could be prosecuted only if the woman he had sex with was married.

In many customary regimes this would also be accompanied with a legitimate demand for return of the bride price that was paid, irrespective of the duration of the marriage, the number of children borne by the wife and the relationship enjoyed for the duration by the divorcing polygamous husband. Failure to refund the bride price by the woman's family would mean that the woman remained married even though she had lost all her rights and claims against the husband as if she was divorced. The husband, on the other hand, under some customary laws, could claim any children she may beget with another man, until his bride price had been repaid and/or a fine paid.[53]

With the coming of HIV/AIDS on the scene, polygamy also puts the women's right to health in jeopardy. Under Article 12 of the ICESCR, states parties recognize the right of everyone to the enjoyment of the highest attainable standard of physical and mental health. Given the attendant problems associated with polygamy, including intra-family violence,[54] unjustified domestic work burdens imposed on women; compromised rights to sex and to a relationship generally, women are denied enjoyment of their rights. Lastly, polygamy also affects women's right to life, particularly in light of increasing their vulnerability to infection with HIV/AIDS, arising from the husband's multiple partners. However, the violation of women's human rights arising from polygamy has continued, as the legal regimes continue to give legal recognition to this practice. Going back to the theme of this chapter, again this practice demonstrates the on-going conflict between culture and the full enjoyment of women's human rights from the resistance to its reform.

Despite the fact that women are the victims, it is worth noting that support for the practice has been voiced by some women. Women have been socialized to perceive it as their duty to marry and to remain 'married' in order to retain their dignity and respect in society. Women's dependency on men is created and perpetuated by the fact that the land, which provides the source of livelihood for the majority of women in Africa, is traditionally owned and controlled by men.

Reforms   Although the practice of polygamy continues, it is worth noting that a number of countries have undertaken reforms in this area, with varying levels of success. These reforms include those countries in Africa that have taken the bold steps to abolish the practice such as Tunisia and Côte d'Ivoire. Others, such as Somalia, Egypt and Morocco, have adopted a midway approach to limit the practice by imposing conditions on the husband to seek permission from courts or a recognized authority to marry a second wife, upon satisfaction of specified conditions; or by giving the wife a right to divorce upon showing that the second marriage has either made her suffer a material or moral injury or will lead to injustice, etc. In Uganda proposals for family law reform along the same lines have been made.[55] However, many countries have so far not made any reforms, allowing coexistence of monogamous and polygamous marriages without the restrictions similar to those highlighted above. The practice is still far from eradication in the near future and should therefore continue to be a concern of human rights activists.

Bride Price

This is the third institution, widely practised in sub-Saharan Africa, which also brings out the tension between culture and women's human rights in Africa. Bride price is a collective name used to refer to various gifts, property, etc. given by the prospective bridegroom and/or his family to the family of the bride-to-be, in consideration of marriage, which either is yet to take place or has taken place. In many Southern African countries this payment is commonly known as 'lobola'. Bride price should be distinguished from dowry, which usually refers to payments originating from the girl's family to the groom-to-be; however, the two are similar in that the payments or gifts are in consideration of marriage. Though widely practised, the practice has continued to be controversial since colonial days, especially with regard to its nature and functions in a customary marriage.[56]

Prevalence Many sub-Saharan African countries recognize the customary marriage as a valid form of marriage. Such a marriage is formed through fulfilling the rites that are usual and customary to the tribe(s) of the parties. Bride price is one single ritual that has been singled out as an essential requirement for contracting a valid customary marriage. Given the fact that the majority of people live in the countryside and marry under their customary law, it is therefore clear that the practice affects a very high number of women. In Uganda, the courts have unanimously held that bride price should have been paid in full before they can recognize a customary marriage as having been contracted. The only exception is if it is shown that it was waived wholly or in part by the girl's family or the groom was forgiven the outstanding balance.[57] The form and amount of payments varies from tribe to tribe, community to community and family to family. So does the period of payment. Factors such as the social status of the respective families of the prospective grooms and bride, educational level and behaviour usually have an impact on the amount of bride price to be paid.

Justification for the institution The institution of bride price has been justified on a number of grounds. It is argued that it signifies the validity of the marriage and legitimizes the children of the marriage.[58] Second, its acceptance serves as conclusive evidence of consent to the marriage by the girl's family.[59] It also serves as a bond to unite the two families and as a stabilizing factor in the marriage.[60] Finally, it is supposed to compensate the girl's family for loss of her services. These reasons notwithstanding, there are some others who also view the practice as amounting to no more than wife-purchase[61] or acquisition of proprietary interests in the wife by her husband. The notion of wife purchase was expounded in the colonial case of *R* v. *Amkeyo*.[62] While it is easy to dismiss this assertion, the view has been exposed in more or less similar terms by men in focus group discussions in recent times.[63] As was seen for the practices of FGM and polygamy, the bride price tradition has also proved difficult to eliminate because of its support from the communities that practise it. Women in particular support the practice despite the fact that it violates their rights, as they erroneously believe that it reflects their value and enhances their respect in the community.

Conclusion

In this chapter, we have highlighted the harmful practices that violate women's rights and the constraints on their elimination. We have also demonstrated that culture remains a very strong force, quite often militating against efforts targeting the eradication of these practices. The cultural dimension manifests itself either as a tool by men and the community to perpetuate the status quo of women's subordination or as a socialization tool to ensure unquestioning compliance by women in a bid to gain respect in their communities or putting fellow women (the circumcisers) at the forefront of the practice and therefore portraying them as the 'custodians' of culture. We have also highlighted how these practices violate women's rights, which are guaranteed in the national constitutions as well as the regional and international human rights instruments and the strategies that have begun to have a positive impact.

Governments have an obligation to do all within their powers to stop these practices. The question therefore should be how this should be done. By recognizing the power of cultural influences on the acts of both men and women, we intended to show that any efforts to eradicate these practices, however well meaning, must be undertaken with a very high level of cultural sensitivity. As Nahid Toubia rightly observes, 'the practice of FGM will not be eradicated unless those who are fighting for change understand the deeply felt beliefs of the people who practise it, particularly with regard to its cultural significance'. For as A. Mohamed and L. Muyah also reaffirmed:

Female genital mutilation is a complex practice which is inextricably intertwined within the rubrics of people's culture. The eradication of FGM, therefore, must begin from a thorough understanding of the complexity of the practice in relation to the people's culture. Since FGM is a societal problem, efforts to eradicate it must involve the participation of key stakeholders in the community, the government, the church, politicians, and individuals who cherish the health and welfare of women and girls.[64]

This is true not only for FGM but also for the other cultural practices that violate the rights of women. For while culture may have its negative side, it does have a positive side as a way of life and practices of a given group, and represents identity, beliefs, norms and values, and acceptable behaviour. It embraces practices impacted upon by the passage of time, which are deep-rooted and entrenched in the value system of a particular community. It also promotes identity and social order. However, the proponents of cultural rights should not assert them at the expense of women's rights. There are other aspects of culture, such as language, dance and music, clothing, food and so on, that the community can continue to enjoy without jeopardizing the enjoyment of women's human rights. Women too should be sensitized to demand from their community respect for their rights guaranteed under the human rights instruments, and to modify their value systems away from cultural practices such as those we have highlighted, which do not permit this to happen.

Appreciating this tension and interrelationship is the starting point for initiating sustainable change, which will ensure not only that women enjoy their rights, but that they can do so as members of their communities. Interventions undertaken in Kenya and Uganda in FGM-practising communities bear witness to the fact that it is possible to work with the community to isolate the harmful aspects of a ritual or practice, while retaining its positive aspects associated with the communities' value systems. Similarly with legislative interventions, this balance can be sought. A case in point is the Tanzanian approach with regard to bride price, which undermines the institution by providing that its payment will not affect the validity of the marriage and that once paid, it should be demanded back at the dissolution of the marriage. Uganda is also tabling similar proposals.

Finally, we should also not lose sight of the need to initiate change in the overall situation of women, as another strategy to tackle these harmful traditional practices, so as to take care of the vacuum that could be created by the eradication of the practice in the community.

Notes

1. See Universal Declaration of Human Rights, the International Covenant of Civil and Political Rights, the International Covenant on Social, Economic and Cultural Rights, the Convention on the Elimination of All Forms of Discrimination against Women, and the African Charter on Human and Peoples' Rights.

2. Nahid Toubia, *Female Genital Mutilation: A Call for Global Action* (1993), at 9 (hereinafter referred to as 'Toubia').

3. World Health Organization, *Female Genital Mutilation: An Overview* (1998), at 6 (hereinafter referred to as 'WHO').

4. Toubia, at 10.

5. Ibid.

6. Ibid.

7. Ibid.

8. Ibid.

9. Ibid.

10. Toubia, at 11.

11. See WHO.

12. Ibid.

13. Ibid.

14. Ibid.

15. Ibid.

16. Toubia, at 26; see also Equality Now, *Awaken Newsletter*, September 1998, at 6 (hereinafter *Awaken*) citing a 1993 survey conducted on obstetricians and gynaecologists facing FGM in Italy, which estimated 27,000 African women to have undergone excision.

17. Toubia, at 5.

18. See *Awaken*, June 1999, at 11, quoting the Somalia *UNDP Human Development Report* (1999).

19. Ibid., Arts 16–17.

20. Ibid.

21. Toubia, at 29; see also *Awaken*, June 1999, at 16–17.

22. Toubia at 29.

23. Toubia at 37.

24. O. Koso-Thomas, *The Circumcision of Women: A Strategy for its Eradication*, Zed Books, London, 1987, pp. 45–9.

25. Ibid.

26. *Awaken*, Vol. 2: 4, December 1999, at 3–4.

27. *The New Vision*, December 6, 1994. But this Resolution was later rescinded.

28. See Rosemary Mburu, 'A tradition better dead', *Women and Health*, Vol. 1, No. 2, Centre for African Family Studies, March 1993.

29. Newsletter No. 14, July 1993.

30. International Planned Parenthood (IPPF) Open File London, June 1993, cited in Tom Kakuba, 'Female genital mutilation, a review of the state of the art', 1995 (unpublished).

31. *Awaken*, December 1998, at 12.

32. Chekweko Jackson, 'Students' attitudes and practices towards female circumcision. a case study of secondary school female students in Tingley County, Kapchorwa District', a dissertation for the Degree of Bachelor of Statistics of Makerere University, 1994, at 49.

33. See CEDAW, Art. 2.

34. See Art. 6.

35. See Art. 24.

36. See e.g. Arts 21 and 33 (6) of the Ugandan Constitution.

37. *Awaken*, December 1998, at 8.

38. Ibid. at 1.

39. See Art. 2 of CEDAW and CRC.

40. Inter Press Service, 19 February 1999.

41. A. Mohamed and L. Muyah, *Alternative Coming of Age Ceremonies: A Viable Strategy for Eliminating Female Genital Mutilation*, reproduced in *Awaken*, December 1998, at 16 (hereinafter Mohamed and Muyah).

42. *Awaken*, December 1998, at 17–19.

43. *Awaken*, December 1998, at 16.

44. The practice has been a subject of another paper, which discusses the issue at great length, particularly from a women's human rights perspective. See Esther N. Mayambala, 'Polygamy and the rights of women in Uganda and Kenya', *EAJPHR*, Vol. 3, No. 2, 200–39 (hereinafter referred to as Mayambala).

45. The Centre for Reproductive Law and Policy and FIDA-(K), *Women of the World: Laws and Policies Affecting their Reproductive Lives – Anglophone Africa* (hereinafter *Women of the World*).

46. Ibid. at 30.

47. Ibid. at 53.

48. Ibid. at 75.

49. Ibid. at 130.

50. Quoted in Mayambala, note 43.

51. E.g. Article 21 of the Uganda Constitution guarantees equality of all persons and prohibits discrimination on the basis of, among other things, sex. Several other articles in the Constitution, such as Articles 31 and 33, reinforce this article by specifically providing for the equality of men and women. Other countries, such as Zambia, Tanzania, Ghana, Ethiopia, all have equality provisions in their constitutions.

52. See UDHR Art. 16; ICESCR Art. 10, CEDAW and ACHPR Art. 2.

53. Mayambala, at 221.

54. For a further discussion on women's intra-familial violence associated with polygamy, see L. Tibatemwa Ekirikubinza, *EAJPHR*, Vol. 4, No. 1, 15–25.

55. See Mayambala.

56. See D. D. Nsereko, 'The nature and function of marriage gifts in customary African marriages', 23 *Jnl of Comp. Law* (1975) pp. 682–704.

57. See e.g. the Ugandan case of *Aiya* v. *Aiya*, Divorce Cause No. 8 of 1973 (unreported).

58. Ibid.

59. Ibid.

60. Ibid.

61. FIDA-K; *Women of the World.*

62. [1917] EAPLR 11.

63. Government of Uganda and Uganda National Council for Children, *Equity and Vulnerability: A Situation Analysis of Women, Adolescents and Children in Uganda* (1994).

64. Mohamed and Muyah, at 17.

11

Modern-day Missionaries or Misguided Miscreants? NGOs, the Women's Movement and the Promotion of Human Rights in Africa

J. Oloka-Onyango

The subject of non-governmental organizations (NGOs) is one that has recently preoccupied scholars from a variety of perspectives. The lawyers are concerned with the rules governing them: rules of association, incorporation, assembly and expression, to mention a few; the sociologists about their link to social movements and the role and place of popular struggle in their evolution and development; the political economist about the fashion in which they are a product of forces from above (the state) or below (the people, howsoever defined). Hence their preoccupation with the prefixes that have come to be attached to the term NGO: GONGO (government-organized NGO); FONGO (foreign-organized NGO); FFUNGO (foreign-funded NGO), and (in the three East African countries of Uganda, Kenya and Tanzania) MUNGOs, MONGOS and MKONGOS (respectively covering Museveni-, Moi-, or Mkapa-organized NGOs)!

For women activists all these issues and many more must be of concern: how sensitive are NGOs to the various questions of gender parity and equality that are of major concern to women? Do NGOs have a key role to play in the democratic struggle? Are we correct to raise them to the pedestal of 'saviour' of the African peoples? What is this animal called 'civil society' that has become the flavour of the month of donors, intellectuals and even governments? Are there no differentials of class, race, ethnicity and religion among these organizations? In other words, are NGOs unproblematic, non-conflictual and undifferentiated? Finally, what is the relevance of the very many diverse discourses about civil society and its importance in contemporary Africa? The problems listed above extend to the discussion about and the definition of the phenomenon of NGOs. Is Claude Welch's presumption about the altruistic character of NGOs, for example, an acceptable one?

Human rights NGOs seek to benefit society, or at least a significant portion of it, without direct benefit to themselves. They constitute both a precondition for, and a supplement to, the constitutionally defined political process and the formal political bodies of the democratic state. As voluntary organizations in large measure, they often pursue idealistic causes. But these causes are crucial to the functioning of a modern society.

This chapter is concerned with analysing the present-day character of NGOs within the context of the political economy of the African situation. It does this first and foremost through a historical examination of the colonial and post-colonial inheritance that has informed the contemporary situation in which associational rights have arisen. It then moves on to examine the specific role, function and impact of NGOs in relation to the main problems they face today, and how they have sought to overcome them. Finally the analysis focuses on women's human rights NGOs in a bid to offer some indication of the place of women's human rights organizations in the democratic struggle.

Non-governmental Human Rights Activity: Background

Contrary to the popular belief that NGOs are a new phenomenon in Africa, their roots date back to the early days of anti-colonial resistance, and can be found in the indigenous agricultural and trade cooperatives that were established to combat racial exclusion and discrimination in the sale and marketing of cash crops. Lawyers, journalists, trade unionists and members of religious organizations have played a prominent role in the struggle for democracy all over the continent. Many of these organizations – the driver's unions, the cotton, cocoa and coffee associations, and the trades unions – were really Africa's first NGOs, and they formed the basis for the nationalist movements that eventually led to the independence of the continent from colonial oppression and domination. Together with the newspapers of those early days, they played an important historical role (a role that should not be forgotten) in the human rights struggle for political emancipation on the continent.

In a historical sense, this period must be viewed as the real first phase of NGOism on the continent. In order to comprehend this role fully, it is essential to go back and critically examine what role they played and whether it was a positive one. It is also important to contrast issues such as their methods of work, sources of financing and linkages to movements and organizations outside the continent. Only through such an exercise can we be sure that there is an African element to the non-governmental struggle and not fall into the trap that assumes that all such activity came from outside the continent. However, following independence the extent and character of NGO activity changed (or was changed dramatically) as a result of both internal and external forces. Internally, human rights activity became proscribed as one-party states became the norm, and military dictatorships abounded. Under the rubric of these systems of governance, the motto became: 'One party, one nation, one people'. The institutional underpinnings of the motto led to the single newspaper to propagandize it, a single women's organization (affiliated to a single party) and a single trade union for all the country's labourers; workers of the country were forced to unite ... behind government! In the midst of the Cold War, Western and Eastern governments were both more concerned with retaining political spheres of influence than they were with fostering democratic struggles from below. Thus, at various stages dictators such as Siad Barre, Idi Amin, Samuel Doe, Marcius Nguema and Jean Bedel Bokassa were aided by external powers in suppressing legitimate opposition to their rule. This process marked a severe decimation of the vigorous non-governmental activity that had previously been in existence.

In the middle to late 1980s, the edifice of these manifestly dictatorial structures began to crumble. Once again, non-governmental activity played a considerable role in bringing them down. With the ending of the Cold War, the collapse of several dictatorships and the increased political space for the expression of various rights and freedoms, a resurgence of non-governmental activity was witnessed. One can thus speak of a second phase of NGO activity, or a renaissance of sorts. The parameters of such activity are complex and not reducible to a single categorization. For the present analysis let us just focus on the relationship between NGOs and the principal official human rights body on the continent – the African Commission on Human and Peoples' Rights (ACHPR).

NGOs and the African Charter and Commission

It is quite clear that there is a major handicap in so far as the continental human rights system is concerned: the weak framework of the Charter, and the medium to mediocre performance of the African Commission. The African Commission is obviously unable to keep track of all the human rights situations in every African country. African NGOs must therefore fill in the gap. However, the number of complaints (human rights petitions) they make to the Commission clearly does not reflect the magnitude of the problems in the field: what are NGOs doing about Somalia, Rwanda and Burundi, Democratic Republic of Congo, etc.? NGOs need not only to pressure the Commission to perform their designated function effectively, they must also attempt to guide the process towards the evolution of a truly African jurisprudence.

In the light of this last point, it is obvious that there is a need to comprehend the influence of the so-called international NGOs (INGOs) on the struggle for human rights in Africa. Based exclusively in the West, the bulk of their work is in the Southern hemisphere. Such work is infused with Western liberal ideals and values about the exact parameters of democratic organization, participation, expression and so on. These groups have significant access to resources and to the structures of political and financial power in the North. Indeed many of them (especially in the Nordic countries) obtained much of their funding from state resources (DANIDA, SIDA, etc.). But INGOs are possessed of a variety of problems, ranging from their methodologies of work to their relationships with their African counterparts. Their methods of work (some have referred to them as 'abolitionist') remind one of the methods of the missionaries of old. They spotlight evils and demand their eradication. For them there is no middle ground or moral dilemma. This may be true in certain instances, but not in all, as for example, in the case of female genital mutilation, in which many African women activists in this area have expressed reservations about the methods and the style of execution adopted by international organizations.

African women know that the issue of FGM is a problem (after all, it affects them, not Western women) and they know how best to deal with it: they should be left to establish the parameters and the framework best suited to the particular problem they may be confronting. In the final analysis, the abolitionist strategy must be informed by much more: a sensitivity to the cultural context in which one is operating. The agenda for the struggle against such heinous practices must, in the first instance, be established and prosecuted by African women and activists. At the same time, it is crucial to be acutely aware of cultural relativism or reductionism – the phenomenon that reduces every human rights problem to an issue of culture versus imperialism. Such antics are simply designed to prevent critical scrutiny of gross human rights violations by prefacing any inquiry with the claim that the issue is 'cultural' and hence beyond external scrutiny. Activists for women's human rights must learn how to negotiate this issue because of the dangers inherent from both sides.

In respect of the African Charter and Commission, individuals and NGOs are permitted to file complaints compelling the Commission to investigate human rights violations. The Commission also has wide powers of interpretation of the Charter principles. In addition, the guidelines formulated by the Commission provide an extremely wide framework for the pursuit not only of traditional civil and political rights, but also of rights of an economic, social and cultural character. Unfortunately the latter, which, it may be argued, are the rights that most greatly affect women's status in society, are very often not given due attention.

NGOs have been fairly active at the African Commission since it began effective operation in the late 1980s. Two features characterize the relation-ship of NGOs to the Commission. First, NGOs were intimately involved in the work of the Commission from the start. It has a simple procedure of accreditation and to date close to two hundred NGOs have obtained status before the Commission, the overwhelming number of which are African. Secondly, biannual ICJ-sponsored workshops have served the purpose of bringing NGOs together, forcing the Commission to become more transparent and effective. Several initiatives and a good deal of networking have occurred at these meetings. This has created a forum for the exchange of views between the Commission and popular and civil opinion in African society at large. There is no doubt that the Commission is sensitive to the many issues that NGOs raise.

The Problems of African NGOs

As with other forms of societal organization, NGOs are not without their problems of internal operation as well as external functioning. Among the most obvious are questions of coordination and collaboration. There is little contact and exchange of experience between NGOs, even within the same country. At the continental level, this phenomenon is duplicated, and made even more debilitating by the over-emphasis on the colonial/linguistic Anglo/Francophone divide. Moreover, the Lusophone countries (Mozambique, Angola, Cape Verde, etc.) suffer an acute marginalization and are invariably excluded from most continental fora that bring NGO activists together. Of course, NGOs are not free of political and personal rivalries, some of which are fostered by governments, and some resulting from ideological and methodological differences in the approach to human rights issues.

Many NGOs have unclear goals and objectives. Thus they take on issues of various kinds and character, leading to a question about the effectiveness of the programmes they pursue. Planning processes are gen-erally of a rudimentary nature, with little critical thought injected into them. Despite operating in a context where economic, social and cultural rights are extremely pertinent, very few African NGOs take up the mandate of championing issues such as the right to shelter, nutrition and food, or the question of health. Instead, they emphasize civil and political rights almost to the exclusion, and sometimes at the expense, of economic, social and cultural rights. An explanation for this can be found in the practice of 'bandwagoning', i.e. simply following the lead of whatever any other organ-ization is doing. But the problem is also related to the fact that the majority of human rights NGOs are based in urban centres, in isolation from the rural parts of the country. This dichotomy is not bridged even when groups carry out para-legal and similar types of programmes in the rural areas.

NGOs are part and parcel of the societies from which they are derived. As such, they too are not free from the societal (ethnic, racial, class and religious) cleavages that characterize the wider society. Such influences may have their bearing on both the manner in which the NGO operates, and in the way in which it relates to the government, or to the opposition. In certain instances, and particularly on account of the absence of political space, NGOs sometimes become actively engaged in the political process, and may in the event compromise their independence. Of course, there are scholars who argue that human rights work is intrinsically political; however, if it becomes overtly partisan, then it is clear that numerous problems may result.

Perhaps the most serious social issue with respect to the operations of human rights NGOs is the question of gender imbalances and the dichotomous approach to women's rights as if they are not human rights. The problem in this respect is twofold. First is the fact that in most instances it is men who dominate in the leadership positions of traditional human rights organizations, with women generally occupying the lower administrative and activist tiers of the bodies. Second, there is also a problem with regard to the approach of human rights NGOs. On the one hand, traditional human rights NGOs rarely take up issues that are of concern to women *qua* women. On the other hand, women's rights organizations do not necessarily perceive that there is a link between their own work and the work of traditional human rights groups. The net result is a lack of consolidated approaches to issues that are of pertinence across the board, such as rights of association, or expression, in which there is little concerted collective action. Scholars such as Sylvia Tamale have nevertheless argued in response that for the moment women's human rights activists are quite in order to put their main focus on the gender aspects of human rights, until such a time as they are considered mainstream and given the prominence they well deserve.

African human rights NGOs suffer a serious problem with obtaining the necessary finances for their operations. Indeed, the question of financial dependency and sustainability are perhaps the most critical in terms of the viability of the African human rights movement. The vast majority of human rights NGOs are foreign-funded. This means that there is a lack of an independent economic foundation for these groups. It also means that, whether directly or otherwise, NGOs are forced to follow the dictates of those who provided them with the finances to organize and operate. The 'flavour-of-the-month' syndrome, whereby donors peripatetically move from one issue to another according to their fancy, greatly affects the operations of African human rights NGOs, who find their programmes compromised, and also their agendas increasingly following the dictates of those who provide the monies for their operations.

African human rights NGOs are part of an international movement, which has played both a positive and a negative role in relation to their operations. Many African groups have adopted some of the very effective mechanisms of advocacy, research and monitoring that their international counterparts pioneered. International organizations assist African groups in both accessing relevant data and connecting with the various international mechanisms, institutions and governments that have a bearing on their domestic operations. At the same time, international groups could be said to be suffering a 'mid-life' crisis. They have long reported on and dominated the human rights scene in African countries, and there is a degree to which their function as watchdogs has been usurped by the local NGOs. And yet their *raison d'être* is human rights violations in countries other than their own. Those tensions may be only implicit, but they have nevertheless led to charges that the international groups have a tendency to monopolize the scene and even to take the work of local groups and pass it off as their own. Of course, just as is the case with African groups, international groups are not free of the racial, class and other discriminatory elements that operate in their own societies.

Finally, African NGOs are in many respects guilty of some of the very practices they condemn as prevalent in the governments they make it their business to criticize. Among them, the issue of undemocratic and unrepresentative organizational structures is a major one. Many human rights NGOs are single-person (often male-) headed, and are operated in the manner of fiefdoms. Certain of these groups have been accused of simply being sites for the petty accumulation of donor finances. African human rights NGOs are not free of the vices of corruption, gross mismanagement, lack of transparency and violation of the rights of expression and association of their own employees. Clearly, the first point of attention in respect of the application of human rights standards must be the human rights NGOs themselves.

The Role of African Women's NGOs in the African Context

Perhaps there is no movement within the African human rights context that is as mature, developed and effective as the women's human rights movement. Their initiatives range from the pre-Beijing organizing of continent-wide sessions to local efforts in a variety of different countries. At the continental level, African women's human rights groups have been involved in the following.

At Lomé, Togo, in 1995, WILDAF organized a workshop on women and the African Charter, recommending the adoption of an additional protocol to the charter that would strengthen the protection of women, and also urged the appointment of a special rapporteur on the issue.

Women's groups have continuously urged the African Commission to take African women's rights seriously; this led to the appointment of the first woman commissioner in November 1993, and the second in 1995. Although this is clearly an insufficient number given the overall representation of women in the continent, it represents first tentative steps.

Collectively, women's groups have forced a critical reconceptualization of the notion of human rights, pushing issues such as domestic violence, rape and defilement, health and education to the forefront of the continental human rights debate. The movement has also forced governments to accord women enhanced positions in the process of decision-making both in the legislature and in the executive. Women NGOs have also been critical in fostering conflict resolution, demanding greater protection for refugees and internally displaced persons and the environment. All of this activity has forced not only government but also traditional human rights groups to reorient their work in the protection and enhancement of human rights.

These are significant achievements. This does not mean that women's NGOs in Africa are without problems. In certain instances their concerns have been narrowly pursued at the expense of the broader human rights question. Consequently, women's rights organizations are reluctant to become involved in issues such as freedom of association, participation or political opposition unless and until they affect them specifically. Such a narrow approach to the attack on human rights essentially facilitates the division of the human rights movement and objectively contributes to the further marginalization or 'ghettoization' of women's organizations. In this way women's rights are divorced from mainstream human rights and the state is able to pursue a policy of divide and rule between the two organs of the movement. At the end of the day, the points that require emphasis are the inseparability of women's rights from the general corpus of human rights and the fact that the different groups in the movement need to adopt a holistic approach to the question. Such a symbiotic approach means two things: first, that traditional human rights groups should adopt a much more gendered and human rights-sensitive approach to their areas of concern. At the same time, women's human rights groups should act in solidarity with their counterparts in the broader movement.

Bibliography

Charlesworth, Hilary, 'Feminist approaches to international law', *American Journal of International Law*, 613 (1991).

Eyango, Vijitha Mahadevan, 'Globalization and international partnerships in Africa: defining the gender-setters', *Development*, 41/4, 63 (1998).

Lawyers Committee for Human Rights, *The World Bank, NGOs and Freedom of Association: A Critique of the World Bank's Draft 'Handbook on Good Practices for Laws Relating to Non-governmental Organizations'* (1997).

Lomo, Z., 'The struggle for the protection of human rights in Uganda: a critical analysis of the work of human rights organizations', *East African Journal of Peace & Human Rights*, 5/2, 161 (1999).

Mamdani, Mahmood, 'Conceptualizing state and civil society relations: towards a methodological critique of contemporary Africanism', in C. Auroi (ed.), *The Role of the State in Development Processes*, London and Portland, OR, F. Cass (1992).

Mohanty, Chandra Talpade (ed.), *Third World Women and the Politics of Feminism*, Bloomington, IN, Indiana University Press (1991).

Mohiddin, Ahmed, 'Partnership: a new buzz-word or realistic relationship?', *Development*, 41/4, 5 (1998).

Mutua, Makau, 'The ideology of human rights', *Virginia Journal of Human Rights*, 36/3, 589 (1996).

Okuku, Juma, 'Non-governmental organizations and the struggle for democratic governance: the case in Uganda', *Mawazo*, 7/2, 83 (1997).

Oloka-Onyango, J., 'The plight of the larger half: human rights, gender violence and the legal status of refugee and internally displaced women in Uganda', *Denver Journal of International Law & Policy*, 24/2, 3, 349 (1996).

Oloka-Onyango, J. and Sylvia Tamale, '"The personal is political," or why women's rights are indeed human rights: an African perspective on international feminism', *Human Rights Quarterly*, 17/4, 691 (1995).

Tamale, Sylvia, *When Hens Begin to Crow: Gender and Parliamentary Politics in Uganda*, Boulder, CO, Westview Press (1999).

Weiss, T. G. and L. Gordenker (eds), *NGOs, the UN and Global Governance*, Boulder, CO, Rienner (1996).

12

Women in the Armed Forces in Uganda: Human Rights Issues[1]

Apollo N. Makubuya

Women across the world are struggling to address the socio-economic injustices and human rights violations they suffer on account of their gender. This chapter deals with a category of women who, either voluntarily or involuntarily, take up arms to protect themselves and their society from repression and abuse of human rights. It aims at exposing a range of human rights issues that affect women in the armed forces, with special reference to Uganda, one of several African countries where women have participated in the struggle to end oppression and dictatorship.

Questions are often raised about women in the armed forces. Should women be in the army at all? Should women be sent to the battle front? Should women be accorded a special status in the army? What is the role of the state regarding women in the army?

Armed forces here refer to, on the one hand, the regular armed institutions such as the army, police and prisons, and on the other hand, to irregular armed forces such as guerrilla movements. Notwithstanding the peculiarities of each of these forces, we examine the common aspects that are relevant to rights of the women therein.

Historical Background

Historically, women have been involved in the army for many centuries. From the seventeenth to the nineteenth centuries, women sold food and drinks to soldiers, while others worked behind the front and devoted themselves to the care of wounded soldiers. In the First World War women started taking part in hostilities more systematically.[2] In the Second World War, women took a more active role in hostilities. In Germany, from 1943 onwards, more than a million women worked in army factories, while 300,000 served as army reserves, with 20,000 in the navy and 130,000 in the air force.[3]

In England, at the end of 1943, women accounted for 9.37 per cent of the country's armed forces. During the Second World War their units had 624 dead, 98 disappeared, 744 wounded and 20 captured.[4] In the Soviet Union, women participated directly in fighting in all units of the army as snipers, rifle women, air pilots, bombardiers, artillerists, etc. It is estimated that about a million women took part in fighting, constituting 8 per cent of the total armed forces.[5] In present times, drafting of women in the armed forces as combatants has generally been marginal with the Soviet Army as an exception. Israel has compulsory military service for women, but in non-combatant roles.

In Uganda, as in many other African countries, the armed forces are dominated by men. According to a public service census on manpower survey in 1987, out of 2,634 employees in the Ministry of Defence, 659 were women, the majority of whom were clerks and service workers. In the police force, out of 5,299 only 611 were women. In the prison service out of a total of 1,907, only 306 were women. According to the National Report for the Fourth World Conference on Women in Beijing in May 1994 the average percentage of women in the police force between 1980 and 1994 was 12.6 per cent. Although the army, police and prisons are not part of the civil service, these figures reveal the poor sex ratios and the low occupational categories in which women are engaged.

In Africa, there are many reasons for the small numbers of women in the armed forces. These include, *inter alia*, socio-cultural attitudes, low educational levels for women, gender discrimination and government policy. For our purposes, we concentrate on human rights issues that affect this number. Despite their small numbers, women play a key role in the army. Women played a key role in the struggle that saw the National Resistance Army capture power in Uganda in 1986.

The Problem

According to Captain Gertrude Njuba, the major handicap for women soldiers in Uganda is that of lack of education. This is coupled with negative social and cultural attitudes and prejudices based on the idea of the inferiority or superiority of either of the sexes or on stereotyped roles for men and women.

Education Lack of education for many women soldiers has many negative implications. First, women are few in number and low in the army hierarchy. Owing to their poor numerical quantity and relative powerlessness they are marginalized in several respects. Further, the male soldiers tend to look upon them simply as a sex resource. In this way many of the women soldiers contract HIV/AIDS and/or unwanted pregnancies. Invariably this denies them many opportunities for promotion and, ultimately, may force them to leave the army.[6] Second, the lack of education means that prospects for promotion are very small. This leads to the third and most significant problem – lack of effective representation in policy and decision-making. Because there are few women in the high command the plight of women soldiers is not effectively articulated and addressed.[7] In Uganda, the formation of women's groups or any other form of sectarian association in the army is seen as subversion and can attract a punishment of life imprisonment.[8] This law effectively denies the marginalized army women from forming groups to advance their cause and ultimately reinforces their discrimination.

Socio-cultural and customary practices   Social, cultural and customary practices, attitudes and prejudices contribute to the marginalized position of women in the army. To many societies in Africa, the army is and remains a man's world. Therefore, a woman who joins the army is seen as a social deviant and is shunned for upsetting social decorum. African society trains girls and women not to do almost all that one has to do as a soldier, including shouting, climbing trees, squatting (*cucuma*), eating while standing, jumping and leaping, etc. A woman who does these things is therefore treated as a social outcast by both the male and her fellow females.

The army as an institution   The nature of the army as a predominantly male institution poses many challenges to women soldiers.[9] These include the lack of effective representation, lack of welfare provisions for women as mothers, lack of supplies that apply only to women, uniforms tailored for women, and family planning provisions. In times of active combat/conflict women's problems are compounded. The lack of provisions necessary for supporting women's social services, healthy and safe working conditions and safeguards for the function of reproduction all prevent women in the army from achieving an effective right to work, to health and to a family.

The Law

Women's international human rights law   The Universal Declaration of Human Rights (UDHR), International Covenant on Civil and Political Rights, the United Nations Charter and regional human rights instruments generally provide for equality and for the application of human rights to all regardless of sex.[10] The Convention on Economic Social and Cultural Rights (ECOSOC), has established a Commission on the Status of Women, whose mandate is to promote women's rights.

The Convention on the Elimination of All Forms of Discrimination against Women (CEDAW Convention),[11] together with the basic rules of the Geneva Conventions and their additional Protocols (ICRC) more specifically address the law that relates to women in the army and in times of conflict. The CEDAW Convention is seen as a standard-setting instrument that provides for legally binding principles and measures to achieve equal rights for women everywhere. The Convention calls for equal rights for all women in all fields and calls for national legislation banning discrimination. It provides for affirmative action to accelerate the achievement of equality in practice and to modify social and cultural patterns that perpetuate discrimination. The Convention emphasizes the equal responsibilities of men and women in the context of family life, stressing the need for combining family obligations with work responsibilities.

The treatment of women combatants and prisoners of war is more specifically provided for under the basic rules of the Geneva Conventions and their additional Protocols. Art. 14 states that women 'shall in all cases benefit by treatment as favorable as that granted to men'. The Third Convention provides in general that prisoners of war must be treated humanely at all times, and it is forbidden to subject them to physical mutilation or to scientific experiments that are not justified by the medical treatment of the prisoner concerned. In a non-international armed conflict, captured combatants do not have the status of prisoners of war but must benefit from the fundamental guarantees of Art. 4.

Women are accorded special protection in an international conflict. Under Art. 72 'pregnant women and mothers having dependant infants who are arrested, detained … for reasons related to the armed conflict, shall have their cases considered with utmost priority'. The third Convention stipulates that women shall be treated with all the regard due to their sex. Article 25, para. 4 states that 'in any camps in which women prisoners of war, as well as men, are accommodated, separate dormitories shall be provided for them'. Furthermore Article 29, para. 2 provides that 'in any camps in which women prisoners of war are accommodated, separate conveniences must be provided for them'. In a non-international armed conflict, Protocol I, Article 5 (2)(a) also specifies that women arrested, detained or interned 'shall be held in quarters separated from those of men and shall be under the immediate supervision of women except when families are united'.

Various conventions of relevance to women have been concluded within the framework of the International Labour Organization.[12] International human rights law as it affects women has come under serious criticism on two serious fronts. Hillary Charlesworth argues that 'the development of international human rights law has been partial and androcentric, privileging a masculine world view ... the structure of the law has been built on the silence of women ... who lack the real power in public or private life. International human rights law, like most economic, social and legal constructs, reinforces this powerlessness.'[13] Further, she argues that

> the structure and institutions of women's international human rights law are more fragile than their apparently more generally applicable counterparts: international instruments dealing with women have weaker implementation obligations and procedures; the institutions designed to draft and monitor them are under-resourced and their roles are often circumscribed compared to other human rights bodies; the widespread practice of states making reservations to fundamental provisions in the instruments is apparently tolerated; as is the failure of states generally to fulfill their obligations under the instruments.[14]

This chapter does not engage in a debate to validate or dismiss these points, but the criticisms raised above are, to an extent, relevant to the entire human rights enforcement mechanism. These problems negate the rapid and universal realization of an effective end to discrimination against women.

National law Uganda's new Constitution addresses the rights of women under Chapter 5 (19 June 1995). Article 62 thereof specifies women's equality and dignity, and recognizes the significant role of women in society and the need to provide opportunities to enhance their welfare and potential. The Constitution takes into account the unique status of women and natural maternal function in society. Furthermore it provides for affirmative action and prohibits laws, cultures and customs or traditions that are against the dignity, welfare or interest of women. The inclusion of women's rights in the Constitution is a new and welcome development. The efficacy of the enforcement mechanisms in the Constitution – the courts and the commission of human rights – is yet to be tested.

We need to point out that the army and police have a strict code of conduct. The military code of conduct and the National Resistance Army Statute (Statute No. 3 of 1992), apply to women members of the army '*as far as may be practicable subject to such modifications as may be necessary*'. This is a very indeterminate and symbolic provision and cannot be relied on to enforce women's rights. Save for this sweeping provision, the Army Statute does not provide for specific protections, rights and safeguards to women soldiers as are provided for in the Constitution and/or in the international instruments discussed above. Like the Army Statute, above, the Police Statute (Statute No. 13 of 1994) has no special provisions to cater for policewomen.

From the above analysis, it is clear that there is in place a legal framework that applies to women in the armed forces at both national and international planes. However, doubt remains as to how effective the existing legal framework is in the protection of the rights of women in the army. We proceed to analyse this point with a few illustrations from Uganda's National Resistance Army.

Women's Rights in the National Resistance Army

Welfare Provisions for women's welfare in the NRM leave a lot to be desired. Often the supplies, including army uniforms and toiletries, do not take into account the special needs of women. Other feminine requirements, such as contraceptive pills, are not provided at all, yet male soldiers are provided with condoms. The denial of these welfare needs amounts to discrimination against women. Women have a right to protection of health benefits, equal treatment and to safety in working conditions, including the function of reproduction (CEDAW Convention, Art. 11).

Family In order to prevent discrimination against women on grounds of marriage or maternity the CEDAW Convention requires states to encourage the provision of the supporting social services to enable parents to combine family obligations with work responsibilities and participation in public life. The Ugandan government is yet to provide supporting social services such as child care facilities. Often, women, unlike their male counterparts, cannot participate in far-away missions because they are looking after their family. Further, married women soldiers forfeit promotions that involve transfers because of the difficulties of getting their families to move along with them. If adequate social services were provided this problem would probably be non-existent.

Maternity and reproduction needs The CEDAW Convention, to which Uganda is a party, obliges states to provide for women appropriate services in connection with pregnancy, confinement and the post-natal period, granting free services where necessary, as well as adequate nutrition during pregnancy and lactation (Art. 12). In Uganda, pregnant women soldiers are 'cared for' at Bombo barracks, which is about 20 miles north of Kampala. The conditions at the barracks do not measure up to the requirements of the CEDAW Convention and hence amount to a denial of human rights.

Conclusion

In conclusion we note that women in the army, like all other women, suffer denial of human rights and equal status. Although Uganda has signed the CEDAW Convention, it still has a long way to go in addressing particular needs, rights and freedoms belonging to women. The law that governs the army, police and prisons has to be revised to provide for women's rights and to integrate a policy of affirmative action as contained in the new Constitution. There is a need for the state to take appropriate measures to modify social and cultural patterns and attitudes that prejudice the position of women, especially those in the armed forces.

Notes

1. Paper presented at a postgraduate course on human rights of women at Mukono in 1995 by A. N. Makubuya, law lecturer, Makerere University, Kampala, Uganda.

2. Françoise Krill, 'Humanitarian Protection of Women in Conflict'.

3. Nancy Loring Goldman and Richard Stites, *Great Britain and the World Wars*, Greenwood Press, London 1982, pp. 24–9.

4. Ibid., pp. 30–5.

5. Ibid., pp. 35–6.

6. The Code of Conduct of the Army, section 2(f), forbids men from developing 'any illegitimate or irresponsible relationship with women'. It is not clear which women are referred to here.

7. In the case of Uganda's National Resistance Army, women are not represented in the highest body, namely, the National Resistance Army High Command, while only one woman soldier (Captain Nalweyiso) represents women's interests at the National Resistance Army Council.

8. S.16 National Resistance Statute No. 3 of 1992.

9. Reference to the army ranks is always to 'officers and men'.

10. See preamble to UN Charter, Article 2, UDHR, preamble to ICCPR, Art. 2A. ACHPR, and Article 1 and Section 1 of the ECHR.

11. Uganda is a signatory to this Convention.

12. These include No. 102 concerning minimum standards of social security including maternity benefits; No. 111 concerning discrimination in respect of employment and occupation and No. 156 concerning equal opportunities and treatment for women and men workers.

13. Hillary Charlesworth 'What are women's international human rights?' in Rebecca J. Cook (ed.), *Human Rights of Women: National and International Perspectives*, University of Philadephia, 1995.

14. Ibid., p. 59.

13

Women Prisoners and Female Staff in Ugandan Prisons

Kurt Neudek

Women in prison seem to be an afterthought of systems run by men for men. They consequently end up accommodated in makeshift circumstances that completely disregard their peculiar unique nature ... Women are the caretakers of families and once imprisoned, it is not only they who suffer but the children, the sick, and the elderly who are dependent on their tender care ... To imprison a woman is to punish society. Women should not go to prison. (Christine Achieng, research officer and coordinator of the Penal Reform Project, Foundation for Human Rights Initiative, Kampala, Uganda, in *Prison Update*, Vol. 3, Issue No. 1, 1997, pp. 5–7)

The way society deals with women who break the law is simply an extension of what is considered appropriate for men. When the policy turns out to be inappropriate for men, it is usually disastrous for women. Imprisonment was created by men for men and although it would be quite simple to introduce a sound penal policy for women's prisons, it has not been done in practice. (Merle Mendonca, Guyana Human Rights Association)

Background

Ugandan prisons are in urgent need of repair and improvement. Thousands of prisoners live in appalling conditions in which they receive inadequate food, water and health care. There are no sewerage systems, no reliable supply of safe water and no facilities for work, education or recreation. These conditions are the result of overcrowding and an absence of funds over many years. These problems are compounded by delay in justice, resulting in the fact that out of about 21,000 prisoners in central government prisons, about 14,000, or two-thirds, await trial for several years.

In view of this and the fact that about 125 local prisons have been taken over by the Central Government Prison Administration (UPS) recently, there is an urgent need to improve the physical infrastructure of the prisons and to have enough resources for the provision of adequate food, sanitation and health services on a daily basis. Within a strict budget limit, the Prison Administration depends on donor funds for the improvement of the physical infrastructure of the prisons and for treatment programmes for inmates and training of staff.

Ugandan prison policy is based on complete openness, transparency and accountability. All prisons are accessible not only to potential donors and NGOs, but also to the general public, politicians and the media. In this context, the generous contributions of several donors deserve to be mentioned, in particular the International Committee of the Red Cross, the Swedish Raoul Wallenberg Institute for Human Rights and Humanitarian Law, Penal Reform International, the European Union and several governments – Austria, Denmark, France, Germany, Ireland, the Netherlands, Norway and the United Kingdom.

Female prisoners In Ugandan prisons, as in most prisons all over the world, women represent a small minority (see Appendix 1). In 1996, their average number was 336, as opposed to 11,205 male prisoners. Out of this total of 336 female prisoners, 232, or more than two-thirds, were on remand. They were mainly accused or convicted of murder, mostly of co-wives, husbands or boyfriends (135), manslaughter (32), theft (58), assault (34) and fraud (17). Most women prisoners were between 18 and 40 years of age, unemployed and poorly educated.

The following are some of the circumstances and situations that cause women in Uganda to come into conflict with the law:

* Domestic quarrels and violence, disrespect and provocation: analysis of the data clearly shows that the majority of women commit murder and manslaughter as a result of violence and provocation. Most of these offences are usually unintended and happen in many cases in self-defence or accidentally through fights and brutal battering by either men 'friends' or husbands.
* Economic effects: unemployment and poverty are other factors related to crime among women, resulting in the commission of thefts, infanticide, child-stealing, etc. In addition, unemployment also places women in a submissive position, leading to very early marriages or irresponsible sex, resulting sometimes in contraction of HIV, etc.
* Denying responsibility for pregnancy is another serious factor related to crime among girls in Uganda. Frequently, girls commit abortions, infanticide and even murder because the fathers of their children refuse to accept responsibility and parents turn girls away from home.

As Mrs Achieng correctly pointed out in *Prison Update*:

Most women are in prison as victims of men's actions in some way. They are either used by men to carry contraband for them; they are prostitutes or they are provoked into fights by men over fellow women. In most theft cases, they steal in order to feed the children for whom the fathers are not providing. Occasionally, they turn brutal or violent in an effort to protect their husbands or partners from having affairs with other women. Their crime, therefore, turns out to be that of reacting to the brutal environment of men's bigotry.

Strict separation of men and women prisoners In accordance with traditional prison rules and regulations as well as Rule 8 of the United National Standard Minimum Rules for the Treatment of Prisoners, men and women prisoners in Uganda are detained either in separate institutions or in institutions that receive both men and women, where the premises allocated to women are entirely separated and guarded only by female staff. From an economic viewpoint, separate prisons for female prisoners in Uganda are disproportionately costly and limited to Luzira in the central region (see Appendix 3) and Mbale, in the eastern part of the country. The economic pressure to mix by gender is strong, but mixing does not in practice eliminate women's disadvantageous position. They will still be the minority within mixed institutions. As it is impossible in Uganda to provide equal and separate facilities for women in all prisons, women are given a choice of separate and equal access to shared facilities, such as water supply, medical services and educational programmes. However, while men sometimes get facilities for job training, women are often limited to sewing, knitting and handicrafts.

Female prison staff In 1997, there were 118 female prison officers working in Uganda Central Government prisons, as compared to 2,303 male officers. Among the female staff, there was one deputy regional prison commander, three officers in charge of prisons and one deputy officer-in-charge. In conformity with national law as well as Rule 53 of the Standard Minimum Rules for the Treatment of Prisoners, in an institution for both men and women, the part of the institution set aside for women is always under the sole authority of the woman officer who has the custody of the keys of all that part of the institution. No male member of the staff is permitted to enter the part of the institution set aside for women prisoners, unless accompanied by women officers. Furthermore, women prisoners have to be attended and supervised only by women officers. This does not, however, preclude male members of the staff, particularly doctors and teachers, from carrying out their professional duties in prisons or parts of prisons set aside for women.

In this context, it may be noticed that some international standards assume almost complete segregation of the sexes. While this is perhaps appropriate for certain countries, others now regard strict distinction between the sexes as outdated. In Uganda women are increasingly securing positions on the labour market and are employed in men's prisons in a number of functions ranging from prison officer to director. Equally, it is not unusual in Uganda for men to be employed in different capacities in women's prisons. It is also in conformity with Uganda prison policy that both sexes enjoy equal opportunities in the field of employment, and that they receive equal pay for doing the same work. Working mothers often have to run a household in addition to their jobs. It is, therefore, Uganda prison policy to make jobs available to female staff on a full-time or part-time basis.

In employing prison officers of both sexes, the Uganda Prison Service has found the experience positive. Female prison officers often reduce the level of aggression shown by male prisoners, and male officers working in a female prison may contribute to better conditions. The presence of both male and female staff has the advantage of creating a situation that more closely resembles society at large. However, the presence of women in a male prison can also create sexual tension. Female officers can be approached not only by prisoners but also by male colleagues in a sexual way. They can experience sexual harassment, sometimes to a degree that makes it impossible for them to carry out their work properly. It is, therefore, the duty of every member of staff in the Uganda Prison Service to guard against the type of intimidating behaviour that seriously affects colleagues in the performance of their duties.

Sexual relations Heterosexual and homosexual relationships sometimes may develop between staff and prisoners in Ugandan prisons, as in prisons in other countries. While the love of two people for each other is no subject of rational discussion, the love affair of a member of staff and a prisoner within an institution cannot be approved, the reason being that the parties are not equal. A prisoner or detainee is strongly dependent on a member of staff. On the other hand, a member of staff may be put under emotional pressure, albeit unintentionally. Although the feelings may be genuine, there is too great a risk of exploitation. The climate and communication opportunities within the Prison Service in Uganda are such that a member of staff can be free and feel free to report such unprofessional feelings for a detainee. The prison authority then determines the measures to be taken, without automatically considering disciplinary punishment or discharge.

Special needs of women prisoners It is clear that special arrangements need to be made for menstruating women prisoners. They should be able to wash themselves and their undergarments as often as they need to, and they should be provided with sanitary materials typically used by menstruating women in the country (such as pads, tampons, cotton cloths, etc.). It is important that these arrangements be available to women under conditions in which they do not need to be embarrassed asking for them (they should be either dispensed by other women or, better yet, accessible whenever needed). In prisons where women live with their children, provisions should be made for adequate hygienic conditions and facilities for infants. However, due to economic constraints, there is, unfortunately, a big gap between these basic requirements and the stark reality of everyday life in Uganda prisons (see Appendix 2).

Imprisoned mothers As regards pregnant women prisoners and mothers with babies, ideally there should be provision for all necessary pre-natal and post-natal care and treatment, which, unfortunately, is deficient in Uganda prisons due to a lack of funds. However, arrangements are made, wherever practicable, for children to be born in a hospital outside the institution. If, exceptionally, a child is born in prison, this fact is not to be mentioned in the birth certificate.

Babies in prison In accordance with international standards where nursing infants are allowed to remain in the institution with their mothers, provision should be made for a nursery staffed by trained persons, where the infants should be placed when they are not in the care of their mothers. Regrettably, this requirement can usually not be met in Ugandan prisons, again due to economic reasons. Neither the United Nations Standard Minimum Rules for the Treatment of Prisoners nor other instruments such as the Convention on the Rights of the Child, which has been ratified by Uganda, address the treatment of babies or small children held in custody with their mothers. The dilemma of whether or not to detain such young children is a real one in Uganda prisons, as well as in prisons in other countries. The interests of the child should be paramount. Bonds with the mother are of great importance at this early stage. When small children are detained with their mothers, they are not prisoners in the ordinary sense and their treatment must reflect that fact. They must be cared for in accordance with recognized outside standards of child care. This includes health care and provision for stimulation. Unless a baby or small child is taken out of the prison environment every week to see the outside world, learning and emotional development may be retarded and adaption to society jeopardized. In practice, in Uganda babies are left with their imprisoned mothers until they reach 18 months of age. In exceptional circumstances, they may stay there even longer, until an appropriate foster care place can be found. *Prisoners in Shadows*, a report on women and children in five Nigerian prisons, published by the Civil Liberties Organization, had this to say:

> For children behind bars, for no fault of theirs, life goes on in the prison. Other women take turns to nurse them, and life to the babies is basically what they observe around them. They have no knowledge of cars, men, schooling, etc. Life is simply waking up, bathing, eating and roving among women while prison life takes its effect on them. They may grow up to hate men, detest cars, or even commit crimes to put them back in the kind of life they are used to.

Guidelines Although in different countries different viewpoints are held about the best solutions with respect to imprisoned mothers, some very basic provisions should be guaranteed. The recommendations of the Human Rights Watch *Global Report on Prisons* (New York, 1993) deserve to be quoted as important guidelines for the Uganda Prisons Service:

- Female inmates should be given sanitary napkins or substitutes and have daily access to showers or their equivalent during menstruation.
- Work and educational opportunities should be available on an equal basis to both men and women prisoners.
- Where visits to female inmates are severely limited because of the long distances relatives must travel, authorities must make efforts to compensate (by subsidizing relatives' travel or through some other system);
- Pregnant prisoners should be given regular pre-natal checkups and an adequate diet;
- Nursing mothers should get an adequate diet;
- Efforts should be made to facilitate mothers' contacts with their children and their right to direct their upbringing.

However, as stated above, in Uganda it is difficult to comply fully with these goals. Further, prisons for women in Uganda are not as poorly differentiated as elsewhere. As a result, the level of security is mostly high, certainly far higher than is generally necessary for women. Prison work for women is little and uninteresting. Prisons are built for men and often poorly adapted to the special needs of women. In Uganda, not even vital needs with respect to menstruation, pregnancy and motherhood can be met, as indicated in Appendix 2. These conditions affect adversely women's health and state of mind. Moreover, women in prisons in all countries are vulnerable to abuse, including rape. Therefore, prison doctors and nurses in Uganda have been urged to pay explicit attention to women, their conditions and their complaints. However, adequate gynaecological care for female prisoners is far from guaranteed in Ugandan prisons. In accordance with the new Draft Prison Act, the hair of women detained in Uganda prisons shall never be cut against their will, expect for demonstrable medical reasons. Moreover, as Uganda women sometimes wear make-up outside prisons, they should be allowed to do so in prisons as well. This is a privilege that does not involve security considerations or require additional expenditures (it is about allowing, not providing, make-up), yet it often can make a big difference in the way female inmates feel about themselves.

Conclusion

The following statement of the officer in charge of the Luzira Women's Prison, Mrs Mary Kaddu (see Appendix 4), based on long-term and first-hand experience, describes the difficult situation of imprisoned women in Uganda:

> The psychological torture which entangles a woman in confinement is un-imaginable. Her mind is always on her children, for she is not sure whether they are under proper care. In most cases, women receive information that the children are out of school and in the streets, that the man has of course taken another woman and has little or no feelings at all for her. This tortures the inmate terribly, because all that she can do is imagine the situation, but she can do nothing to control or to stop it. She is worried about her property, if any, and the men sometimes even give the inmates' clothes to the new lovers. With all these imaginations, a woman takes time to settle and accept the new situation of imprisonment. However, after some time, and with the help of the rehabilitational activities carried out in the prison's institutions, the female prisoner eventually accepts the situation. But when it is about time for release, she becomes totally disturbed again. She does not know where to go, because, if she is married, there may be already another woman at home. If she has killed her husband, the latter's relatives may be waiting for revenge or, at least, refuse to accept her back. The ex-inmate's parents, too, may be economically unable to have an extra burden of care. Her friends may also have had enough of her problems and may not be prepared for additional expenditure. She is worried that the public, too, may not willingly accept her back. How can she make the public change their traditional beliefs, attitudes and practices to re-adopt her as an ex-prisoner?

In view of this difficult situation, and considering the lack of funds for assistance to detained or released female prisoners on the part of the prison service, outside support from donors and concerned NGOs, as well as churches and other interested parties, is greatly appreciated. In this context, special mention deserves to the made of the pioneering Port Bell Resettlement Project, organized by members of the National Association of Women's Associations in Uganda (NAWOU) and the Prison Women's Association. It is generously funded by the European Union, through Penal Reform International as the implementing agency. Under this scheme, if a women is stranded after release, she is absorbed in the Resettlement Project and attends a six-months course in different skills, such as bakery, mushroom-growing, catering, weaving, poultry, tailoring, etc. At the end of the course, she undergoes an examination, writes up a proposal and, if successful, receives a certificate. Many of those who have gone through this scheme have obtained work, while others have started their own businesses and are able to pay school fees for their children. Most significantly, the public needs to be sensitized, so that people change their attitude towards ex-prisoners and accept them back into the community. Special bodies, such as the Uganda Human Rights Commission and the Foundation for Human Rights Initiative, make efforts to change traditional beliefs, attitudes and practices and promote the re-adoption of female ex-offenders into society.

Recommendations

The following suggestions may be made with a view to alleviating the plight of female prisoners in Uganda.

- Women's rights are human rights and should be observed as such in and outside prisons.
- Family values need to be strengthened. In particular family violence should be prevented to avoid murders, grievous harm, assaults, suicide, etc.
- The linkage between female inmates and their families must be maintained. Special attention should be paid to avoid 'secondary victimization' of other family members, especially small children, through imprisonment of their mothers. Prosecutors, judges and magistrates should be sensitized to this possibility.
- Men should be made responsible for their notions as fathers and husbands, in order to avoid abortions and infanticide as a consequence of pregnancies of women.
- Non-custodial penal sanctions, such as community service, suspended sentences and probation, should be applied to women convicted of petty offences.

Let me end by recalling an incident that occurred recently on the occasion of one of my visits to a Ugandan prison up-country. When I asked the officer-in-charge (male) how many female prisoners were detained in this prison, he replied instantly: 'We have 16 ladies, Sir.' At this point, the regional prison commander (male) reprimanded him: 'Prisoners are not ladies!' Whereupon the officer-in-charge apologetically remarked: 'Sorry, Sir, for the slip of the tongue.' This story demonstrates in a nutshell the attitude some of the male staff in the Uganda Prison Service as well as the general public still entertain towards female detainees. To change this attitude and fully to secure and promote the human rights and the dignity of female prisoners in Uganda will be one of our main challenging tasks in the years to come.

Appendix 1

Comparison of daily average of inmates by year and sex, 1987–96

Year	Male	Female	Total
1987	11.311	228	11.539
1988	11.968	296	12.264
1989	12.694	315	13.009
1990	11.099	376	11.475
1991	11.299	351	11.650
1992	11.016	350	11.366
1993	9.905	381	10.286
1994	10.063	382	11.445
1995	11.155	379	11.534
1996	10.869	336	11.205

Appendix 2

May Karooro Okurut, 'Female prisoners won't be celebrating Women's Day' (*The Monitor*, 7 March 1997, p. 11)

Tomorrow is Women's Day. The theme is 'women and empowerment'. But as we celebrate, let us remember that women have many problems. Being a woman prisoner is one of them. The women behind bars face innumerable problems, almost tragic. Imagine that very delicate time of the month – when the woman 'sees the moon'. For women prisoners, it is one of the most humiliating and agonizing moments of their lives. Visit the women's section of any prison and ask them what they use when they see the moon. You will get the same answer.

Somehow, these women manage to find a tiny bit of cloth, and it has to serve as a sanitary pad for the whole lot of them. Fortunately, they don't all have their periods at the same time. So one uses it, washes it and passes it on to the next woman. Can you imagine this happening at the dawn of the 21st century? Even refugee camps now realize that sanitary towels are as important as cooking oil and posho (maize) in the life of a woman. How then can our prison system be so insensitive to the needs of women that they do not provide pads?

The pity is that most women prisoners are there for minor offences. For instance, many are arrested when police officers swoop down on people engaged in petty trade on street verandahs, selling sweets, chewing gum, roasted groundnuts, simsim, and the like. You have probably seen many such women selling merchandise, one child strapped on the neck, another constantly sucking from a breast that does not have much milk in it because the mother cannot afford a wholesome meal. Then like a bolt of lightning, the uniformed officers strike. Naked fright springs into the eyes of the women as they try to salvage what little they can of their already scanty merchandise. But it is too late.

Moreover, these women cannot match the might or speed of the officers. In the ensuing stampede, their goods are trampled upon, turning into a bizarre paste. Whatever the law enforcement officers can put their hands on is confiscated and the woman, with the remaining merchandise, is bundled on to a pick-up and taken to court. Her crime? She has not paid taxes. Never mind that millionaires are busy evading taxes under the very noses of bigger law enforcement officers or even Uganda Revenue Authority bosses.

In court she is fined. This is the biggest irony of all for if she cannot raise Shs 1,000 for a simple meal, how is she expected to produce the fine? Here are people who are trying to stand on their own, *to kulembeka* (tap resources) in their own small way so that they do not have to become beggars or prostitutes. Yet they are thrown behind bars because they are unable to pay a fine. What sort of justice is this?

Once in prison, the unhygienic practice of sharing menstrual cloth is not the only hardship women prisoners encounter. In several prisons a door does not exist between the female and the male prisoners' cells. Or if it does exist, it is not in working order. The male prisoners or the warders kick this door open to rape the women. It is amazing how many women prisoners have become pregnant in this despicable manner. Imagine somebody's wife is taken prisoner and by the time she leaves she is pregnant. She will probably lose her husband and home – a double punishment. It is equally bad if the woman is single. She is sexually exploited by both the male prisoners and the warders.

What human rights are we talking of in Uganda? As we celebrate Women's Day tomorrow and once more bask in what women have achieved in this country, let us remember those women who feel they are living in an eclipse of the new order. Yes, we shall rejoice, sing and boast of a woman vice-president, deputy speaker and so on. Rightly so.

But have we tried to improve the lot of the many disadvantaged women? Unless we do that, all the changes we have made will be merely cosmetic and only one section of women will dance, sing and ululate. The rest will be silent, poverty-stricken watchers. Looking with envy at those at the banquet table.

Appendix 3

Ellis Oundo-Jeyo, 'Luzira women "cooler" sets example' (*The Prisoner*, May 1998, Vol. 1, No. 1, p. 20, published by Uganda Prisoners' Aid Foundation)

Despite logistical handicaps and administrative bureaucracy, Luzira Women's Prison has set a nationwide example as a perfect haven for incarceration. Female inmates who talked to *The Prisoner* were reserved despite harsh prison conditions. They all however concede that conditions in the country's leading women prison are conducive to reformation.

Barbs from the female coolers can only be pointed at a few wardressess like Corporals Betty 'Smart' Alyang, Aio and Asio, who have meted out corporal punishments to the women convicts. According to one, Betty Nantaba, who served sentence from 1995 to 1996, the behaviour of wardresses is very unpredictable. The worst moods are noticed when prisoners receive expensive and quality items from relatives which the wardresses cannot afford.

Another barb is directed to the officer-in-charge (OC), who has 'failed' to ensure that inmates received their entitlements. This is especially when the women have their menstrual periods (MPs). Although sanitary pads are regularly supplied to prison authorities for that purpose, the women inmates are left at God's mercy. Their only salvation is old pieces of blankets which they resort to for convenience.

However, in general, Luzira Women's Prison is commended for being clean, with adequate toilet facilities, ventilated cells, regular supply of uniforms and a functional clinic.

The prison also allows inmates to keep personal clothes, which are locked up in stores and are used when one is being taken to court. Another thumbs-up is to allow those inmates who have health problems to be served a special diet and the acceptance of a cash account to be opened at the reception for the convict.

Justine Nankinga of Nabukalu zone in Kawempe, who served a sentence for four years (1992–96), only laments the type of manual labour women are subjected to. She complains that women are given heavy labour which even men cannot do, like splitting heavy and hard stumps of firewood, working long hours on the farm and, worse, being made to carry heavy bags of posho. She also deplores the harsh treatment of prison wardresses, especially when they find out that the inmate has a rich background or is receiving many visitors.

Research carried out by *The Prisoner* showed that Luzira Women's Prison has a very well-planned workshop where female inmates made all sorts of handicrafts, such as sewing and weaving. However, money accruing is allegedly not used to support the welfare of the inmates, who should be beneficiaries of their labour.

The accusation is that the OC and her team of prison administrators divert the funds and other materials to their own benefit. Even transport money inmates are supposed to be given at the end of their sentence instead finds its way into the pockets of the prison's authorities.

Acknowledgement from both prison authorities and inmates alike goes to organizations such as the Uganda Human Rights Initiative (UHRI), the Uganda Prisoners' Aid Foundation, Sisters of Nsambya and Kamwokya and other local and international human rights organizations that have helped improve conditions. Their assistance has been in the form of blankets, beds, sanitary pads, bug-sprays, etc., and has helped to restore some human dignity in the cells.

Appendix 4: 'Women prisoners in good hands'

Mary Kaddu is a senior superintendent of prisons and an officer-in-charge of Luzira Women's Prison. She took a management course of four months in Yorkshire, Great Britain. Later, she returned to Britain for a three-month advanced prison course. Mary also trained as a counsellor in 1993 and is now an international trainer of counsellors. In August this year, she returned from her second trip to Nigeria, where Mildmay International train people on care and management of people with AIDS. Kaddu is also the director of the Care and Management of People with HIV/AIDS course in all prisons. Jane Nandawua talked to her at her office in Luzira Women's Prison.

How did you get into the prison service?

I have a relative who worked in prisons. He told me how interesting working for prisons is, and that is how I decided to train for the service in 1973. Later, I was confirmed superintendent of prisons while in Mbale, I worked so efficiently that in 1996, I was awarded a Chevening Scholarship by the British government to take an Advanced Prison Management course in Worthing. There were only four of us [awarded the scholarship] that year; the others are from different fields.

What do you have to say about the poor sanitation and other health conditions in the prisons?

People always say that the sanitation here is bad but they do not know what takes pace here. You have seen the compound, is it dirty? Many Ugandans have not been in prisons. For example, some lady recently alleged that prisoners are raped. I made efforts and invited the press to interview the prisoners. And what did they find? Nothing! In fact, the prisoners become very angry when they hear such allegations being made about them, but these allegations do not worry me because our reason and objective is to make the prisoners' lives better than before. We want to rehabilitate them and if anything, society is worse than the prisoners.

It is alleged that the spread of AIDS in prisons is very high. What's the truth in this?

It is not true, AIDS does not spread here. The few prisoners who have AIDS come with it and we take the trouble to treat them while they stay with us. Another point is that female and male prisoners never mix. All the officers who work in this prison are women, so how can AIDS spread? There is no way the women can get in touch with the male inmates. Elsewhere in the world, in Britain for example, they mix but here it does not happen. Currently, we have a care and management course of people with HIV/AIDS sponsored by the British Department for International Development. We want to cover all the 50 prisons in Uganda. We have completed six phases and have covered 24 prisons so far. We train the ward leaders [prisoners' leaders] who go back and train all their colleagues in groups at specific times. Each phase goes for one month and covers four prisons. We also train staff members. We have just completed [another] phase and the next one is due in December. I won't tell you which prisons we shall cover next but it is somewhere in the east.

How did you conceive of the idea of enlightening prisoners about AIDS?

We wanted them to live comfortably. We want them to develop together with others. The aim is that prisoners who do not have AIDS do not get it here.

What is the course all about?

The course is on HIV/AIDS. We train the prisoners on the management of AIDS patients with symptoms like malaria, diarrhoea, TB, etc. The prisoners should know how to get along with the AIDS patients. We teach them about opportunistic infections and caution them on how to use things like razors. The course also emphasizes needs assessment and helping skills. We teach them palliative care.

How has the course helped prisoners?

Oh, it has really helped a lot. They have learned to be friends to each other. You know everybody here is from a different place. The course has taught them that they are relatives to each other and therefore they have to care for each other. It has instilled love in them. The prisoners sit together with staff members during the lessons and this gives them great joy. They feel free and human. This is a miracle to them. They are now so much together like father and daughter. The food they eat in that one month is also another source of appreciation to what we have done for them. They eat meat and drink sodas during the training.

What's the estimated number of women prisoners and how do you cope in terms of feeding, dressing, sleeping, etc.?

I don't usually say the number but they are in the range of two hundred. As for feeding, the government provides posho and beans. But I also have friends who give us rice, bread and sugar once in a while. Some organizations have really been sympathetic and they have been of great help. Our friends have donated a mattress to each of the inmates. The British government has donated a weaving loom for the inmates to make their own blankets. Some of my prisoners have even more than two blankets. The French government donated us blankets while the British High Commissioner has promised toys to babies of prisoners. I want to particularly thank the British organizations for looking after us.

What special problems do women prisoners face?

The prison tries to minimize the likely problems. We let them do all sorts of leisure activities. They sing about AIDS and practise church music. They have a salon where they treat their hair. Yes, we want them to enjoy their femininity. In fact, the [Prisons] Act says women prisoners should remain as feminine as they wish. This is why they are not caned and handcuffed like men.

Do you have any rehabilitation programmes for prisoners so that they get out of prison having learnt something useful?

We have a literacy class and we teach them cattle-keeping. We have a mushroom ground where they plant mushrooms. There is a big demand for them and we sell a kilo at Shs 7,000. They are about to start weaving blankets for themselves. They have a busy programme every day. Monday is an AIDS day. They sit in groups to discuss issues related to AIDS. Tuesday and Wednesday are Bible days. They clean the compound every morning while others go for gardening. Some do handicraft.

Are prisoners of any use to the nation or are they just a liability as most people believe?

The prisoners are part and parcel of society. They are of great importance to the society. This is why we train them for self-sustenance. Most of them start businesses when they go out of here. They open up shops and others start hawking. When they are released, they become part of us. I like prisoners and I feel it is my responsibility to develop them. They are human beings and can be better Ugandans. I appeal to society to appreciate prisoners. Most of them go back when their families no longer have anything to do with them. You know Ugandan men can hardly wait for three months. So when the women go back, they find their marriages already taken over and everybody shuns them. The relatives should welcome prisoners back home.

Select Bibliography

Achterberg, Angeline van (ed.), *Out of the Shadows. The first African Indigenous Women's Conference*, Amsterdam: International Books/NCIV, 1998.

Afkhami, Mahnaz (ed.), *Faith and Freedom. Women's Human Rights in the Muslim World*, Syracuse: Syracuse University Press, 1995.

Afkhami, Mahnaz and Haleh Vaziri, *Claiming our Rights. A Manual for Women's Human Rights in Muslim Societies*, Montreal: Sisterhood Is Global Institute, 1996.

Afkhami, Mahnaz and Erika Friedl (eds), *Muslim Women and the Politics of Participation. Implementing the Bejing Platform*, Syracuse: Syracuse University Press, 1997.

Afkhami, Mahnaz, Greta Hofmann Nemiroff and Haleh Vaziri, *Safe and Secure. Eliminating Violence against Women and Girls in Muslim Societies*, Montreal: Sisterhood Is Global Institute, 1999.

Afshar, Halef (ed.), *Women and Politics in the Third World*, New York: Routledge, 1996.

Agger, Inger, *The Blue Room. Trauma and Testimony among Refugee Women*, London: Zed Books, 1994.

Alexander, M. Jacqui and Talpade Chandra Mohanty (eds), *Feminist Genealogies, Colonial Legacies and Democratic Futures*, New York: Routledge, 1996.

Alfredsson, Gudmundur (ed.), *A Thematic Guide to Documents on Human Rights of Women*, Amsterdam: Raoul Wallenberg Institute, and Martinus Nijhoff, 1995.

Altink, Sietske, *Stolen Lives. Trading Women into Sex and Slavery*, London: Scarlet Press, 1996.

Amadiume, Ife, *Re-inventing Africa. Matriarchy, Religion and Culture*, London: Zed Books, 1997.

Amnesty International, *It's About Time. Human Rights are Women's Rights*, London: Amnesty International, 1995.

Anderson, Mary B., *Focusing on Women. UNIFEM's Experience in Mainstreaming*, New York: UNIFEM, 1993.

Anita and Gouri Salvi (eds), *Beijing! UN Fourth World Conference on Human Rights of Women*, New Delhi: Women's Feature Service, 1998.

Anker, Richard, *Gender and Jobs. Sex Segregation of Occupations in the World*, Geneva: International Labour Office, 1998.

Ankumah, Evelyn, *The African Commission on Human and Peoples' Rights*, The Hague: Martinus Nijhoff, 1996.

Armstrong, Alice, *Culture and Choice. Lessons from Survivors of Gender Violence in Zimbabwe*, Harare: Violence Against Women in Zimbabwe Research Project, 1998.

Armstrong, Alice (ed.), *Struggling over Scarce Resources. Women and Maintenance in Southern Africa*, Harare: University of Zimbabwe Publications, 1992.

Ballara, Marcela, *Women and Literacy*, London: Zed Books, 1992.

Bandarage, Asoka, *Women, Population and Global Crisis. A Political-Economic Analysis*, London: Zed Books, 1997.

Basu, Amrita (ed.), *The Challenge of Local Feminists. Women's Movement in Global Perspective*, Boulder, CO: Westview Press, 1995.

Beneria, L. and S. Feldman (eds), *Unequal Burden. Economic Crisis, Persistent Poverty and Women's Work*, Boulder, CO: Westview Press, 1992.

Berer, Marge with Sunada Ray, *Women and HIV/Aids*, London: Pandora, 1993.

Best Practices for Gender Integration in Organizations and Programs from the Interaction Community, Washington, DC: InterAction, 1996.

Bhasin, Kamla, *What is Patriarchy?*, Boserup: Kali for Women, 1993.

Bodman, Herbert and Nayereh Tohidi (eds), *Women in Muslim Societies. Diversity within Unity*, Boulder, CO: Lynne Rienner, 1998.

Boland, Reed and Anika Rahman, *Promoting Reproductive Rights. A Global Mandate*, New York: Center for Reproductive Law and Policy, 1997.

Boris, Eileen and Elisabeth Prügl (eds), *Homeworkers in Global Perspective. Invisible No More*, New York: Routledge, 1996.

Boserup, Ester, *Woman's Role in Economic Development*, Covelo: Island Press, 1989.

Boylan, Ester, *Women and Disability*, London: Zed Books, 1991.

Braidotti, R., E. Charkiewicz, S. Hausler and S. Wieringa, *Women, the Environment and Sustainable Development*, London: Zed Books/INSTRAW, 1994.

Brasileiro, Ana Maria (ed.), *Building Democracy with Women*, New York: UNIFEM, 1996.

— (ed.), *Women's Leadership in a Changing World*, New York: UNIFEM, 1996.

— (ed.), *Gender and Sustainable Development. A New Paradigm*, New York: UNIFEM, 1997.

— (ed.), *Women against Violence. Breaking the Silence*, New York: UNIFEM, 1997.

Brill, Alida (ed.), *A Rising Public Voice. Women in Politics Worldwide*, New York: Feminist Press, 1995.

Brooke, Pamela, *Traditional Media for Gender Communication*, New York: Pact Publications, 1996.

Bujis, Gina (ed.), *Migrant Women. Crossing Boundaries and Changing Identities*, Oxford: Centre for Cross-cultural Research on Women, 1993.

Bullock, Susan, *Women and Work*, London: Zed Books, 1994.

Bunch, Charlotte, 'Women's rights as human rights: towards a re-vision of human rights', *Human Rights Quarterly*, Vol. 12, No. 4, 1991, pp. 486–98.

Bunch, Charlotte and Niamh Reilly, *Demanding Accountability. The Global Campaign and Tribunal for Women's Human Rights*, New York: UNIFEM, 1994.

Buvinic, M., C. Gwin and L. M. Bates (eds), *Investing in Women. Progress and Prospects for the World Bank*, Baltimore, MD: Johns Hopkins University Press, 1996.

Bystydzienski, Jill, *Women Transforming Politics*, Bloomington: Indiana University Press, 1992.

Carillo, R., *Battered Dreams: Violence against Women as an Obstacle to Development*, New York: UNIFEM, 1992.

Center for Reproductive Law and Policy, *Women of the World. Formal Laws and Policies Affecting their Reproductive Lives*, New York: CRLP, 1995.

Center for the Study of Human Rights, *Woman and Human Rights. The Basic Documents*, New York: Columbia University, 1996.

Center for Women's Global Leadership, *Gender Violence and Women's Human Rights in Africa*, New Brunswick: Center for Women's Global Leadership, 1994.

— *Testimonies of the Global Tribunal on Violations of Women's Human Rights*, New Brunswick: Center for Women's Global Leadership, 1994.

Centre for Development and Population Activities, *Project Design for Project Managers, Vol. 2*, Washington: CEDPA, 1994.

— *Training Trainers for Development, Vol, I*, Washington, DC: CEDPA, 1995.

— *Gender Equity. Concepts and Tools for Development*, Washington, DC: CEDPA, 1996.

— *Gender and Development, Vol. 3*, Washington, DC: CEDPA, 1996.

Chambers, Robert, *Whose Reality Counts? Putting the first Last*, London: Intermediate Technology Publications, 1997.

Chatty, Dawn and Annika Rabo, *Organizing Women*, Oxford and New York: Berg, 1998.

Chinkin, C. and K. Workman, *CEDAW #12: The Committee on the Elimination of Discrimination Against Women, the Convention on the Elimination of All Forms of Discrimination Against Women, and Women's Human Rights*, Minneapolis: International Women's Human Rights Action, 1993.

Clarke, Roberta: *Violence against Women in the Caribbean*, New York: UNIFEM, 1998.

Cock, Jacklyn, *Colonels and Cadres. War and Gender in South Africa*, Oxford and New York: Oxford University Press, 1991.

Cockburn, Cynthia, *The Space between Us. Negotiating Gender and National Identities in Conflict*, London: Zed Books,1998.

Collet, Berit (ed.), *Guide to Women-specific Policies and Programmes within UN Departments*, New York: Quaker United Nations Office, 1994.

Conway, J. K. and S. C. Bourque (eds), *The Politics of Women's Education*, Ann Arbor, University of Michigan Press, 1994.

Conway-Turner, Kate and Suzanne Cherin, *Women, Families and Feminist Politics. A Global Exploration*, New York: Haworth Press, 1998.

Cook, Rebecca, *Women's Health and Human Rights*, Geneva: World Health Organization, 1994.

— *Human Rights of Women. National and International Perspectives*, Philadelphia: University of Pennsylvania Press, 1994.

— *Human Rights Package*, New York: Women, Ink.,1995.

Correa, Sonia with Rebecca Reichmann, *Population and Reproductive Rights. Feminist Perspectives from the South*, London: Zed Books/DAWN/Kali for Women, 1994.

Council of Europe, *The Gender Perspective*, Strasbourg: Council of Europe Publishing, 1995.

— *Women in the Working World. Equality and Protection within the European Social Charter*, Strasbourg: Council of Europe Publishing, 1995.

Culbertson, Debbie (ed.), *Doing the Gender Boogie. Power, Participation and Economic Justice*, Toronto: Ten Days for World Development, 1995.

D'Amico, F. and P. R. Beckman (eds), *Women in World Politics*, Westport, CT: Bergin and Garvey, 1995.

Davies, Miranda (ed.), *Woman and Violence. Realities and Responses Worldwide*, London: Zed Books, 1994.

Davison, J., *Voices from Mutira. Lives of Rural Gikuyu Women*, Boulder, CO: Lynne Rienner, 1989.

Dixon-Mueller, Ruth, *Population Policy and Women's Rights*, Westport, CT: Praeger, 1993.

Dorkenoo, E. and S. Elworthy, *Female Genital Mutilation: Proposals for Change*, London: Minority Rights Group, 1992.

Dorkenoo, Efua, *Cutting the Rose. Female Genital Mutilation*, London: Minority Rights Group, 1995.

Dutt, Malika, Lena Martin and Helen Zia, *Migrant Women's Human Rights in G7 Countries. Organizing Strategies*, New Brunswick: Center for Women's Global Leadership, 1997.

Eade, Deborah, *Capacity Building. An Approach to People-centered Development*, Oxford: Oxfam Publishing, 1997.

Elson, Diane (ed.), *Progress of the World's Women*, New York: UNIFEM, 2000.

Fallon, Helen, *WOW: Women on the Web. A Guide to Gender-related Resources on the Internet*, Dublin: Women's Education Research and Resource Centre, University College, 1997.

Farmer, P., M. Connors and J. Simmons (eds), *Women, Poverty and Aids*, Monroe: Common Courage Press, 1996.

Fawzi, El-Solh and Judy Camillaand Mabro (eds), *Muslim Womens' Voices*, Providence, RI: Berg, 1994.

fisher, Elizabeth and Linda Gray MacKay, *Gender Justice. Women's Rights are Human Rights*, Cambridge: Unitarian Universalist Service Committee, 1996.

Forbes Martin, Susan, *Refugee Women*, London: Zed Books, 1991.

Friedlander, Eva (ed.), *Look at the World through Women's Eyes*, New York: NGO Forum on Women, 1996.

Getecha, Ciru and Jesimen Chipika (eds), *Zimbabwe Women's Voices*, Harare: Zimbabwe Women's Resource Centre and Network, 1995.

Gianotten, V., V. Goverman, E. Van Walsum and L. Zuidberg, *Assessing the Gender Impact of Development Projects*, Amsterdam: Royal Tropical Institute, 1994.

Goetz, Anne Marie (ed.), *Getting Institutions Right for Women in Development*, London: Zed Books, 1997.

Gopal, Gita and Maryam Salim (eds), *Gender and Law. Eastern Africa Speaks*, Washington, DC: World Bank, 1998.

Gordon, April A., *Transforming Capitalism and Patriarchy. Gender and Development in Africa*, Boulder, CO: Lynne Rienner, 1996.

Guijt, Irene and Meera Kaul Shah, *The Myth of Community*, London: Intermediate Technology Publications, 1998.

Harcourt, Wendy (ed.), *Power, Reproduction and Gender. The Intergenerational Transfer of Knowledge*, London: Zed Books, 1997.

— (ed.), *Feminist Perspectives on Sustainable Development*, London: Zed Books, 1994.

Hardon, Anita and Elizabeth Hayes (eds), *Reproductive Rights in Practice. A Feminist Critique on the Quality of Care*, London: Zed Books, 1997.

Hedman, Birgitta, Francesca Perucci and Pehr Sundström, *Engendering Statistics. A Tool for Change*, New York: Women, Ink., 1996.

Heise, L. L. with J. Pitanguy and A. Germain, *Violence against Women. The Hidden Health Burden*, World Bank Discussion Papers No. 255, Washington, DC: World Bank, 1994.

Heyzer, Noeleen (ed.), *A Commitment to the World's Women. Perspectives on a Development Agenda for Beijing and Beyond*, New York: UNIFEM, 1995.

Holland, Jeremy with James Blackburn, *Whose Voice? Participatory Research and Policy Change*, London: Intermediate Technology Publications, 1998.

Hosken, Fran P., *Stop Female Genital Mutilation. Women Speak: Facts and Action*, Lexington, MA: WIN News, 1995.

Hughes, Donna M. and Claire Roche (eds), *Making the Harm Visible. Global Sexual Exploitation of Women and Girls: Speaking Out and Providing Services*, Rhode Island: CATW, 1999.

Imam, Ayesha, Amina Mama and Fatou Sow (eds), *Engendering African Social Sciences*, Dakar: Codesria, 1997.

International Labour Office, *International Labour Standards and Women Workers. Information Kit*, Geneva: ILO, 1993.

International Women's Tribune Center, *Rights of Women. A Guide to the Most Important United Nations Treaties on Women's Human Rights*, New York: IWTC, 1998.

ISIS International, *Directory of Third World Women's Publications*, Quezon City: ISIS International, 1990.

Jackson, Cecile and Richard Palmer-Jones, *Work Intensity, Gender and Well-being*, Geneva: UNDP/SIDA, 1998.

Jahan, Rounaq, *The Elusive Agenda. Mainstreaming Women in Development*, London: Zed Books, 1995.

Jalal, Imrana, *Law for Pacific Women. A Legal Rights Handbook*, Suva, fiji: fiji Women's Rights Movement, 1997.

James, Valentine Udoh (ed.), *Women and Sustainable Development in Africa*, Westport, CT: Praeger, 1995.

Jaquette, Jane S. and Sharon L. Wolchik (eds), *Women and Democracy. Latin America and Central and Eastern Europe*, Baltimore, MD: Johns Hopkins University Press, 1998.

Jensen, M. and K. Poulsen, *Human Rights and Cultural Change: Women in Africa*, Copenhagen: Danish Centre for Human Rights, 1993.

Jimenez-David, Ria (ed.), *Women's Experience in Media*, Manila: WACC/ISIS, 1996.

Joekes, Susan and Ann Weston, *Women and the New Trade Agenda*, New York: UNIFEM, 1995.

Kabeer, Naila, *Reversed Realities. Gender Hierarchies in Development Thought*, London: Verso, 1994.

Karam, Azza (ed.), *Women in Parliament. Beyond Numbers*, Stockholm: International IDEA, 1998.

Karl, Marilee, *Women and Empowerment. Participation and Decision-making*, London: Zed Books, 1995.

Kempadoo, Kamala and Jo Doezema (eds), *Global Sex Workers. Rights, Resistance and Redefinition*, New York and London: Routledge, 1998.

Kerr, Joanna (ed.), *Ours by Right. Women's Rights as Human Rights*, Ottawa: North-South Institute/Zed Book, 1993.

King, Elizabeth and M. Anne Hill, *Women's Education in Developing Countries. Barriers, Benefits and Policies*, Baltimore, MD: Johns Hopkins University Press, 1998.

Koblinsky, M., J. Timyan and J. Gay (eds), *The Health of Women*, Boulder, CO: Westview Press, 1993.

Kurz, Kathleen M. and Cynthia J. Prather, *Improving the Quality of Life of Girls*, Washington, DC: AWID and New York: UNICEF, 1995.

Kyeremeh, Kwasi Ansu, *Communication, Education and Development*, Accra: Ghana Universities Press, 1997.

Landsberg–Lewis, Ilana, *Bringing Equality Home. Implementing the Convention on the Elimination of All Forms of Discrimination against Women*, New York: UNIFEM, 1998.

Lean Lim, Lin, *The Sex Sector*, Geneva: International Labour Office, 1998.

Macdonald, Mandy (ed.), *Gender Planning in Development Agencies*, Oxford: Oxfam, 1994.

Macdonald, Mandy, Ellen Sprenger and Irene Dubel, *Gender and Organizational Change. Bridging the Gap between Policy and Practice*, Amsterdam: Royal Tropical Institute, 1997.

Marchand, Marianne and Joe Parpart, *Feminism/Postmodernism/Development*, New York: Routledge, 1995.

Martens, M. H. and S. Mitter (eds), *Women in Trade Unions. Organizing the Unorganized*, Geneva: International Labour Office, 1994.

Meena, Ruth (ed.), *Gender in Southern Africa*, Harare: SAPES Books, 1992.

Meer, Shamin (ed.), *Women Speak. Reflections on our Struggles 1982–1997*, London: Kwela Books and Oxfam, 1998.

Mernissi, Fatima, *Women's Rebellion and Islamic Memory*, London: Zed Books, 1996.

Mertus, Julie with Mallika Dutt and Nancy flowers, *Local Action/Global Change. Learning about the Human Rights of Women and Girls*, New York: UNIFEM, 1999.

Meyer, Mary K. and Elizabeth Prügl (eds), *Gender Politics in Global Governance*, New York: Rowman and Littlefield, 1999.

Mies, Marie and Vandana Shiva, *Ecofeminism*, London: Zed Books and Halifax: Fernwood Press, 1993.

Mikell, Gwendolyn, *African Feminism. The Politics of Survival in Sub-Saharan Africa*, Philadelphia: University of Pennsylvania Press, 1997.

Miller, Carol and Shahra Razavi (eds), *Missionaries and Mandarins. Feminist Engagement with Development Institutions*, London: Intermediate Technology Publications in Association with the United Nations Research Institute for Social Development, 1998.

Mobility International, *Loud, Proud and Passionate. Including Women with Disabilities in International Development*, Eugene: Mobility International, 1997.

Moffat, Linda, Yolande Geadah and Ricky Stuart (CCIC/MATCH), *Two Halves Make a Whole. Balancing Gender Relations in Development*, Ottawa: Bonanza Press, 1991.

Moore Harbour, P. and L. Twist (eds), *Voices of Women. Forward with Dignity and Wholeness*, Kalamazoo: Fetzer Institute, 1996.

Morgan, Robin (ed.), *Sisterhood is Global*, New York: Feminist Press at The City, 1996.

Moser, Caroline O. N., *Gender Planning and Development. Theory, Practice and Development*, London: Routledge, 1993.

Mosse, Julia Cleves, *Half the World, Half the Change*, Oxford: Oxfam, 1993.

Murphy, Joseph, *Mainstreaming Gender in World Bank Lending. An Update*, Washington, DC: World Bank, 1997.

Narayan, Uma, *Dislocating Cultures. Identities, Traditions and Third World Feminism*, New York: Routledge, 1997.

Neft, Naomi and Ann Levine, *Where Women Stand. An International Report on the Status of Women in 140 Countries*, New York: Random House, 1997.

Nelson, Barbara J. and Najima Chowdhury (eds), *Women and Politics Worldwide*, New Haven, CT: Yale University Press, 1994.

NGO Forum 95 Newspapers, New York: Women, Ink., 1996.

Nnaemeka, Obioma, *Sisterhood, Feminism and Power in Africa*, Trenton, NJ: Africa World Press, 1997.

Nowak, Manfred (ed.), *Report on the Contribution of the NGO Community to the 1993 World Conference on Human Rights*, Vienna: Ludwig Boltzmann Institute for Human Rights, 1993.

Nussbaum, Martha and Jonathan Glover (eds), *Women, Culture and Development. A Study of Human Capabilities*, Oxford: Oxford University Press, 1996.

O'Connell, Helen, *Women and the Family*, London: Zed Books, 1994.

Omvedt, Gail, *Violence against Women. New Movements and New Theories in India*, New Delhi: Kali for Women, 1990.

Owen, Margret, *A World of Widows*, London: Zed Books, 1996.

Packer, Carinne A. A., *The Right to Reproductive Choice: A Study in International Law*, Turku: Abo Akademi University Institute for Human Rights, 1996.

Pala, Achola O., *Connecting Across Cultures and Continents. Black Women Speak Out on Identity, Race and Development*, New York: UNIFEM, 1995.

Parker, Rani A., *Another Point of View. A Gender Analysis Training Manual for Grassroots Workers*, New York: UNIFEM, 1993.

Parker, Rani A., Itziar Lozano and Lyn A. Messner, *Gender Relations Analysis. A Guide for Trainers*, Washington: Save the Children Fund, 1995.

Peiris, Kamala, *Weaving a Future Together. Women and Participatory Development*, Utrecht: International Books, 1997.

Penn, Shana, *Women's Guide to a Wired World*, New York: The Feminist Press, 1997.

Petchesky, Rosalind and Karen Judd (eds), *Negotiating Reproductive Rights. Women's Perspectives across Countries and Cultures*, London and New York: Zed Books, 1998.

Peterson, V. Spike and Anne Sisson Runyan, *Global Gender Issues* (2nd edn), Boulder, CO: Westview Press, 1998.

Pietilä, Hilkka and Jane Vickers, *Making Women Matter. The Role of the United Nations* (3rd edn), London: Zed Books, 1996.

Rao, Aruna (ed.), *Women's Studies International. Nairobi and Beyond*, New York: The Feminist Press, 1991.

Razavi, Shahra, *Gendered Poverty and Social Change*, Geneva: UNRISD/UNDP/SIDA, 1998.

Razavi, Shahra and Carol Miller, *Gender Mainstreaming. A Study of the Efforts by the UNDP, the World Bank and ILO to Institutionalize Gender Issues*, New York: UNIFEM, 1995.

Riano, P. (ed.), *Women in Grassroots Communication*, London: Sage, 1994.

Rodda, Annabel, *Women and the Environment*, London: Zed Books, 1991.

Rosenbloom, Rachel (ed.), *Unspoken Rules. Sexual Orientation and Women's Rights*, London and New York: Cassell Academic, 1996.

Ross, Andrew (ed.), *No Sweat. Fashion, Free Trade and the Rights of Garment Workers*, New York: Verso, 1997.

Rowbotham, S. and S. Mitter (eds), *Dignity and Daily Bread*, London: Routledge, 1994.

Royal Tropical Institute, *Women and Development. An Annotated Bibliography*, Amsterdam: RTI, 1992.

— *Advancing Women's Status. Women and Men Together? Critical Reviews and a Selected Annotated Bibliography*, Amsterdam: RTI, 1995.

Royal Tropical Institute and Oxfam, *Gender Training. The Source Book*, Oxford: RTI/ Oxfam, 1998.

Saith, Ruth and Barbara Harriss-White, *Gender Sensitivity of Well-being Indicators*, Geneva: UNRISD, 1998.

Sajor, Indai Lourdes, *Common Grounds. Violence against Women in War and Armed Conflict Situations*, Quezon City: Asian Centre for Women's Human Rights, 1998.

Schuler, Margaret (ed.), *Empowerment of the Law. Strategies for Third World Women*, Washington, DC: OEF International, 1986.

— (ed.), *Women, Law and Development*, 1990.

— (ed.), *Claiming our Place. Working the Human Rights System to Women's Advantage*, 1993.

— (ed.), *From Basic Needs to Basic Rights. Women's Claim to Human Rights*, Women, Law and Development International, 1995.

Schuler, Margaret and Sakuntala Kadirgamar-Rajasingham (eds), *Legal Literacy. A Tool for Women's Empowerment*, New York: PACT Communications, 1992.

Scott, Catherine V., *Gender and Development. Rethinking Modernization and Dependency Theory*, Boulder, CO: Lynne Rienner, 1996.

Scott, Joan, Cora Kaplan and Debra Keates (eds), *Transitions, Environments, Translations. Feminism in International Politics*, London: Routledge, 1997.

Seager, Joni, *The State of Women in the World Atlas*, London: Penguin, 1997.

Sen, G. and R. C. Snow (eds), *Power and Decision. The Social Control of Reproduction*, Cambridge, MA: Harvard University Press, 1994.

Sen, Gita, Adrienne Germain and Lincoln C. Chen (eds), *Population Policies Reconsidered. Health, Empowerment and Rights*, Cambridge, MA: Harvard University Press, 1994.

Shami, S., L. Taminian, S. A. Morsley, Z. B. El Bakri and E. M. Kameir, *Women in Arab Society: Work Patterns and Gender Relations in Egypt, Jordan and Sudan*, Paris: Berg/ UNESCO, 1990.

Shiva, V. (ed.), *Close to Home. Women Reconnect Ecology, Health and Development Worldwide*, London: Earthscan, 1994.

Silliman, Jael and Ynestra King (eds), *Dangerous Intersections. Feminist Perspectives on Population, Environment and Development*, Cambridge: South End Press, 1999.

Sinclair, M. Thea (ed.), *Gender, Work and Tourism*, London and New York: Routledge, 1997.

Singh, Naresh and Vangile Titi (eds), *Empowerment. Towards Sustainable Development*, London: Zed Books, 1995.

Sittirak, Sinith, *The Daughters of Development. Women in a Changing Environment*, London: Zed Books, 1998.

Sivard, Ruth, *Women. A World Survey*, Washington, DC: World Priorities, 1995.

Skrobanek, Siriporn, Nattaya Boonpadee and Chutima Jantateroo, *The Traffic in Women. Human Realities of the International Sex Trade*, London: Zed Books, 1997.

Slocum, Rachel, Lori Wichhart, Dianne Rocheleau and Barbara Thomas-Slayter, *Power, Process and Participation. Tools for Change*, London: Intermediate Technology Publications, 1995.

Smyke, Patricia, *Women and Health*, London: Zed Books, 1991.

Snyder, Margaret, *Transforming Development. Women, Poverty and Politics*, London: Intermediate Technology Publications, 1995.

Snyder, Margaret C. and Mary Tadesse, *African Women and Development. A History*, London: Zed Books/Witwatersrand University Press, 1995.

Sohoni, Neera Kuckreja, *The Burden of Girlhood. A Global Inquiry into the Status of Girls*, Oakland: Third Party Publishing, 1995.

South African Women's Health Book, The, Oxford: Oxford University Press, 1996.

Sparr, Pamela (ed.), *Mortgaging Women's Lives. Feminist Critiques of Structural Adjustment*, London: Zed Books, 1994.

Staudt, Kathleen (ed.), *Women, International Development and Politics. The Bureaucratic Mire* (2nd edn), Philadelphia: Temple University Press, 1997.

— *Policy, Politics and Gender. Women Gaining Ground*, West Hartford, CT: Kumarian Press, 1998.

Steady, F. S. (ed.), *Women and Children first. Environment, Poverty and Sustainable Development*, Rochester: Schemkman Books, 1993.

Steiner Moseley, Eva (ed.), *Women, Information and the Future. Collecting and Sharing Resources Worldwide*, Fort Atkinson: Highsmith Press, 1995.

Sweetman, Caroline (ed.), *Women and Rights*, Oxford: Oxfam, 1995.

— *Women, Employment and Exclusion*, Oxford: Oxfam, 1996.

— *Gender in Development Organizations*, Oxford: Oxfam, 1997.

— (ed.), *Gender and Migration*, Oxford: Oxfam, 1998.

— (ed.), *Gender, Education and Training*, Oxford: Oxfam, 1998.

— (ed.), *Gender, Religion and Spirituality*, Oxford: Oxfam, 1998.

— (ed.), *Violence against Women*, Oxford: Oxfam, 1998.

Thomas-Slayter, Barbara, Rachel Polestico, Andrea Esser, Octavia Taylor and Elvina Mutua, *A Manual for Socio-economic and Gender Analysis. Responding to the Development Challenge*, Worcester: ECOGEN-Project/Clark University, 1995.

Tomasevski, Katarina, *Women and Human Rights*, London: Zed Books, 1993.

Toubia, Nahid, *Female Genital Mutilation. A Call for Global Action*, New York: Rainbow, 1993.

Tucker, Judith E. (ed.), *Arab Women. Old Boundaries, New Frontiers*, Bloomington: Indiana University Press, 1993.

Turshen, Meredith and Clotilde Twagiramariya, *What Women Do in Wartime. Gender and Conflict in Africa*, London: Zed Books, 1998.

United Nations Development Programme, *Human Development Report*, 1998.

UNIFEM, *Advocacy Kit on CEDAW*, UNIFEM and UNICEF, 1995.

United Nations, *Strategies for Confronting Domestic Violence. A Resource Manual*, New York and Geneva: UN Publications, 1993.

— *Methods of Measuring Women's Economic Activities*, New York: United Nations, 1993.

— *WISTAT. Women's Indicators and Statistics Database*, New York: United Nations, 1995.

— *The World's Women. Trends and Statistics*, New York: United Nations, 1995.

— *The United Nations and the Advancement of Women*, New York: United Nations.

— *Handbook for Producing National Statistical Reports on Women and Men*, New York: United Nations, 1997.

— *1999 World Survey on the Role of Women in Development: Globalization, Gender and Work*, New York: United Nations, 1999.

United Nations High Commissioner for Human Rights, *Vienna Declaration and Programme of Action*.

UNRISD, *Gender Mainstreaming*, Geneva: UNRISD, 1995.

— *Working Towards a More Gender-equitable Macro-economic Agenda*, Geneva: UNRISD, 1997.

Vickers, Jane, *Women and War*, London: Zed Books, 1993.

Visvanathan, Nalini, Lynn Duggan, Laurie Nisonoff and Nan Wiegersma (eds), *The Women, Gender and Development Reader*, London: Zed Books, 1997.

Wallace, Helen M., Kanti Giri and Carlos V. Serrano, *Health Care of Women and Children in Developing Countries*, Oakland: Third Party Publishing, 1995.

Walters, Shirley and Linzi Manicom (eds), *Gender in Popular Education. Methods for Empowerment*, London: Zed Books, 1996.

Weis Bentzon, Agnete, Anne Hellum, Julie Stewart, Ncube Welshman and Torben Agersnap, *Pursuing Grounded Theory in Law. South–North Experiences in Developing Women's Law*, Harare: Tano Aschehoug/Mond Books, 1998.

Wieringa, Saskia (ed.), *Subversive Women. Women's Movement in Africa, Asia, Latin America and the Caribbean*, New Delhi: Kali for Women, 1996.

Wijers, Marjan and Lin Lap-Chew, *Trafficking in Women. Forced Labour and Slavery-like Practices in Marriage, Domestic Labour and Prostitution*, Utrecht: STV, 1997.

Williams, Suzanne with Janet Seed and Adeline Mwau, *The Oxfam Gender Training Manual*, Oxford: Oxfam, 1994.

Wolper, Andrea and Julie S. Peters, *Women's Rights, Human Rights*, New York and London: Routledge, 1995.

Women, Law and Development International, *State Responses to Domestic Violence. Current Status and Needed Improvements*, Washington, DC: Women, Law and Development International, 1996.

— *Women's Human Rights Step by Step. A Practical Guide for Using International Law and Mechanisms to Defend Women's Human Rights*, Washington, DC: Women, Law and Development International, 1997.

— *Gender Violence. The Hidden War Crime*, Washington, DC: Women, Law and Development International, 1998.

Women's Environment and Development Organization, *Risks, Rights and Reforms. A 50 Country Survey of Government Actions five Years after the International Conference on Population and Development*, New York: WEDO, 1999.

Women's Media Watch, *Whose Perspective? A Guide to Gender-sensitive Analysis of the Media*, Kingston: Women's Media Watch, 1998.

World Health Organization: *Female Genital Mutilation. An Overview*, Geneva: WHO, 1998.

Yatbeck Haddad, Yvonne and John L. Esposito (eds), *Islam, Gender and Social Change*, Oxford: Oxford University Press, 1997.

Young, G., V. Samarsinghe and K. Kuster, *Women at the Center. Development Issues and Practices for the 1990s*, West Hartford, CT: Kumarian Press, 1993.

Index

152–3; provisions and meaning of, 34–4; reporting procedures under, 131–8; reservations, 126–9; submission of reports, 133–5; use of, in courts, 145

Convention on the Elimination of Racial Discrimination, 14, 15, 124–5, 127, 129

Convention on the Nationality of Married Women (1957), 10, 33, 62, 247

Convention on the Political Rights of Women (1952), 10, 33, 62, 247

Convention on the Rights of the Child, 128, 244, 306

Conventional Weapons Convention, 187

Coomaraswyma, Radhika, 64

Copenhagen conference *see* World Conference of the UN Decade of Women

Costa Rica, 150

Cote d'Ivoire: FGM in, 275; polygamy in, 279

Council of Europe, 7, 210–28 *passim*; Committee of Ministers, 213, 217; Human Rights Charter, 210; Statute of, 210

credit, access to, 38, 236

culture, 89–91; cultural identities of women, 90

customary law, 277

death penalty, 195, 232; abolition of, 212

Declaration of Philadelphia, 71

Declaration of St Petersburg, 183

Declaration of the Rights of Man and Citizen (1789), 215

Declaration of the Rights of Woman and Citizen, 215

Declaration on the Elimination of Discrimination Against Women (1967), 11, 12, 34–44, 44–5, 52, 62, 119

Declaration on Equality of Women and Men (Europe, 1988), 214, 217–18

Declaration on Freedom of Expression and Information (Europe, 1982), 214

Declaration on Policies for Combating Violence Against Women in a Democratic Europe (Europe, 1993), 214

Declaration on the Protection of Women and Children in Emergency and Armed Conflict (1974), 33

Declaration Regarding Intolerance (Europe, 1981), 214

Delors, Jacques, 86

detention of women, 197

disabled women, 125

discrimination: concept of, 34, 123–9; gender-specific, prohibition of, 105–18; multiple forms of, 125

divorce, 253, 254, 256, 257, 258

Dow, Unity, 146, 234, 238

dowry, 39–40, 254

dress, freedom of, 251

drugs, trafficking of, 75

Ducci, Maria Angelica, 81

dum-dum bullets, banning of, 187

earnings of women, 37

Earth Summit (Rio de Janeiro, 1990), 7, 176

Echard, Nicole, 95

education of women, 16, 38, 51, 212, 236, 276

Egypt, polygamy in, 279

Eisemann, Pierre Michel, 97

employment opportunities of women, 16

empowerment of women, 50

environmental considerations in war, 186–7

equal opportunity, 42

equal pay, 73, 76, 77, 222

equality: between men and women, 107–8, 115; in Islam, 249, 250; male-based model of, 125–6; principle of, 50; standards of, 23–4 *see also* law, equality before

Eritrea, women fighters in, 177

Ethiopia, FGM in, 273, 274

ethnic cleansing, 199

European Commission, 'New Opportunities for Women' (NOW), 222

European Commission of Human Rights, 216